RIGHT TO INFORMATION
An Act for Best Citizenry

About the Author

Dr. E.M.S. Natchiappan Minister of State for Commerce and Industry, Sr Advocate in Supreme Court of India, President, Indian Society of International Law, New Delhi. He is elected member for 13th Lok Sabha, elected Second time Member of Rajya Sabha representing State of Tamil Nadu, and on Panel, Vice Chairman, Rajya Sabha. Chairman Parliamentary department related Standing Committee on Personnel, Public Grievances, and Law and Justice and has formulated 36 Reports in various issues including Equal Property Rights to Women through Amendment of Hindu Succession Act, Reservation of seat for Women in Parliament and Assembly, CBI, UPSC, Electoral Laws , Supreme Court and High Courts etc. He has written to his credit many books including *World Trade Organisation - Indian Parliament, Executive and Judiciary*. He addressed United Nations General Assembly and other UN Committees. Founder President, Parliamentarians Forum of Human Rights for Global Development. New Delhi.

RIGHT TO INFORMATION

An Act for Best Citizenry

E.M.S. Natchiappan

CONCEPT PUBLISHING COMPANY PVT. LTD.
NEW DELHI-110059

ISBN-13: 978-93-5125-089-0

First Published 2014

Published and Printed by

Concept Since 1974

Concept Publishing Company Pvt. Ltd.
A/15-16, Commercial Block, Mohan Garden
New Delhi-110059 (India)
T: 25351460, 25351794, *F*: 091-11-25357109
E: publishing@conceptpub.com, W: www.conceptpub.com
Editorial Office: H-13, Bali Nagar, New Delhi-110 015, India.

Cataloging in Publication Data—*Courtesy:* D.K. Agencies (P) Ltd. <docinfo@dkagencies.com>

Sudarsana Natchiappan, E. M., 1947-
Right to information : an act for best citizenry / E.M.S. Natchiappan.
p. cm.
Includes bibliographical references and index.
ISBN 9789351250890

1. Freedom of information—India. I. Title.

DDC 342.540853 23

वजाहत हबीबुल्लाह
अध्यक्ष
Wajahat Habibullah
Chairperson

सत्यमेव जयते

भारत सरकार
Government of India
राष्ट्रीय अल्पसंख्यक आयोग
National Commission for Minorities

Foreword

The Right to Information is increasingly recognised the world over as a basic freedom which must underpin any governance system that claims to be a system representing the will of its people. As Kofi Annan, former Secretary General of the United Nations so succinctly put it:

> *"The great democratising power of information has given us all the chance to effect change and alleviate poverty in ways we cannot even imagine today. Our task, your task ... is to make that change real for those in need, wherever they may be. With information on our side, with knowledge of a potential for all, the path to poverty can be reversed".*

The right to information is now a 'Fundamental Right' of a free citizenry, from which other basic human rights can flow, and no society can claim to be truly free unless it has both the instrument and the practice of this right, whether it be called the freedom of information as it is in most countries where it is practiced at present, or the right to information which it has become after it has been so declared in the world's largest and most intense democracy with the enforcement of India's Right to Information Act in October 2005, which brings within its spread the entire span of governance including the executive, the legislature and the judiciary. EMS Natchiappan's Handbook presents in some detail the form and practice that this legislation has taken in India and in countries across the continents

EMS Natchiappan, himself Chair of the Department Related Parliamentary Standing Committee on Personnel, Public Grievances Law and Justice, 2005, which was instrumental in arriving at the draft of the Bill that became Act No 22 of 2005 has, therefore, made an important contribution to the literature on this innovative law by presenting an assessment of what went into the thinking contributing to devising this law, the history of the use of this freedom and the experience of different societies and diverse nations in its actual implementation.

The Right to Information Act in India has been described by many as the most radical legislation in this country since the passage of the Constitution of India in 1950. Even if one were not to agree with this definition, which the author rightly considers to be a premature conclusion, the test of the law's acceptance by the public in general came in mid-2006 when the very Government which had passed this legislation through India's Parliament sought to bring amendments which many thought of as curtailing of the Right guaranteed by the original Act. The widespread public debate both in the visual and written media as well as the general public outcry in neighbourhoods which included slum areas persuaded the Government of India that no amendment would be considered in future without wide public consultation. In other words, the Government that, in fact, sponsored the Act recognised that this Legislation had passed beyond its domain and had been accepted by India's public as its own. No legislature could have wished for more from any legislation.

Although the exercise of the freedom of information has now matured and even fully developed in several societies, yet it is relatively nascent in most developing countries. These countries moreover are in many cases those which are only now emerging from the incubus of a colonial hierarchy, structured to exploit the skills of its people at the least cost to the colonial masters and the economic ruin of the colonised populace. In such a system transparency was of no account and accountability encouraged only to itself, never to the public. Hence we have insidious legislations like India's Official Secrets Act of 1923, which clearly defined the public as enemy of the State. It is for this reason that India's experimentation with this Right, which is in its ninth year of operation, and seen varying results within the federal structure of India, has been put under such close scrutiny by the international community.

Most recently there has been in India much debate arising from the decision of the Central Information Commission of June 3, 2013 on two complaints moved by one Subhash Chandra Agrawal, reproduced in full in this Handbook, regarding the application of RTI to political parties holding that "the AICC/INC, BJP, CPI (M), CPI, NCP and BSP are public authorities u/s 2(h) of the RTI Act". Also included is the full text of the proposed amendment of the Act, introduced in the Lok Sabha as Bill No 112 of 2013, intended to reverse this decision.

This Handbook will form an essential reference work for all those seeking to mould such a right in their societies, both those where none has been recognised so far, and those where such a legislation is already in operation, and help chart a roadmap to further strengthen the basis of the exercise of this right by all.

Wajahat Habibullah
Former Chief Information Commissioner
India

Preface

When I was nominated by Chairman of Rajya Sabha on the customary recommendation of Political Party, it was a pleasant surprise for as Second term Member of Parliament. Because the name was suggested by Madam Sonia Gandhi, as President of the Congress Party to make me Chair of the newly formed Department related Standing Committee Personnel, Public Grievances, Law and Justice, which was earlier with the department related Parliamentary Standing Committee for Home Affairs Chaired by Mr Pranab Mukerjee. This committee was consisting of very experienced Parliamentarians from Bureaucracy, Law, Politics, Science and variety of discipline representing both Lok Sabha (20) and Rajya Sabha (11). This committee has to discharge the work with close interaction with Bureaucracy to monitor their performance, accountability, implementation of the mandated programmes and deliver the Goods and Services to the people as 'Mini Parliament'. If any law is introduced in the parliament it used to be referred to the concerned department related Parliamentary Committee for detailed discussion, examination of witnesses from Bureaucracy, stack holders, public by invitation on perusing memoranda submitted and requesting the audience of committee. This system has strengthened consultation process with common man, experts and open up opportunity to interested parties to partake in the process of law making.

This healthy procedure followed by Parliament enables the individual's ideas become the Government programmes. I feel that I have to record my experience as Member of Opposition in NDA Government, I was in the department related Parliamentary Standing Committee for Science and Technology, Environment and Forest (1999-2002). When Demands for Grants to the department of Space was considered on 10th April 2001, by this committee Dr. Kasturirengan, then Secretary for Department of Space gave the evidence that Department of Space was then developed cryogenic engine indigenously to take a payload to space and bring it back to earth safely. As a member of the Committee I suggested to him 'why don't the knowledge of indigenously developed knowledge on cryogenic engine be used to send the first Indian to Moon'. On hearing this Secretary was thrilled with emotion and said "we are ready to do if the committee recommends to the Government for the programme". These verbatim report on 10th April 2001 is in the Parliamentary record. The system started to work. By the recommendation of the Committee in report No. 91, paragraph 38, submitted to Parliament on 24-4-2001 and followed by Action Taken Report 92 'Lunar Mission to moon' accelerated with public criticism. (Para 44-47) Report 100 dated 2/5/2002, Report 108 para 46. Report 114 dated 2/5/2003 taken up as 'Indian Mission for Moon' 47-51. Report 129th dated 26/8/2004 (para 10) Chandrayaan 1 becomes official programme for 2007. In the meantime the department of space constituted the Task Force of the scientist and the progress of their work was monitored and they finally submitted the report demanding 650 crore for the implementation of the programmes. The Prime Minister Mr Vajpayee declared in his Independence Day speech on 2003 coining the name of the project as 'Chandrayaan' which was implemented in Congress led UPA Government 2007 led by Dr. Manmohan Singh. This is a specimen case to show that how our Parliamentary system works and prove that on giving best solutions into the system it is ready to be absorbed and implemented irrespective of the person who suggested and which political party heading the Government.

With such faith upon the department related Parliamentary Committee system of Parliament I chaired the committee (2004-2009) and brought 36 historical reports with the help of Members, officials, citizens of the world, media and Madam Sonia Gandhi, Chairperson of UPA. On 12 January 2001, I received a surprise call from Mrs. Sonia Gandhi enquiring about the steps taken for considering the Right to Information Bill. I explained the situation as to cancellation of trip to Mumbai as the Chairman of Rajya Sabha banned all tours of the Committees because of the tsunami and aftermath of the natural calamity. But I explained the road map laid by the committee to complete the open enquiry for participation of interested groups and citizens to put their ideas before the committee and submit a comprehensive Report to the Parliament before March. She was satisfied on the priority being given by committee on historical Bill.

This shows the interest bestowed by high level leaders to empower the citizens through Right to Information. As Chairperson of the National Advisory Committee Smt. Sonia Gandhi and experts have gone in depth steady on various issues. Many NGO's were doing field study and collected opinions and experiences of various states where the state level legislations and executive orders were implemented with lively participation of stakeholders

This book is written with purpose of making world understand how the evolution of Right to Information Act 2005 came into force after understanding the compulsions externally and domestically to bring the real power of people in a practicing democratic country. India is alone working on adult franchise for every citizen who crossed 18 years of age as the only qualification to vote and bring government of his or her choice. This shows how the young to old,' large spectrum of voters', are to be informed of the happening in the Government to get concurrence and authenticity of democracy.

The formation of the chapters of the book are explaining various stages of historical, sociological, Archaeological and political evidences to prove that the Right to Information Act 2005 showed the long path of evolution. The verbatim Report of the department related Parliamentary Standing Committee of Personnel, Public Grievances and Law and Justice is made as the Annexures. Since the main source of understanding pith and substance of the Law through the questions of different political parties belonging to National and State Parties, Former Judge, Senior Lawyers, Senior Administrators, Governors, Active Politicians, Representatives from Public, NGOs and the replies given by the Government Secretaries from various departments. As the Chairman of the Committee I feel every body has played crucial role in giving inputs in the law making process. I could make certain crucial changes in bringing various spectrum of representatives of the people (Sec 13) as members of the National and

State Information Commission members by removing the provisions for holding the post by exclusively retired administrators. This type of inclusion is first ever attempt in India legislation. Similarly I could bring "Human Rights issue" in Sec 24(4) proviso within the Law of Right to Information even though strong opposition came from makers of earlier Bill. Mr Jethmilani played the crucial role to bring the Preamble to the true sprit of the law. These type of individual thoughts and the response from Administrators on the issue of bring the jurisdiction of State and all other Public money invested and aided Institutions and organisations within the preview of law will be transparent enough in the verbatim report. This is the way law could be interpreted on the sprit of law makers.

The final amendments and correction numbering around 113 which were well received by Cabinet Committee of Group of Ministers Chaired by Mr. Pranab Mukerjee, and then by Union Cabinet presided by Dr. Manmohan Singh. Only one suggestion by the Parliamentary Standing Committee to punish the chronicle violator in the Information desk with the punishment of imprisonment was not accepted by CGM and all the rest of amendments were carried through and Lok Sabha and Rajya Sabha made an excellent debate and finally passed through, without objections but appreciation and President of India gave assent and notified as Act.

The Right to Information Act was implemented by every Panchayat, State, Union Government and all other organisations as explained in the Act and Rules. Our committee took note of certain difficulties and hesitations during the course of implementation of the Act but it can be seen as teething trouble and not the real difficulties. The officials have started to taste first time the democratic questioning in many sources and angle which they were never entertaining. On the other hand the questions as to how many trips the official car used for private visits, how many tea cups were served very day for visitors, were some of the harassment so to the officials. But they have forgotten that they have to maintain log books for every vehicle and even try expenses should be accounted for the prevailing system. On the other hand the failed service candidates used the RTI to know the system of promotion or giving leave on discretionary powers. These can be well addressed by transparent system and the availability of these information in official web site which was already mentioned in voluntary disclosure under Section 2(4) of RTI Act.

But one thing made us to go for parallel system of Public Grievances Redressal System as in built system with in the Institution to stop the litigating mind of the employee. Hence in Department related Parliamentary Standing Committee on Personnel, Public Grievances and Law and Justice, Report 29 the following recommendation was made.

"3.50. The Committee further feels that a wrong notion has entered into the mind of the public that the Right to Information Act is an instrument to solve their grievances by giving/providing them information written/oral required by them. The Committee feels that this wrong notion needs to be changed because information seeking is altogether different from the redressal of grievances and need to be looked in a different manner. The Committee, therefore, recommends that Government should immediately take some urgent steps like taking the help of NGOs working in the field of Right to Information, print and electronic media, organising nukkad natak in the rural and urban area on the subject to educate people about their rights etc. The Committee also recommends that in order to solve the problems of the people, the Government must give statutory backing to the Public Grievances Redressal Mechanism on same line that of the Right to Information Act, the both will work parallel to each other and help in solving the grievances. Hence we examined witnesses and discussed on Citizens Charter by visiting various cities and found the necessity of Separate law so that Right to Information Act should be stand alone legislation instead of using it for Redressal of Grievances."

I had my mind on including the political parties also within the system of Right to Information Act. Here we have to differentiate between pure information and hidden information being brought out by law. The very purpose of Right to Information Act is to empower citizens and public to get clear Information of usage and availability of goods and services generated by Tax payers public money. It should be developed to such an extent by self generating information under Section 4 (2) leading to a day of 'nil receipt of application,' so that the public have minimum resort to the use of this Act to obtain information.'

The Representative of Peoples Act is exclusively for the Public elected representatives to regulate the registration of Political party, conducting election and monitoring the behaviour before and after election. The management of Party and it's fund and utilisation of public property and private money are all comprehensively covered under the authority the Election Commission, a Constitutional body. This is similar to any organisation crated by law and overseeing its actions within the law. If the Information Commissioners reasoning for bringing the Political activities within the RTI regime then the system will crack loose it's importance.

Regarding the Supreme Court observation that Judicial mind alone can lead RTI dispute resolution system is also misplaced in application. The Information Commission is purely 'Jury system' to declare whether a person is entitled to information as per law and interpretation of courts. The Grand Jury is not interpreting the law. It is having limited role of applying law to the request.

The RTI is within a decade took kaleidoscopic visuals to the interested parties making and unmaking Governments by sensationalism added highly by the new born liberty to media and specifically electronic media. Time tested observation is 'Liberty coupled with accountability', is the spirit of democracy.

In the North Block of Central Secretariat with Rashtrapathi Bhawan, New Delhi there is an engraved statement

"Liberty will not descend to a People. A People must raise themselves to Liberty: It is blessing that must be earned before it can be enjoyed"

India enjoys unlimited 'liberty', but democracy will have to mature to show the other side of the coin the 'accountability.'

Contents

CHAPTER – 1
Introduction

Democracy is a political system in which all the members of the society have an equal share of formal political power. In modern representative democracy, this formal equality is embodied primarily in the right to information to get the vote for governance by such elected persons.

It is generally believed that democracy and Constitution were created in one particular place and time – identified as "Ancient Athens" about the year 508 BC. In a broad sense, they may have existed in several areas of the world well before the turn of the fifth century. 'Primitive democracy', is identified in small communities or villages when the following take place: face to face discussion in the village council or a headman whose decisions are supported by village elders or other cooperative modes of government. British colonial governance used this basic structure by imposing its laws and bureaucratic super hierarchy based on 'Official Secret Act'. This was new to India and incompatible with its ethics, heritage and culture of grassroots democracy.

Indian governance is ancient and culture based. Villages are the heart and soul of Governance. Village level democracy allows every citizen to participate in decision making and the implementation of the said decision. This power is the basic strength of the 'Gram Rajya'. In the parlance of modern governance "Legislature-Executive-Judiciary", all the three pillars were with the citizens in the 'Gram Sabha' (village Assembly) and 'Panchayat' (village executive and judiciary). They were self-sufficient and potential in rendering justice—political, economic, social, and cultural rights.

This way of governance was the cultural heritage of India from Vedic days and it continued in the contemporary period too. Many invasions by Mohammedans and Europeans had not changed this system. But British colonial rule had attempted to destabilize this village governance by gradual interference using the rule of law in place of customary law based on the traditional culture of 'Dharma'. Local Self-Government in India and more specifically in Tamil Nadu which has a long history as is evident from the Uthiramerur stone inscriptions in Kancheepuram district. In a way, in those days, it was a land of village republics, with community groups undertaking many activities for their area development. This tradition reached its peak during the tenth-eleventh centuries under the reign of the Cholas when Village Councils used to levy taxes, improve community life and administer justice in their limited area. *Kuda Olai Murai* was the process of secret ballot exercised to select members to the Village Councils. These Village Councils had effective links with the Chola rulers.

The assumption of democratic governance is that of the consent of the people in favour of a class of people to govern on their behalf for their welfare. The knowledge of the governance is the qualification of the class of people in governance. Furthermore the governance should be to the knowledge of the people who are governed. There cannot be any 'space' for secrecy in between them.

The beginning of the century is marked with the developments in the field of information and technology. The primary role of information is to equip the consumer to make informed choices. As a citizen of a democratic country, a person has a right to know about the policies, laws and other information that may affect one directly or indirectly. This right to information also co-exists with our right to vote. A citizen is not only entitled to select the government by exercising his or her franchise but he/she is also expected to know how the selected candidate is performing.

Right to information is the fundamental right of the citizen to know the happenings in the state. If the state enters into multilateral agreements with countries as the part of the WTO obligation its features must be known to the people. The executive feels that the citizen does not have the expertise to know such features. This is the colonial mind of the authority. Similarly, the executive down to the level of the grassroots official thinks has the information till it is withheld by him from the eyes of the citizen. Moreover, he feels that the information empowers the individual or group of such people. Hence it carries a value which has to be bought or paid for by the beneficiary which in common parlance we call "corruption".

It is accepted by democrats that the people in a democratic country are the master who allocate the work for different Institutions and the individual. This allocation of jobs is done through electing representatives. The elected representatives should ensure that the mandates of the people are carried out in all sincerity and thus the elected representatives are accountable for the responsibility bestowed on them by the people. Since India has adopted a permanent secretarial or bureaucratic system to do the job as per the direction of the mandate of the people they are answerable to the people. This is the ethic of democratic governance. But the genetic defect of bureaucracy inherited through the British colonial system, the Indian Civil Services (ICS) reborn as the Indian Administrative Services (IAS) retains secrecy as part of governance which is contradictory in democratic governance based on 'transparency and accountability'. This secrecy crept into the Parliament and the Judiciary too. This is where the 'Right to Information Act' comes into play to rectify the genetic defect which crippled the development of India for the past sixty years of democratic republic governance.

Information

The original root of the word "information" is the Latin word *informare*, which means to fashion, shape, or create, to give form to. Information is an idea that has been given form, such as the spoken or written word. It is a means of representing an image or thought so that it can be communicated from one mind to another. Rather than worrying about all the information afloat in the world, we must ask ourselves what matters to us, what do we want to know. It's having ideas and learning to deal with issues that is important, not accumulating lots and lots of data.

Right to Information, globally, is an old concept whose evolution can be traced to efforts mainly in the eighteenth century which later, with more and more countries becoming its votaries, became universal towards the end of the nineteenth century. Now more than sixty countries have comprehensive laws relating to RTI. Efforts made by the international community and the United Nations have played a very important role in bringing a paradigm shift in governance from secrecy in government functioning to openness and accountability. At the international level, various instruments were adopted imposing duty on states to disclose and disseminate information leading to the evolution of the international law in this regard. With consequent efforts at the regional and national levels, informed citizenry and a transparent government are considered as essentials for a democratic nation. Initially, in India RTI took a back seat and it was secrecy in matters of government functioning that was emphasized in British India. Nonetheless, after Independence, the judiciary played a commendable role in interpreting constitutional provisions relating to RTI and brining a new dawn of RTI law in India.

Right to information is increasingly being recognized as a necessary condition to achieve accountable, transparent and participatory governance and people-centred development. While in India, a conducive legal and constitutional environment in support of this right always existed, as reflected in the Constitution and various Supreme Court judgments among others, it was the work of the civil society organizations at grassroots level and their strong advocacy that led to the enactment of right to information legislation in India—first at the regional and local and then at the national level.

As we know that the information has an unlimited potential, it is the life-blood that sustains political, social and business decisions. Power resides in those entities that control the communication system and consequently the gathering, processing, distribution, and storage of information. Information is a key to keep pace with progressive trends in the post modern world. We need information when we buy some product from the market. It may pertain to quality, quantity, purity, standard potency and prices of product or service that are needed to make informed choices or decisions. During the last three decades a vast number of human rights have found place in constitutions and bills of rights of more than eighty countries and of supra national entities. The countries which enacted their new constitutions have had the benefit of all developments in the human rights jurisprudence which have taken place since 1950.

Disclosure of Government Information in India is governed by a law enacted during the British rule, the Official Secrets Act of 1889 which was last amended in 1923. Though the intent of this law was to secure only information related to security of the State, sovereignty of the country and friendly relations with foreign states, it contained provisions which could make it a crime to disclose even non-classified information. Civil service conduct rules and the Indian Evidence Act put further restrictions on government officials' powers to disclose information to the public.

In 1975, the Supreme Court delivered a judgment that has been described as "landmark", which held that " the people.... have a right to know every public act, everything that is done in a public way, by their public functionaries".

Freedom of Information Act

Freedom of Information Act (FOIA) was passed by Congress in 1966 and became effective on 4 July, 1967. Amended in 1974 in the light of the Watergate scandal and again by the Freedom of Information Reform Act of 1986, FOIA provides citizen access to documents held by agencies in the federal government's executive branch, including government and government-controlled corporations. The law does not apply to elected officials or the federal judiciary. FOIA requests may be denied only if they pertain to any of the following types of information: classified national security materials; matters relating to internal personnel rules and practices; information exempt under other laws; confidential business information obtained from private sector sources; internal communications regarding the formation of policy; personnel and medical files of individuals; law enforcement investigatory records; information about government-regulated financial institutions; or geological and geophysical data on oil and natural-gas wells. A requester may file an administrative appeal for access to withheld documents and if denied, may file a judicial appeal in a U.S District Court, where the burden of justifying withholding of information lies with the government.

With the rise in the 1930s of the modern administrative state and its proliferating agencies and bureaucracies, executive responsibility expanded in an often bewildering manner, the security interests of the Cold War compounded matters. A minor freedom of information movement in Congress culminated in the 1966 legislation, but the law lacked force until the events of Vietnam and Watergate discredited claims of executive privilege based on national security or separation of powers. During the 1980s, the administration of President Ronald Reagan sought to reduce the use of FOIA. The result was a reduction of personnel responsible for reviewing documents. In 1982, Executive Order 12356 required reviewers to consider security needs more important than the public's right to know. Congressional amendments in 1986 further narrowed the scope of releasable information. In 1994, President Bill Clinton reversed the policy on nine previous presidents and declared that because the National Security Council, which advises the president on security matters, is not an agency of the federal government; its records must be considered strictly as presidential papers not subject to the FOIA and other record laws. Although FOIA has its flaws, such as its use by felons to obtain appeals, it has led to greater public access to government information. When used by journalists covering current events and scholars probing the origins and working of laws and administrations, it has brought the nation closer to its founders' ideals. "A popular government without popular information or the means of acquiring it," wrote James Madison in 1822, "is but a prologue to a force or a Tragedy or perhaps both".

Passage of a national level law, however, proved to be a difficult task. Given the experience of state governments in passing practicable legislation, the Central Government appointed a working group under H.D. Shourie and assigned it the task of drafting legislation. The Shourie draft, in an extremely diluted form, was the basis for the Freedom of Information Bill, 2000 which eventually became law under the Freedom of Information Act, 2002. This Act was severely criticized for permitting too many exemptions, not only under the standard grounds of national security and sovereignty, but also for requests that would involve "disproportionate diversion of the resources of a public authority". There was no upper limit on the complying with a request for information. The FoI Act, consequently, never came into effective force.

In India, the pioneering steps were taken by the Mazdoor Kishan Shakti Sangathan (MKSS). The MKSS has fought diligently on the issues of accountability and transparency and has succeeded in demonstrating that critical link between lack of transparency and corruption and in initiating substantiate changes. The MKSS succeeded in ensuring minimum wages for daily wage workers in Rajasthan, and forced muster rolls, bills and vouchers pertaining to construction activity undertaken in past years to be opened to public scrutiny.

In Delhi the people's movement against corruption, Parivartan has successfully demonstrated the mismanagement and corruption in the Public Distribution Scheme in Delhi. Parivartan through the use of Right to Information has brought to the public domain startling discoveries of subsidized ration grains being black-marketed. Having acquired records of ration shop owners across the city and having mobilized the urban poor to access information and demand their dues the group has been successful in initiating a process of reforms to rectify the inefficiencies within the system.

Since 1997 a silent revolution is sweeping across the whole country. In one state after another governments are granting citizens the rights to demand information, inspect government works and take copies of tenders, contracts issued for development works. Currently nine states in India have passed Right to Information Acts—these include, Rajasthan, Maharashtra, Delhi, Karnataka, Madhya Pradesh, Tamil Nadu, Goa, Assam and Jammu & Kashmir.

Several groups have also focused their attention on the Central Government's Freedom of Information Bill. The National Campaign for People's Right to Information (NCPRI) in the late 1990s became a broad based platform for this purpose, with members from diverse sections of the society. The National Advisory Council (NAC), chaired by Sonia Gandhi sent 36 proposed amendments for the un-notified Freedom of Information Act in August 2004. The Freedom of Information Bill, 2004 was tabled in the Lok Sabha in December 2004 and was passed in May 2005. This Bill is intended to replace the old Freedom of Information Act, 2002. The enthusiasm and fervor generated by the Right to Information among citizens expresses public recognition of its power in making government actions accountable. Several known and unknown groups, organizations and individuals are helping citizens increasingly realize their right to participate in their own governance. Gradually, through the use of Right to Information it is being understood that the leaders that the citizens elect bear great responsibility towards enabling their exercise of their right to know.

Since its passage in October 2001 the Delhi Right to Information Act has come a long way in addressing accountability and transparency issues in several government departments across Delhi. Non-government Organizations, Citizens' groups, Resident Welfare Associations, Students and Individual citizens have utilized the Act to highlight mismanagement and corruption in various departments such as the Municipal Corporation, Delhi Jal Board, Registrar of Cooperative Societies, MCD Slum and JJ, Education, Food and Supplies and many more. Some of these experiences have received considerable amount of media coverage and helped propel the Act and the experiences of using Right to Information in the wider public domain.

However, these initiatives and experiences associated with the Right to Information movement here in Delhi and in other states in India require to be more focused and consistent to experience this trend in participatory governance firsthand. With the passage of the Central Right to Information Bill in May 2005 the importance of taking this effective governance tool to the masses becomes even more significant.

CHAPTER – 2

RTI and a Sovereign India

India is a sovereign country. Whether this statement is true and in which way the Right to Information Act is contemplated to realize the declaration in the Preamble of the Constitution that India is a 'Sovereign Democratic Republic' can be verified. Customary law as defined, "results from a general and consistent practice of states followed by them from a sense of legal obligation".[1]Sovereignty is a legal institution that authenticates a political order based on independent states whose governments are the principal authorities, both domestically and internationally.[2]

State sovereignty has been claimed on many grounds: divine sovereignty (in the name of God or His anointed agent on earth); monarchical sovereignty (in the name of the king or queen); parliamentary sovereignty (in the name of the people).

Does our organization enable its members to effectively carry out a strategy and meet their goals? The first requirement of an organizational fitness for purpose is that the organization's structure should be aligned with its goals. What this means is that the organization's structure should reflect the nature of its business and its aims. It has to be able to direct resources—people, money, technology, raw materials where they are needed and where they can be effective.

Organizations that are fit for purpose enable quick, clear communication, both vertically and laterally. This means that information gets passed around and reaches the places where it is needed. People thus know what to do and when to do it. They can give each other advice and information and help each other complete their tasks. An organization where people communicate freely and easily is a whole greater than the sum of its parts. An organization where communication channels are blocked will eventually grind to a halt as its members are unable to act or work towards goals.[3]

Organizations have to adapt and change as their circumstances change. However this ability to adopt is also has to be built into the organization. Making an organization flexible and adaptable is not easy. Largely, this is a matter of culture. Innovation is also a part of an organization to meet the goals. Careful planning, constant monitoring and substantial investment in time coupled with a well managed process, will be repaid many times over in the form of greater efficiency and greater effectiveness.

Corruption was well under control in the ancient period in India. A well-evolved democratic system was functional, starting at the Saba level, between the eighth and the sixteenth centuries in South India, irrespective of the ruling dynasties: the Cheras, Cholas, Pallavas, Pandyas and Vijaynagar.

> "The members of a Saba were elected by the whole community of the village by a system peculiarly known as 'Kuda Olai' system (Kudam-Pot and Olai-Palm leaf). The village was divided into wards called 'Kudumbus', and every ward had to write the eligible person's names on the palm leaves. The bundle of palm leaves was emptied in a pot. The member was chosen by draw of lots."

The most important point to note here was the issuance of strict guidelines by the rulers; inscriptions give fair indication of the clarity of thought and zero tolerance towards financial bungling.

Among the inscriptions three are very important which belong to the tenth century AD. Two inscriptions are found in Vaykundanatha Perumal temple at Uttramerur, Kanchipuram district and another one is from Pallipakkam village of Tanjore in Tamil Nadu state belonging to the rule of Parantaka Chola Ist, Chandni explains.

The crimes committed by the members of the Saba are divided into three categories. The swindling of funds or public property and those who failed to submit their accounts have been considered as crime number two. Such members were not eligible to contest the Saba election for life. Not only they but their relatives too could not contest elections, such as children, in-laws, brothers and their children, grand-parents, grand- children, relations through wife etc., for nearly three generations. They were called as 'Grama Dhurogis'.

"While murder of even Brahmins was considered pardonable, crimes like cheating or swindling public funds were unpardonable even by gods. Political crime was not pardonable but other crimes could be punished with penalties or performance of penance and charitable deeds, to become eligible for elections again."

There were established codes of conduct laid down for the Saba members as found in an inscription from Mannur village of Tirunelveli district. Among them, the most interesting one relates to obstructing the political processes or functioning of the Saba deliberately. In such cases a penalty of five Kasu (Rupees) was imposed for every such act of mis-conduct, on such members. Yet they were permitted to stay and participate in the proceedings of the Saba. Generally, the Kings' orders were executed by passing in the Saba.

To prevent political power getting concentrated in one family leading to dynastic tendencies, rules were framed. According to this rule, the present members of the Saba cannot contest the election for next 2 to 10 years. In the same way none of their relatives should have contested for the past five years if one wanted to contest for membership of Saba. There is also a sub-rule to provide equal opportunity for everybody stipulating induction of two new members without any previous experience as members of the Saba.

The Sabas had to be dissolved before the election of the new one and the elections were generally conducted by the village accountant and a judge called 'Madhyasthan'. In the public services there were no holidays and therefore, no one in authority could neglect public duty. "It was categorically mentioned that the elected members should provide their service for 360 days. The elected members' term of office was only one year and automatically they should resign after completion of the term.

They also actively practised the right to recall. "In those days if an elected member of the Saba committed a crime or violated law, he was immediately sacked. Such has been our rich and exemplary past. Let us bring it back instead of looking to the west for solutions".

Governance in India is based on democratic process and principles, even from the ancient times. Ancient India has a proud claim to distinction. Its oldest civilization antedates any other advanced culture found in Asia, even in China, and is far more venerable than the oldest civilizations of Europe or the Americas. India claim to be one of the mothers of civilization along with Egypt in Nile Valley and Mesopotamia in the valley of the Tigris and Euphrates rivers. It was in these three areas between 4000 and 2000 B.C. that men, for the first time, began building and living in cities. They invented writing, organized government on a large scale, erected great buildings, forged metal tools, and carried on commerce with other people. The **Brahminy bull**, bronze **dancing girl,** sacred tree and monster are all in the steatite seal of Mohenjo-daro archaeology findings which could show the informative nature of governance in those ancient days. During the Vedic period a group of families constituted the village (*grama*) which was the unit of organization. It was a little republic, with headman and hereditary officers, and its stretch of common pastureland. The head of the Indo-Aryan tribe was the *Raja* or king.

The king surrounded by his nobles (*rajanyas*) and mounted on his chariot, led his people in war. The king's power was not absolute. He had to win for his acts the approval of the popular assembly (*sabha*) consisting of males of fighting-age, who, no doubt, ratified his election in the first instance. The king was the administrator of justice; the punishment for murder was the payment of blood-money, which varied according to the victim; the fine for the slaughter of a man of high rank might be a hundred cows, paid to the dead man's relatives. Minor cases, criminal and civil, were doubtless settled by the village council according to custom. Thus the people's participation in governance was the basis of Indian culture. The Aryan invasion of India continued intermittently from about 2000 to 1000 B.C. and the only source of information comes from the ancient Vedas, and this period is called the Vedic Age. The terms of various administrative posts like *adhyaksa, duta,nidhapati, rathaspati, senam* etc. would be abundantly clear that the Vedic society was neither nomadic nor in a merely rural stage, as has been assumed by many. It had long passed those stages and was dealing with kings and kingdoms, as having an organized administrative machinery, fortified towns and was engaged in both land and sea trade. Just as there were cities, towns and villages in the Harappan ensemble (as there are even today in any society) there were both rural and urban components in the Vedic times.

From 1000 to 500 B.C. considerable progress was made by Aryans in developing a civilization which is called the Epic Age, as most of the information comes from two epic poems: the *Mahabharata* and *the Ramayana*. In the Mahabaratha, Shanti Parva, chapter LV111.verse 11 declares "The eternal duties of kings are to make their subjects happy, to observe truth, and to act sincerely".

After the Aryans the Persians invaded India next to Afghanistan in the year 518 B.C. Persian rule continued for two centuries, only to be brought to an end by another invader, Alexander the Great, whose Greeks conquered the Persian empire and marching eastwards crossed over the mountains into northern India in 326 B.C.l[2] (India, Wall Blank Henry Holt and Company, 1948, USA). The Chandragupta Maurya dynasty (two centuries), Asoka (273-232 B.C.), Moslem Arabs early eighth century to 1000A.D.Babur and Akbar ruled India.

From 1498 onwards Europeans invaded various parts of India. Even after suffering so many centuries of invasion on India, its basic structure of village republics withstood the time. It may be over reaching or an illogical claim since throughout the last century the Western world could establish that they founded democracy by historical necessity. But one thing is clear, the basic of Indian life is communication between the ruler and ruled more so to the succeeding generation by way of erecting temples, arches and monuments where the information about the ruling of the country and such other day-to-day needs of the citizens were percolated through sculptures and drawings in temples and monuments. Lord Macaulay said in the British Parliament in 1835:

> "I have travelled across the length and breadth of India and I have not seen one person who is a beggar, who is a thief, such wealth I have seen in this country, such high moral values, people of such calibre, that I do not think we would ever conquer this country, unless we break the very backbone of this nation, which is her spiritual and cultural heritage, and, therefore, I propose that we replace her old and ancient education system, her culture, for if the Indians think that all that is foreign and English is good and greater than their own, they will lose their self-esteem, their native culture and they will become what we want them, a truly dominated nation."

THE ETHNOLOG I CAL SURVEY OF INDIA 1875-1901: The colonial intentions were well revealed by the letter by the Secretary of State commenting on the importance of investigations. "It has come to be recognized of late years that India is a vast storehouse of social and physical data which only need to be recorded in order to contribute to the solution of the problems which are being approached in Europe with the aid of material much of which is inferior in quality...It is the entire framework of native life in India is made up of groups of this kind, and the status and conduct of individuals are largely determined by the rules of the group to which they belong. For the purpose of legislation, of judicial procedure, of famine relief, of sanitation and dealing with epidemic disease, and of almost of every form of executive action, an ethnographic survey of India and a record of the customs of the people is as necessary an incident of good administration as a cadastral survey of the land and a record of right of its tenants. The census provides the necessary statistics: it remains to bring out and interpret the facts which lie behind the statistics."[3] No clearer statement could be made of the colonial uses of anthropology, of how by the late nineteenth century the British in India recognized that the task of colonial rule was essentially ethnographic. Virtually no area of governmental policy or activity could be conducted without benefit of extensive anthropological knowledge. The late colonial state was genuinely an ethnographic state.

It was part of the culture and heritage of India to have democratic governance at every level more so at village level. Mahatma Gandhi wrote in the *Harijan*, 26 July, 1942: "There will be a compulsory service of village guards who will be selected by rotation from the register maintained by the village. Since there will be no system of punishments in the accepted sense, this Panchayat will be the legislature, judiciary and executive combined to operate for its year of office. Here there is perfect democracy based upon individual freedom. The individual is the architect of his own government. He and his village are able to defy the might of a world, for the law governing every villager is that he will suffer death in the defense of his and his village's honour." It was the way of life to allow every citizen to participate in decision-making and implementation of the same. This power was the basic strength of the "Gram Rajya". In the parlance of modern governance—Legislature, Executive and Judiciary—all the three pillars of governance were with the citizens in *Gram Rajya*. They were self-sufficient and potential in rendering justice—social, political, cultural and economic.

This way of governance, the cultural heritage of India from Vedic days continued in the contemporary period too. Many invasions by European and Mohammedans have not changed this system. But British colonial rule had attempted to destabilize the village governance by gradual interference using the rule of law in place of customary law (*Dharma*). The peace and tranquillity of local self-governance of the people, by the people, and for the people was not tolerable to the British rulers. The 'rule of law' was neither made with the consent of people nor by the participation of the people in making the laws. The reason behind making such laws was not even explained to the people. Simply making the law in London or Delhi or the Provincial capital was made binding by just publishing in the Government Gazetteer. The presumption of law was that everybody knews it. Ignorance of law was no excuse as a defense when it was violated and for which the executive applied penal provisions. Democracy is for the people, of the people and by the people. If it is true then every citizen should know what is happening, how it is happening, who is making it happen and for whose welfare it is happening. These principles were gradually and systematically taken away by the British system of governance. The Village officers in the name of Head Man (*Patel*) and *Karnam* (village accountant) aided by the village Constable was the first attempt of the British Government to destabilize the *Gram Rajya*. The very Village Head who was looked upon by hereditary acceptance as the Community leader to manage the community wealth and the individuals as Chief of the village was made a statutory officer under 'The Village Munssif and Karnam Act'. The hierarchy of officials from bottom to the top as District Collector to Governor General made the complete set-up of secrecy that was colonial Governance. Even after decades of democratic governance the mindset of the bureaucracy remains the same.

Self-Government—*Gram Swaraj* was the dream of Gandhiji and made as the part of the Constitution—Article 40: "Organisation of village panchayats: The State shall take steps to organize village panchayats and endow them with such powers and authority as may be necessary to enable them to function as units of self-government". When democracy and the free market have fused into a single predatory organism with a thin constricted imagination that revolves almost entirely around the idea of maximizing profit the very democratic principle itself becomes one other commodity for trading.

The movement on right to information in India, spearheaded by a small grassroots organization in rural Rajasthan, was the first major people's movement against misappropriation in public expenditure and for gaining access to official information as a right. This was the first influential attempt to reclaim development and the first movement that brought about a conceptual shift in the right to information debate in at least four respects.

Firstly, it shifted the focus of the right to information debate from one that was in the past concerned with "freedom of speech and expression" or "media's freedom of access to information" to the citizens' "right to information". Much of the debate in the past had focused on right to free expression and freedom of the press.

Although the media clearly is an important source of information for people, it cannot be the only source. Media has its own internal problems imposed by market interests, political leanings of the owners, private agendas and urban slant, and has failed to utilize the space for reflecting the concerns of the ordinary people. There was thus a need to recognize that apart from the media's right to information, there was the people's right to information to demand government transparency. The intensity of this need led to the remark that "Right to information is too important to be left to the press and media." This was a remarkable shift in the debate that raised right to information to a different footing. Secondly, it rooted the right to information debate within the constitutionally guaranteed right to life and liberty. It highlighted the underpinning nature of right to information for the realization of other rights. It brought out the linkage between information and livelihoods and hence survival. From an abstract notion, right to information became a living and practical tool for people to protect their life and livelihoods.

Thirdly, it looked upon information as a public good, generated for the public with public money and held by public officials. The civil society's work led to people realizing that the public expenditure incurred in their name was in fact their money and they had a right to demand how that money was being used. This encouraged them to ask for records held by public officials. This was the beginning of the concept of 'social audit' in India. Civil society empowered people to demand direct accountability of civil servants as distinct from their accountability to people through their superiors, courts or elected representatives. This redefined the whole concept of accountability. Fourthly, civil society in India has also used right to information as an instrument for greater citizen participation in governance. Along with transparency and accountability, this is a key component of democratic governance. In the context of globalization, where people are losing control over decision-making in matters that affect their lives, one thing that can have a countervailing effect is greater participation in local governance which makes free access to information a prerequisite. People can then not only demand information on how their money is being spent by government officials, but actually determine what development activities their money should be spent on. With the tremendous emphasis on decentralization and local governance in India, the participatory angle provided by civil society is an important aspect of the right to information movement.

In India before the Official Secrets Act, (OSA) 1923, the Indian Official Secrets Act, 1889 and the Official Secrets Act, 1911 (passed by British Parliament) were in force. Subsequently, The Public Record Act, 1993 was enacted to regulate the management, administration and preservation of public record of the Central Government, UT administration, PSU, statutory bodies and corporations, commissions and committees constituted by the Central Government or UT Administrations. Under this Act, Record Officers were authorized to take appropriate action in case of unauthorized removal or destruction of record in his custody.

Utmost importance was given to secrecy in government working under the Official Secrets Act, 1923. In addition to OSA other statutes also provided for secrecy, i.e. Indian Evidence Act, 1872 prohibited the giving of evidence from unpublished official record without permission of Head of relevant Department. Further Supreme Court of India in *R.K. Jain* vs. *Union of India*, provided that Section 123 of Indian Evidence Act, 1872 gives right to the government or immunity from disclosure of unpublished official state documents in public interest. However, under some statutes right to access information was granted in restricted form, i.e. The Indian Evidence Act, requires public officials to provide copies of public documents to anyone who has right to inspect them.

Further the Factory Act, 1948 provides that factory workers have the right to know regarding dangers including health hazards and measure of protection.

In 1948, the Press Laws Enquiry Committee recommended certain amendments in OSA 1923. For the first time movement towards RTI started in early 1990 in Rajasthan when the Mazdoor Kisan Shakti Sangthan's (MKSS) members fought for their wages during famine and wanted transparency in records. The MKSS demanded the copies of all documents released to public works important of which were muster roll, wages due paid. It was accepted by the collector but the village development officer refused to comply. MKSS started *dharnas* which continued for 52 days when the Deputy Chief Minister of Rajasthan announced in May 1997 that the State Government had issued notification allowing people to have information relating to panchayat or village local government institutions. Copies of muster rolls were given but the order was not fully implemented. The MKSS movement led to the national campaign for drafting RTI Bill, i.e. RTI law was proposed by the Consumer Education and Research Council, Ahmedabad in 1993; the Shourie Committee prepared freedom of Indian law.

> "It will be interesting to mention that Press Council of India prepared a draft Bill in 1996 to make a provision for securing RTI. This draft Bill was named RTI Bill, 1996. The Institute of Rural Development, Hyderabad also prepared a bill in 1997. Both the bills initiated a national debate on the issue of Effective and Responsive Administration. The Government of India appointed a working group on January 2, 1997. The terms of reference of the Working Group included the examination of feasibility and need to introduce a full-fledge RTI Bill. This group recommended that a legislation in this regard is not only

> feasible but is also vitally necessary. The Working Group recommended that the Bill should be named as Freedom of Information Bill as the RTI has already been judicially recognised as a part of the fundamental right to free speech and expression."

However, in the meantime in 1997, Tamil Nadu and Goa, passed the RTI law.

Ultimately Freedom of Information Bill, 2000 was introduced in Parliament and Freedom of Information Act, 2002 was enacted to promote transparency in government activity. Unfortunately, notification for enforcement of Freedom of Information Act, 2002 was not issued by the Central Government. So it never came into operation. In 2004, a new government, UFA promised to give a more progressive, participatory and meaningful RTI Law.

Accordingly the National Advisory Council (NAC) was set up to implement the government's common minimum programme. In the meantime public interest litigation was filed in the Supreme Court of India to compel government to notify the enforcement of Freedom of Information Act, 2002. The Supreme Court of India in September 2004 directed government to advise as to when the Act will be notified.

In 2004, sincere effects of NAC resulted in enactment of RTI Bill, 2002, which was passed by both the Houses of Parliament in May 2005 and received assent of President A.P.J. Abdul Kalam on 15 June, 2005. Ultimately it came into force on 12 October, 2005.

Constitutional Provisions and Judicial Trends on RTI in India

After Independence, "Article 19(1) (a) of the Constitution guarantees the fundamental rights to free speech and expression. The prerequisite for enjoying this right is knowledge and information. The absence of authentic information on matters of public interest will only encourage wild rumours and speculations and avoidable allegations against individuals and institutions. Therefore, the RTI becomes a constitutional right, being an aspect of the right to free speech and expression which includes the right to receive and collect information. This will also help the citizens to perform their fundamental duties as set out in Article 51A of the Constitution. A duly informed citizen will certainly be better equipped for the performance of these duties. Thus, access to information would assist citizens in fulfilling these obligations."

Significantly, the United States Supreme Court opined that, "The construction and guarantee of freedom of speech and press are not for the benefit of press so much as far as the benefit of all the people." Further, "freedom of speech and press include not only the right to utter or to print but the right to read". In India before enactment of RTI Act in 2005, judiciary had mainly laid emphasis on RTI as regards disclosure of information/documents; right to know; right to acquire information and disseminate information and direction on voter's RTI.

Regarding RTI, the Supreme Court of India in *B.C. and Co. v. UOI*, opined that freedom of speech and expression under Article 19(1)(a) of the Constitution of India includes two-fold right: the right of the citizen to speak and the right of the community to hear or know. Amongst the other, main function of the newspaper is to disseminate information. "Newspaper is the most potent means of educating the people as it is read by those who read nothing else and in politics, common man gets his education mostly from, newspaper."

Justice A.M. Ahmadi and Sujata v. Manohar 1997 of the Apex Court of India, in *Dinesh Trivedi M.P.* v. *UOI*, held that "to ensure continued participation of people in democratic process, they must be kept informed of the vital decisions taken by the government. Democracy, therefore, expects openness and openness in a concomitant of a free society. Sunlight is the best disinfectant. But it is equally important to be alive to the dangers that lie ahead."

Justice S.B. Sinha and V.N. Khare of the Apex Court of India in 2004 in *People's Republic for Civil Liberties* v. *Union of India* opined that "RTI is a facet of freedom of "speech and expression" under Article 19(1)(a) of the Constitution thus is a fundamental right". However, the state under Article 19(2) of the Constitution is entitled to impose reasonable restriction in the interest of the state. How far and to what extent the same should be balanced was the question involved in this appeal.

Regarding disclosure of information/documents Methew, J., of the Supreme Court in *State of UP* v. *Raj Narain* held that "the people of this country have a right to know every public act, everything that is done in a public way, by their public functionaries. They are entitled to know which is derived from the concept of freedom of speech, though not absolute is a factor which should make one wary, when secrecy is claimed for transactions which can, at any rate, have no repercussion on public security."

Further Bhagwati, P.N., J., Gupta, A.C., *et al.* of the Apex Court in a landmark case of *S.P. Gupta* v. *UOI*, went one step further and held that the "Open government is the new democratic culture of an open society towards which every democratic society is moving and our country should not be an exception. In a country like India which is committed to socialistic pattern of society, right to know becomes a necessity for the poor, ignorant and illiterate masses (*emphasis mine*)." Further, the Apex Court held that "no democratic government can survive without accountability and the basic postulate of accountability is that the people should have information about the functioning of government. It is only if people have information about the functioning of government. It is only if people know how government is functioning that they can fulfil the role which democracy assigns to them and make democracy a really effective participatory democracy (*emphasis mine*)".

On Right to acquire information and disseminate information, Sawant, P. B., Jeevan Reddy, B.P. and Mohan, S. — Judges of the Apex Court of India in a leading case of *Secretary, Ministry of Information and Broadcasting of India* v. *Cricket Association of Bengal* opined that, "The freedom of speech and expression includes Right to acquire information and disseminate it. Freedom of speech and expression is necessary for self-fulfilment and it enables the people to contribute to debate on social and moral issues… Equally important is the role it plays in facilitating artistic and scholarly endeavours of all sorts." The right to communicate includes right to communicate through any media, i.e. print, electronic or audiovisual such as advertisement, movie, article, speech etc. Therefore, freedom of speech and expression includes freedom of press also.

Explaining, the Apex Court opined that the freedom of speech and expression includes freedom of press which in turn includes freedom to communicate or circulate one's opinion without interference to as large population in the country, as well as abroad, as is possible to reach. Further Government's power to pre-censor films and to granting licence has to be exercised in conformity with Article 19(2) of the Constitution (reasonable restriction).

Regarding Directions on Voter's RTI in 2002 the *SC of India in UOI* v. *Association of Democratic Republic* opined that democracy cannot survive without free and fair election, without free and fair informed voters. Votes cast by uninformed voters in favour of any candidate would be meaningless. Because one-sided information, disinformation, misinformation and non-information all equally create an uninformed citizenry and makes democracy a farce. Therefore, the Election Commission was directed to exercise its power under Article 324 and call for following information from each candidate seeking election to Parliament or state legislature; whether convicted/acquitted/discharged of any criminal offence in past, prior to six months of filing nomination, whether candidate is accused of any pending case of any offence where punishment is imprisonment of two years or more and in which charge is framed or cognizance was taken by the court; assets of candidate and his/her spouse or that of dependent; liabilities and educational qualification.

Right to Information in India: An Effective Governance

A democratic society survives by accepting new ideas, experimenting with them, and rejecting them if found unimportant. Therefore, it is necessary that whatever ideas the government or its other members hold must be freely put before the public. The free flow of information is a must for a democratic society in particular because it helps the society to grow and flourish. It is now recognized that the right to information is vital to democracy for ensuring transparency and accountability in governance. It, therefore, ensures that governance is more participatory being a vital component of successful democracy.

The right to information gained an impetus when UDHR was adopted in 1948 providing everyone the right to seek, receive, information and ideas through any media and regardless of frontiers.[1] Also the International Covenant on Civil and Political Rights 1966 says that "Everyone shall have the right to freedom of expression, the freedom to seek and impart information and ideas of all kind, regardless of frontiers."[2]

The legislature and the judiciary function as open. More openly the legislature by way of open debate by the representatives of the people to which press and people both have access. In a very similar manner the judiciary decides the cases only after giving both the parties to the cases, a chance of hearing. These two wings of government never normally carry out their operation in secrecy.

On the other hand the Executive always carries out its work in secret chambers and people or press hardly have access or control over it. Now-a-days the executive, apart from discharging its normal function of executing laws, promulgates, delegates legislative functions and also adjudicates on controversial matters.

As Justice Krishna Iyer in the *Maneka Gandhi case*[3] said "a government which functions in secrecy not only acts against democratic decency, but also buries itself with its own burial." Therefore, if look at the concept of power, we can note that power corrupts and absolute power corrupts absolutely. There is a certain danger that despite several efforts for welfare purposes, the power may be used arbitrarily and for corrupt goals.

Therefore, a right to know is necessary to handle effectively the affairs related to the executive and provides a platform for people to participate in governance with proper knowledge.

Has Right to Information Emerged from Our Constitution?

Rightly as one of the significant objectives of the Constitution of India as the Preamble describes, is to secure liberty of thought and expressions to the citizens of India. The Article 19(1)(a) of the Constitution, the fundamental right to speech and expression can never be exercised until and unless the information regarding public matters is being circulated.

The right to information is an inalienable component of freedom of speech and expression guaranteed by Article 19(1)(a) of the Constitution of India as held in the respective cases of *Bennet Colman* v. *UOI*[4], *SP Gupta* v. *UOI*[5], and *Secretary, Ministry of Information and Broadcasting* v. *Cricket Assn. of Bengal*[6]. The Supreme Court of India in the *Bennet Coleman case* while taking into account the News Print Control Order, allotment of newsprint to a newspaper was restricted, held that such restriction had not only infringed newspapers, right to freedom of speech but also readers' right to read was cut down. And the reader's right to access the newspaper was his right to information which was implicit in the Right of Freedom of Speech. Similarly, in the *SP Gupta case* the SC observed that "the people of this country have a right to know every public act, everything that is done in a public way, by those functionaries. They are entitled to know all the very particulars of every public transaction. Also in *Secretary, Ministry of Information & Broadcasting* v. *Cricket Assn. of Bengal*, the SC held that the airwaves were a public property and their distribution among the government media and the private channels should be done on equitable basis as the freedom of speech included the right to impart and receive information from the electronic media.

Besides Article 19(1)(a), the other articles which give right to information under the Constitution of India are Articles 311(2) and 22(1). Article 311(2) provides for a government servant to know why he is being dismissed or removed or being demoted and representation can be made against the order. By way of Article 22(1) a person can know the grounds for his detention. In *Essar Oil Ltd v. Halar Utkarsha Samiti,* the SC held that right to information emerges from right to personal liberty guaranteed by Article 21 of the Constitution[7].

Restrictions Under Indian Law on Right to Know

There are laws which are contrary to the right to know in India and need to be amended in order to preserve the right to know. Sections 123, 124, and 162 of the Indian Evidence

Act provide to hold the disclosure of documents. Section 123 provides that any head of department may refuse to provide information on affairs of state and only swearing that it is a state secret will not entitle to disclose the information. In a similar manner Section 124 states that no public officer shall be compelled to disclose communications made to him in official confidence. Section 162 provides for the court not to inspect a document relating to matters of state.

The Atomic Energy Act, 1912 provides that it shall be an offence to disclose information restricted by the Central Government. The Central Civil Services Act provides that a government servant will not communicate or part with any official documents except in acçordance with a general or special order of government.

The Official Secrets Act as evident from its name, under Section 5, provides that any government official can mark a document as confidential so as to prevent its publication.

Legislation in India for Right to Information

India might be a super power in the IT sector but still sixty years have passed after independence, the government has never been serious on legislating the right to know. Merely declaring that Right to know is a constitutional right will not do. There is an utmost need to practically apply this right. In the year 2002 the Indian parliament passed the Freedom of Information Act. After obtaining the assent of the President this Bill could not come into force due to the want of a notification by the Central Government.

The Bill being unable to fulfil the purpose, the UPA Government, in the year 2005 enacted a new legislation on the same with the title "Right to Information Act, 2005", which came into effect from 12 October, 2005. The procedure for asking information is very simple; anybody can make a request on a plain paper in writing with a nominal fee. And the information as per the Act needs to be provided within 30 days of such request. Many states have established State Information Commissions for appealing purposes. A Central Information Commission is also established under the Act.

NOTES

1. Article 19, Universal Declaration of Human Rights (1948).
2. Article 19, International Covenant on Civil and Political Rights (1966).
3. A.I.R. 1978 SC 597.
4. AIR1973 SC 106.
5. AIR1982 SC 149.
6. (1995) 2 SCC 161.
7. AIR 2004 SC 1834.

CHAPTER – 3

Constitutional Protections of the Right to Information : Global Perspective

The right of access to official information is now protected by the constitutions of some 60 countries. At least fifty, and arguably fifty seven of these expressly guarantee a "right" to "information" or "documents," or else impose an obligation on the government to make information available to the public. The top courts of six of these countries[1] have interpreted the constitution to recognize the right implicitly.

Almost all these countries also have statutes that elaborate and implement a right to information. In countries with such laws, the question as to whether the right also has constitutional status may have little practical significance. Nonetheless, we suggest that the fact that so many countries have afforded the right constitutional status is noteworthy, and provides support for strengthening the status of the right under international and regional law. The fundamental status of the right has been particularly recognized in Latin America, even before the Inter-American Court's landmark judgment in the *Claude Reyes case*[2].

Constitutions that guarantee less than a general right to government-held information are not included in this count. For instance, we do not include constitutions that guarantee a right only to personal information, or to environmental information, or extend the right only to journalists. Nor do we include in this count constitutions that recognize a "right to freely seek and receive information," or variations of that phrasing, for instance as part of the right to freedom of expression, unless case-law, actual practice and/or assessments of in-country experts support the conclusion that the right includes a general right to information. We do, however, include in this count a right to government-held information that is limited to information of public interest (as found, e.g. by Canada's Supreme Court in a 2010 judgment[3] (see under Canada), and by the European Court of Human Rights.[4])

We note that the constitutional status of the right to information is disputed in at least seven European countries that we include in our list. In Austria and Belgium, the constitutional provision is viewed by some as imposing important duties on government but not as conferring an enforceable right on individuals. The constitutions of Azerbaijan, Georgia, Macedonia, Russia and Ukraine all guarantee the right to freely receive information but not, explicitly, a right to receive information from public bodies. A few lower courts in some of those countries have ruled that their constitution does impose a right to receive, or a duty to provide, information. Moreover, all of the seven countries have laws that implement a general right to information, although the laws of

Austria and Ukraine are relatively weak. We have included these seven countries in our list on the ground that the right is accorded special importance in those countries, sometimes as a right of the citizen, sometimes as a democratic imperative. Also, in all the countries, at least some access to information advocates and/or other experts claim that the right does have constitutional status. While such claims are not decisive, we have allowed them to tip the scales in favor of inclusion. We welcome readers' comments and feedback and, in particular, any authoritative interpretations, such as relevant case-law or academic analysis.

According to the above criteria, the constitutions of the following fifty seven countries guarantee a right to information:

- Eleven countries in the Americas (Brazil, Chile, Colombia, Costa Rica, Ecuador, Mexico, Nicaragua, Panama, Paraguay, Peru and Venezuela);
- Seventeen in Europe clearly grant a right to information (Albania, Bulgaria, Czech Republic, Estonia, Finland, Greece, Hungary, Lithuania, Moldova, Norway, Poland, Portugal, Romania, Serbia, Slovakia, Slovenia, Sweden);
- Seven in Europe arguably guarantee a right to information (Austria, Azerbaijan, Belgium, Georgia, Macedonia, Russia, Ukraine);
- Six in Asia and the Pacific (Nepal, New Zealand, Pakistan, Papua New Guinea, Philippines, Thailand); and
- Sixteen in Africa (Burkina Faso, Cameroon, Democratic Republic of Congo, Eritrea, Ghana, Guinea Bissau, Kenya, Madagascar, Malawi, Morocco, Mozambique, Senegal, Seychelles, South Africa, Tanzania, and Uganda).

The top courts of at least six additional countries have interpreted their constitutions or other basic laws to protect the right to information implicitly: Argentina, Canada, France, India, Israel and South Korea. Courts below the top courts have interpreted their constitutions to give rise to the right to information in several additional countries including Paraguay, Uruguay and Russia.

Top courts of at least nine of these countries have ruled that the constitutional right is enforceable in court even without enactment of an implementing law. These include Chile, Costa Rica, India, Paraguay, the Philippines, South Africa, South Korea, Uganda and Uruguay. Of these countries, Chile, India, South Africa, South Korea, Uganda, and Uruguay have adopted ATI laws. In three countries – Costa Rica, Paraguay, and the Philippines – which have yet to adopt ATI laws, the actionable constitutional right is all the more important.

The constitutions of a few additional countries – including Fiji – call for enactment of legislation to guarantee a statutory right of access to information.

At least five constitutions – of Kenya, Panama, Poland, Serbia and South Africa – expressly extend the right to information to state owned enterprises and/or private entities that exercise public functions as well as to public authorities. Indeed, the constitutions of South Africa and Kenya guarantee a right of access to "any information that is held by another person and that is required for the exercise or protection of any rights" (South Africa) or "for the exercise or protection of any right or fundamental freedom" (Kenya).

Several countries that provide a right to information in their constitutions also have constitutional procedures that enable the right to be directly enforced by the courts. For instance, in several Latin American countries (including Costa Rica, Honduras, Nicaragua, Panama and Peru) the constitutional right to information may be enforced *via* a habeas data petition or amparo.

Of the 57 constitutions that expressly guarantee the right to information, at least 24 extend that right to "everyone": six in the Americas—Brazil, Colombia, Mexico, Panama, Peru, Venezuela; 14 in Europe—Albania, Armenia, Austria, Azerbaijan, Bulgaria, Czech Republic, Estonia, Finland, Georgia, Greece, Lithuania, Moldova, Norway, Romania, Slovenia; and four others: New Zealand, Mozambique, Seychelles and Uganda. Several constitutions—including those of Hungary, Kenya, Macedonia, Morocco, Nepal, Pakistan, the Philippines, Poland, Portugal, Spain and Sweden—expressly limit the right to citizens. Other constitutions are ambiguous on this point.

Constitutions and courts have set forth several lines of reasoning underlying or giving rise to the right to information:

- Several emphasize the importance of the right as the foundation for a democratic society, recognizing that citizens' need information if they are to be able to participate effectively in decision-making and holding officials accountable (e.g., Argentina, Chile, Costa Rica, Hungary, Mexico, Peru).
- Several courts have interpreted the right to information to be an implicit component of the right to freedom of expression. For instance, South Korea's Constitutional Court ruled that the right to information is implicit in the right to freedom of speech and press, given that free expression and communication of ideas requires free formation of ideas as a precondition, and that "[f]ree formation of ideas is in turn made possible by guaranteeing access to sufficient information."[5] Colombia's Constitutional Court has advanced similar reasoning in several cases[6]. Freedom of speech and access to official documents in Sweden have been viewed as closely related since at least the original Freedom of the Press Act of 1766.
- Some constitutions note the particular importance of the right for journalists and the media (e.g. Ecuador).
- Colombia's Constitutional Court has noted the close relationship between the right and the rights of victims of serious human rights violations to truth, reparation and justice.
- India's Supreme Court concluded that the right to know arises not only from the right to freedom of expression but also, importantly, from the right to life[7].
- South Africa's Constitution recognizes the importance of the right to information in exercising and protecting all other rights.

The above-summarized reasoning, unusual provisions, tallied information and more, as well as citations, are supported by or supplied in the following country paragraphs.

Africa and the Middle East

In Africa, 16 out of 54 countries (the 53 countries of the African Union plus Morocco) have expressly guaranteed the right to information in their constitutions: seven countries in the Southern Africa Development Community (SADC) (Democratic Republic of Congo, Madagascar, Malawi, Mozambique, Seychelles, South Africa and Tanzania); three in east Africa (Eritrea, Kenya and Uganda); five in west Africa (Burkina Faso, Cameroon, Ghana, Guinea Bissau, and Senegal), and one in north Africa (Morocco).

An additional 14 countries have protected the right to information within the context of the broader right to freedom of expression, which includes the right to "seek, receive and impart information". These include eight in the SADC region (Angola, Botswana, Lesotho, Mauritius, Namibia, Swaziland, Zambia and Zimbabwe), one in east Africa (Tanzania), two in West Africa (Nigeria and Sierra Leone); and Ethiopia, whose constitution (in Art. 29) recognizes the right to information within the broader right to freedom of the press, mass media and artistic creativity.

African Union

The Declaration of Principles on Freedom of Expression in Africa, adopted by the African Commission on Human and Peoples' Rights in 2002,[8] is widely considered to constitute an authoritative interpretation of Article 9 of the African Charter on Human and Peoples' Rights, which is binding on the 53 countries of the African Union. The Declaration's strong statement of the right to information is premised, in part, on the recognition that "the right of access to information held by public bodies and companies will lead to greater public transparency and accountability, as well as to good governance and the strengthening of democracy" (preambular paragraph 4) and that " [public bodies hold information not for themselves but as custodians of the public good" [Article 4(1)].

Burkina Faso

Article 8 of the Constitution provides:

> Freedom of opinion, freedom of the press and right to information are guaranteed.

Cape Verde

Article 245d of the Constitution of Cape Verde provides:

> Access to administrative records and files, without prejudice to the provisions concerning the law on internal and external security of the state, criminal investigation, the secrecy, state secrecy and personal privacy[9].

Congo, Democratic Republic of

Article 24 of the Constitution provides:

> La liberté de presse, la liberté d'information et d'émission par la radio et la télévision, la presse écrite ou tout autre moyen de communication sont garanties sous réserve du respect de l'ordre public, des bonnes mœurs et des droits d'autrui.

Eritrea

Article 19(3) of the Constitution provides:

> Every citizen shall have the right of access to information.

Ethiopia

Article 29 of the Constitution provides:

> 1. Everyone shall have the right to hold opinions without any interference.
> 2. Everyone shall have the right to freedom of expression without interference. This right shall include freedom to seek, receive and impart information and ideas of all kinds, regardless of frontiers, either orally, in writing or in print, in the form of art, or through other media of his choice.

Guinea Bissau

Article 34 of the Constitution states:

> Everyone has the right to information and legal protection under the law.

Ghana

Article 21(1) of the Constitution of Ghana states:

> All persons shall have the right to... (f) information, subject to such qualifications and laws as are necessary in a democratic society...

Israel

The Supreme Court held in 1990 that the public has a right to be informed of the content of coalition agreements negotiated by political parties participating in an election.[10] Acting in the absence of explicit constitutional or statutory recognition of the right of access, the Court nonetheless held that:

> Freedom of public opinion and knowledge of what is happening in the channels of government are an integral part of a democratic regime, which is structured on the constant sharing of information about what is happening in public life with the public itself. Withholding of information is justifiable only in exceptional cases where security of the State or foreign relations may be impaired or where there is a risk of harming some vital public interest.[11]
>
> [...]

There is a third source [for the obligation to disclose] which is entrenched in the public's right to know. It has been her[e] that freedom of expression is one of the basic principles of our system of law. Freedom of expression is a complex value, at the crux of which is the freedom "to express one's thoughts and to hear what others have to say." In order to realize this freedom the law vests the holder thereof with additional rights derived from the freedom of expression. Among these additional rights it [*sic*] the "right to receive information." As against the individual's right to receive information is the governing body's study [*sic*] to provide that information.[12]

Kenya

The Constitution of Kenya adopted in 2010 is the second constitution in the world, besides South Africa's Constitution, that provides for a comprehensive right of access to privately-held information. Article 35 of the Bill of Rights states: "Every citizen has the right to access to information held by the state or any information that is held by another person and that is required for the exercise or protection of any right or fundamental freedom."

Madagascar

According to Article 11 of the Constitution of Madagascar:

(1) Information in all forms shall be subject to no prior restraint.
(2) Conditions of freedom of information and its responsibility shall be determined by law and by codes of professional ethics.

Malawi

Article 37 of the Constitution of Malawi states:

> Subject to any Act of Parliament, every person shall have the right of access to all information held by the State or any of its organs at any level of Government in so far as such information is required for the exercise of his rights.

Morocco

Article 27 of the 2011 Constitution of Morocco states:

> Citizens have the right to access information held by public bodies, elected institutions and bodies performing public service. Access to information can be limited only by the law with the purpose of protecting everything concerning national defence, internal and external security of the State, and private life; of preventing violation of any rights and liberties declared in the present Constitution and protecting the sources and domains expressly determined by the Constitution.[13]

Mozambique

Article 74 of the Constitution of Mozambique states:

1. All citizens shall have the right to freedom of expression and to freedom of the press as well as the right to information.

Senegal

Article 8 of the Constitution provides:

> La République du Sénégal garantit à tous les citoyens les libertés individuelles fondamentales, les droits économiques et sociaux ainsi que les droits collectifs. Ces libertés et droits sont notamment:
>
> [...]
>
> le droit à l'information plurielle

Seychelles

Article 28 of the Constitution provides for the "right of access to official information:"

(1) The state recognises the right of access of every person to information relating to that person and held by a public authority which is performing a governmental function and the right to have the information rectified or otherwise amended, if inaccurate.

(2) The right of access to information contained in clause (1) shall be subject to such limitations and procedures as may be prescribed by law and are necessary in a democratic society including—
   (a) for the protection of national security;
   (b) for the prevention and detection of crime and the enforcement of law;
   (c) for the compliance with an order of a court or in accordance with a legal privilege;
   (d) for the protection of the privacy or rights or freedoms of others.

(3) The state undertakes to take appropriate measures to ensure that information collected in respect of any person for a particular purpose is used only for that purpose except where a law necessary in a democratic society or an order of a court authorises otherwise.
(4) The state recognises the right of access by the public to information held by a public authority performing a governmental function subject to limitations contained in clause (2) and any law necessary in a democratic society.

South Africa

Section 32(1) of the 1996 Constitution of South Africa reads:

Everyone has the right of access to –

(a) any information that is held by the state; and
(b) any information that is held by another person and that is required for the exercise or protection of any rights.

National legislation must be enacted to give effect to this right, and may provide for reasonable measures to alleviate the administrative and financial burden on the state.

Section 32(1)(b) was the first constitutional provision that provided for a comprehensive right of access to privately-held information. Kenya's Constitution now also provides for such a right. Moreover, it is uncontested that the phrase "another person" includes juristic as well as natural persons.

The transitional arrangements for the final Constitution provided that until the national legislation mandated under Section 32(2) was enacted, the provision relating to the right of access to information contained in the Interim Constitution (the Constitution that was negotiated as a part of the final political settlement ahead of South Africa's first post-apartheid democratic election of April 1994) would remain in force.[14] The Promotion of Access to Information Act, 2000 (PAIA) was enacted in January 2000 (and came into effect in March 2001). Thus, between 1994 and January 2000, the right of access to information was the right as set forth in Section 23 of the Interim Constitution: "Every person has the right of access to all information held by the state or any of its organs in any sphere of government in so far as that information is required for the exercise or protection of any of their rights."

The Interim Constitution differs from the Constitution in that the Interim Constitution (a) makes no provision for access to privately-held information and (b) includes the caveat even regarding access to information held by the state that the information must be "required for the exercise and protection of any ... rights."[15]

It is now well-accepted that the term "any rights" (in both the Interim and 1996 Constitutions) is not limited to fundamental rights protected in Chapter 3 of the Constitution (the South African Bill of Rights). In Claase, for example, the Supreme Court of Appeal found that access to the passenger records of a certain commercial flight was required for the protection of the contractual (retirement) rights of a former pilot of South African Airways (SAA).[16]

In another case, the High Court ruled that applicant requesters, who sought to protect their rights to trust property which were potentially threatened by the building of a large steel mill, were entitled to copies of the records held by the Minister of Environmental Affairs relevant to the proposed rezoning and planning permission.[17]

Tanzania

Article 18(1) of the Constitution of Tanzania includes the right to seek, receive and impart information as part of the right to freedom of opinion and expression. Article 18(2) guarantees every citizen the right to be informed at all times of various events in the country and in the world at large which are important to the lives and activities of people and of issues of importance to society. The Commonwealth Human Rights Initiative deems these provisions to constitute an explicit guarantee of the right to information. In late 2006 the Government released a draft Freedom of Information Bill, 2006. Stakeholders responded by rejecting the Government Bill and drafting their own alternative Stakeholder Bill to take to Government.[18]

Uganda

Article 41(1) of the Constitution of Uganda reads:

> Every citizen has a right of access to information in the possession of the state or any other organ or agency of the state except where the release of the information is likely to prejudice the security or sovereignty of the state or interfere with the right to privacy of any other person.

Zimbabwe

Article 20 of the Constitution provides:

1. Except with his own consent or by way of parental discipline, no person shall be hindered in the enjoyment of his freedom of expression, that is to say, freedom to hold opinions and to receive and impart ideas and information without interference, and freedom from interference with his correspondence.

Americas and the Caribbean

Argentina

The Supreme Court of Justice has ruled that Article 1 of the Constitution of Argentina, which establishes a republican form of government, gives rise to an obligation of transparency because a republic requires that government actions be available to the public.[19] Furthermore, Article 75.22 ensures the domestic application of international human rights treaties, including the American Convention on Human Rights (ACHR), the International Covenant on Civil and Political Rights (ICCPR), and the American Convention Against Corruption (ACAC). The Supreme Court has interpreted that, in light of these provisions, there is a duty to ensure access to information.[20]

Brazil

Article 5, paragraph XIV of the 1998 Constitution of Brazil reads, "[A]ccess to information is ensured to everyone and the confidentiality of the source shall be safeguarded, whenever necessary to the professional activity."

Canada

The Constitution of Canada does not expressly provide for a right of access to information. However, Canadian courts have held that freedom of expression, found in section 2(b) of the Canadian Charter of Rights and Freedoms ("the Charter"), includes the right to receive as well as to convey information. As the Supreme Court held in *Edmonton Journal* v. *Alberta* (*Attorney General*), "listeners and readers, as members of the public, have a right to information pertaining to public institutions and particularly the courts."[21] Several courts, including the Supreme Court of Canada, have reasoned that FOI legislation, given its connection with the concept of democracy, has a quasi-constitutional status.[22] For instance, Justice Laforest concurring with the Supreme Court majority on this point, noted, in the landmark case of *Dagg* v. *Canada*, that the overarching purpose of access to information legislation, then, is to facilitate democracy. It does so in two related ways. It helps to ensure first, that citizens have the information required to participate meaningfully in the democratic process, and secondly, that politicians and bureaucrats remain accountable to the citizenry.[23]

In *Ontario (Public Safety and Security)* v. *Criminal Lawyers' Association*[24] the Supreme Court recognized a limited constitutional right to have access to government-held documents. Similar to previous cases, the Court found that freedom of expression under section 2(b) of the Charter includes the right to information. This time, however, it particularly specified that section 2(b) includes the right to request access to government documents:

[T]here is a *prima facie* case that section 2(b) may require disclosure of documents in government hands where it is shown that, without the desired access, meaningful public discussion and criticism on matters of public interest would be substantially impeded.[25]

The Federal Court of Appeal has suggested that the right to access and correct one's personal information could engage section 7 of the Charter, in light of the emerging view that an individual's right to privacy (and to access and correct his or her private information) is enshrined in one's liberty interest set forth in section 7. This is so because the protection of private life is considered to be at the heart of liberty in a democratic society.[26]

Furthermore, the Ontario Court of Appeal, in a 2007 decision, found that the right to freedom of expression protected by section 2(b) of the Charter was not possible if the information was not provided and as such the public interest override contained in the Ontario Freedom of Information and Protection of Privacy Act was held to apply to all of the Act's provisions.[27] In spite of this, the courts have yet to find a general constitutional right to information, and lower courts and Information Commissioners have been reluctant to accept that a right to access information is guaranteed by the Charter.

Cayman Islands

The Constitution of the Cayman Islands provides the following:

> 122. A law enacted by the Legislature shall provide for a right of access to information held by public authorities, for the conditions for the exercise of that right, and for restrictions and exceptions to that right in the interests of the security of the Cayman Islands or the United Kingdom, public safety, public order, public morality or the rights or interests of individuals.

Chile

Article 19, No. 12 of the Constitution of Chile guarantees the right to freedom of expression, including the "right to seek and impart" information. However, this protection, unlike in several other constitutions of Latin America, does not include a "right to receive" information. In addition, the Constitution (Art. 19, No. 14) enshrines a right to petition, which in some other jurisdictions has been considered to be a means to ensure access to information. In 2005, Article 8 of the Chilean Constitution was amended to read: "The acts and decisions of the state authorities, as well as their reasoning and the procedures they use, shall be public." The provision continues to state that exceptions are permissible as long as they are established by a qualified law (a law that requires a super-majority of votes to be approved), and only if disclosure would have a negative effect on the functioning of a state body, the rights of individuals, state security or national interests. This article does not, on its face either (a) guarantee a right of access to information, or (b) apply to all information held by public authorities (but only to acts, decisions, reasoning and the procedures used to reach decisions).

The Constitutional Tribunal (the highest court on constitutional questions) ruled in August 2007, in *Casas Cordero and Others* v. *National Customs Service*, that the right of access to government information is implicitly protected by the Constitution's guarantee of freedom of expression and the constitutional principle of a democratic republic.[28] The case arose when a Chilean company filed a request for information from Chile's Customs Department regarding alleged irregularities in the setting of customs tariffs. The Department refused the request without even consulting the private party or considering the public's interest in publication of the information. In finding for the applicant, the Tribunal ruled that the right of access, even though not explicitly recognized by the Chilean Constitution, was implicitly protected. In the words of the Tribunal, the right of access is an integral part of the broader right of freedom of expression and "an essential mechanism for [ensuring] the full effectiveness of the democratic regime" which promotes "the adequate exercise and protection of [other] fundamental rights."[29] The Tribunal further held that any restrictions on the right of access must be defined and construed narrowly. Turning to the specific facts of the case, the tribunal found that the statute at stake granted agencies impermissibly broad discretion to withhold third party information, the disclosure of which might arguably harm their confidentiality interests. In particular, the Tribunal held that agencies cannot withhold such information without first consulting with, or receiving objections from, the third party involved. Interestingly, even though the Inter-American Court on Human Rights had issued its landmark judgment in the *Claude Reyes case*[30] against Chile nearly a year earlier (in September 2006), the Court did not refer to that case.

Colombia

Articles 74, 20 and 23 of the Constitution of Colombia enshrine the rights to: (a) access public documents, (b) impart and receive impartial and accurate information, and (c) obtain a prompt response to requests for information.

> Article 74 of the Constitution states that: "Every person has the right to access public documents, with exceptions provided by law."
> Article 20 guarantees the right to freedom of expression and information: "Every person is guaranteed the freedom to express and disclose his thoughts and opinions, to impart and to receive impartial and truthful information, and to found broadcasting media."
> Article 23 states that: "Every person has the right to respectfully request information from the authorities for reasons of general or particular interest and to obtain an expeditious response. The Legislative Branch may regulate the exercise of this right with respect to private organizations to guarantee fundamental rights."

In addition, Article 15 recognizes the action of habeas data, concerning personal information, as a fundamental right.

Numerous decisions of the Constitutional Court refer to the fundamental nature of the right of access to information. Some note the close relationship between the right to information and the right to freedom of information given that "it is undeniable that the guarantee of the free flow of information requires access to public documents."[31] The Court has also noted the link between the right of access to information and the rights of victims to truth, reparations and justice.[32] Moreover, the Constitutional Court established that, in a democratic society, the general rule is to allow access to all public documents, and that public authorities have a duty to provide clear, complete, timely, truthful and updated information about any state activity. Every public body should also have a policy to maintain documents, particularly those related to serious and systematic human rights and humanitarian law violations.[33] The Court has further ruled that exceptions to the general principle of disclosure should be allowed only in unusual circumstances, must be authorized by a legislative act,[34] and should aim to protect another legitimate purpose set forth in the Constitution, such as a fundamental right (e.g., the right to life or privacy) or the protection of national security.[35] The restrictions must be reasonable and proportionate to the legitimate objective, in the context of a democratic society.[36]

Costa Rica

Article 30 of the Constitution of Costa Rica states that: "The free access to administrative departments for the purposes of obtaining information on matters of public interest is guaranteed. State secrets are exempt from this provision."

The Constitutional Chamber of the Supreme Court of Costa Rica held in a 2002 case that the Central Bank's refusal to disclose a report of the International Monetary Fund, requested by a newspaper, violated the constitutional right to information "to the detriment of all Costa Rican citizens." The Court reasoned that "the State must guarantee that information of a public character and importance is made known to the citizens and, in order for this to be achieved, the State must encourage a climate of freedom of information. … In this way, the State … is the first to have an obligation to facilitate not only access to this information, but also its adequate disclosure and dissemination, and towards this aim, the State has the obligation to offer the necessary facilities and eliminate existing obstacles to its attainment."[37]

In reaching its decision, the Court relied emphatically on the symbiotic relationship between the right to information and the rights of democratic participation, arguing that "the right to information … implicates the citizens' participation in collective decision-making, which, to the extent that freedom of information is protected, guarantees the formation and existence of a free public opinion, which is the very pillar of a free and democratic society."[38]

The Constitutional Chamber of the Supreme Court reaffirmed the right of access to state-held information in a 2003 case concerning access to banking information of political parties held by the Central Bank.[39] See Section on Information about Elections, Political Parties and Candidates.

Ecuador

Article 81 of the Constitution of Ecuador provides for a right to access information sources, as well as a right to "seek, receive, examine and disseminate objective, accurate, pluralistic and timely information, without prior censorship, on matters of general interest," consistent with community values; and gives particular relevance to the enjoyment of this right by journalists and communications professionals.[40] Paragraph 3 of Article 81 establishes that information from public archives should not be reserved, except when national security or other laws so provide. This right is implemented both by the constitutional right to petition and by the Transparency and Access to Public Information Act, 2004.

The first and third paragraphs of Article 81 state:

The state shall guarantee the right, in particular for journalists and social commentators, to obtain access to sources of information; and to seek, receive, examine, and disseminate objective, accurate, pluralistic, and timely information, without prior censorship, on matters of general interest, consistent with community values. ...

Information held in public archives shall not be classified as secret, with the exception of documents requiring such classification for the purposes of national defence or other reasons specified by law.

Mexico

Since 1977, the Constitution of Mexico has established, in Article 6, an obligation on the federal state to guarantee access to information.[41] The Supreme Court has established that this provision is closely linked to the right to truth, understood as a right of the public to be provided truthful information to enhance its participation in the decision-making process. The Supreme Court has established that authorities who provide manipulated or incomplete information, or information that is biased towards particular interests, and that limits informed participation in public matters, violate constitutional rights.[42] The Constitution also provides for a right of petition.

In June 2007, a second paragraph was added to Article 6 of the Constitution requiring all 32 states and the Federal District to revise their local ATI laws within a one-year period and to introduce electronic systems for offering information within two years. Article 6(2) now reads as follows (translation approximate):[43]

(1) All information in possession of state institutions is public and only in exceptional cases may information be temporally reserved, in the public interest and as defined by law.
(2) Private information and personal data will be protected according to the law.
(3) All persons will have free access to public information without the need for justification or proving interest. All persons will have free access to their personal information and will be able to correct mis-information.
(4) Procedures for accessing and revising information must be established. These procedures are to be conducted before specialized and impartial organs, which have operational, administrative and decision-making autonomy.
(5) The obliged entities will have to maintain their documents in updated archives and will have to publish through available electronic media full and actual information regarding their management indicators and the management of public resources.
(6) The laws will define the form in which the obliged entities will have to make public the information related to public resources which they give to legal or moral persons.
(7) Sanctions will be administered to those not fulfilling their obligations regarding ATI. These sanctions will be defined by law.

Nicaragua

Article 66 of the Constitution of Nicaragua provides that Nicaraguans have the right to truthful information and, in exercising that freedom, may seek, receive, and disseminate information and ideas, orally, in writing, in graphic form, or by another medium of their choice. In addition, Article 26 of the Constitution provides a right to personal information, in the following terms: "All persons have the right to … (4) Knowledge of all information about them registered by state authorities, as well as the right to know why and for what purpose this information is held." These rights were implemented by Law No. 621 of 2007 on Access to Public Information.

Panama

The Constitution of Panama was amended in 2004 to provide, in Article 43, for the right to access information held by the state or by private companies involved in work of a public nature. It allows that such a right might be limited but only by written law. Articles 42 and 44 also guarantee judicial remedies to ensure the exercise of the right of access to information, along with habeas data procedures.

Paraguay

Article 28 of the 1992 Constitution of Paraguay, titled "About the Right to Obtain Information," reads as follows:

(1) The people's right to receive true, responsible, and equitable information is hereby recognized.
(2) Everyone has free access to public sources of information. The laws will regulate the corresponding procedures, deadlines and sanctions in order to make this right effective.

Although no law has been adopted to implement this provision, in 2007, the District Court of Asuncion ruled that Paraguay's Constitution guarantees the right of access to state held information, and that the right is judicially enforceable.[44] The case, brought by Instituto de Derecho y Economía Ambiental (IDEA), started when a member of the office of the Public Defender twice requested, in person, from the Rectorate of the National University of Asuncion, a copy of certain amendments to the scholarship regulations. The Rectorate denied the request on technical grounds (because not signed by the proper official in the Public Defender's Office and not submitted in proper format). The information was eventually provided, but the Public Defender sued anyway over the initial refusal. The Court, ruling that the suit was not moot, concluded that there is a constitutional right of access to state-held information in Paraguay which was violated in this case. The Court relied on the constitutional right to petition the authorities (Article 40) and to receive information from publicly available sources (Article 28). The Court interpreted these provisions in light of Article 13 of the American

Convention on Human Rights and the Claude Reyes judgment[45], which is considered binding law for Paraguay.

Peru

The right to public information is protected under Section 5 of Article 2 of the 1993 Constitution of Peru. Under this section, any person[46] has the right to request, without stating a specific cause, information from a government entity except for that expressly prohibited by law or the Constitution such as personal or private information or information pertaining to national security. There are limits to these exceptions, such as Article 96, which guarantees any member of Congress the right to request from public officials any reports that he or she deems necessary including those considered to be of a confidential nature.

Peru's Tribunal of Constitutional Guarantees has interpreted Article 2 to be a fundamental right of all persons as well as a collective right given that an informed public serves as the foundation for a democratic society in which all participate in the process of elaboration, search, selection and promulgation of public information.[47] Access to information is the foundation for an authentic democratic society, necessary for citizens to be able to develop free and informed public opinion about government activities and hold their government accountable.[48] In order to fulfil this constitutional mandate, the Tribunal has held that government entities must provide information, that is "complete, precise, correct, current, timely, and accurate."[49] While Section 5 declares the intent to promote open and transparent government as the basis for a democratic society, the second half of Section 5 protects against the unlawful disclosure of private or personal information. The Constitutional Tribunal has held that private information can become public when it is requested and subsequently possessed and used by an administrative entity.[50] In addition to a general right to public information, the Constitution's authors also contemplated the need to enumerate specific rights to information regarding public functionaries. See section on Asset Declarations.

United States

In the United States, the right to freedom of information is considered central to the concept of democratic accountability. James Madison, a leading figure in the drafting of the US Constitution, eloquently described the importance of an informed citizenry to democratic governance:

> A popular Government, without popular information, or the means of acquiring it, is but a prologue to a farce or a tragedy; or, perhaps, both. Knowledge will for ever govern ignorance; and a people who mean to be their own governors must arm themselves with the power which knowledge gives.[51]

The Supreme Court ruled in 1978 that, while the right of access to information clearly is guaranteed by statute, there is no constitutional underpinning to the right:

> [T]here is no constitutional right to have access to particular government information, or to require openness from the bureaucracy.... The Constitution itself is neither a Freedom of Information Act nor an Official Secrets Act.[52]

Justice Stevens, dissenting from the majority, cited various sources that recognize constitutional protections of the media's right to collect information and the public's right to know.[53] In the *Richmond case*, (in which the Court ruled that holding a closed criminal hearing to prevent public attendance violated the First Amendment's right to freedom of speech), he noted:

> Today... for the first time, the Court unequivocally holds that an arbitrary interference with access to important information is an abridgment of the freedoms of speech and of the press protected by the First Amendment.
> It is somewhat ironic that the Court should find more reason to recognize a right of access today than it did in Houchins.[54]

The Sixth Circuit, in the *Detroit Free Press case*,[55] concluded that the Supreme Court's various pronouncements do signify the existence of a constitutional right to freedom of information, albeit limited:

> [T]here is a limited constitutional right to some government information.... [A]lthough First Amendment Coalition and Capital Cities Media recognize Houchins as holding that there is no general right of access to government information, the line of cases from Richmond Newspapers to Press—Enterprise II recognize that there is in fact a limited constitutional right to some government information...[56]
> Nonetheless, most commentators view the Houchins decision as the most decisive ruling in the United States on the question of whether the right of access to information receives constitutional protection.[57]

Uruguay

In a 2002 decision, a Court of Appeals ordered the executive branch to release information related to an arrest request by Argentina concerning two former members of the military and an ex-policeman for alleged human rights abuses. The information included reports of the Public Prosecutor and the Attorney General. The Court ruled that exceptions to the principle of access to information shall be clearly stated, noting the importance of international human rights provisions, freedom of information as a means to build public opinion, and the essential character of public opinion in a democratic society.[58] (Editor's note: We have not counted Uruguay among the countries whose top courts have interpreted the Constitution to guarantee a right to information given that the Court of Appeals is not a top court.)

Venezuela

Article 28 of the Constitution of Venezuela, amended in 1999, provides:

> All persons have the right of access to information and data held in government or private files referring to them or to their property, except where the law provides otherwise; to know why and for what purpose the information is kept; and to file requests before the competent court for the updating, rectification, or destruction of information that is erroneous or that illegitimately affects their rights. They may also obtain access to documents of any kind containing information of interest to communities or groups of individuals.
>
> Article 51 of the Constitution establishes the right to submit petitions to the authorities. According to this provision, all persons have the right to address petitions to any authority or public official on matters within their purview and to obtain a timely and adequate response. Violations of this right are punishable by law and can result in dismissal. The Oıganic Law on Public Administration and other laws implement at least parts of the right to information.

Asia and Pacific Islands

Fiji

Article 174 of the 1997 Constitution of Fiji states: "As soon as practicable after the commencement of this Constitution, the Parliament should enact a law to give members of the public rights of access to official documents of the Government and its agencies." Article 30(1) guarantees to "everyone" a general "right to freedom of speech and expression," including "(a) freedom to seek, receive and impart information and ideas." We have, however, not included Fiji in our count of countries whose Constitution guarantees a right to information given that (a) the Constitution only calls for legislation, and a law has yet to be enacted; (b) Article 174 is in the part of the Constitution titled "Accountability," rather than the Bill of Rights; and (c) the Commonwealth Human Rights Initiative holds the view that Fiji's Constitution does not guarantee a right to information.[59]

In October 2007, Fiji's High Court cited Article 174 as partial basis for its ruling that Fiji TV Ltd. had to be allowed to broadcast information about a financial audit of the Fiji National Provident Fund (FNPF), a statutory body which is Fiji's largest financial institution.[60] Under the FNPF Act, all employers make compulsory monthly contributions to the fund equal to 16 per cent of monthly wages. Fiji TV aired excerpts of an audit by the accounting firm of Ernest and Young on September 19, 20 and 21 by which date the FNPF obtained a temporary injunction. It then filed an application for a permanent injunction. In dismissing the application, Justice Coventry of the High Court concluded that the findings of the audit were a matter of clear public interest and that the FNPF had failed to prove that the report was confidential. Furthermore, he ordered the FNPF to pay FJD $ 13,500 (US $ 8,812) in costs to Fiji TV. Justice Coventry reasoned that the FNPF could not seek to prevent the public from knowing the contents of a report concerning the conduct of its affairs when it involved the investment of millions of dollars of their money. Justice Coventry cited the Fiji Constitution's "Bill of Rights," which exhorts the courts to "promote the values that underlie a democratic society".[61] Drawing attention to Article 174 on Freedom of Information, he noted: "It is now nearly 10 years since the Constitution came into being. Parliament has not yet enacted a law giving members of the public rights to access official documents of the government and its agencies. In my judgment, this is a grave shortcoming and should be rectified at the earliest opportunity."[62] The ruling is considered to set a precedent allowing the media to publish any government or statutory body information no matter how it is obtained so long as it is in the public interest according to the Constitution.

India

The Constitution of India does not contain an explicit reference to the right to information. The Supreme Court has established in several decisions that the citizen's right to know arises from two fundamental rights guaranteed by the Constitution – the right to freedom of speech and expression, guaranteed by Article 19(1) and the right to life, guaranteed by Article 21.[63] The Supreme Court addressed the issue as early as 1975. In ruling that the government had to disclose documents regarding security arrangements for the Prime Minister's travels within the country, despite growing tensions in the country, so long as disclosure did not endanger his security or public order, the Court reasoned as follows:

> In a government of responsibility like ours, where all the agents of the public must be responsible for their conduct, there can be but few secrets. The people of this country have a right to know every public act, everything that is done in a public way, by their public functionaries. They are entitled to know the particulars of every public transaction in all its bearing. The right to know, which is derived from the concept of freedom of speech, though not absolute, is a factor which should make one wary when secrecy is claimed for transactions which can, at any rate, have no repercussion on public security.[64]

In 1982, the Supreme Court ordered the government to release intra-agency correspondence regarding transfers and dismissals of judges. Recognizing a "right to know which seems implicit in the right of free speech and expression," the Indian Court reasoned that,

> [w]here a society has chosen to accept democracy as its creedal faith, it is elementary that the citizens ought to know what their government is doing. The citizens have a right to decide by whom and by what rules they shall be governed and they are entitled to call on those who govern on their behalf to

> account for their conduct. No democratic government can survive without accountability and the basic postulate of accountability is that the people should have information about the functioning of government. ... The citizens' right to know the facts, the true facts, about the administration of the country is thus one of the pillars of a democratic State.[65]

The Court further reasoned that the citizen's right to know forms an integral part of the right to life and liberty guaranteed under Article 21 of the Constitution.[66]

Japan

There is no reference to freedom of information in the Constitution of Japan, however, the Supreme Court ruled that the right to information is protected by Article 21, which guarantees freedom of assembly, organization, speech and the press together with any other form of expression.[67] The Court stated:

> In order that the contents of the reports of such mass media may be correct, the freedom to gather news for informational purposes, as well as the freedom to report must be accorded due respect in light of the spirit of Article 21 of the Constitution.[68]
> The Court concluded that the right to information enjoys constitutional protection due to its instrumental role in realizing the freedom of the press.[69]

Kazakhstan

The Constitution of the Republic of Kazakhstan of 30 August, 1995, amended by Law No. 284 of 7 October, 1998, does not recognize general right to government-held information. Rather, it includes three articles that provide a public access to certain limited categories of information. Article 18(3) imposes an obligation on "state bodies, public associations, officials, and the mass media" to "provide every citizen with the possibility to obtain access to documents, decisions and other sources of information" but only "concerning his rights and interests." Article 20(2) guarantees the "right to freely receive and disseminate information by any means not prohibited by law." Article 31(2) provides that "[o]fficials shall be held accountable for the concealment of facts and circumstances endangering the life and health of the people in accordance with law."

Korea, Republic of (South)

The Constitutional Court issued a landmark ruling in 1989, recognizing an actionable, constitutional right of the public to government-held information, even though Korea's Constitution does not expressly guarantee such a right.[70] In ruling that a municipal office had to grant the applicant access to certain real estate records, the Court reasoned as follows:

> Freedom of speech and press guaranteed by Article 21 of the Constitution envisages free expression and communication of ideas and opinions that require free formation of ideas as a precondition. Free formation of ideas is in turn made possible by guaranteeing access to sufficient information. Right to access, collection and processing of information, namely the right to know, is, therefore, covered by the freedom of expression. The core of the right to know is the people's right to know about the information held by the government, that is, the general right to request disclosure of information from the government. The right to know is given effect directly by the Constitution without any legislation implementing it. Therefore, if the complainant requested disclosure of information and had a legitimate interest in it, and the government failed to respond without any review, his freedom of speech and press, or freedom of expression of Article 21 or its component right to know, was abridged. However, the right to know is not absolute, and can be reasonably restricted. The limit on the extent of restriction must be drawn by balancing the interest secured by the restriction and the infringement on the right to know. Generally, the right to know must be broadly protected to a person making the request with interest as long as it poses no threat to public interest. Disclosure, at least to a person with direct interest, is mandatory.[71]

Following this case, known as the *Forests Survey Inspection Request case*, the National Assembly adopted the Official Information Disclosure Act in late 1996.

Mongolia

The Mongolian Constitution guarantees to its citizens the following rights and freedoms:

> Article 16 (17): The right to seek and receive information except that which the state and its bodies are legally bound to protect as secret. In order to protect human rights, dignity and reputation of persons and to ensure State defence, national security and public order secrets of the State, organization or individuals, which are not subject to disclosure shall be determined and protected by law.

Nepal

Article 27 (Right to Information) of the Interim Constitution of Nepal states: "(1) Every citizen shall have the right to demand or obtain information on any matters of his/ner own or of public importance."

New Zealand

Section 14, on freedom of expression, of the Bill of Rights Act, 1990 reads: "Everyone has the right to freedom of expression, including the freedom to seek, receive, and impart information and opinions of any kind in any form." Prior to passage of this Act in 1990, the New Zealand Court of Appeal had already described New Zealand's freedom of information legislation as "an Act of constitutional significance."[72] The Bill of Rights affirms and extends that position, for example, influencing public access to court records.[73]

Pakistan

The 18th Amendment, adopted in April 2010, inserted a new Article 19A in the Constitution of Pakistan that states: "Every citizen shall have the right to have access to information in all matters of public importance subject to regulation and reasonable restrictions imposed by law."

Papua New Guinea

Article 51 of the Constitution of Papua New Guinea provides: "(1) Every citizen has the right of reasonable access to official documents, subject only to the need for such secrecy as is reasonably justifiable in a democratic society." Article 51 sets forth a list of 10 permissible exceptions to the right, including an unusual one for "(j) geological or geophysical information and data concerning wells and ore bodies." This is similar to the ninth exemption to the US Freedom of Information Act, which excludes from the Act's coverage "geological and geophysical information and data, including maps, concerning wells. A Draft Freedom of Information Bill was developed by civil society, but had not been acted upon by Government as of 2006.[74]

Philippines

The right to information is recognized as a distinct Constitutional guarantee. Article III (Bill of Rights), Sec. 7 of the 1987 Constitution of the Philippines,[75] which remains in force, states:

> The right of the people to information on matters of public concern shall be recognized. Access to official records, and to documents and papers pertaining to official acts, transactions, or decisions, as well as to government research data used as basis for policy development, shall be afforded to the citizen, subject to such limitations as may be provided by law.

The Supreme Court declared the right to be enforceable in 1987, in a case involving access to information regarding the civil service eligibility of certain individuals:

> These constitutional provisions [re the right to information] are self-executing. They supply the rules by means of which the right to information may be enjoyed... by guaranteeing the right and mandating the duty to afford access to sources of information. Hence, the fundamental right therein recognized may be asserted by the people upon the ratification of the

> Constitution without need for any ancillary act of the Legislature.... What may be provided for by the Legislature are reasonable conditions and limitations upon the access to be afforded which must, of necessity, be consistent with the declared State policy of full public disclosure of all transactions involving public interest...[76]

The Court continued by noting the importance of the right to information for democratic decision-making:

> The incorporation in the Constitution of a guarantee of access to information of public concern is a recognition of the essentiality of the free flow of ideas and information in a democracy.... In the same way that free discussion enables members of society to cope with the exigencies of their time..., access to information of general interest aids the people in democratic decision-making ... by giving them a better perspective of the vital issues confronting the nation.[77]

The 1987 Constitution also contains a provision in Article II (Declaration of Principles and State Policies), Section 28, which reads:

> Subject to reasonable conditions prescribed by law, the State adopts and implements a policy of full public disclosure of all its transactions involving public interest.

For many years, this latter provision was regarded merely as providing emphasis to the guarantee under the Bill of Rights. However, in the recent case of *Chavez* v. *NHA*[78], the Supreme Court for the first time gave this Section 28 an independent construction. The Court distinguished between "the duty to permit access to information," which is required by Section 7 of the Bill of Rights, and "the duty to disclose information," which is what Section 28 mandates. The Court stated:

> Sec. 28, Art. II compels the State and its agencies to fully disclose "all of its transactions involving public interest." Thus, the government agencies, without need of demand from anyone, must bring into public view all the steps and negotiations leading to the consummation of the transaction and the contents of the perfected contract. Such information must pertain to "definite propositions of the government," meaning official recommendations or final positions reached on the different matters subject of negotiation. ....
> The other aspect of the people's right to know apart from the duty to disclose is the duty to allow access to information on matters of public concern under Sec. 7, Art. III of the Constitution. The gateway to information opens to the public the following: (1) official records; (2) documents and papers pertaining to official acts, transactions, or decisions; and (3) government research data used as a basis for policy development.

> Thus, the duty to disclose information should be differentiated from the duty to permit access to information. There is no need to demand from the government agency disclosure of information as this is mandatory under the Constitution; failing that, legal remedies are available. On the other hand, the interested party must first request or even demand that he be allowed access to documents and papers in the particular agency. A request or demand is required; otherwise, the government office or agency will not know of the desire of the interested party to gain access to such papers and what papers are needed. The duty to disclose covers only transactions involving public interest, while the duty to allow access has a broader scope of information which embraces not only transactions involving public interest, but any matter contained in official communications and public documents of the government agency.[79]

However, while the guarantee in the Bill of Rights is self-executing, the Court stated that Section 28 requires implementing legislation. Advocates in the Philippines for the passage of a Freedom of Information Act have strengthened provisions on "the duty to disclose" to conform to this latest Supreme Court ruling.

In addition to the foregoing provisions spelling out general rights and duties, there are also specific classes of information that the Constitution requires to be made public. These include information on foreign loans obtained or guaranteed by the government. Article XII (National Economy and Patrimony), Sec. 21 of the 1987 Constitution states: "Foreign loans may only be incurred in accordance with law and the regulations of the monetary authority. Information on foreign loans obtained or guaranteed by the government shall be made available to the public."

The constitutional guarantee is applied to all branches of government (legislative, judicial, and executive) including all their instrumentalities.[80] For constitutional guarantees regarding the public's right of access to declarations by public officers or employees of their assets and liabilities see section on Asset Declarations.

Thailand

The current Constitution of Thailand was passed by referendum of the voters on 19 August 2007 and enacted by the King on 24 August, 2007. Its legitimacy has been challenged given that it was drafted by an Assembly selected by the junta and installed by King Bhumibol Adulyadej following the September 2006 coup. In any event, Part 10, encompassing Sections 56-62, contains strong affirmations of the right to information, including a general right to information held by public agencies, state enterprises and local governments (Section 56), as well as specific rights to certain kinds of information. Section 57 guarantees a right to information concerning activities that "may affect the quality of the environment, health and sanitary conditions, the quality of life or any other material interest concerning such person [the requester] or a local community," and Section 61 guarantees a right to consumer information. Section

62 recognizes a right to information about "the performance of duties of persons holding political positions, State agencies and State officials" and extends protection to whistleblowers. Following is the language of these sections:

Section 56

A person shall have the right to know and have access to public data or information in possession of a Government agency, a State agency, a State enterprise or a local government organization, unless the disclosure of such data or information shall affect the security of the State, public safety or interests of other persons which shall be protected or purport to be personal data, as provided by law.

Section 57

A person shall have the right to receive data, explanations and reasons from a Government agency, a State agency, a State enterprise or a local government organization prior to the approval or the operation of any project or activity which may affect the quality of the environment, health and sanitary conditions, the quality of life or any other material interest concerning such person or a local community and shall have the right to express his or her opinions to agencies concerned, for assisting further consideration of such matters.

In planning social, economic, political and cultural development, or in undertaking expropriation, town and country planning, zoning and making bylaws likely to have impacts on essential interests of the public, the State shall cause to be held comprehensive public hearings prior thereto.

Section 61

The right of a person as a consumer shall be protected in respect of the acquisition of rightful information and a person as such shall have the right to make a complaint for a remedy of loss suffered as well as the right to assemble in an endeavour to protect rights of consumers.

Section 62

A person shall have the right to monitor and make a request for an examination of the performance of duties of persons holding political positions, State agencies and State officials.

The person who *bona fide* provides to an agency responsible for the scrutiny of the exercise of State powers or to a State agency information in connection with the performance of duties of persons holding political positions, State agencies or State officials shall be protected.

Europe

Council of Europe

The Council of Europe Convention on Access to Official Documents, adopted by the Council of Europe Committee of Ministers on 27 November, 2008, provides in preambular paragraph 6 that exercise of the right to access official documents:

(i) provides a source of information for the public;
(ii) helps the public to form an opinion on the state of society and on public authorities; [and]
(iii) fosters the integrity, efficiency, effectiveness and accountability of public authorities, so helping affirm their legitimacy …

Albania

Article 23 of the Constitution of Albania reads:

1. The right to information is guaranteed.
2. Everyone has the right, in compliance with law, to get information about the activity of state organs, as well as of persons who exercise state functions.
3. Everybody is given the possibility to follow the meetings of collectively elected organs.

Austria

Article 20(4) of the Federal Constitutional Law of Austria imposes an obligation on civil servants "entrusted … with administrative duties" and "functionaries of public law corporate bodies" to "impart information about matters pertaining to their sphere of competence in so far as this does not conflict with a legal obligation to maintain secrecy".[81] Article 20(3) sets forth a presumption of secrecy if concealment is required to protect an enumerated list of interests, unless otherwise provided by law.[82]

Azerbaijan

Article 50(1) of the Constitution of Azerbaijan is almost identical to the first sentence of Article 29 of Russia's Constitution. Article 50(1) reads: "Everyone is free to look for, acquire, transfer, prepare and distribute information."

Belgium

Article 32 of the Constitution of Belgium guarantees a right of access to administrative documents: "Everyone has the right to consult any administrative document and to have a copy made, except in the cases and conditions stipulated by the laws, decrees, or rulings referred to in Article 134."[83] Administrative information is defined as "any information in any form whatsoever, which the administration possesses". This includes all information recorded in any form, regardless of the information's source. Whatever the origin of a document, when it is in possession of an administrative body, it is considered to be an administrative document.

Bulgaria

Article 41 of the Constitution of Bulgaria reads:

(1) Everyone shall be entitled to seek, obtain and disseminate information. This right shall not be exercised to the detriment of the rights and reputation of others, or to the detriment of national security, public order, public health and morality.

(2) Everyone shall be entitled to obtain information from state bodies and agencies on any matter of legitimate interest to them which is not a state or official secret and does not affect the rights of others.

This language is based on Article 19 of the Universal Declaration of Human Rights. The Constitutional Court held[84] that this constitutional right (a) entitles every citizen to seek and obtain information from government bodies without the need for special justification of his/her interest, and (b) imposes an obligation on the state to provide public information. The constitutional provision and the above decision are constantly referred to by the Supreme Administrative Court in cases of information denial. Access to information is recognized as both a constitutional and a statutory right.

Czech Republic

The 1993 Charter of Fundamental Rights and Freedoms, Article 17 states: "Freedom of expression and the right to information are guaranteed."

Estonia

Article 44 of the Constitution of Estonia states:

(1) Everyone shall have the right to freely receive information circulated for general use.

(2) At the request of Estonian citizens, and to the extent and in accordance with procedures determined by law, all state and local government authorities and their officials shall be obligated to provide information on their work, with the exception of information which is forbidden by law to be divulged, and information which is intended for internal use only.

(3) Estonian citizens shall have the right to become acquainted with information about themselves held by state and local government authorities and in state and local government archives, in accordance with procedures determined by

law. This right may be restricted by law in order to protect the rights and liberties of other persons, and the secrecy of children's ancestry, as well as to prevent a crime, or in the interests of apprehending a criminal or to clarify the truth for a court case.

(4) Unless otherwise determined by law, the rights specified in Paragraphs (2) and (3) shall exist equally for Estonian citizens and citizens of other states and stateless persons who are present in Estonia.

Finland

Section 12 of the 2000 Constitution of Finland states:

(1) Everyone has freedom of expression. Freedom of expression entails the right to express, disseminate and receive information, opinions and other communications without prior prevention by anyone. More detailed provisions on the exercise of the freedom of expression are laid down by an Act. Provisions on restrictions relating to pictorial programmes that are necessary for the protection of children may be laid down by an Act.

(2) Documents and recordings in the possession of the authorities are public, unless their publication has for compelling reasons been specifically restricted by an Act. Everyone has the right of access to public documents and recordings.

France

The Conseil d'État has affirmed in two cases that the right of access to administrative documents is a "fundamental guarantee, accorded to citizens for the exercise of their public liberties in the sense of Article 34 of the Constitution of France."[85] Article 34 reads in relevant part: "Statutes shall determine the rules concerning … civic rights and the fundamental guarantees granted to citizens for the exercise of their public liberties …." The full statement by the Conseil d'État, in Case No. # 237203, paragraph 6, reads as follows:

> Considérant que la définition des modalités concrètes de communication de documents administratifs ne met en cause ni le principe ni l'étendue du droit d'accès aux documents administratifs, qui constitue une garantie fondamentale accordée aux citoyens pour l'exercice des libertés publiques au sens de l'article 34 de la Constitution; que le pouvoir réglementaire était donc compétent, dans le silence de la loi du 17 juillet 1978, pour décider que les frais d'acheminement postal des copies de documents administratifs seraient mis à la charge du demandeur….[86]

Georgia

Article 24(1) of the 1995 Constitution of Georgia, as amended through December 27, 2006, guarantees to everyone "the right to freely receive and impart information."

Article 41 guarantees the right to privacy of personal information including "the right to become acquainted ... with the information about him/her stored in state institutions as well as official documents existing there."

Greece

Article 5A of the Constitution of Greece states:

(1) All persons are entitled to information, as specified by law. Restrictions to this right may be imposed by law only in so far as they are absolutely necessary and justified for reasons of national security, of combating crime or of protecting rights and interests of third parties.

Hungary

Article VI (2) of the 2011 Fundamental Law of Hungary states: "Everyone shall have the right to the protection of their personal data, as well as to access and disseminate data of public interest." The Constitutional Court ruled in 1992 that freedom of information is a constitutional right essential for citizen oversight:

> The publicity and accessibility of data of public interest is a fundamental right guaranteed by the Constitution, which also happens to arise directly from it. Free access to information of public interest promotes democratic values in elected bodies, the executive power, and public administration by enabling people to check the lawfulness and efficiency of their operations. Because of the complexity of the civic sphere, the citizens' sway over administrative decisions and the management of public affairs cannot be effective unless public authorities are willing to disclose pertinent information.[87]
>
> In 1994, the Court struck down a state secrets law, ruling that it imposed impermissible restrictions on the right to information. In so doing, the Court found that free access to data of public interest, including those held by the state, is one of the preconditions for the exercise of the right to free expression.[88]

Italy

The Constitution of Italy is silent on the matter, but the Constitutional Court has declared that transparency is a general principle that binds domestic authorities as it is part of the common European constitutional heritage.[89]

Lithuania

Article 25 (paragraphs 2 and 3) of the Constitution of the Republic of Lithuania, adopted by referendum on 25 October, 1992, guarantees a right to information in the following terms:

(2) The human being must not be hindered from seeking, receiving and imparting information and ideas.

(3) Freedom to express convictions, to receive and impart information may not be limited otherwise than by law, if this is necessary to protect the health, honour and dignity, private life, and morals of a human being, or to defend the constitutional order.

Inclusion of the 3rd paragraph in Article 25 establishes the right as more than a right to gather information free from government interference; instead, paragraph 3 declares that receipt of information is the norm, and limitations, which must be specified by law and be necessary to protect a short list of enumerated interests, are the exception. Moreover, the list of permissible limitations is narrower than those allowed by Article 10 of the European Convention on Human Rights: they do not include "disclosure of information received in confidence" or "maintaining the authority and impartiality of the judiciary." For these reasons, we count the constitutional provision as one that guarantees a right to information, and not merely freedom of information.

The fifth paragraph of Article 25 guarantees citizens (as distinct from "human beings," who are the holders of the general right to information) the right to receive personal information:

(5) The citizen shall have the right to receive, according to the procedure established by law, any information concerning him that is held by State institutions.

Macedonia

Article 16 of the Constitution of Macedonia provides, in relevant part that

(2) The freedom of speech, public address, public information and the establishment of institutions for public information is guaranteed.

(3) Free access to information and the freedom of reception and transmission of information are guaranteed.

Moldova

Article 34 of the Constitution of Moldova provides for a right of access to information:

(1) Having access to any information of public interest is everybody's right that may not be curtailed.

(2) According to their established level of competence, public authorities shall ensure that citizens are correctly informed both on public affairs and matters of personal interest.

(3) The right of access to information may not prejudice either the measures taken to protect citizens or national security.

(4) The State and private media are obliged to ensure that correct information reaches the public. ...

Montenegro

The new Constitution of Montenegro, adopted October 2007, includes the right to information in Article 51:

> Everyone shall have the right to access information held by the state authorities and organizations exercising public authority.
> The right to access to information may be limited if this is in the interest of the protection of life; public health; morality and privacy; carrying of criminal proceedings; security and defence of Montenegro; foreign, monetary and economic policy.
> In addition, Article 23 guarantees environmental rights, including access to environmental information, and Article 49 guarantees freedom of public information.

Netherlands, The

Article 110 of the Constitution of the Netherlands states: "In the exercise of their duties government bodies shall observe the right of public access to information in accordance with rules to be prescribed by Act of Parliament." There are two views as to whether this provision guarantees a right to public information or only imposes a duty on public bodies to make information available consistent with statutes. The prevailing view within the Netherlands is that the Constitution does not guarantee a right to information, based in part on the fact that Article 110 is not included in the Bill of Rights but rather in that part of the Constitution titled "Legislation and Administration." A minority contend that the right is of constitutional stature. The courts have not expressed an opinion on the matter and are unlikely to do so, given that the courts may not set aside a law, or declare an action of an administrative body illegal, on the ground that it contradicts the Constitution. In any event, the issue is not significant given that the FOI law provides a relatively strong statutory protection of the right. For these reasons, we do not include the Netherlands in our count of countries that recognize a constitutional right to information.

Norway

The Constitution of Norway, as amended in 2004, provides in Article 100 that

> Everyone has a right of access to the documents of the State and of the municipal administration and a right to be present at sittings of the courts and elected assemblies. The law may prescribe limitations to this right in regard to the right to privacy or other weighty considerations.

Poland

Article 61 of the Constitution of Poland states:

(1) A citizen shall have the right to obtain information on the activities of organs of public authority as well as persons discharging public functions. Such right shall also include receipt of information on the activities of self-governing economic or professional organs and other persons or organizational units relating to the field in which they perform the duties of public authorities and manage communal assets or property of the State Treasury.
(2) The right to obtain information shall ensure access to documents and entry to sittings of collective organs of public authority formed by universal elections, with the opportunity to make sound and visual recordings.
(3) Limitations upon the rights referred to in Paragraphs (1) and (2), may be imposed by statute solely to protect freedoms and rights of other persons and economic subjects, public order, security or important economic interests of the State.

Portugal

The Constitution of Portugal has included a right of access to information since 1976. Article 268 of the 1989 Constitution states:

(1) Citizens shall possess the right to be informed by the Administration whenever they so request as to the progress of the processes in which they are directly interested, as well as to be made aware of such decisions as are taken in relation to them.
(2) Without prejudice to the law governing matters of internal and external security, criminal investigation and personal privacy, citizens shall also possess the right of access to administrative files and records.

Romania

Article 31 of the Constitution of Romania on the Right of Access to Information, reads, in relevant part:

(1) A person's right of access to any information of public interest shall not be restricted.
(2) The public authorities, according to their competence, shall be bound to provide correct information to the citizens in public affairs and matters of personal interest.
(3) The right to information shall not be prejudicial to the measures of protection of young people or national security. …

Russian Federation

Article 29(4) of the Constitution of the Russian Federation states:

> Everyone shall have the right to freely look for, receive, transmit, produce and distribute information by any legal way. The list of data comprising state secrets shall be determined by a federal law.

In addition, Article 24(2) guarantees the right of everyone to review personal information about him- or herself: "The bodies of state authority and local self-government, their officials shall ensure for everyone the possibility of acquainting with the documents and materials directly affecting his or her rights and freedoms, unless otherwise provided for by law."

The leading Russian freedom of information NGO, the Institute for Information Freedom Development (IIFD), takes the position that Article 29 guarantees citizens the right to access any information, including information about activities of government bodies. The Institute recognizes that many governmental agencies do not agree with this interpretation and instead take the position that citizens have a right only to information that directly affects their rights and freedoms, according to Article 24 of the Constitution. A few courts have expressly adopted the Institute's position, in particular, concerning government websites and standards. In their decisions, the courts quoted Article 29, but did not provide any explanation or interpretation of the Article.[90]

Serbia

Article 51 of the Constitution of Serbia reads:

> Everyone shall have the right to be informed accurately, fully and timely about issues of public importance. The media shall have the obligation to respect this right.
>
> Everyone shall have the right to access information kept by state bodies and organizations witn delegated public powers, in accordance with the law.

Slovakia

The 1992 Constitution of Slovakia provides for a general right of access to information and a specific right of access to environmental information.

Article 26 of the Constitution reads in relevant part:

> (1) The freedom of speech and the right to information are guaranteed.
> (2) Everyone has the right to express his views in word, writing, print, picture, or other means as well as the right to freely seek out, receive, and spread ideas and information without regard for state borders. ...
> (3) The freedom of speech and the right to seek out and spread information can be restricted by law if such a measure is unavoidable in a democratic society

to protect the rights and liberties of others, state security, public order, or public health and morality.

(4) Public authorities are under an obligation to provide information on their activities in an appropriate manner and in the state language. The conditions and manner of execution will be specified by law.

Article 45 states: "Everyone has the right to timely and complete information about the state of the environment and the causes and consequences of its condition."

The Constitutional Court ruled that the right to make an audio recording of a session of a municipal legislative body follows from the Constitution. The Court reasoned as follows:

> From the definition in the Constitution, it follows that the right to information has three components—seeking out, receiving, and disseminating information. (...) Receiving information is collecting data into its own disposition sphere so that the information can be processed by the subject for his/her needs or for the needs of others. Acquiring information can be done by sensual organs as well by various technical means – under present conditions, audio, visual, as well as audiovisual records, but also by every other means.[91]
>
> In a similar case, the Constitutional Court ruled that prohibiting a citizen from taking photographs of members of the municipal legislative body during the process of a vote on an important issue violated the constitutional right to receive information[92]. In findings nr II. ÚS 28/96, II. ÚS 7/00 and III. ÚS 169/03, the Constitutional Court similarly ruled that the right to make an audio recording of a public court session follows from the Constitution.

The Constitutional Court, in its finding no. II. ÚS 44/00, ruled that the right to make a video recording of members of the police during a police action similarly follows from the Constitution. The police took action against people demonstrating for the freedom of Tibet on the square in the town of Prešov in order to prevent them from continuing the demonstration. When people began to make a video recording of the police action, the police prevented them from doing so, arguing that making a video recording of their action violated their right to privacy and their right to protection of personality. The Constitutional Court ruled:

> [T]he execution of power regulated by law in a public place can be considered neither as a component of the basic right to privacy, nor as an expression of a personal nature (§ 11 of the Civic Code) of the members of the city police. (...) Public officials must be aware of the fact that they will face the attention of the public, and they must accept the execution of the right to information by the public minimally in the extent of executing their constitutional or lawful powers in public or in contact with the public.[93]

Slovenia

Access to public information is guaranteed in the second paragraph of Article 39 of the Constitution of Slovenia, titled Freedom of Expression. This second paragraph reads: "Except in such cases as are provided by law, everyone has the right to obtain information of a public nature in which he has a well-founded legal interest under law." A "legal interest" no longer needs to be proven or even stated, given that the Act on Access to Information of Public Character, adopted in 2003, explicitly so provides. Moreover, Article 15, paragraph 4 of the Constitution makes clear that nothing in the Constitution shall be interpreted to restrict a human right recognized by a law in force: "No human right or fundamental freedom regulated by legal acts in force in Slovenia may be restricted on the grounds that this Constitution does not recognize that right or freedom or recognizes it to a lesser extent."

Sweden

Sweden provides the oldest, and one of the strongest, constitutional protections of the right to information. The core of the principle, dating from the 1766 Constitution of Sweden, is that all government documents are public in the absence of a statute that expressly regulates otherwise.[94] This presumption of openness is considered one of the most important foundations of Swedish democracy.[95] The Freedom of the Press Act (Tryckfrihetsförordningen, TF), first proclaimed in the Constitution of 1766, was suspended only from 1772 to 1809. Article 1 of Chapter 2 of the current version, adopted in 1949, on the public nature of official documents, reads: "Every Swedish citizen shall be entitled to have free access to official documents, in order to encourage the free exchange of opinion and the availability of comprehensive information." Article 2 states that the right may be restricted only if "necessary" to protect one of seven enumerated interests and only if "scrupulously specified" by a special act. Indeed, until 1937, any restrictions to the right of access to official documents had to be in constitutional law.

The Instrument of Government (1974), another constitutional document, stipulates in Chapter II, on Fundamental Rights and Freedoms, Article 1(2) that:

> [Every citizen shall be guaranteed] freedom of information: that is, the freedom to procure and receive information and otherwise acquaint oneself with the utterances of others.

Article 13 sets forth a list of the permissible restrictions on freedom of information.

Switzerland

The Federal Constitution of Switzerland, as amended through 15 October, 2002, contains only a guarantee of freedom of information, and not a right to government-held information (and thus is not included in our list of constitutions that guarantee a right to information). Article 16 reads:

(1) The freedom of opinion and information is guaranteed.
(2) All persons have the right to form, express, and disseminate their opinions freely.
(3) All persons have the right to receive information freely, to gather it from generally accessible sources and to disseminate it.

Ukraine

The 1996 Constitution of Ukraine was strongly influenced by the European Convention on Human Rights. Fortunately, regarding the right to information, the Constitution was also influenced by Article 19 of the International Covenant on Civil and Political Rights. Article 34 guarantees the right to information in the following terms:

- Everyone is guaranteed the right to freedom of thought and speech, and to the free expression of his or her views and beliefs.
- Everyone has the right to freely collect, store, use and disseminate information by oral, written or other means of his or her choice.
- The exercise of these rights may be restricted by law in the interests of national security, territorial indivisibility or public order, with the purpose of preventing disturbances or crimes, protecting the health of the population, the reputation or rights of other persons, preventing the publication of information received confidentially, or supporting the authority and impartiality of justice.

The Constitution also includes the right to inspect and correct personal information,[96] and the right to environmental information.[97]

NOTES

1. Argentina, Canada, France, India, Israel and South Korea.
2. Inter-American Court of Human Rights, Claude Reyes *et al. v.* Chile, September 19, 2006. Open Society Justice Initiative filed an *Amicus Brief* in the case.
3. Supreme Court of Canada, Ontario (Public Safety and Security) *v.* Criminal Lawyers' Association, 2010 SCC 23, 17 June, 2010.
4. E.g., Társaság a Szabadságjogokért *v.* Hungary, (Application No. 37374/05), 14 April 2009.
5. Forests Survey Inspection Request Case, (1989) 1 KCCR 176, 88Hun-Ma22 (S. Kor.).
6. See the paragraph on Colombia below.
7. S.P. Gupta v. Union of India, A.I.R. 1982 S.C. 149, 234 (India).
8. 32nd Session, 17-23 October, 2002: Banjul, The Gambia.
9. Informal translation. The Portuguese version reads: "aceder aos arquivos e registos administrativos, sem prejuízo do disposto na lei em matéria relativas à segurança interna e externa do Estado, à investigação criminal, ao segredo de justiça, ao segredo do Estado e à intimidade das pessoas".

10. HCJ 1601/90 Shalit *v.* Peres 48(3) PD 353 [1990] (Isr.).
11. HCJ 1601/90 Shalit *v.* Peres 48(3) PD 353 [1990] (Isr.)., at 214.
12. HCJ 1601/90 Shalit *v.* Peres 48(3) PD 353 [1990] (Isr.)., at 353.
13. Translation by the editors. The original French version states: Les citoyennes et les citoyens ont le droit d'accéder à l'information détenue par l'administration publique, les institutions élues et les organismes investis d'une mission de service public. Le droit à l'information ne peut être limité que par la loi, dans le but d'assurer la protection de tout ce qui concerne la défense nationale, la sûreté intérieure et extérieure de l'Etat, ainsi que la vie privée des personnes, de prévenir l'atteinte aux droits et libertés énoncés dans la présente Constitution et de protéger des sources et des domaines expressément déterminéspar la loi.
14. Section 23(2)(a) of Schedule 6 (Transitional Arrangements) to the Final Constitution – The Constitution of South Africa Act, 1996, Act 108 of 1996.
15. Section 23 of the Interim Constitution, 1994.
16. Claase *v.* Information Officer of South African Airways [2006] SCA 163 (RSA). The retired pilot was entitled to a certain number of business class flights per year as a part of his contractual retirement package. Arriving in New York to fly to South Africa, he was informed that there were no such seats available. He disbelieved this assertion and, by successfully accessing the computer records relating to the flights and its passenger assignments, was able to show that at the point he sought the seat, he was unlawfully denied one in breach of his contractual rights.
17. Van Huyssteen and Others NNO *v.* Minister of Environmental Affairs and Tourism and Others 1996 (1) SA 283 (C).
18. Information from website of the Commonwealth Human Rights Initiative.
19. Acordada de la Corte Suprema de Justicia de la Nación No. 1/2004 Exp. 315/2004 Adm. Gral.
20. Corte Suprema de Justicia de la Nación, S.622.XXXIII "S.,V. c/ M., D.A. s/medidas precautorias" 3 April, 2001, at 25.
21. [1989] 2 S.C.R. 1326 at 1336.
22. See MacDonnell *v.* Quebec (Commission d'accès à l'information) [2002] S.C.J. No. 71(S.C.C.); Canada (Attorney General) *v.* Canada (Information Commissioner), 2004 FC 431 (F.C.) at para 194 (Dawson J: "The investigation is conducted in furtherance of the quasi-constitutional right of access that has as its purpose the facilitation of democracy"); and Canada (Attorney General) v. Canada (Information Commissioner), [2002] F.C.J. No. 225 (Fed. T.D.) (McKeown J: "I recognize that the Access to Information Act is quasi-constitutional legislation and the Information Commissioner has an important role to play in our society ...").
23. Dagg *v.* Canada (Minister of Finance), [1997] 2 S.C.R. 403 (S.C.C.) at 433, per La Forest J. (dissenting, but not on this point).
24. Ontario (Public Safety and Security) *v.* Criminal Lawyers' Association, [2010] 1S.C.R. 815. For an opinion on the case, see Paul Schabas and Ryder Gilliland, Supreme Court of Canada Recognizes Limited Right to Access Government Documents.
25. Ontario (Public Safety and Security) *v.* Criminal Lawyers' Association, [2010] 1S.C.R. 815 at 37.
26. Ruby *v.* Canada (Solicitor General) [2000] F.C.J. No. 779 (F.C.A.), at para. 165. The Court held that the specific paragraphs of the Privacy Act at issue in the case

did not engage section 7 of the Charter. Although the case was appealed to the Supreme Court of Canada, the Supreme Court did not address the liberty/privacy issue.

27. The Criminal Lawyers' Association v. The Ministry of Public Safety and Security (formerly The Solicitor General) et al. (2007) 86 O.R. (3d) 259 (C.A) [Contra: Ontario (Attorney General) *v.* Fineberg [1994] O.J. No. 1419 (S.C.J.)].
28. Casas Cordero and Others *v.* the National Customs Service. For a copy of the judgment in Spanish, as well as comments submitted to the Constitutional Tribunal, in English and Spanish, by the Justice Initiative with the *pro bono* assistance of the law firm of Ropes & Gray LLP. The Chilean transparency NGO Pro Acceso brought the case and were represented before the Constitutional Tribunal by the Chilean law firm of Colombara & Olmedo.
29. Casas Cordero and Others *v.* the National Customs Service.
30. Inter-American Court of Human Rights, Claude Reyes *et al. v.* Chile, September 19, 2006. Open Society Justice Initiative submitted an Amicus Brief in the case.
31. Constitutional Court, T-216/05, para. 17. See also Constitutional Court, T-473/92.
32. Constitutional Court, C-872/03.
33. Constitutional Court, C-872/03; and Constitutional Court, T-227/03.
34. Constitutional Court, C-872/03. The Court considered that the establishment of exceptions to the right of access to information may be established by a simple majority of the house.
35. Constitutional Court, C-872/03; and Constitutional Court, T-227/03.
36. Constitutional Court, C-872/03; and Constitutional Court, C-038/96.
37. Navarro Gutiérrez v. Lizano Fait, Judgment of April 2, 2002, as translated in the 2003 Report of the Special Rapporteur for Freedom of Expression, at 107.
38. Navarro Gutiérrez v. Lizano Fait, Judgment of April 2, 2002, para. VI.
39. Appeal for constitutional protection presented by the Representative José Humberto Arce Salas against the Bank of Costa Rica. File: 02-009167-0007-CO, Res. 2003-03489.
40. Political Constitution of Ecuador, Decreto Legislativo No. 000 RO/1 11 August 1998, Art. 81.
41. Article 6 was included by a reform published on December 6, 1977. See: Semanario Judicial de la Federación y su Gaceta, Novena Época, Pleno, XI abril de 2000, p.72, tesis: P.XLV/2000, IUS 191981.
42. Semanario Judicial de la Federación y su Gaceta, Novena Época, Pleno III, June 1996, tesis: P. LXXXIX/96; IUS: 200111.
43. Decreto por el que se adiciona un segundo párrafo con siete fracciones al Artículo 6 de la Constitución Política de los Estados Unidos Mexicanos, published in the Official Gazette, July 20, 2007.
44. Elizabeth Flores Negri *v.* Rector of the National University of Asunción, Sentencia Definitiva No. 40 of 31 July 2007.
45. Inter-American Court of Human Rights, Claude Reyes et al. v. Chile, September 19, 2006. Open Society Justice Initiative submitted an Amicus Brief in the case.
46. Person includes corporate entities. Sentencia del Tribunal Constitucional, Exp. No. 0644-2004. Oct. 17, 2005.
47. Sentencia del Tribunal Constitucional, Exp. No. 1797-2002 HD/TC, Jan. 29, 2003,

at 9-10. Estado actual de la pagina web del Poder Judicial de acuerdo con la Ley de Transparencia y Acceso a la Información, Informe del Consorcio Justicia Viva.

48. Sentencia del Tribunal Constitucional, Exp. No. 2579-2003-HD/TC, Apr. 6, 2005, 5.
49. Sentencia del Tribunal Constitucional, Exp. No. 0959-2004-HD/TC, Nov. 19, 2004, 6.
50. Sentencia del Tribunal Constitucional, Exp. No. 0644-2004 HD/TC, Oct. 17, 2005, 5.
51. Letter from James Madison to William T. Barry (4 Aug. 1822), in 3 Letters and Other Writings of James Madison 276 (R. Worthington ed., 1884).
52. Houchins *v*. KQED, Inc., 438 U.S. 1, 14 (1978).
53. Houchins *v*. KQED, Inc., 438 U.S. 1, 14 (1978), Justice Stevens, dissenting.
54. Richmond Newspapers, Inc. *v*. Virginia, 448 U.S. 555 (1980) (Justice Stevens, concurring).
55. Detroit Free Press *v*. Ashcroft, 303 F.3d 681, 684-85 (6th Cir. 2002).
56. Detroit Free Press *v*. Ashcroft, 303 F.3d 681, 695, 700 (citing First Amendment Coal. *v*. Judicial Inquiry & Review Bd., 784 F.2d 467, 473 (3d Cir. 1986) (en banc); Capital Cities Media, Inc. *v*. Chester 797 F.2d 1164, 1167 (3d Cir. 1986) (en banc); Press-Enterprise Co. *v*. Sup. Ct. of Cal., 478 U.S. 1, 13 (1986).
57. Roy Peled and Yoram Rabin, The Constitutional Right to Information, *Columbia Human Rights Law Review*, Vol. 42(2), pp. 375-78.
58. A. Alsina c. Estado, 4 March 2002, paras XVIII to XX.
59. See Status of the Right to Information in the Commonwealth.
60. See news report, Court Strikes Blow For Right to Information, Nov. 6, 2007, Inter Press Service.
61. Article 43(2).
62. See news report, Court Strikes Blow For Right to Information, Nov. 6, 2007, Inter Press Service.
63. The relevant cases of the Supreme Court are Bennett Coleman & Co. *v*. Union of India, AIR 1973 SC 783, dissenting judgment of Justice KK Matthew in particular; State of UP *v*. Raj Narain, AIR 1975 SC 865.
64. State of Uttar Pradesh *v*. Raj Narain, A.I.R. 1975 S.C. 865, 884. Accordingly, despite the fact that tensions within the country were growing, the Court ordered the government to disclose documents regarding security arrangements for the Prime Minister's travels within the country so long as they did not endanger his security or public order. See also Handbook, supra note 24, § 6.2.4 (discussing this case).
65. S.P. Gupta *v*. Union of India [1982] AIR (SC) 149, at 232. See also Reliance Petrochemicals Ltd. *v*. Proprietors of Indian Express Newspapers, Bombay Pvt. Ltd., AIR 1989 SC 190; Indian Express Newspapers (Bombay) Pvt. Ltd. *v*. India (1985) 1 SCC 641; Secretary, Ministry of Information & Broadcasting, Govt. of India, and Others, *v*. Cricket Association of Bengal Anaothers, 1995(002) SCC 0161 SC People's Union For Civil Liberties (PUCL) And Another *v*. Union of India, 2003(001) SCW 2353 SC.
66. S.P. Gupta *v*. Union of India [1982] AIR (SC) 149, at 232.
67. Peled, Rabin, The Constitutional Right to Information, *Columbia Human Rights Law Review*, Vol. 42(2), p. 373.
68. Kaneko *v*. Japan, 23 Keishu 1490 (Sup. Ct., Nov. 26, 1969).
69. Peled, Rabin, The Constitutional Right to Information, *Columbia Human Rights Law Review*, Vol. 42(2), p. 373.

70. Forests Survey Inspection Request case, 1 KCCR 176, 88 Hun-ma22, Sept. 4, 1989.
71. Forests Survey Inspection Request case, 1 KCCR 176, 88 Hun-ma22, Sept. 4, 1989.
72. Commissioner of Police *v.* Ombudsman [1988] 1 NZLR 385.
73. See, e.g. Mafart *v.* Television New Zealand Ltd., Sup. Ct no. SC70/2006, [2006] NZSC 78, (2006) 18 PRNZ 394.
74. Information from website of the Commonwealth Human Rights Initiative.
75. The guarantee was first recognized in the 1973 Constitution. Article IV (Bill of Rights), Section 6, of the 1973 Constitution reads: "The right of the people to information on matters of public concern shall be recognized. Access to official records, and to documents and papers pertaining to official acts, transactions, or decisions, shall be afforded the citizen subject to such limitations as may be provided by law."
76. Legaspi *v.* Civil Service Commission, 150 S.Ct. Rpts. Ann. 530, G.R. No. 72119 (May 29, 1987) (en banc).
77. Legaspi *v.* Civil Service Commission, 150 S.Ct. Rpts. Ann. 530, G.R. No. 72119 (May 29, 1987) (en banc).
78. G.R. No. 164527; August 15, 2007.
79. G.R. No. 164527; August 15, 2007.
80. Information supplied by Nepomuceno Malaluan, Action for Economic Reforms.
81. Article 20(4) provides in full: "All functionaries entrusted with Federation, Länder and municipal administrative duties as well as the functionaries of other public law corporate bodies shall impart information about matters pertaining to their sphere of competence in so far as this does not conflict with a legal obligation to maintain secrecy; an onus on professional associations to supply information extends only to members of their respective organizations and this inas much as fulfilment of their statutory functions is not impeded. The detailed regulations are, as regards the Federal authorities and the self-administration to be settled by Federal law in respect of legislation and execution, the business of the Federation; as regards the Länder and municipal authorities and the self-administration to be settled by Land law in respect of framework legislation, they are the business of the Federation while the implemental legislation and execution are Land business."
82. Article 20(3) provides: "All functionaries entrusted with Federal, Länder, and municipal administrative duties as well as the functionaries of other public law corporate bodies are, save as otherwise provided by law, pledged to secrecy about all facts of which they have obtained knowledge exclusively from their official activity and whose concealment is enjoined in the interest of the maintenance of public peace, order and security, of universal national defence, or external relations, in the interest of a public law corporate body, for the preparation of a ruling or in the preponderant interest of the parties involved (official secrecy). Official secrecy does not exist for functionaries appointed by a popular representative body if it expressly asks for such information."
83. Article 134 reads: "Laws executed on the basis of Article 39 determine the judicial force of the rules which the organs that they create may take in matters which they determine. They may confer the power to decree with force of law to these organs, with the responsibilities and in the manner which they establish."
84. Decision No 7 of 1996 on constitutional case No 1 from 1996.

85. Conseil d'Etat 9 / 10 ssr 13 décembre 2002 n°237203 & Conseil d'Etat 7 / 5 ssr 29 avril 2002 no 228830.
86. Translation by the editors: "Considering that the specific form of providing administrative documents does not threaten either the principle or the scope (extent) of the right of access to administrative documents, which constitutes a fundamental guarantee accorded to citizens for the exercise of their public liberties in the sense of Article 34 of the Constitition; that the regulatory power is therefore competent, the law of 17 July, 1978 being silent [on the matter], to decide that the costs for postal transport of administrative documents will be charged to the requestor ...."
87. In re to Constitutionality of Act LXV of 1990 on Local Governments, 32/1992 (V.29) AB, at 183-184 (as translated by the Office of the Hungarian Parliamentary Commissioner for Data Protection and Freedom of Information).
88. Decision 34/1994 (VI.24) AB.
89. Italian Constitutional Court, Judgment No. 104 of 2006.
90. Information provided by Ivan Pavlov, Executive Director, Institute for Information Freedom Development. Court decisions in Russian can be found in the Institute's.
91. Finding of the Constitutional Court, no. I. ÚS 57/00, 2000.
92. Finding of the constitutional Court, no. IV. ÚS40/03, 2003.
93. Finding of the Constitutional Court, no II. ÚS 44/00, 2000.
94. Constitution of Sweden (The Freedom of the Press Act) Chapter 2: "The Principle of Public Access to Official Records."
95. Hans-Gunnar Axberger, "Freedom of the Press in Sweden," *in Press Law and Practice: A Comparative Study of Press Freedom in European and Other Democracies*, edited by S. Coliver (Article 19: March 1993), at 160.
96. Article 32 provides, in part: "Every citizen has the right to examine information about himself or herself, that is not a state secret or other secret protected by law, at the bodies of state power, bodies of local self-government, institutions and organisations. Everyone is guaranteed judicial protection of the right to rectify incorrect information about himself or herself and members of his or her family, and of the right to demand that any type of information be expunged, and also the right to compensation for material and moral damages inflicted by the collection, storage, use and dissemination of such incorrect information."
97. Article 50 states: "Everyone has the right to an environment that is safe for life and health, and to compensation for damages inflicted through the violation of this right. Everyone is guaranteed the right of free access to information about the environmental situation, the quality of food and consumer goods, and also the right to disseminate such information. No one shall make such information secret."

Important Cases

Case Title	*Country*	*Year*
Claude Reyes *et al.* *v.* Chile	Inter-American Court of Human Rights	2006
Társaság a Szabadságjogokért *v.* Hungary	European Court of Human Rights	2009
Acordada de la Corte Suprema de Justicia de la Nación No. 1/2004 Exp. 315/2004 Adm. Gral.	Argentina	2004
Decision No 7 of 1996 on Constitutional case No 1 from 1996	Bulgaria	1996
Canada (Attorney General) *v.* Canada (Information Commissioner)	Canada	2004
Dagg *v.* Canada (Minister of Finance)	Canada	1997
Edmonton Journal *v.* Alberta (Attorney General)	Canada	1989
MacDonnell *v.* Quebec	Canada	2002
Ontario (Public Safety and Security) *v.* Criminal Lawyers' Association	Canada	2010
Ruby *v.* Canada	Canada	2000
The Criminal Lawyers' Association *v.* The Ministry of Public Safety and Security (formerly The Solicitor General) *et al.*	Canada	2007
Casas Cordero and Others *v.* the National Customs Service	Chile	2007
Constitutional Court decision C-872/03	Colombia	2003
Constitutional Court decision T-227/03	Colombia	2003
Constitutional Court decision C-038/96	Colombia	1996
Constitutional Court decision T-216/05	Colombia	2005
Constitutional Court decision T-473/92	Colombia	1992
Appeal for constitutional protection presented by the Representative José Humberto Arce Salas against the Bank of Costa Rica	Costa Rica	2003
Navarro Gutiérrez *v.* Lizano Fait	Costa Rica	2002
Fiji National Provident Fund (FNPF) *v.* Fiji Television Ltd.	Fiji	2007
Case No. # 237203	France	2002
In re to Constitutionality of Act LXV of 1990 on Local Governments [(32/1992 (V 29) AB)]	Hungary	1992
Decision 34/1994 (VI.24) AB	Hungary	1994
Bennett Coleman & Co. *v.* Union of India	India	1975
Indian Express Newspapers (Bombay) Pvt. Ltd. *v.* India	India	1985
People's Union For Civil Liberties (PUCL) And Another, *v.* Union of India	India	2003
Reliance Petrochemicals Ltd. *v.* Proprietors of Indian Express Newspapers Bombay Pvt. Ltd.	India	1989
Secretary, Ministry of Information & Broadcasting, Govt. of India, And Others, *v.* Cricket Association of Bengal and Others	India	1995
S.P. Gupta *v.* Union of India	India	1982

Case Title	*Country*	*Year*
State of Uttar Pradesh *v.* Raj Narain	India	1975
Shalit *v.* Peres	Israel	1990
Judgment No. 104 of 2006	Italy	2006
Forests Survey Inspection Request case	Japan	1989
Kaneko *v.* Japan	Japan	1969
Tesis: P. LXXXIX/96, IUS: 200111	Mexico	1996
Commissioner of Police v. Ombudsman	New Zealand	1988
Mafart v. Television New Zealand Ltd.	New Zealand	2006
Elizabeth Flores Negri *v.* Rector of the National University of Asunción	Paraguay	2007
Sentencia del Tribunal Constitucional, Exp. No. 0644-2004. Oct. 17, 2005	Peru	2005
Sentencia del Tribunal Constitucional, Exp. No. 1797-2002 HD/TC, Jan. 29, 2003	Peru	2003
Sentencia del Tribunal Constitucional, Exp. No. 2579-2003-HD/TC, Apr. 6, 2005	Peru	2005
Sentencia del Tribunal Constitucional, Exp. No. 0959-2004-HD/TC, Nov. 19, 2004	Peru	2004
Sentencia del Tribunal Constitucional, Exp. No. 0644-2004 HD/TC, Oct. 17, 2005	Peru	2005
Chavez *v.* NHA	Philippines	2007
Legaspi *v.* Civil Service Commission	Philippines	1987
Finding of the Constitutional Court, no. I. ÚS 57/00, 2000	Slovakia	2000
Finding of the Constitutional Court no. IV. ÚS40/03, 2003	Slovakia	2003
Finding of the Constitutional Court, no II. ÚS 44/00, 2000	Slovakia	2000
Claase *v.* Information Officer of South African Airways	South Africa	2006
Van Huyssteen and Others NNO v. Minister of Environmental Affairs and Tourism and Others	South Africa	1996
Capital Cities Media, Inc. *v.* Chester	United States	1986
Detroit Free Press *v.* Ashcroft	United States	2002
Houchins *v.* KQED	United States	1978
Press-Enterprise Co. *v.* Sup. Ct. of Cal	United States	1986
Richmond Newspapers, Inc. *v.* Virginia	United States	1980
A. Alsina c. Estado	Uruguay	2002

Chapter – 4

RTI Act : An Overview

The Act specifies timeframes for complying with the request.

- If the request has been made to a PIO, compliance is expected within 30 days.
- If the request has been made to an APIO, compliance is expected within 35 days.
- If the PIO transfers the request to some other department (better concerned with the information requested), the time allowed is 35 days.
- Information about Human Rights violations by Security agencies has to be provided within 45 days.
- However, in any of the above cases, if life or liberty is involved, the PIO has to comply within 48 hours.

Since the information is to be paid for, the time between the reply of the PIO and the time taken to deposit the further fees for information is excluded from the time allowed.

If information is not provided within this period, it is treated as a refusal. Refusal with or without reasons may be ground for appeal.

For Central departments as of 2006, there is a fee of Rs. 10 for filing the request, Rs. 2 per page of information and Rs. 5 for each hour of inspection after the first hour. States fix their own rules.

Provisions

- Obligations of public authorities [S.4(1)]
- Designation of Public Information Officers and Assistant Public Information Officers [S.5(1) and 5(2)]
- Constitution of Central Information Commission (S.12 and 13)
- Constitution of State Information Commission (S.15 and 16)
- Non-applicability of the Act to Intelligence and Security Organisations (S.24)
- Power to make rules to carry out the provisions of the Act (S.27 and 28)

Information Defined

In terms of the section 2(f) of the Act, information has been defined as any material in any form including records, documents, memos, e-mails, opinions, advices, press releases, circulars, orders, logbooks, contracts, reports, papers, samples, models, data material held in any electronic form and information relating to any private body which can be accessed by a public authority under any other law for the time being in force.

The Union Cabinet, on 20 July, 2006 gave its nod to an amendment to restrict access to file notes under the RTI law. Restrictions on access to material on the basis of which Cabinet takes decisions CIC will have powers to undertake research and conduct conferences to promote RTI. This means the citizens can at best seek what decisions were taken—almost never why.

Right to Information

Right to Information is a part of fundamental rights under Article 19(1) of the Constitution. Article 19(1) says that every citizen has freedom of speech and expression. As early as in 1976, the Supreme Court said in the case of *Raj Narain v. State of UP*, that people cannot speak or express themselves unless they know. Therefore, right to information is embedded in Article 19. In the same case, the Supreme Court further said that India is a democracy. People are the masters. Therefore, the masters have a right to know how the governments, meant to serve them, are functioning. Further, every citizen pays taxes. Even a beggar on the street pays tax (in the form of sales tax, excise duty etc.) when he buys a piece of soap from the market. The citizens, therefore, have a right to know how their money was being spent. These three principles were laid down by the Supreme Court while saying that RTI is a part of our fundamental rights.

Under the Act Section 2(j), right to information includes the right to:

- Inspect works, documents, records.
- Take notes, extracts or certified copies of documents or records.
- Take certified samples of material.
- Obtain information in the form of printouts, diskettes, floppies, tapes, video cassettes or in any other electronic mode or through printouts.

What is not Open to Disclosure?

The following is exempt from disclosure [S.8]

- information, disclosure of which would prejudicially affect the sovereignty and integrity of India, the security, strategic, scientific or economic interests of the State, relation with foreign State or lead to incitement of an offence;
- information which has been expressly forbidden to be published by any court of law or tribunal or the disclosure of which may constitute contempt of court;
- information, the disclosure of which would cause a breach of privilege of Parliament or the State Legislature;
- information including commercial confidence, trade secrets or intellectual property, the disclosure of which would harm the competitive position of a third party, unless the competent authority is satisfied that larger public interest warrants the disclosure of such information;

- information available to a person in his fiduciary relationship, unless the competent authority is satisfied that the larger public interest warrants the disclosure of such information;
- information received in confidence from foreign Government;
- information, the disclosure of which would endanger the life or physical safety of any person or identify the source of information or assistance given in confidence for law enforcement or security purposes;
- information which would impede the process of investigation or apprehension or persecution of offenders;
- cabinet papers including records of deliberations of the Council of Ministers, Secretaries and other officers;
- information which relates to personal information the disclosure of which has no relationship to any public activity or interest, or which would cause unwarranted invasion of the privacy of the individual;
- notwithstanding any of the exemptions listed above, a public authority may allow access to information, if public interest in disclosure outweighs the harm to the protected interests.

Why is it that RTI works when no other law has woɪked?

There have been many good laws in this country but none of those laws worked. Why do you think this law would work?

This law is already working. This is because for the first time in the history of independent India, there is a law which casts a direct accountability on the officer for non-performance. If concerned officer does not provide information in time, a penalty of Rs. 250 per day of delay can be imposed by the Information Commissioner. If the information provided is false, a penalty of a maximum of Rs. 25000 can be imposed. A penalty can also be imposed for providing incomplete information or for rejecting your application for *mala fide* reasons. This fine is deducted from the officer's personal salary.

Has any penalty been imposed so far?

Yes, some officers have been penalized by the Central as well as State Information Commissioners.

Does the Applicant get the amount fined to the PIO?

No. The amount fined is deposited in the government treasury. However, under section 19, the applicant can seek compensation.

Partial Disclosure

In terms of section 10 of the Act, only that part of the record which does not contain any information which is exempt from disclosure and which can reasonably be severed from any part that contains exempt information, may be provided.

Exclusions

Central Intelligence and Security agencies specified in the Second Schedule such as IB, RAW, Directorate of Revenue Intelligence, Central Economic Intelligence Bureau, Directorate of Enforcement, Narcotics Control Bureau, Aviation Research Centre, Special Frontier Force, BSF, CRPF, ITBP, CISF, NSG, Assam Rifles, Special Service Bureau, Special Branch (CID), Andaman and Nicobar, the Crime Branch-CID-CB, Dadra and Nagar Haveli and Special Branch, Lakshadweep Police. Agencies specified by the State Governments through a Notification will also be excluded. The exclusion, however, is not absolute and these organizations have an obligation to provide information pertaining to allegations of corruption and human rights violations. Further, information relating to allegations of human rights violations can be given but only with the approval of the Central or State Information Commission.

Right to Information Act

The Right to Information Act 2005 (Act, No. 22/2005) is a law enacted by the Parliament of India giving Indians (except those in the State of Jammu and Kashmir who have their own special law) access to Government records. Under the terms of the Act, any person may request information from a "public authority" (a body of Government or instrumentality of State) which is expected to reply expeditiously or within thirty days. The Act also requires every public authority to computerize their records for wide dissemination and to proactively publish certain categories of information so that the citizens need minimum recourse to request for information formally. This law was passed by Parliament on 15 June, 2005 and came into force on 13 October, 2005.

Main Features of Right to Information Act

The Right to Information Act is a codification of this important right of citizens. The right existed since the time India became a republic, but was difficult to enforce without going to Court. The Act and its rules include the following:

- Define a format for requisitioning information.
- A time period within which information must be provided, namely 30 days.
- Method of giving the information.
- Some charges for applying. The principle is that charges should be minimum, — more as a token. They are not representative of the costs, which may be incurred.
- Some exemptions of information, which will not be given.
- Citizens can ask for information by getting Xerox copies of documents, permissions, policies and decisions.

- Inspection of files can also be done and samples can be asked for.
- All administrative officers of public authorities have to appoint 'Public Information Officers (PIO).'
- Citizens apply for information to the Public Information Officer of the concerned office.
- If information is not provided or wrongly refused, the citizen can go in appeal to an Appellate Authority who would be an official in the same department, senior to the PIO. The Appellate Authority has to give a decision in 30 days.
- If this too does not give a satisfactory result, one can appeal to the State or Central Information Commissioner, which is an independent Constitutional Authority, established under the Act.
- The Act provides for a penalty for delay on the PIO at a rate of Rs. 250 per day of delay, or for *mala fide* denial of information. In case of information being delayed, no charges for information are to be paid.
- Information can be demanded from all Public authorities, i.e. all Government bodies and organizations substantially financed by Government including NGOs. Each State has the right to frame its rules in terms of fees, procedures and forms, which have to be in consonance with the Act.
- Thus RTI provides for a time bound and defined process for citizens to access information about all actions taken by Public authorities.
- The penal provisions on the PIO are the real teeth of the Act, which ensure that the PIO cannot treat a Citizen's demands for information in a cavalier manner.

State-level Laws

The RTI Laws were first successfully enacted by the state governments – Tamil Nadu (1997), Goa (1997), Rajasthan (2000), Karnataka (2000), Delhi (2001), Maharashtra (2002), Madhya Pradesh (2003), Assam (2002) and Jammu and Kashmir (2004).

The Maharashtra and Delhi State level enactments are considered to have been the most widely used. The Delhi and Jammu & Kashmir RTI Acts are still in force.

Role of the Government

As stated in section 26 of the Act, the Act enjoins upon the federal government, as also the state governments of the Republic of India to initiate necessary steps to:

- Develop educational programmes for the public especially disadvantaged communities of RTI.
- Encourage Public Authorities to participate in the development and organization of accurate information to the public.
- Promote timely dissemination of accurate information to the public.
- Train officers and develop training materials.

Compile and disseminate a User Guide for the public in the respective official languages.

- Publish names, designations, postal addresses and contact details of PIOs and other information such as notices regarding fees to be paid, remedies available in law if request is rejected etc.

Power to Make Rules

- Central Government, State Governments and the Competent Authority as defined in S.2(e) are vested with powers to make rules to carry out the provisions of the Right to Information Act, 2005. (S.27 & S.28)

Who has the power to deal with the difficulties while implementing this Act?

- If any difficulty arises in giving effect to the provisions in the Act, the Central Government may, by Order published in the Official Gazette, make provisions necessary/expedient for removing the difficulty. (S.30)

Effects

In the first year of the National RTI, 42,876 (not yet official) applications for information were filed to Central (i.e. Federal) Public Authorities. Of these 878 were disputed at the final appellate stage—the Central Information Commission at New Delhi. A few of these decisions have thereafter been mired in further legal controversy in the various High Courts of India. The first stay order against a final appellate decision of the Central Information Commission was granted on 3 May, 2006 by the High Court of Delhi in WP(c)6833-35/2006 cited as "NDPL & Ors. *Versus* Central Information Commission & Ors". The Indian government planned to amend the RTI in 2006 but was compelled to abandon the changes owing to public outery.

Impact of RTI Act on Panchayati Raj and Gram Panchayats

Participation in governance is at the heart of any successful democracy. As citizens, they need to participate not only at the time of election but on a day-to-day basis—when decisions on policy, laws and schemes are being made and projects and activities are being implemented. Public involvement not only enhances the quality of governance but also promotes transparency and accountability in government functioning. Panchayati Raj Institutions (PRIs) in India are a home grown effort to decentralize government to promote greater participation by the ordinary public in their own governance. This process of decentralization was set in motion with the 73rd Constitution Amendment Act, which enabled decentralized governance through PRIs in rural areas.

The Right to Information Act allows access to information held by all "Public authorities", including those that have been constituted or established by the Constitution. This means that Panchayati Raj Institutions, which are in Part IX of the Constitution of India, are covered by the Act, thereby giving the citizens an additional tool to access information from these local bodies. The right to information imposes a positive duty on government to disseminate information to the people and extends the right for people to seek and receive information held by government bodies (and some information from private bodies). Generally, information is disclosed to the public in two different ways, i.e. proactively and upon request. The Act provides citizens the right to access government-held information, which includes panchayat information. Citizens can inspect works, documents and records, take notes, extracts or certified copies of documents or records, take certified samples of materials, and obtain information in electronic form from PRIs.

Panchayati Raj

In order to facilitate at the panchayat level, in 1997 the Government of India issued a circular stating that each State should consider passing orders implementing three different aspects of transparency in local governance.

1. PRIs, especially Gram Panchayats, should display all vital information pertaining to development projects (especially receipt of funds and how they are being spent) in panchayat offices or on a prominent board outside the local school,
2. All relevant records should be open to inspection, and
3. Members of the public should be able to obtain photocopies of documents pertaining to development projects (including all bills, muster rolls, vouchers, estimates, measurement books, the criteria and procedures for selection of beneficiaries and lists of beneficiaries), as well as matters of general public interest, on payment of a nominal charge.

Gram Panchayat

Gram Panchayats are the smallest unit of elected local self-governance, situated at the village level. Each Gram Panchayat area is divided into not less than ten and not more than twenty wards and each ward elects one Panch. The Gram Panchayat consists of the elected Panchs plus a Sarpanch, who is the head of the Gram Panchayat. An Up-Sarpanch is also elected, who acts as the Sarpanch's deputy. Each Gram Panchayat also has a Secretary, who may service one or more Gram Panchayats.

Gram Sabha

There is a Gram Sabha for every village. The Gram Sabha consists of all the people who are registered in the list of voters of a village. The basic philosophy that underlies the concept of the Gram Sabha is that of participatory democracy. Gram Sabhas provide a local platform for people to meet and discuss local development problems and analyse the development and administrative actions of their elected representatives, thus ensuring transparency and accountability. Most importantly, a Gram Sabha provides an opportunity for the participation of all sections of the village-women, *dalits*, tribals and other marginalized groups in planning and implementation of local development programmes.

The Gram Sabha is a general body of electors, whereas the Gram Panchayat is an executive, elected body. The executive has to perform its duties as per directions given by the general body.

The National Institute of Rural Development (NIRD) has released a publication, Implementation of Rural Development Programmes, Role of PRI in the context of the Right to Information Act, which is meant to provide information to locals about how to access information from panchayats about all major rural development schemes run by the Ministry of Rural Development (MoRD). MoRD implements a number of rural development and poverty alleviation programmes, which support infrastructure in villages, offer employment and provide subsidized food grains, shelter and drinking water to villagers.

The Indira Awaas Yojana (JAY) scheme targets rural BPL families who are either totally houseless or live in unserviceable *kutcha* houses. The Central Ministry of Rural Development took out a half page advertisement in *The Hindu* national news paper proactively disclosing information about the scheme. This is exactly the kind of information that needs to be published under section 4 of the RTI Act.

In practice, the right to information provides that people should be able to access information from PRIs upon request, and that PRIs have a duty to proactively publish important information, for example, through sharing information in Gram Sabha meetings, by pasting information on notice boards, *via* the village loudspeaker or by publication in the official gazette or local newspapers.

CHAPTER – 5

Role of Indian Judiciary on Right to Information

Introduction

The Indian response towards conferment of right to information can be classified under the following two categories:

(a) Constitutional Response, and
(b) Statutory Response.

(A) *Constitutional Response*

This includes:

(i) Freedom of information under Article 19(1)(a), and
(ii) Right to know under Article 21.

(i) Freedom of information under Article 19(1)(a)

Article 19(1)(a) of the Constitution guarantees to all citizens freedom of speech and expression. At the same time, Article 19(2) permits the State to make any law in so far as such law imposes reasonable restrictions on the exercise of the rights conferred by Article 19(1)(a) of the Constitution in the interest of sovereignty and integrity of India, the security of the State, friendly relations with foreign States, public order, decency, morality, contempt of court, defamation and incitement of offence. Thus, a citizen has a right to receive information and that right is derived from the concept of freedom of speech and expression comprised in Article 19(1)(a).[1] It must, however, be noted that freedoms under Article 19, including Article 19(1)(a), are available only to citizens of India. An alien or foreigner has no rights under this Article because he is not a citizen of India. Thus to confer protection upon non-citizens one has to depend upon and apply Article 21 which is available to all persons, whether citizen or non-citizen.

(ii) Right to Know under Article 21

Article 21 enshrines right to life and personal liberty. The expressions "right to life and personal liberty" are compendious terms, which include within themselves a variety of rights and attributes. Some of them are also found in Article 19 and thus have two sources at the same time.[2] In *R.P. Limited* v. *Indian Express Newspapers*[3] the Supreme Court read into Article 21 the right to know. The Supreme Court held that right to know is a necessary ingredient of participatory democracy. In view of transnational developments when distances are shrinking, international communities are coming together for cooperation in various spheres and they are moving towards a global perspective in various fields including Human Rights, the expression "liberty" must receive an expanded meaning. The expression cannot be limited to mere absence of bodily restraint. It is wide enough to expand to a full range of rights including right to hold a particular opinion and right to sustain and nurture that opinion. For sustaining and nurturing that opinion it becomes necessary to receive information. Article 21 confers on all persons a right to know which includes a right to receive information. The ambit and scope of Article 21 is much wider as compared to Article 19(1)(a). Thus, the courts are required to expand its scope by way of judicial activism. In *P.U.C.L* v. *U.O.I*[4], the Supreme Court observed that Fundamental Rights themselves have no fixed contents, most of them are empty vessels into which each generation must pour its contents in the light of its experience. The attempt of the court should be to expand the reach and ambit of the Fundamental Rights by process of judicial interpretation. There cannot be any distinction between the Fundamental Rights mentioned in Chapter-III of the Constitution and the declaration of such rights on the basis of the judgments rendered by the Supreme Court.

Further, it is well settled that while interpreting the constitutional provisions dealing with Fundamental Rights the courts must not forget the principles embodied in the international conventions and instruments and as far as possible the courts must give effect to the principles contained in those instruments. The courts are under an obligation to give due regard to the international conventions and norms while construing the domestic laws, more so when there is no inconsistency or conflict between them and the domestic laws.

(B) Statutory Response

Besides constitutional provisions we have certain statutory provisions also, which confer right to information upon the citizens. The notable ones among them are:

(1) Right to Information in Case of Food and Drugs

Section 23 r/w Rule 32[5] of the Prevention of Food Adulteration Act, 1954 confers on consumers of food products a right to be informed whether or not the article of food is vegetarian or non-vegetarian. As regards drugs and cosmetics, necessary amendments have not been made in the relevant statute. In *Ozir Husain* v. *U.O.I*[6] a division bench of the Delhi High Court observed that it is the Fundamental Right of the consumers to know whether the food products, cosmetics and drugs are of non-vegetarian or vegetarian origin, as otherwise it will violate their Fundamental Right under Articles 19(1) (a), 21 and 25 of the Constitution. The packages of non-vegetarian products should bear a symbol giving their non-vegetarian origin; and a package of a vegetarian product should also bear a symbol. To enable a person to practise the beliefs and opinions, which he holds, in a meaningful manner, it is essential for him to receive the relevant information; otherwise he may be prevented from acting in consonance with his beliefs and opinions. In case a vegetarian consumer does not know the ingredients of the drugs or food products which he/she wishes to buy, it will be difficult for him/her to practise vegetarianism. Moreover, reading Article 19(1) (a) along with International Covenant on Civil and Political Rights, it must be recognized that right to freedom of speech and expression includes freedom to seek, receive and impart information of ideas. Further Article 21 confers on every person the right to receive information and also a right to know the ingredients or the constituents of drugs and food products. However, as far as life saving drugs are concerned a limited exception will apply because a patient, who is suffering from a serious ailment, which can be fatal if a life saving drug is not administered to him, need not be informed in his own interest as to whether or not the drug contains part of any animal as it is conducive to the preservation of life and, therefore, in tune with Article 21 of the Constitution. Thus the High Court issued certain directions about declarations and different coloured symbols to be displayed on packages of drugs and cosmetics regarding their vegetarian or non-vegetarian origin, till amendments are made in the Act.

(2) Right to Information in Cases of Venereal or Infectious Diseases

The welfare of the society is the primary duty of every civilized State. Sections 269 to 271 of the Indian Penal Code 1860 make an act which is likely to spread infection, punishable by considering it as an offence. These sections are framed in order to prevent people from doing acts which are likely to spread infectious diseases. Thus a person suffering from an infectious disease is under an obligation to disclose the same to the other person and if he fails to do so he will be liable to be prosecuted under these sections. As a corollary, the other person has a right to know about such infectious diseases. In *Mr. X* v. *Hospital Z*[7] the Supreme Court held that it was open to the hospital authorities or the doctor concerned to reveal such information to the persons related to the girl whom he intended to marry and she had a right to know about the HIV Positive status of the appellant. A question may, however, be raised that if the person suffering from HIV Positive marries with a willing partner after disclosing the factum of disease to that partner, will he still commit an offence within the meaning of Sections 269 and 270 of I.P.C? It is submitted that there should be no bar for such a marriage if the healthy spouse consents to marry despite being aware of the fact that the other spouse is suffering from the said disease. The courts should not interfere with the choice of two consenting adults who are willing to marry each other with full knowledge about the disease. It must be noted that in *Mr. X* v. *Hospital Z* a three-judge bench of the Supreme Court held that once the division bench of the Supreme Court held that the disclosure of HIV Positive status was justified as the girl has a right to know, there was no need for this court to go further and declare in general as to what rights and obligations arise in such context as to right to privacy or whether such persons are entitled to marry or not, or in the event such persons marry they would commit an offence under the law, or whether such right is suspended during the period of illness. Therefore, all those observations made by the court in the aforesaid matter were unnecessary. Thus, the court held that the observations made by this court, except to the extent of holding that the appellant's right was not affected in any manner by revealing his HIV Positive status to the relatives of his fiancée, are uncalled for. It seems that the court has realized the untenability of the earlier observations and the practical difficulties which may arise after the disclosure of HIV status.

(3) Right to Know about the Information under the Control of a Public Authority

In our present democratic framework, free flow of information for the citizens suffers from several bottlenecks including the existing legal framework, lack of infrastructure at the grassroots levels and an attitude and tendency of maintaining secrecy in the day-to-day governmental functioning. To remove these unreasonable restrictions the Right to Information Act, 2005 (RTIA-05) has been enacted by the Parliament. The Act provides for freedom to every citizen to secure access to information under the control of public authorities consistent with public interest, in order to promote openness, transparency and accountability in administration and in relation to matters connected therewith or incidental thereto. The Act is in accord with Article 19 of the Constitution as well as Article 19 of the Universal Declaration of Human Rights, 1948. The Act will enable citizens to have an access to information on a statutory basis. With a view to further this objective, Section 3 of the Act specifies that subject to the provisions of this Act, every citizen shall have the right to freedom of information. Obligation is cast upon every public authority under Section 4 to provide information and to maintain all records consistent with its operational requirements duly catalogued, indexed and published.

It must be noted that right to receive information from public authorities, which includes the judiciary, is not an absolute right but is subject to statutory and constitutional restrictions. For instance, freedom of speech and expression as provided under Article 19(1)(a) of the Constitution is subject to reasonable restrictions as provided under Article 19(2). Similarly, right to know under Article 21 can be restricted by a procedure established by law which is just, fair and reasonable. On the statutory side, under the Right to Information Act, 2005 (RTIA-05), a citizen is not entitled to an absolute freedom of information. In certain cases information can be withheld from a citizen. Besides the RTIA-05 there may be other statutes also where information may be withheld from a citizen. For instance, the report of an inquiry made against a judge of a High Court under the provisions of the Judges Enquiry Act, 1968 may be withheld from the public by the Chief Justice of India (CJI). In *Indira Jaising* v. *Registrar General, Supreme Court of India*[8] an inquiry report was made by the committee to the CJI, in respect of alleged involvement of sitting judges of the High Court of Karnataka in certain incidents. The petitioner sought the publication of the inquiry report. The Supreme Court held that it was not appropriate for the petitioner to approach this court for relief or direction for release of the report, for what the CJI had done was only to get information from peer judges of those who were accused and the report made to the CJI was wholly confidential. It was purely preliminary in nature, *ad hoc* and not final. The Court further held that in a democratic framework free flow of information to the citizens is necessary for proper functioning, particularly in matters which form part of public record. The right to information is, however, not absolute. There are several areas where such information need not be furnished. Even the Freedom of Information Act, 2002 (now RTIA-05) does not say in absolute terms that information gathered at any level, in any manner and for any purpose shall be disclosed to the public. The inquiry ordered and the report made to the CJI being confidential and discreet is only for the purpose of his information and not for the purpose of disclosure to any other person. The court thus rejected the contention to release the said report. The Court, however, made it clear that if the petitioner can substantiate that any criminal offence has been committed by any of the judges mentioned in the course of the petition, appropriate complaint can be lodged before a competent authority for taking action by complying with requirements of law.

(4) Right to Information and Electronic Governance

Digital technologies and new communication systems have made dramatic changes in our lives. Business transactions are being made with the help of computers. Information stored in electronic form is cheaper and easier to store. Thus, keeping in view the urgent need to bring suitable amendments in the existing laws to facilitate electronic commerce and electronic governance, the Information Technology Act, 2000 was enacted by the Parliament. The aim of the e-governance is to make the interaction of the citizens with the government offices hassle free and to share information in a free and transparent manner. It further makes the right to information a meaningful reality. In a democracy, people govern themselves and they cannot govern themselves properly unless they are aware of social, political, economic and other issues confronting them. To enable them to make a proper judgment on those issues, they must have the benefit of a range of opinions on those issues. This plurality of opinions, views and ideas is indispensable for enabling them to make an informed judgment on those issues, to know what is their true interest, to make them responsible citizens, to safeguard their rights as also the interests of society and the State. All the constitutional courts of leading democracies have recognized and reiterated this aspect. In *U.O.I* v. *Association for Democratic Reforms*[9] the Supreme Court observed that the citizens of India have a right to know every public act, everything that is done in a public way by the public functionaries. Public education is essential for functioning of the process of popular government and to assist the discovery of truth and strengthening the capacity of an individual in participating in the decision making process. The right to get information in a democracy is recognized all throughout and it is a natural right flowing from the concept of democracy. Thus e-governance and right to information are interrelated and are two sides of the same coin. With the enactment of the Information Technology Act, 2000 more and more transparency is expected in governmental functioning by keeping people aware of the State's plan, policies, objectives and achievements.

(5) Right to Know about Antecedents of Election Candidates

In a democratic form of government, voters are of utmost importance. They have a right to elect or re-elect on the basis of the antecedents and past performance of the candidate. For maintaining purity of elections and a healthy democracy, voters are required to be educated and well informed about the contesting candidates. Such information would include assets held by the candidate, his qualification including educational qualification and antecedents of his life including whether he was involved in a criminal case and if the case was decided, its result, if pending –whether charge has been framed or cognizance has been taken by the court. There is no necessity of suppressing the relevant facts from the voters.

In *U.O.I* v. *Association for Democratic Reforms*[10] the Supreme Court recognized this right of the voter. The Court held that the decision making process of a voter would include his right to know about the public functionaries who are required to be elected by him. Moreover, Article 19(1)(a) of the Constitution provides for freedom of speech and expression. Voter's speech and expression in case of election would include casting of vote. For this purpose, information about the candidate to be selected is a must. In *P.U.C.L* v. *U.O.I*[11] the Supreme Court held that in an election petition challenging the validity of an election of a particular candidate, the statutory provisions would govern the respective rights of the parties. However, the voter's Fundamental Right to know antecedents of a candidate is independent of statutory rights under the election laws. Members of a democratic society should be sufficiently informed so that they may cast their votes intelligently in favour of persons who are to govern them. There can be little doubt that exposure to public gaze and scrutiny is one of the surest means to cleanse our democratic governing system and to have competent legislatures. The court further observed that securing information on the basic details concerning the candidates contesting for elections to the Parliament or State legislatures promotes freedom of expression and therefore, the Right to information forms an integral part of Article 19(1)(a). This Right to Information is, however, qualitatively different from the right to get information about public affairs or the right to receive information through the press or e-media, though, to a certain extent, there may be overlapping. The right to vote is a constitutional right but not merely a statutory right; freedom of voting as distinct from right to vote is a facet of the Fundamental Right enshrined in Article 19(1)(a).

There was a time when the Courts in India, particularly the Supreme Court waxed eloquent about the "Right to Information", being a part of the constitutionally enshrined right to speech and expression. Thus, while rejecting the government's claim of privilege on the Blue book containing the security instructions for the Prime Minister in *Indira Gandhi's case*, the Court said, "In a government of responsibility like ours, where all the agents of the public must be responsible for their conduct, there can be but few secrets. The people of this country have a right to know every public act, everything, that is done in a public way by their public functionaries."

Thereafter, while rejecting the government's claim of privilege on the correspondence between the Chief Justice and the Law Minister on the appointment and transfer of judges, the Court said, "Where a society has chosen to accept democracy as its creedal faith, it is elementary that the citizens ought to know what their government is doing. The citizens have a right to decide by whom and by what rules they shall be governed and they are entitled to call on those who govern on their behalf to account for their conduct. No democratic government can survive without accountability and the basic postulate of accountability is that the people should have information about the functioning of the government. It is only if people know how government is functioning that they can fulfil the role which democracy assigns to them and make democracy a really effective participatory democracy."

It was on the basis that the Right to Information is a fundamental right of people, that the Court ordered that even candidates contesting elections would be obligated to publicly disclose information about their criminal antecedents and their income and assets etc. Yet, though the courts' general pronouncements on the right to information have been very liberal, its practices have often not been in conformity with the declared right. Thus, for example, the courts often follow the practice of asking the government and public authorities to file reports in sealed covers in court. These reports are then perused only by judges and often not given to the opposite parties or their lawyers. Often the orders and judgements of courts are based on their perception formed on the basis of these "confidential reports", which is not only a violation of the right to information of the opposite party, but also in violation of the principles of Natural Justice, considered to be sacrosanct.

The double standards of the courts on Right to Information have become even more obvious after the Right to Information Act has come into force. Though the Act clearly applies to courts which are obviously included in the definition of Public Authorities, most High Courts did not even appoint Public Information Officers (PIOs) even months after the Act came into force. Some have still not appointed them, thus effectively denying the right to information to the people about the courts. Moreover, many of even those which appointed PIOs have framed their own rules which effectively deny information about administrative or financial matters. Thus, the Delhi High Court Rules provide that:

> "5. *Exemption from disclosure of information*: The information specified under Section 8 of the Act shall not be disclosed and made available and in particular the following information shall not be disclosed:
> (a) Such information which is not in the public domain or does not relate to judicial functions and duties of the Court and matters incidental and ancillary thereto."

Thus, information sought regarding the appointment of Class 3 and 4 employees by the High Court, who are reported to have been appointed on extraneous considerations, without any public advertisement or selection, was denied by the High Court, citing this rule. This rule means that no information will be given about the expenditures incurred by the High Court (from public funds) or about any appointments or transfers. This is in total violation of the RTI Act which allows exemption from disclosure only on certain grounds specified in Section 8 of the Act and on no other ground. No public authority can refuse to disclose information which does not fall under the exemptions permissible under Section 8 of the Act. Rule 5 of the Delhi High Court rules clearly violates the Act and is thus liable to be struck down.

Not only this, the High Court rules have increased the application fees from the normal ₹ 10 to near ₹ 500. And the penalty for non-disclosure has been reduced from the maximum of ₹ 25,000 as provided in the Act to ₹ 500, which is hardly likely to deter any information officer from wantonly denying information. Thus every attempt has been made to dilute the Act and make it as difficult as possible for citizens to access information about the courts. They have been emboldened to do all this in the secure knowledge that to challenge such illegal rules, the citizen would have to approach the same courts.

The Supreme Court has recommended to the government that so far as the Supreme Court is concerned, the decision of the Registrar General of the Court should be final and not subject to any independent appeal to the Central Information Commission. They have further recommended that the Chief Justice should have the unfettered right to interdict the disclosure of any information, which in his opinion, might compromise the independence of the Judiciary. The Chief Justice has already gone on record to say that even the disclosure of income and assets by judges or the formation of any independent disciplinary authority over judges, would compromise the independence of the Judiciary. Going by this, it is obvious that no information about complaints against judges or about their incomes and assets would be available under the Right to Information. Thus while the Supreme Court decrees that even candidates aspiring to become public servants (MLAs or MPs), would be required to disclose their assets, when it comes to sitting judges, such disclosure would violate the independence of the Judiciary! There cannot be a more glaring case of double standards.

The track record of the courts on cases arising out of the RTI Act is also not very inspiring. Even the occasional progressive orders of the Central Information Commission ordering various public authorities to disclose information have been stayed by the Delhi High Court and the matter remains pending for months and years thereafter. Thus, even the order of the CIC to merely peruse the correspondence between the then President and the Prime Minister on the Gujarat genocide of 2002 has been stayed by the High Court, though the Act specifically provides that no information will be withheld from the CIC. Similarly, the order of the CIC asking the UPSC to disclose the marks obtained by candidates in the preliminary examination has also been stayed by the High Court, as have various other orders of the CIC.

All this shows that while the courts have been liberal in making pronouncements about the citizen's right to information in a democracy, and have also in cases implemented it with regard to others, they have been very reluctant to practice what they preach. The dictum appears to be that transparency and accountability is good for others, but the courts and judges are *sui generis*, and in their case transparency would compromise their independence. The want of "Independence of the Judiciary" has always been waived by the Judiciary to shield themselves from accountability, going to the extent of saying that not even an FIR can be registered against judges for any offence without the prior written permission of the Chief Justice of India. On top of all this, they enjoy the power of Contempt, where they can send any person who accuses any judge to jail.

It is not surprising then that the voices to make the judiciary accountable are growing louder and are now beginning to take the shape of a public campaign. The common people are beginning to realize that they are the main stakeholders in the judicial system and they must bring grassroots pressure on the authorities for them to reform the system.

The Supreme Court in case of *Secretary, Ministry of Information and Broadcasting, Government of India* v. *Cricket Association of Bengal*[12] narrowly expanded its view on the provision of Article 19(1)(a) towards the right to information. It held that the right to freedom of speech and expression includes the right to receive and impart information. For ensuring the free speech right of citizens of this country, it is necessary that the citizens have the benefit of plurality of views and a range of opinions on all public issues. A successful democracy posits an unaware citizen's diversity of opinions, views, ideas and ideologies is essential to enable the citizens to arrive at informed judgment on all issues touching them. This Court made more clear of the provision of right to information that is inferred itself in Article 19(1)(a). It held in the case of *S.P. Gupta* v. *Union of India*[13], that right to know is implicit in right of free speech and expression. Disclosure of information regarding functioning of the government must be the rule.

In going back to 1975 this Court in the case of *State of Uttar Pradesh* v. *Raj Narain*[14] observed that freedom of speech and expression includes right of citizens to know every public act, everything that is done in a public way, by their public functionaries. In the year 1997 the Court also held that freedom of speech and expression includes right of the citizens to know about the affairs of government. *Dinesh Tribedi* v. *Union of India*[15]. Freedom of speech and expression, has been held repeatedly by the Supreme Court as basic to and indivisible from a democratic polity. It includes right to impart and receive information. The restrictions to the said could only be as provided in Article 19(2). This Article provides that nothing in sub-clause (i) of clause (1) shall affect the operation of any existing law or prevent the State from making any law, in so far as such law imposes reasonable restrictions on the exercise of the right conferred by the said sub-clause in the interests of the sovereignty and integrity of India, the security of the State, friendly relations with the foreign States, public order, decency or morality. The grounds upon which reasonable restrictions can be placed upon the freedom of speech and expression are designed firstly to ensure that the said right is not exercised in such a manner as to threaten the sovereignty and integrity of India, security of the State, friendly relations with foreign State, public order, decency or morality. The existing laws providing such restrictions are saved and the State is free to make laws in future imposing such restrictions. The grounds aforesaid are conceived in the interest of ensuring and maintaining conditions in which the said right can meaningfully and peacefully be exercised by the citizens of this country.

Hence the right to know or be informed is the foundation of democracy and is derived from the plenary provisions of Article 19(1)(a) of the Constitution of India. The Supreme Court, in another case of *Peoples Union for Civil Liberties* v. *Union of*

India[16]) held that true democracy cannot exist unless the citizens have a right to participate in the affairs of the policy of the country. The right to participate in the affairs of the country is meaningless unless the citizens are well informed on all sides of issues in respect of which they are called upon to express their views. One-sided information, disinformation, misinformation and non-information all equally create uninformed citizens which makes democracy a farce when medium of information is monopolised either by a part in a central authority or by private individuals or oligarchy organisations. This is particularly so in a country like ours where 65 per cent of the population is illiterate.

It is obvious from the Constitution that India has adopted a democratic form of government where a society has chosen to accept democracy as its creedal faith. It is elementary that the citizen's right to know what their government is doing. The citizens have a right to decide by whom and by what rules they shall be governed and they are entitled to call on those who govern on their behalf to account for their conduct. No democratic government can survive without accountability and the basic postulate of accountability is that the people should have information about the functioning of the government. It is only if the people know how government is functioning that they can fulfil the role which democracy assigns to them and make democracy a really effective participatory democracy.

A popular government without popular information or the means of obtaining it, is but a prologue to a farce or tragedy or perhaps both. The citizen's right to know the facts, the true facts about the administration of the country is thus one of the pillars of a democratic State. And that is why the demand for openness in the government is increasingly growing in different parts of the world. Any important role people can fulfil in a democracy only if it is an open government where there is full access to information in regard to the functioning of government. Enlightened and informed citizens would undoubtedly enhance democratic values. In the absence of law on right to information, the Supreme Court observed in the case of *Union of India* v. *Association for Democratic Reforms*[17], wherein it gave the directives that were included to operate only till the law was made by the Legislature and in that sense *"pro tempore"* in nature. Once legislation is made, the Court has to make an independent assessment in order to evaluate whether the items of information statutorily ordained are reasonably adequate to secure the right to information available to the citizens. The Court has to take a holistic view and adopt a balanced approach in examining the legislation providing for right to information and laying down the parameters of that right.

In a government of responsibility, where all the agents of the public must be responsible for their conduct, there can be but few secrets. The people of this country have a right to know every public act, everything that is done in a public way, by their public functionaries. They are entitled to know the particulars of every public; transaction in all its bearing *State of Uttar Pradesh* v. *Raj Naraian*[18].

The Supreme Court earlier in 1950 also has observed that the freedom lay at the foundation of all democratic organisations, for without free political discussion on public education, so essential the proper functioning of the processes of popular government. A freedom of such amplitude might involve risks of abuse. But it is better to leave a few of its noxious branches to their luxuriant growth, than, by pruning them away, to injure the vigour of those yielding the proper fruits (*Romesh Thapar* v. *State of Maharashtra*[19]).

The fundamental rights involved are the people's right to know. Freedom of speech and expression should, therefore, receive a generous support from all those who believe in the participation of people in the administration (*Attorney General* v. *Times News Papers Ltd*[20]). The members of the democratic society should be sufficiently informed so that they may influence intelligently the decisions which may affect them. Further the right to get information in democracy is recognised all throughout and it is a natural right flowing from the concept of democracy (*Union of India* v. *Association for Democratic Reform*[21]). The public interest in freedom of discussion stems from the requirement that members of a democratic society should be sufficiently informed (*Indian Express News Papers (Bombay)* v. *Union of India*[22]).

It is apparent that from the opinions and observations of the Supreme Court in *Keshavanand Bharati* case, that India is in need of law on the right to information. The Court in the case of *Union of India* v. *Association of Democratic Reforms*[23] issued the directives to the Election Commission of India regarding voters' right to know the antecedents of the election candidates. Between these periods a plethora of sensitive judgments followed the Supreme Court's concern on the right to know. In 2002 the Law Commission of India's 179th Report was on public interest disclosure and protection of informer followed the Freedom of Information Act, 2002 and finally, the Indian Parliament passed the law on Right to Information in May 2005.

Interpretation by the Indian Judiciary on Right to Information

Bennett Coleman & Co. v. *Union of India*

The judges in this case remarked, it is indisputable that by freedom of the press they meant the right of all citizens to speak, publish, and express their views…Freedom of speech and expression includes within its compass the right of all citizens to read and be informed.

Prabha Dutt v. *Union of India*

The Court held that there could be no reason for refusing permission to the media to interview prisoners on death row. Repeated violations of civil rights by the police and other law enforcement agencies have compelled the courts to give directions to the concerned agencies for ensuring transparency in their functioning.

Sakal Newspapers (Private) Ltd. v. *Union of India*

The Supreme Court held that the impugned Act and the Order imposed unconstitutional restriction on the freedom of the press. The Court also held that restriction upon freedom of speech was to be examined with lesser presumption of constitutionality than the restrictions upon freedom of trade or business. The Court brought in the preferred freedom doctrine in the Constitution of India.

Romesh Thappar v. *State of Madras*

One of the earliest cases where the Supreme Court laid emphasis on the people's right to know. There the petitioner had challenged an order issued by the then Government of Madras under Section 9(1-A) of the Madras Maintenance of Public Order Act, 1949 imposing a ban on the circulation of the petitioner's journal *Cross Roads* that was struck down as violative of the right to freedom of speech and expression under Article 19(1)(a).

S.P. Gupta v. *Union of India*

This case is popularly known as Judges Transfer case, Bhagwati, J. had advised in the landmark case that it is essential for the people to have as much information about governmental operations as possible. Participation in government by the people is regarded as an important aspect of democracy and people cannot participate unless they have information as to what is going on in the country.

In this case a seven judge bench of the Supreme Court observed: Where a society has chosen to accept democracy as its creedal faith, it is elementary that the citizens ought to know what their government is doing. The citizens have a right to decide by whom and by what rules they shall be governed and they are entitled to call on those who govern on their behalf to account for their conduct. No democratic government can survive without accountability and the basic postulate of accountability is that the people should have information about the functioning of the government. It is only if the people know how the government is functioning that they can fulfil the role which democracy assigns to them and make democracy a really effective participatory democracy.

Reliance Petrochemicals Ltd. v. *Indian Express Newspapers Bombay (P) Ltd.*

Justice Mukharji recognized the right to know as emanating from the right to life. The question which arose was whether Reliance Petrochemicals Ltd. was entitled to an injunction against *Indian Express* which had published an article questioning the reliability of the former's debenture issue. The learned Judge observed:

> We must remember that the people at large have a right to know in order to be able to take part in a participatory development in the industrial life and democracy. Right to know is a basic right to which citizens of a free country aspire in the broader horizon of the right to live in this age on our land under Article 21 of our Constitution. That right has reached new dimensions and urgency. That right puts greater responsibility upon those who take upon themselves the responsibility to inform.

Tata Press Ltd. v. *MTNL*

The Supreme Court, while considering the scope of Article 19(1)(a) in the context of advertising or commercial speech, held that the public has a right to receive information. The question which arose in that case was whether advertisements being for commercial gain could avail of the protection guaranteed under Article 19(l)(a). The Supreme Court held: Advertising as a 'commercial speech' has two faces. Advertising which is no more than a commercial transaction, is nonetheless dissemination of information regarding the product advertised. The public at large is benefited by the information made available through the advertisements. In a democratic economy free flow of commercial information is indispensable. There cannot be honest and economical marketing by the public at large without being educated by the information disseminated through advertisements. The economic system in a democracy would be handicapped without there being freedom of commercial speech. Examined from another angle, the public at large has a right to receive the 'commercial speech'. Article 19(1)(a) not only guarantees freedom of speech and expression, it also protects the rights of an individual to listen, read and receive the said speech. So far as the economic needs of a citizen are concerned, their fulfilment has to be guided by the information disseminated through the advertisements. The protection of Article 19(l)(a) is available to the speaker as well as to the recipient of the speech. The recipient of a commercial speech may be having much deeper interest in the advertisement than the businessman who is behind the publication. An advertisement giving information regarding a life-saving drug may be of much more importance to the general public than to the advertiser who may be having purely a trade consideration.

In *Secretary, Ministry of Information and Broadcasting* v. *Cricket Association of Bengal*, The Supreme Court, while considering the rights of a person to telecast a sports event on television through the use of air waves held that the right under Article 19(1)(a) includes the right to receive and acquire information and that viewers have the right to be informed adequately and truthfully. In support of this right, the Court quoted from Article 10 of the European Commission on Human Rights. The Court held that although a person seeking to telecast a sports event when he himself is not participating in the game is not exercising his right to self-expression, he is seeking to educate and entertain the public which is part of the freedom of expression. The Court held that the right of the viewer to be entertained and informed is also, likewise, integral to the freedom of expression. The Court observed:

> True democracy cannot exist unless all citizens have a right to participate in the affairs of the polity of the country. The right to participate in the affairs of the country is meaningless unless the citizens are well informed on all sides of the issues, in respect of which they are called upon to express their views. One-sided information, misinformation and non-information all equally create an uninformed citizenry which makes democracy a farce when it is a medium of information publication. An advertisement giving information regarding a life-saving drug may be of much more importance to the general public than to the advertiser who may be having purely a trade consideration.

Dinesh Trivedi v. *Union of India*

This concerned the questions of the disclosure of the Vohra Committee Report. The Supreme Court once again acknowledged the importance of open Government in a participative democracy. The Court observed that: In modern constitutional democracies, it is axiomatic that citizens have a right to know about the affairs of the Government which, having been elected by them, seeks to formulate sound policies of governance aimed at their welfare. It went on to observe that democracy expects openness and openness is the concomitant of a free society and sunlight is a disinfectant.

Indira Jaising v. *Registrar General, Supreme Court of India*

A Senior Advocate practising in the Supreme Court filed a petition demanding the publication of the inquiry report. The Court declined disclosure with a reasoning that is difficult to reconcile with its own bold pronouncements in the past: A report made on such inquiry if given publicity will only lead to more harm than good to the institution as judges would prefer to face inquiry leading to impeachment. In such a case the only course open to the parties concerned if they have material is to invoke the provisions of Article 124 or Article 217 of the Constitution, as the case may be. The said report is only for the purpose of satisfaction of the Chief Justice of India that such a report has been made. It is purely preliminary in nature, *ad hoc* and not final... the only source and authority by which the Chief Justice can exercise this power of inquiry is moral or ethical and not in exercise of powers under any law. Exercise of such power of the Chief Justice of India based on moral authority cannot be made the subject-matter of a writ petition to disclose a report made to him.

Association for Democratic Reforms v. *Union of India*

The Delhi High Court has emphasized that the right to information acquires great significance in the context of elections. It is now common knowledge that there is criminalization of politics in India. It is a matter of great concern that anti-social elements and criminals are seeking to enter the political arena through the mechanism of elections to State Legislatures and even to Parliament. Parliament has not yet been able to enact a law to uproot this evil. In this scenario, the Delhi High Court has sought to cleanse the electoral process through the mechanism of the right to know of the people and laid down certain conditions which the Apex Court also agreed on appeal. The Apex Court went on to say that one-sided information, disinformation, mis-information and non-information will equally create an uninformed citizenry which makes democracy a farce. Freedom of speech and expression includes right to impart and receive information which includes freedom to hold opinions.

M. Nagaraj v. *Union of India*

It was held that right to know and right to access information is implicit in the right of free speech and expression guaranteed under Article 19(1)(a). The right to information has both intrinsic and instrumental value. Its intrinsic value comes from the fact that citizens have a right to know. It is a crucial step towards a deeper, more meaningful democracy. More tangibly, in a country like India it can promote action for development and therefore, has considerable instrumental value. Information enables people to make enlightened choices, and keep tabs on elected representatives and officials who claim to act on their collective behalf. Thus, accountability and transparency are both enhanced radically.

PUCL v. *Union of India*

It was held to be *intra vires* Articles 14, 19, 20(3) and 21. Neither a lawyer can claim professional communication beyond what is permitted under Section 126 of Indian Evidence Act, nor is there any law permitting a newspaper or a journalist to withhold relevant information from courts, nor can withholding of such information be traced to the right to privacy, which itself is not an absolute right. The need for Right to Information has been widely felt in all sectors of the country and this has also received judicial recognition through some landmark judgments of Indian courts.

Judiciary also not Exempted from RTI Purview

Besides the RTIA-05, there may be other statutes also where information may be withheld from a citizen. For instance, the report of an inquiry made against a justice of the High Court under the provisions of the Judges Enquiry Act, 1968 may be withheld from the public by the Chief Justice of India. In *Indira Jaising* v. *Registrar General*, Supreme Court of India an inquiry report was made by the Committee to the CJI, in respect of alleged involvement of sitting judges of the High Court of Karnataka in certain incidents. The petitioner sleeked the publication of the inquiry report. The Supreme Court held that it is not appropriate for the petitioner to approach this court for relief for direction for release of the report, for what the CJI has done is only to get information from judges of those who are accused and the report made to the CJI is wholly confidential. It is purely preliminary in nature, *ad hoc* and not final. The Court further held that in a democratic framework free flow of information to the citizens is necessary for proper functioning, particularly in matter, which forms part of public record. The right to information is, however, not absolute. There are several areas where such information need not be furnished. Even the Freedom of Information Act, 2002 (Now RTIA-05) does not say in absolute terms that information gathered at any level, in any manner and for any purpose shall be disclosed to the public. The inquiry ordered and the report made to the CJI being confidential and discreet is only for the purpose of his information and not for the purpose of disclosure to any other person. The Court thus rejected the contention to release the said report. The Court, however, made it clear that if the petitioner can substantiate that any criminal offence has been committed by any of the judges mentioned in the course of the petition, appropriate complaint can be lodged before a competent authority for taking action by complying with requirements of law.

Now the big question is whether Section 22 of the RTIA-05 will override any other provision to the contrary. If an application under RTIA-05 has been made to the High Court for obtaining certain information in possession of the High Court, the PIO of the HC cannot refuse the concerned information by contending that it should be obtained as per HC rules as the matter is Judicial. There is nothing "Judicial" about such information. One is not asking about any certified copies of a judgment or order. What one is doing is simply asking for information lying exclusively with the High Court. It is at most "administrative information" and the same cannot be refused on the basis of judicial argument. In fact, if something is "judicial" it becomes a "public document" and anybody can ask for it after complying with the procedural requirements.

However, since the case is "Pending", the court may legitimately refuse its disclosure after giving reasons in writing. This is so because a premature disclosure may "prejudice the interest of the parties". Perhaps, that must be the implied contention of the PIO. All that he/she wants is that a "judicial permission" and not a RTIA-2005 application is the correct procedure, in the peculiar facts and circumstances of the case. The information sought in the present case is two reports submitted by a Committee appointed by the High Court in a PIL (said case is pending) for which they applied as an RTI application.

Now a big question arises as to the immunity of the Judiciary from the scope of RTIA- 2005. There is nothing either under the Constitution or under any statutory enactment, including RTIA-2005 that exempts the Judiciary from such administrative disclosures. However, when it comes to "Judicial matter", some leverage must be given to it. For instance, if a court is trying a case where the identity of the victim must not to be disclosed, then none can ask for the same or any information related to it. This will be so irrespective of Section 22 of the RTIA-2005, overriding force has been created in favour of that Act. But it must be harmoniously construed with other provisions of various statutes. The first attempt of the court should be to reconcile two conflicting provisions of two statutes. If such reconciliation is not possible then only the overriding provision under section 22 can be invoked. Thus, RTIA-05 cannot be read in isolation and a holistic interpretation is the need of the hour.

Now whatever may be the interpretation, one thing is sure. The Judiciary is not out of the reach of RTIA-05 except on the limited grounds mentioned under the Constitution of India, RTIA-05 and other statutes. In fact, people of India have great faith in the Judiciary of India. This is natural as well since it is functioning as per the Constitutional norms. Now what is expected from the Judiciary at this stage is to throw away extraneous applications under the RTIA-05 at the threshold and to allow all other genuine applications to the maximum possible extent. The Judiciary must voluntarily come forward to meet this democratic ideal. The same is expected from the Judiciary and it will once again meet our expectations: WE, THE PEOPLE OF INDIA.

Conclusion

Apart from these leading cases there are many cases where people's right to know and right to information have been upheld. The purpose of discussing all these is to show that we already have the right to information as guaranteed by Article 19(1)(a) of the Constitution of India. Moreover, as an extended part of the freedom of speech and expression, the right to know and to be known is our Fundamental right as ensured by Chapter III of the Constitution. As per the Constitution if there is violation of Fundamental Right by the state, the aggrieved person may go to the Supreme Court under Article 32 or to the High Court under Article 226 directly. But after passing of the Right to Information Act, 2005, this Fundamental Right becomes only a statutory right.

It is too early to say whether RTIA will be a "great and revolutionary act." Whether the RTIA fulfils the hopes of the people of India hinges largely on how it is implemented. It is difficult to predict whether India is at last at the verge of the passage of a landmark law which would explicitly guarantee the people's right to information. The rapid legislation of FOIA-style laws in many countries both developed and developing has caused increasing problems of implementation. But the implementation in India has been examined more persistently and stubbornly than in any other country. Corruption and mismanagement have been reduced and the governmental responsiveness has improved according to reports as the civil society organizations and the common man have started using the RTI Act. Provisions in the law to promote "proactive disclosure" of key information are often disregarded. It has been seen that due to the non-compliance by public officials the number of cases complaining for the same have quietly gone up making the commissions to struggle, which are established for the enforcement of law.

If these challenges are not adequately grappled with then it would mean that the law is meant to serve only those people who are wealthy and have knowledge and resources to get the law enforced in their favour. The same has been seen in many other countries also where a law was adopted to meet and serve progressive aims in public interest ultimately serves interests of already advantaged people by reinforcing their position. Like the other countries, in India also, the advocates of RTI Act have been continuously facing attempts at amending the Act launched by the ministers and bureaucrats so as to restrict the right to information.

Bureaucratic habits as well as administrative practices in India are built up over decades owing to traditions and British colonial rule. Indeed, it is to some extent still true that India is struggling with its administrative system. Introduction of Right to Information Act in India is a good practical with FOIA-style laws. This is because of mainly two reasons: the vast population of the country which is going to be benefited and much more difficult circumstances under which the law is introduced as compared to the other nations who had adopted it earlier. Numberless challenges are still waiting to come across and the adoption of an FOIA-style law is merely a step towards the long way to transparency. This is not possible until the judiciary in the country, especially the higher judiciary recognizes its responsibility towards the people's right to information. Because, ultimately it will be one best way for the judiciary maintain to the confidence and trust of the common man of the country in it.

"Judicial independence doesn't mean that judges are above the law—Lord MacKay." This decision showed that the higher judiciary could only preach accountability to other organs of state, viz. legislature and executive (sometimes it includes the lower judiciary also), but when it comes to following their own preaching they are fearful. The Apex Court has itself mentioned in several cases that society's demand for honesty of a judge is exacting and absolute, therefore, a judge must keep himself absolutely above suspicion. The confidence of the common man in honesty and impartiality was destroyed after seeing the panic and apprehension among the judges, when they were asked to disclose their assets. Instead of keeping themselves absolutely above suspicion, the act of opposing disclosure of assets brought them into the centre of suspicion.

It is appreciable that the Judiciary has used its craftsmanship to harness the right to information to achieve an extremely laudable social objective, viz. that of preventing criminalization of Indian politics. It seems to be really unfortunate to say that the judicial system in India has proved itself to be an instrument not really meant for protecting the rights of the oppressed and poor, rather it has become an instrument to harass the common man. The system functions with great speed and eagerness when it is invoked by a powerful and rich man, while its functioning becomes abnormal and impaired in the case of the weak and the poor. The courts are increasingly displaying their elitist bias and it appears that they have seceded from the principles of the Constitution which set up a republic of the people who were guaranteed "Justice—social, economic and political". It is again hard to digest why the higher judiciary insists so much for taking itself out of the realm of the Right to Information Act because only those who are guilty of errors, incompetence, misbehaviour, dereliction of duty and malpractice may be concerned and wish that the fact relating to such matters are not made public.

We have got a very good tool in the form of the Right to Information Act to ensure transparency in public working, but all depends upon its proper implementation. If an executive is not working properly then we can trust the Judiciary, but now who will tackle the Judiciary when they are not ready to consider their responsibility towards the nation in terms of the Right of Information of the people of India. Modern democratic government means government of the people, by the people and for the people and if they are ignorant of the issue to be resolved the argument for and against different solutions and the facts underlying those arguments the business of the government is not an activity about which only those professionally engaged are entitled to receive information and expression opinion. It is or should be a participatory process, but there can be no assurance that government is carried out for the people unless the facts are made known and the issues are publicly ventilated.

Since right to information is not absolute, a report made by the Committee of Judges regarding the conduct of High Court Judges to the Chief Justice of India is wholly confidential and is only for the purpose of satisfaction of the Chief Justice of India. It is purely preliminary in nature, *ad hoc* and not final. The authority by which the Chief Justice of India can exercise this power of inquiry is moral or ethical and not in the exercise of powers under any law. Exercise of such power of the Chief Justice of India based on moral authority cannot be made the subject matter of a writ petition to disclose a report made to him.

Suggestions

1. The role of the Information Commission has to go beyond the hearing of the appeals. As per the Act, they are expected to issue orders/directions to the Public Authorities to carry out their duties as per the mandate of the Act. However, till the time the Information Commission assumes the role of ensuring the compliance of the RTI Act by the various Public Authorities, there would not be any control mechanism.
2. The efforts made by appropriate Governments and Public Authorities have been restricted to publishing of rules and FAQs on websites. As compared to the RTI Act the common citizens (and disadvantaged communities) are significantly more aware of other Government schemes focused on socio-economic development. Analyzing the issues highlighted in the section, it is clear that the appropriate Governments and the Public Authorities have taken inadequate steps to make the RTI process citizen-friendly.
3. The process of RTI application submission should be so designed as to suit the needs, aspirations and convenience of the citizens. The quality of response provided can be a direct consequence of the record management practices within the Public Authority, the transparency in its processes, the training provided to the concerned PIO, drafting of the RTI application itself.
4. The higher Judiciary should understand its responsibility towards the nation. They must know how much trust the people of this country repose in them and they must keep themselves above any sort of suspicion. Ultimately, the Government of India consists of three wings, i.e. Legislative, Judiciary and Executive. Hence the judiciary, irrespective of higher or lower, is well within the need for transparency. This fact should be understood by our higher judiciary. It is the right time for the Judiciary to introspect and save its independence, which it itself has established as part of the basic structure of the Constitution of India.
5. There is a need to make the laws stringent against the public officers erring in giving the information under this section. An amendment should be made in Cr.PC. so as to make a provision for appeal under the cases in which disclosing of information is denied or is given wrongly by the public authority. The District Court should be given power to hear the appeals under such cases.
6. An amendment in Section 166 of Indian Penal Code should be made so as punish the public officers who try to conceal the relevant information and give wrongful, *mala fide* and misleading information. Failure to provide information by a public servant must be considered as a non-bailable offence; and there should be a provision service degradation.

NOTES

1. State of U.P. v. Raj Naraian, AIR 1975 SC 865; P.V. Narsimha Rao v. State AIR 1998 SC 2120.

2. Kharak Singh v. State of U.P., AIR 1963 SC 1295.
3. AIR 1989 SC 190.
4. JT 2003 (2) 528.
5. As amended in 2001.
6. AIR 2003 Delhi 103.
7. (1998) 8 SCC 296.
8. 2003 (4) SCALE 643.
9. (2002) 5 SCC 294.
10. *ibid*.
11. JT 2003 (2) SC 528.
12. AIR 1995 SC 1236.
13. 1981 Supp SCC 87.
14. 1975 4 SCC 428.
15. 1974 SCC 306.
16. AIR 2003 SC 2363.
17. AIR 2002 SC 2112.
18. 1975 4 SCC 428.
19. AIR 1950 SC 124.
20. 1973 3 ALL ER 54.
21. AIR 2002 SC 2112.
22. AIR 1986 SC 515.
23. AIR 2002 SC 2110.

Annexures

Annexure – I

Comparative Table of the Provisions in the Freedom of Information Act, 2002/NAC's Right to Information Bill, 2004 [1]Right to Information Bill, 2004 as Introduced in Lok Sabha

Sl. No.	*Freedom of Information Act, 2002*	*NAC's Right to Information Bill, 2004*	*Right to Information Bill, 2004 as Introduced in Lok Sabha*
1	2	3	4
	Preamble	*Preamble*	*Preamble*
	An Act to provide for freedom to every citizen to secure access to information under the control of public authorities, consistent with public interest, in order to promote openness, transparency and accountability in administration and in relation to matters connected therewith or incidental thereto.	A Bill to operationalise the right to information by setting out the practical regime for people to secure access to information under the control of public authorities, consistent with public interest, in order to promote openness, transparency and accountability and in relation to matters connected therewith or incidental thereto.	A Bill to provide for setting out the practical regime of right to information for people to secure access to information under the control of public authorities, in order to promote transparency and accountability in the working of every public authority, the constitution of a Central Information Commission and for matters connected therewith or incidental thereto.
	Chapter 1: Preliminary	**Chapter 1: Preliminary**	**Chapter 1: Preliminary**
1.	1. (1) This Act may be called the Freedom of Information Act, 2002.	(1) This Act may be called the Right to Information Act, 2004.	(1) This Act may be called the Right to Information Act, 2004.
2.	(2) It extends to the whole of India except the State of Jammu and Kashmir.	(2) It extends to the whole of India except the State of Jammu and Kashmir.	(2) It extends to the whole of India except the State of Jammu and Kashmir.
3.	(3) It shall come into force on such date as the Central Government may, by notification in the Official Gazette, appoint.	(3) It shall come into force within 120 days of it being enacted.	(3) It shall come into force on the one hundred and twentieth day of its enactment.

Contd…

Sl. No.	*Freedom of Information Act, 2002*	*NAC's Right to Information Bill, 2004*	*Right to Information Bill, 2004 as Introduced in Lok Sabha*
1	2	3	4
4.	Does not exist in the present Act.	(4) Where State legislation exists dealing with the right to access information, a person will have the right to seek information under the State law as well as under this Act, if the information pertains to a subject under the State List in Schedule 7 of the Constitution of India.	
5.	Does not exist in the present Act.	(5) Objectives of the Act: The objectives of the Act are to (i) give effect to the Fundamental Right to Information, which will contribute to strengthening democracy, improving governance, increasing public participation, promoting transparency and accountability in Union, State and Local Self Government Institutions. (ii) establish voluntary and mandatory mechanisms or procedures to give effect to right to information in a	

Contd...

Sl. No.	*Freedom of Information Act, 2002*	*NAC's Right to Information Bill, 2004*	*Right to Information Bill, 2004 as Introduced in Lok Sabha*
1	2	3	4
		manner which enables persons to obtain access to records of public authorities in a swift, effective, inexpensive and reasonable manner. (iii) promote transparency, accountability and effective governance of all public authorities by, including but not limited to, empowering and educating all persons to: – understand their rights in terms of this Act in order to exercise their rights in relation to public authorities; – understand the functions and operation of public authorities; and – effectively participating in decision making by public authorities that affects their rights.	
6.	2. In This Act, unless the context otherwise requires: (a) "appropriate Government",	2. In This Act, unless the context otherwise requires: (a) "appropriate Government",	2. In This Act, unless the context otherwise requires: (c) "Government", means in relation

Contd...

Sl. No.	*Freedom of Information Act, 2002*	*NAC's Right to Information Bill, 2004*	*Right to Information Bill, 2004 as Introduced in Lok Sabha*
1	2	3	4
	means in relation to a public authority established, constituted, owned, substantially financed by funds provided directly or indirectly or controlled— (i) by the Central Government, the Central Government; (ii) by the State Government, The State Government; (iii) by the Union territory, The Central Government.	means in relation to a public authority established, constituted, owned, substantially financed by funds provided directly or indirectly or controlled— (i) by the Union Government, the Union Government; (ii) by the State Government, The State Government; (iii) by the Union territory, The Central Government.	to a public authority established, constituted, owned, substantially financed by funds provided directly or indirectly or controlled by the Central Government or a Union territory administration, means the Central Government.
7.	(b) "competent authority" means— (i) the Speaker in the case of the House of the People or the Legislative Assembly and the Chairman in the case of the Council of States or the Legislative Council; (ii) The Chief Justice of India in the case of the Supreme Court; (iii) The Chief Justice of the High Court in the case of a High Court;	(b) "competent authority" means— (i) the Speaker in the case of the House of the People or the Legislative Assembly and the Chairman in the case of the Council of States or the Legislative Council; (ii) The Chief Justice of India in the case of the Supreme Court; (iii) The Chief Justice of the High Court in the case of a High Court;	(b) "competent authority" means— (i) the Speaker in the case of the House of the People or the Legislative Assembly of a Union Territory and the Chairman in the case of the Council of States; (ii) the Chief Justice of India in the case of the Supreme Court; (iii) the Chief Justice of the High Court of Delhi; (iv) the President in the case of other authorities created by or under the Constitution;

Contd...

Sl. No.	Freedom of Information Act, 2002	NAC's Right to Information Bill, 2004	Right to Information Bill, 2004 as Introduced in Lok Sabha
1	2	3	4
	(iv) The President or the Governor, as the case may be, in case of other authorities created by or under the Constitution; (v) the administrator appointed under Article 239 of the Constitution;	(iv) The President or the Governor, as the case may be, in case of other authorities created by or under the Constitution; (v) the administrator appointed under Article 239 of the Constitution;	(v) the administrator appointed under Article 239 of the Constitution;
8.	(c) "freedom of information" means the right to obtain information from any public authority by means of.— (i) inspection, taking of extracts and notes— (ii) Certified copies of any records of such public authority; (iii) Disketts, floppies or in any other electronic mode or through printouts where such information is stored in a computer or in any other device;	(d) "right to information" means the right to access information held by, legally accessible by or under the control of any public authority and includes: (i) Inspection of works, documents, records; (ii) Taking notes and extracts and obtaining certified copies of documents or records; (iii) Taking certified samples of material; (iv) Obtaining information in the form of diskettes, floppies, tapes, video cassettes or in any other electronic mode or through printouts where such information is stored in a computer or in any other	(j) "right to information" means the right to Information accessable under its Act which is held by or under the control of any public authority and includes the right to- (i) Inspection of works, documents, records; (ii) taking notes, extracts or certified copies of documents or records; (iii) taking certified samples of material; (iv) Obtaining information in the form of diskettes, floppies, tapes, video cassettes or in any other electronic mode or through printouts where such information is stored in a computer or in any other device.

Contd...

Sl. No.	Freedom of Information Act, 2002	NAC's Right to Information Bill, 2004	Right to Information Bill, 2004 as Introduced in Lok Sabha
1	2	3	4
		device.	
9.	Does not exist in present Act.	(c) "Chief Information Commissioner", "Information Commissioner" and "State Information Commissioner" means the authorities so appointed under this act.	(a) "Commission" means the Central Information Commission constituted under section 12; (e) "Information Commissioner" and "Deputy Information Commissioner" means the Information Commissioner and the Deputy Information Commissioner appointed under sub-section (3) of section 12;
10.	(d) "information" means any material in any form relating to the administration, operations or decisions of a public authority;	(e) "information" means any material in any form, including records, documents, file notings, memos, emails, opinions, advices, press releases, circulars, orders, logbooks, contracts, reports, papers, samples, models, data, material held in any electronic form and any information relating to a private body which can be accessed by a public authority under any law;	(d) ."information". means any material in any form, including records, documents, memos, emails, opinions, advices, press releases, circulars, orders, logbooks, contracts, reports, papers, samples, models, data, material held in any electronic form and any information relating to a private body which can be accessed by a public authority under any other law for the time being in force;
11.	(e) "prescribed" means prescribed by rules made under this Act by the appropriate Government or the competent authority, as the case may be;	(f) "prescribed" means prescribed by rules made under this Act by the appropriate Government or the competent authority, as the case may be;	(f) "prescribed" means prescribed by rules made under this Act by the Government or the competent authority, as the case may be;

Contd…

Sl. No.	*Freedom of Information Act, 2002*	*NAC's Right to Information Bill, 2004*	*Right to Information Bill, 2004 as Introduced in Lok Sabha*
1	2	3	4
12.	(f) "public authority" means any authority or body established or constituted,— (i) by or under the Constitution; (ii) by any law made by the appropriate Government, and includes any other body owned, controlled or substantially financed by funds provided directly or indirectly by the appropriate Government;	(f) "public authority" means any authority or body established or constituted,— (i) by or under the Constitution; (ii) by any law made by the appropriate Government, and includes any other body owned or controlled by the appropriate Government and includes Panchayati Raj Institutions and other community bodies, like district councils, and village or locality durbars, performing public functions in areas notified under schedule 5 and 6 of the Constitution.	(g) .'public authority' means any authority or body established or constituted, (i) by or under the Constitution; (ii) by any law made by Parliament; (iii) by notification issued or order made by the Government, and includes any other body owned or controlled by the Government;
13.	(g) "Public Information Officer" means the Public Information Officer appointed under sub-section (I) of section 5;	(h) "Public Information Officer" means the Public Information Officer appointed under sub-section (1) and/or (1)(a) of section 5;	(h) "Public Information Officer". means the Public Information Officer appointed under sub-section (1), and, includes an Assistant Information Officer designated as such under sub-section (2) of section 5;

Contd....

Sl. No.	*Freedom of Information Act, 2002*	*NAC's Right to Information Bill, 2004*	*Right to Information Bill, 2004 as Introduced in Lok Sabha*
1	2	3	4
14.	(h) "record" includes— (i) any document, manuscript and file; (ii) any microfilm, microfiche and facsimile copy of a document; (iii) any reproduction of image or images embodied in such microfilm (whether enlarged or not); and (iv) any other material produced by a computer or by any other device.	(i) "record" includes— (i) any document, manuscript and file; (ii) any microfilm, microfiche and facsimile copy of a document; (iii) any reproduction of image or images embodied in such microfilm (whether enlarged or not); and (iv) any other material produced by a computer or by any other device.	(i) "record" includes— (i) any document, manuscript and file; (ii) any microfilm, microfiche and facsimile copy of a document; (iii) any reproduction of image or images embodied in such microfilm (whether enlarged or not); and (iv) any other material produced by a computer or by any other device.
15.	(i) "third party" means a person other than the person making a request for information and includes a public authority.	(j) "third party" means a person other than the person making a request for information and includes a public authority.	(k) "third party" means a person other than the person making a request for information and includes a public authority.
	CHAPTER II	**CHAPTER II**	**CHAPTER II**
	FREEDOM OF INFORMATION AND OBLIGATIONS OF PUBLIC AUTHORITIES	**FREEDOM OF INFORMATION AND OBLIGATIONS OF PUBLIC AUTHORITIES**	**RIGHT TO INFORMATION AND OBLIGATIONS OF PUBLIC AUTHORITIES**
16.	3. Subject to the provision of this Act, all citizens shall have freedom of information.	3. Subject to the provision of this Act, all citizens shall have right to information.	3. Subject to the provision of this Act, all citizens shall have the right to information.
17.	4. Every public authority shall— (a) maintain all its records, in such	4. Every public authority shall— (a) maintain all its records, duly	4. (1) Every public authority shall— (a) mintain all its records, duly

Contd…

Sl. No.	Freedom of Information Act, 2002	NAC's Right to Information Bill, 2004	Right to Information Bill, 2004 as Introduced in Lok Sabha
1	2	3	4
	manner and form as is consistent with its operational requirements duly catalogued and indexed;	catalogued and indexed, in a manner and form which facilitates the right to information as provided for in this Act, including ensuring that all records, covered by the Act that are appropriate to computerise, are within a reasonable time and subject to availability of resources, computerised and connected through a network all over the country on different systems so that authorised access to such records is facilitated;	catalogued and indexed, in a manner and form which facilitates the right to information under this Act and ensure that all records that are appropriate to be computerised are, within a reasonable time and subject to availability of resources, computerised and connected through a network all over the country on different systems so that authorised access to such records is facilitated;
18.	(b) publish at such intervals as may be prescribed by the appropriate Government or competent authority,— (i) the particulars of its organisation, functions and duties. (ii) the powers and duties of its officers and employees and the procedure followed by them in the decision	(b) publish within 6 months of this Act coming into force and thereafter update at least every 12 months— (i) The particulars of its organisation, functions and duties. (ii) The powers and duties of its officers and employees. (iii) Procedures followed	(b) publish before the commencement of this Act,— (i) the particulars of its organisation, functions and duties. (ii) the powers and duties of its officers and employees. (iii) the procedures followed in the decision-making process, including channels of supervision and

Sl. No.	*Freedom of Information Act, 2002*	*NAC's Right to Information Bill, 2004*	*Right to Information Bill, 2004 as Introduced in Lok Sabha*
1	2	3	4
	making process. (iii) the norms set by the public authority for the discharge of its functions. (iv) rules, regulations, instructions, manual and other categories of records under its control used by its employees for discharging its functions. (v) the details of facilities available to citizens for obtaining information, and (vi) the name, designation and other particulars of the Public Information Officer;	during the decision making process, including chains of supervision and accountability. (iv) The norms set by the public authority for the discharge of its functions. (v) Rules, regulations, instructions, manual and records held by or under its control used by its employees for discharging its functions. (vi) A statement of the categories of documents that are held by or under the control of the public authority. (vii) Particulars of any arrangement that exists for consultation with, or representation by, members of the public in relation to the formulation of policy in,	accountability. (iv) the norms set by the public authority for the discharge of its functions. (v) the rules, regulations, instructions, manuals and records, held by it or under its control or used by its employees for discharging its functions. (vi) a statement of the categories of documents that are held by it or under its control; (vii) the particulars of any arrangement that exists for consultation with, or representation by, the members of the public in relation to the formulation of its policy or implementation thereof. (viii) a statement of the boards, councils, committees and other bodies consisting of two or more persons constituted as its part of its advise, and as to whether

Contd…

Sl. No.	*Freedom of Information Act, 2002*	*NAC's Right to Information Bill, 2004*	*Right to Information Bill, 2004 as Introduced in Lok Sabha*
1	2	3	4
		or in the administration of, the public authority. (viii) A statement listing all boards, councils, committees and other bodies constituted by two or more persons, that are part of, or that have been established for the purpose of advising, the public authority, and whose meetings are open to the public, or the minutes of whose meetings are available for public inspection; (ix) A directory of their public servants, from the level of the head of the department or his/her equivalent and below; (x) The monthly remuneration received for each position, including the system of compensation as established in regulations;	meeting of those boards, councils, committees and other bodies are open to the public, or the minutes of such meetings are accessible for public; (ix) a directory of its officers and employees; (x) the monthly remuneration received by each of its officers and employees, including the system of compensation as established in its regulations; (xi) the budget collection to each of its agency, indicating the particulars of all plans, proposed expenditures and reports on disbursements made; (xii) the manner of execution of subsidy programmes, including the amounts allocated and the details of beneficiaries of such programmes;

Contd....

Sl. No.	*Freedom of Information Act, 2002*	*NAC's Right to Information Bill, 2004*	*Right to Information Bill, 2004 as Introduced in Lok Sabha*
1	2	3	4
		(xi) Information concerning the budget assigned to each agency, including all plans, proposed expenditures and reports on disbursement; (xii) The design and execution of subsidy programmes, including the amounts allocated to them, criteria for access, implementation details and beneficiaries; (xiii) All concessions, permits or authorizations; granted, with their recipients specified; (xiv) All information available to the public authority in electronic form or capable of being reduced to electronic form which is not exempt under this Act, subject to availability of resources;. (xv) the details of facilities available to citizens for	(xiii) particulars of concessions, permits or authorisations granted by it; (xiv) details in respect of the information, available to or held by it, reduced in an electronic form; (xv) the particulars of facilities available to citizens for obtaining information, including the working hours of a library or reading room, if maintained for public use; (xvi) the names, designations and other particular of the Public Information Officers; (xvii) such other information as may be prescribed; and thereafter update these publications within such intervals in each year as may be prescribed. (2) It shall be a constant endeavour of every public authority to take steps in accordance with the requirements of clause (b) of sub-section (1) to provide as much information *suo moto* to the

Contd....

Sl. No.	*Freedom of Information Act, 2002*	*NAC's Right to Information Bill, 2004*	*Right to Information Bill, 2004 as Introduced in Lok Sabha*
1	2	3	4
		obtaining information, including if the public authority maintains a library or reading room that is available for public use, a statement of that fact including details of the address and hours of opening of the library or reading room; (xvi) the name, designation and other particulars of the Public Information Officer; (xvii) such other information as prescribed by the appropriate government or Information Commissioner from time to time which would promote transparency across public authorities or in specific public authorities, as appropriate; on the basis that it shall be a constant endeavour of public	public at regular intervals through various means of communications so that the public have minimum resort to the use of this Act to obtain information.

Contd....

Sl. No.	*Freedom of Information Act, 2002*	*NAC's Right to Information Bill, 2004*	*Right to Information Bill, 2004 as Introduced in Lok Sabha*
1	2	3	4
		authorities to take steps to provide as much information to the public *suo moto* at regular intervals through various means of communication so that the public have minimum resort to the use of this Act to obtain information.	
19.	(c) publish all relevant facts concerning important decisions and policies that affect the public while announcing such decisions and policies;	(c) publish all relevant facts concerning important decisions and policies that affect the public while announcing such decisions and policies;	(c) publish all relevant facts while formulating important policies or announcing the decisions which affect policies;
20.	(d) give reasons for its decisions, whether administrative or quasi-judicial to those affected by such decisions;	(d) give reasons for its decisions, whether administrative or quasi-judicial to those affected by such decisions;	(d) provide reasons for its administrative or quasi-judicial decisions to affected persons;
21.	(e) before initiating any project, publish or communicate to the public generally or to the persons affected or likely to be affected by the project in particular, the facts available to it or to which it has reasonable access which in its opinion should be known to them in the best interests	(e) before initiating any project, publish or communicate to the public generally or to the persons affected or likely to be affected by the project in particular, the facts available to it or to which it has reasonable access which in its opinion should be known to them	(e) before initiating any project, publish or formulating any policy, scheme, programme or law, publish or communicate to the public in generally or to the persons likely to be affected thereby in particular, the facts available to it or to which it has reasonable access which in its opinion

Contd....

Sl. No.	*Freedom of Information Act, 2002*	*NAC's Right to Information Bill, 2004*	*Right to Information Bill, 2004 as Introduced in Lok Sabha*
1	2	3	4
	of natural justice and promotion of democratic principles.	in the best interests of natural justice and promotion of democratic principles.	should be known to them in the best interests of natural justice and promotion of democratic principles.
22.	Does not exist in the present Act.	(f) For the purpose of this section, information should be disseminated widely and in a form and manner which is easily accessible and comprehensible to the public. "Disseminated" shall mean appropriately making known to the public the information to be communicated through notice boards, newspapers, public announcements, media broadcasts, the internet or other such means and shall include inspection at all of the bodies offices. All materials shall be disseminated keeping in mind cost effectiveness, the local language and the most effective method of communication in that local area. Such information should be easily accessible, with the Public Information Officer, where possible in electronic format, which shall be available free or at the cost of the medium, or in print at cost price.	(3) For the purpose of sub-section (1), every information shall be disseminated widely and in such form and manner which is easily accessible and comprehensible to the public. (4) All materials shall be disseminated taking into consideration the cost effectiveness, local language and the most effective method of communication in that local area and the information should be easily accessible, to the extent possible in electronic format with the Public Information Officer, available fee or at such cost of the medium or in print cost price may be prescribed. *Explanation* For the purposes of sub-sections (3) and (4), 'disseminated'. means making known or communicated the information to the public through notice boards, newspapers, public announcements, media broadcasts, the internet or any other means, including inspection of offices of any public authority.

Contd....

Sl. No.	*Freedom of Information Act, 2002*	*NAC's Right to Information Bill, 2004*	*Right to Information Bill, 2004 as Introduced in Lok Sabha*
1	2	3	4
23.	5. (1) Every public authority shall for the purposes of this Act, appoint one or more officers as Public Information Officers.	5. (1) Every public authority shall for the purposes of this Act, designate as many officers as Public Information Officers, in all administrative units and offices under such authority, as are necessary to render the public body as accessible as reasonably possible for requesters of information, within one month of this Act coming into force. (a) An officer at each sub-divisional level or other appropriate sub-district level, shall be designated a Public Information Officer, within three months of this Act coming into force, for the purposes of this Act. He/she shall receive all requests for information, and appeals, both under the state and the central acts, and pass them on to a designated authority for onward transmission to the relevant department/agency.	5. (1) Every public authority shall, within one hundred days of the enactment of this Act, designate as many officers as Public Information Officers in all administrative units or offices under it as may be necessary to provide information to persons requesting for the information under this Act. (2) Without prejudice to the provisions of sub-section (1), every public authority shall designate an officer, within one hundred days of this Act, at each sub-divisional level or other sub-district level as an Assistant Public Information Officer to receive the applications for information or appeals under this Act for forwarding the same forthwith to it or to the Government: Provided that where an application for information or appeal is given to an Assistant Public-Information Officer, a period of five days shall be added in computing the period for response specified under sub-section (1) of section 7.

Contd....

Sl. No.	*Freedom of Information Act, 2002*	*NAC's Right to Information Bill, 2004*	*Right to Information Bill, 2004 as Introduced in Lok Sabha*
1	2	3	4
		(b) Where applications/appeals are handed over at the sub-divisional or sub-district level, an additional period of five days would be added to the time of response specified under this Act, in order to enable the request/appeal to be communicated to the relevant authority.	
24.	(2) Every Public Information Officer shall deal with requests for information and shall render reasonable assistance to any person seeking such information.	(2) Every Public Information Officer shall deal with requests for information and shall render reasonable assistance to any person seeking such information.	(2) Every Public Information Officer shall deal with requests from person seeking information and render reasonable assistance to the persons seeking such information.
25.	(3) The Public Information Officer may seek the assistance of any other officer as he considers necessary for the proper discharge of his duties.	(3) The Public Information Officer may seek the assistance of any other officer as he considers necessary for the proper discharge of his duties.	(3) The Public Information Officer may seek the assistance of any other officer as he or she considers it necessary for the proper discharge of his or her duties.
26.	(4) Any officer whose assistance has been sought under sub-section (3), shall render all assistance to the Public Information Officer seeking his assistance.	(4) Any officer whose assistance has been sought under sub-section (3), shall render all assistance to the Public Information Officer seeking his/her assistance and be treated as a Public Information Officer for the purposes of the	(4) Any officer whose assistance has been sought under sub-section (4), shall render all assistance to the Public Information Officer seeking his or her assistance and for the purpose of any contravention of the provisions of this Act such other

Contd....

Sl. No.	*Freedom of Information Act, 2002*	*NAC's Right to Information Bill, 2004*	*Right to Information Bill, 2004 as Introduced in Lok Sabha*
1	2	3	4
		penalty provisions in this Act.	officer shall be treated as a Public Information Officer.
27.	6. A person desirous of obtaining information shall make a request in writing or through electronic means, to the concerned Public Information Officer specifying the particulars of the information sought by him:	6. (1) A person desirous of obtaining information shall make a request in writing or through electronic means in English or in the official language of the area in which the application is being submitted, to: (a) the Public Information Officer of the relevant public authority; (b) other designated Public Information Officers, as specified in 5 (1a) specifying the particulars of the information sought by him/her:	6. (1) A person who desirous to obtain any information under this Act shall make a request in writing or through electronic means in English or in the official language of the area in which the application is being made, accompanying such fee as may be prescribed, to: (a) the Public Information Officer of the concerned public authority; (b) the Assistant Public Information Officer, specifying the particulars of the information sought by him or her:
28.	Provided that where such request cannot be made in writing the Public Information Officer shall render all reasonable assistance to the person making the request orally to reduce it in writing.	Provided that where such request cannot be made in writing the Public Information Officer shall render all reasonable assistance to the person making the request orally to reduce it in writing.	Provided that where such request cannot be made in writing the Public Information Officer shall render all reasonable assistance to the person making the request orally to reduce the same in writing.
29.	Does not exist in present Act.	6 (2) An applicant for access to information shall not be required to give any reason for requesting	6 (2) An applicant making request for information shall not be required to give any reason for requesting the

Contd....

Sl. No.	*Freedom of Information Act, 2002*	*NAC's Right to Information Bill, 2004*	*Right to Information Bill, 2004 as Introduced in Lok Sabha*
1	2	3	4
		access to that information or any other personal details except those necessary for contacting the applicant.	information or any other personal details except those that may be necessary for contacting him.
30.	Does not exist in the present Act.	6 (3) (1) Where an application is made to a Public Authority for information: (a) which is held by another Public Authority; or (b) the subject matter of which is more closely connected with the functions of another Public Authority, the first mentioned Public Authority shall transfer the application or such part of it as may be appropriate to that other Public Authority and shall inform the applicant immediately of the transfer.	6. (3) (1) Where an application is made to a Public Authority requesting for an information: (i) which is held by another Public Authority; or (ii) the subject matter of which is more closely connected with the functions of another Public Authority, The Public Authority, to which such application is made, shall transfer the application or such part of it as may be appropriate to that other public authority and inform the applicant immediately about such transfer:
		(2) A transfer of an application pursuant to sub-section (1) shall be made as soon as practicable but not later than	Provided that the transfer of an application pursuant to this sub-section (1) shall be made as soon as practicable but in no case

Contd....

Sl. No.	*Freedom of Information Act, 2002*	*NAC's Right to Information Bill, 2004*	*Right to Information Bill, 2004 as Introduced in Lok Sabha*
1	2	3	4
		5 days after the date of receipt of the application.	later than 5 days after the date of receipt of the application.
31.	7. (1) On receipt of a request under section 6, the Public Information Officer shall as expeditiously as possible and in any case within thirty days of the receipt of the request either provide the information requested on payment of such fee as may be prescribed or reject the request for any of the reasons specified in sections 8 and 9: Provided that where the information sought for concerns the life and liberty of a person, the same should be provided within forty-eight hours of the receipt of the request:	7(1) Subject to section 5, sub-section (1b) above and section 7, sub-section (3)(a) below, on receipt of a request under section 6, the Public Information Officer shall as expeditiously as possible and in any case within fifteen days of the receipt of the request, either provide the information requested on payment of such fee as may be prescribed or reject the request for any of the reasons specified in sections 8 and 9: Provided that where the information sought for concerns the life and liberty of a person, the same should be provided within forty-eight hours of the receipt of the request; 7(2) If a Public Information Officer fails to give the decision on a request for access to the requestor concerned within the period contemplated in section 7(1), the Public Information Officer would,	7(1) Subject to proviso to sub-section (2) of section 5 or the proviso to sub-section (3) of section 6, the Public Information Officer on receipt of a request under section 6 shall, as expeditiously as possible the information on payment of such fee as may be prescribed or reject the request for any of the reasons specified in sections 8 and 9: Provided that where the information sought for concerns the life or liberty of a person, the same shall be provided within forty-eight hours of the receipt of the request; 7(2) If the Public Information Officer fails to give the decision on the request for information within the period specified under sub-section (1), the Public Information Officer shall be deemed to have refused the request.

Contd....

Sl. No.	Freedom of Information Act, 2002	NAC's Right to Information Bill, 2004	Right to Information Bill, 2004 as Introduced in Lok Sabha
1	2	3	4
		for the purposes of this Act, be regarded as having refused the request.	
32.	Provided further that where it is decided to provide the information on payment of any further fee representing the cost of providing the information, he shall send an intimation to the person making the request, giving the details of the fees determined by him, requesting him to deposit the fees and the period intervening between the dispatch of the said intimation and payment of fees shall be excluded for the purpose of calculating the period of thirty days referred to above.	7 (3) Where it is decided to provide the information on payment of any further fee representing the cost of providing the information, the Public Information Officer shall send an intimation to the person making the request, giving: (a) the details of such fees as determined by him, showing the calculations as per the Act, at prescribed rates, requesting him to deposit the fees, and the period intervening between the dispatch of the said intimation and payment of fees shall be excluded for the purpose of calculating the period of fifteen days referred to above;	7 (3) Where a decision is taken to provide the information on payment of any further fee representing the cost of providing the information, the Public Information Officer shall send an intimation to the person making the request, giving: (a) the details of further fees representing the cost of providing the information as determined by him, together with the calculations made to arrive at the amount in accordance with fee prescribed under sub-section (1) requesting him to deposit that fees, and the period intervening between the dispatch of the said intimation and payment of fees shall be excluded for the purpose of calculating the period of thirty days referred

Contd....

Sl. No.	*Freedom of Information Act, 2002*	*NAC's Right to Information Bill, 2004*	*Right to Information Bill, 2004 as Introduced in Lok Sabha*
1	2	3	4
		(b) information concerning his/her rights with respect to review the decision as to the amount of fees charged and/or the form of access provided, including the contact details of the appellate authority, time limits, process and any relevant forms.	to in that sub-section; (b) information concerning his or her rights with respect to review the decision as to the amount of fees charged or the form of access provided, including the particular of the appellate authority, time limits, process and any other forms.
33.	Does not exist in the present Act.	7 (4) Where access to a record or a part thereof is to be given under this Act and the person to whom access is to be given has a sensory disability, the public authority will provide assistance to enable access to the information, including providing assistance with inspection as appropriate.	7 (4) Where access to a record or a part thereof is required to be provided under this Act and the person to whom access is to be provided is sensorily disabled, the public authority shall provide assistance to enable access to the information, including providing such assistance as may be appropriate for the inspection.
34.	Does not exist in the present Act.	7 (5) (a)Subject to sub-sections (b) and (c) below, where access to information is to be given in the form of printed copies, or copies in some other form, such as on tape, disk, film or	7 (5) Where access to information is to be provided in the printed or in any electronic format, the applicant shall, subject to the provisions of sub-section (6), pay such fee as may be prescribed.

Contd....

Sl. No.	*Freedom of Information Act, 2002*	*NAC's Right to Information Bill, 2004*	*Right to Information Bill, 2004 as Introduced in Lok Sabha*
1	2	3	4
		other material, the applicant shall pay the prescribed fee. (b) Any fees payable by the applicant shall be reasonable, and shall in no case exceed the actual cost of copying the information or in the case of samples of materials the cost of obtaining the sample, and shall be set *via* regulations at a maximum limit taking account of the general principle that fees should not be set so high that they undermine the objectives of this Act in practice. (c) Notwithstanding sub-section (a), where a public authority fails to comply with the time limits specified in section 7; any access to information to which the applicant is entitled pursuant to his request shall be provided free of charge.	(6) Notwithstanding anything contained in sub-section (5), the person making request for the information shall be provided the information free of charge where a public authority fails to comply with the time limits specified in sub-section (1).

Contd....

Sl. No.	*Freedom of Information Act, 2002*	*NAC's Right to Information Bill, 2004*	*Right to Information Bill, 2004 as Introduced in Lok Sabha*
1	2	3	4
35.	7(2) Before taking any decision under sub-section (1), the Public Information Officer shall take into consideration the representation made by a third party under section 11.	7(6) Before taking any decision under sub-section (1), the Public Information Officer shall take into consideration the representation made by a third party under section 11.	7(7) Before taking any decision under sub-section (1), the Public Information Officer shall take into consideration the representation made by a third party under section 11.
36.	7(3) Where a request is rejected under sub-section (2), the Public Information Officer shall communicate to the person making request, (i) the reasons for such rejection; (ii) the period within which an appeal against such rejections may be preferred; (iii) the particulars of the appellate authority.	7(7) Where a request is rejected under sub-section (2), the Public Information Officer shall communicate to the person making request, (i) the reasons for such rejection; (ii) the period within which an appeal against such rejections may be preferred; (iii) the particulars of the appellate authority.	7(8) Where a request is rejected under sub-section (2), the Public Information Officer shall communicate to the person making request, (i) the reasons for such rejection; (ii) the period within which an appeal against such rejections may be preferred; (iii) the particulars of the appellate authority.
37.	7(4) Information shall ordinarily be provided in the form in which it is sought unless it would disproportionately divert the resources of the public authority or would be detrimental to the safety or preservation of the record in question.	7(8) Information shall ordinarily be provided in the form in which it is sought unless it would disproportionately divert the resources of the public authority or would be detrimental to the safety or preservation of the record in question.	7(9) An information shall ordinarily be provided in the form in which it is sought unless it would disproportionately divert the resources of the public authority or would be detrimental to the safety or preservation of the record in question.

Contd....

Sl. No.	*Freedom of Information Act, 2002*	*NAC's Right to Information Bill, 2004*	*Right to Information Bill, 2004 as Introduced in Lok Sabha*
1	2	3	4
38.	8. (1) Notwithstanding anything herein before contained, the following information not being information relating to any matter referred to in sub-section (2), shall be exempted from disclosure, namely:— (a) information, the disclosure of which would prejudicially affect the sovereignty and integrity of India, security of the State, strategic scientific or economic interest of India or conduct of international relations; (b) information, the disclosure of which would prejudicially affect public safety and order, detection and investigation of an offence or which may lead to an incitement to commit an offence or prejudicially affect fair trial or adjudication of a pending case;	8 (1) Notwithstanding anything contained in this Act, there shall be no obligation to give any person: (a) information, disclosure of which would prejudicially affect the sovereignty and integrity of India, the security, strategic, scientific or economic interests of the State, relation with foreign State or lead to incitement of an offence; (b) information which has been expressly forbidden to be published by any court of law or tribunal or the disclosure of which may constitute contempt of court ; (c) information, 'the disclosure of which would cause a breach of privilege of Parliament or the State Legislature ; (d) information including	8 (1) Notwithstanding anything contained in this Act, except as otherwise provided hereof, the following information shall be exempted from disclosure, namely: (a) information, the disclosure of which would: (i) prejudicially affect the sovereignty and integrity of India, security, strategic, scientific or economic interests of the State, relation with foreign State; or (ii) lead to incitement of an offence; (b) information which has been expressly forbidden to be published by any court of law or tribunal or the disclosure of which may constitute contempt of court ; (c) information, 'the disclosure of which may result in a breach of privilege of Parliament or the Legislature of a State;

Contd....

Sl. No.	*Freedom of Information Act, 2002*	*NAC's Right to Information Bill, 2004*	*Right to Information Bill, 2004 as Introduced in Lok Sabha*
1	2	3	4
	(c) information, the disclosure of which would prejudicially affect the conduct of Centre-State relations, including information exchanged in confidence between the Central and State Governments or any of their authorities or agencies; (d) Cabinet papers including records of deliberation of the Council of Ministers, Secretaries and other officers; (e) Minutes or records of advice including legai advice, opinions or recommendations made by any officer of a public authority during the decision making process prior to the executive decision or policy formulation; (f) Trade or commercial	commercial confidence, trade secrets or intellectual property, the disclosure of which would harm the competitive position of a third party, unless the Competent Authority is satisfied that larger public interest warrants the disclosure of such information; (e) information available to a person in his fiduciary relationship, unless the Competent Authority is satisfied that the larger public interest warrants the disclosure of such information; (f) information received in confidence from foreign government; (g) information, the disclosure of which would endanger the life or physical safety of any	(d) information including commercial confidence, trade secrets or intellectual property, the disclosure of which would harm the competitive position of a third party: Provided that such information may be disclosed, if the Public information Officer is satisfied that larger public interest warrants the disclosure of such information; (e) information available to a person in his fiduciary relationship, unless the Competent Authority is satisfied that the larger public interest warrants the disclosure of such information; (f) information received in confidence from foreign government; (g) information, the disclosure of which would endanger the life or physical safety of any

Contd....

Sl. No.	*Freedom of Information Act, 2002*	*NAC's Right to Information Bill, 2004*	*Right to Information Bill, 2004 as Introduced in Lok Sabha*
1	2	3	4
	secrets protected by law or information, the disclosure of which would prejudicially affect the legitimate economic and commercial interests or the competitive position of a public authority; or would cause unfair gain or loss to any person; and (g) Information, the disclosure of which may result in the breach of privileges of Parliament or the Legislature of a State, or contravention of a lawful order of a court.	person or identify the source of information or assistance given in confidence for law enforcement or security purposes ; (h) information which would impede the process of investigation or apprehension or prosecution of offenders ; (i) cabinet papers including records of deliberations of the Council of Ministers, Secretaries and other officers, provided that the decisions of Council of Ministers, the reasons thereof, and the material on the basis of which the decisions were taken shall be made public after the decision has been taken, and the matter is complete, or over; provided further	person or identify the source of information or assistance given in confidence for law enforcement or security purposes ; (h) information which would impede the process of investigation or apprehension or prosecution of offenders ; (i) cabinet papers including records of deliberations of the Council of Ministers, Secretaries and other officers: Provided that the decisions of Council of Ministers, the reasons thereof, and the material on the basis of which the decisions were taken shall be made public after the decision has been taken, and the matter is complete, or over: Provided further that those matters which come under the exemptions listed in

Contd....

Sl. No.	*Freedom of Information Act, 2002*	*NAC's Right to Information Bill, 2004*	*Right to Information Bill, 2004 as Introduced in Lok Sabha*
1	2	3	4
		that those matters which come under the exemptions listed in Section 8 shall not be disclosed. (j) information which relates to personal information the disclosure of which has no relationship to any public activity or interest, or which would cause unwarranted invasion of the privacy of the individual unless the Information Officer or the appellate authority, as the case might be, is satisfied that the larger public interest justifies the disclosure of such information: Provided that the information, which cannot be denied to the Parliament or a State Legislature, shall not be denied to any person.	Section 8 shall not be disclosed. (j) information which relates to personal information, the disclosure of which has no relationship to any public activity or interest, or which would cause unwarranted invasion of the privacy of the individual: Provided that such information may be disclosed, if the Public Information Officer or the appellate authority, as the case may be, is satisfied that the larger public interest justifies the disclosure of such information. (2) An information which cannot be denied to Parliament or Legislature of a State, as the case may be, shall not be denied to any person. (3) A public authority may, notwithstanding the exemptions specified in sub-section (1), allow access to information if public

Contd....

Sl. No.	*Freedom of Information Act, 2002*	*NAC's Right to Information Bill, 2004*	*Right to Information Bill, 2004 as Introduced in Lok Sabha*
1	2	3	4
		Notwithstanding anything in the Official Secrets Act, 1923 nor any of the exemptions permissible in accordance with section 8 (1), a public authority may allow access to information, if public interest in disclosure outweighs the harm to the protected interests.	interest in disclosure of the information outweighs the harm to the public authority.
39.	8(2) Subject to the provisions of clause (a) of sub-section I, any information relating to any occurrence, event or matter which has taken place, occurred or happened twenty-five years before the date on which any request is made under section 6 shall be provided to any person making a request under that section:	8(2) Subject to the provisions of clause (a) and (i) of sub-section I of section 8, any information relating to any occurrence, event or matter which has taken place, occurred or happened ten years before the date on which any request is made under section 6 shall be provided to any person making a request under that section: Provided that the matters covered by sub-section 8(a) and sub-section 8(i) may be disclosed after twenty-five years:	8(4) Subject to the provisions of clause (a) and (i) of sub-section (1), any information relating to any occurrence, event or matter which has taken place, or occurred ten years before the date on which any request is made under section 6, shall be provided to the person making the request under that section:

Contd....

Sl. No.	*Freedom of Information Act, 2002*	*NAC's Right to Information Bill, 2004*	*Right to Information Bill, 2004 as Introduced in Lok Sabha*
1	2	3	4
40.	Provided that where any question arises as to the date from which the said period of twenty-five years has to be computed, the decision of the Central Government shall be final.	Provided that where any question arises as to the date from which the said period of ten years or twenty-five has to be computed, the decision of the Union Government shall be final, subject to the usual appeals provided for in this Act.	Provided that where any question arises to the date from which the said period of ten years has to be computed, the decision of the Central Government shall be final.
41.	9. Without prejudice to the provisions of section 8, a public information officer may reject a request for information also where such request— (a) is too general in nature or is of such a nature that, having regard to the volume of information required to be retrieved or processed would involve unreasonable diversion of the resources a public authority or would adversely interfere with the functioning of such authority: Provided that where such request is rejected on the ground that the request is too general, it would be the duty of the Public Information Officer to render	9. Without prejudice to the provisions of section 8, a Public Information Officer may reject a request for information where such a request for providing access would involve an infringement of copyright subsisting in a person other than the State.	9. Without prejudice to the provisions of section 8, a Public Information Officer may reject a request for information where such a request for providing access would involve an infringement of copyright subsisting in a person other than the State.

Contd....

Sl. No.	*Freedom of Information Act, 2002*	*NAC's Right to Information Bill, 2004*	*Right to Information Bill, 2004 as Introduced in Lok Sabha*
1	2	3	4
	help as far as possible to the person making request to reframe his request in such a manner as may facilitate compliance with it; (b) relates to information that is required by law, rules, regulations or orders to be published at a particular time and such information is likely to be so published within thirty days of the receipt of such request; or (c) relates to information that is contained in published material available to public; (d) relates to information which would cause unwarranted invasion of the privacy of any person.		
42.	10 (1) If a request for access to information is rejected on the ground that it is in relation to information which is exempted from disclosure, then notwithstanding anything contained in this Act, access may be given to that	10 (1) If a request for access to information is rejected on the ground that it is in relation to information which is exempted from disclosure, then notwithstanding anything contained in this Act, access may be given to	10 (1) Where a request for access to information is rejected on the ground that it is in relation to information which is exempted from disclosure, then notwithstanding anything contained in this Act, access may

Contd....

Sl. No.	*Freedom of Information Act, 2002*	*NAC's Right to Information Bill, 2004*	*Right to Information Bill, 2004 as Introduced in Lok Sabha*
1	2	3	4
	part of the record which does not obtain any information that is exempted from disclosure under this Act and which can reasonably be severed from any part that contains exempted information.	that part of the record which does not obtain any information that is exempted from disclosure under this Act and which can reasonably be severed from any part that contains exempted information.	be provided to that part of the record which does not obtain any information which is exempted from disclosure under this Act and which can reasonably be severed from any part that contains exempt information.
43.	10 (2) Where access is granted to a part of the record in accordance with subsection (1), the person making the request shall be informed: (a) that only part of the record requested, after severance of the record containing information which is exempted from disclosure, is being furnished; and (b) of the provisions of the Act under which the severed part is exempted from disclosure.	10 (2) Where access is granted to a part of the record in accordance with sub-section (1), the Public Information Officer shall send a notice to the applicant, advising: (a) that only part of the record requested, after severance of the record containing information which is exempted from disclosure, is being furnished; and (b) The reasons for the decision; including any findings on any material questions of fact, referring to the material on which those findings were based;	10 (2) Where access is granted to a part of the record under sub-section (1), the Public Information Officer shall send a notice to the applicant, informing: (a) that only part of the record requested, after severance of the record containing information which is exempted from disclosure, is being provided; (b) the reasons for the decision; including any findings on any material questions of fact, referring to the material on which those findings were based; (c) the name and designation of the person giving the decision;

Contd....

Sl. No.	*Freedom of Information Act, 2002*	*NAC's Right to Information Bill, 2004*	*Right to Information Bill, 2004 as Introduced in Lok Sabha*
1	2	3	4
		(c) The name and designation of the person giving the decision; and (d) Details of the fees determined by him/her and requesting the applicant to deposit the fees; (e) Information concerning his/her rights with respect to review of the decision regarding non-disclosure of part of the information, the amount of fees charged and/or the form of access provided, including the contact details of the appellate body, time limits, process and any relevant forms.	(d) the details of the fees determined by him or her and the amount of fee which the applicant is required to deposit; and (e) his or her rights with respect to review of the decision regarding non-disclosure of part of the information, the amount of fees charged or the form of access provided, including the particulars of the appellate body, time limits, process and any relevant forms.
44.	(11)(1) Where a public authority intends to disclose any information or record, or part thereof on a request made under this Act which relates to, or has been supplied by a third party and has	11 (1) Where a public authority intends to disclose any information or record, or part thereof on a request made under this Act which relates to, or has been supplied by a	11 (1) Where a public authority intends to disclose any information or record, or part thereof on a request made under this Act which relates to or has been supplied by a third party and has

Contd....

Sl. No.	*Freedom of Information Act, 2002*	*NAC's Right to Information Bill, 2004*	*Right to Information Bill, 2004 as Introduced in Lok Sabha*
1	2	3	4
	been treated as confidential by that third party, the Public Information Officer shall, within twenty-five days from the receipt of a request, give written notice to such third party of the request and of the fact that the public authority intends to disclose the information or record, or part thereof: Provided that except in the case of trade or commercial secrets protected by law, disclosure may be allowed if the public interest in disclosure outweighs in importance any possible harm or injury to the interests of such party. (2) where a notice is given by the public information officer under sub-section (1) to a third party in respect of any information or record or part thereof, the third party shall, within twenty days from the date of issuance of notice, be given the opportunity to make representation against	third party and has been treated as confidential by that third party, the Public Information Officer shall, within five days from the receipt of a request, give written notice to such third party of the request and of the fact that the public authority intends to disclose the information or record, or part thereof and invite the third party to make a submission, in writing or orally, regarding whether the information should be disclosed, which submission shall be taken into account when determining whether to disclose the information: Provided that except in the case of trade or commercial secrets protected by law, disclosure may be allowed if the public interest in disclosure outweighs in importance any possible	been treated as confidential by that third party, the Public Information Officer shall, within five days from the receipt of the request, give a written notice to such third party of the request and of the fact that the public authority intends to disclose the information or record, or part thereof and invite the third party to make a submission in writing or orally, regarding whether the information should be disclosed, and such submission of the third party shall be kept on view while taking a decision about disclosure of information: Provided that except in the case of trade or commercial secrets protected by law, disclosure may be allowed if the public interest in disclosure outweighs in importance any possible harm or injury to the interests of such third party. (2) where a notice is served by the public information officer under

Contd....

Sl. No.	*Freedom of Information Act, 2002*	*NAC's Right to Information Bill, 2004*	*Right to Information Bill, 2004 as Introduced in Lok Sabha*
1	2	3	4
	the proposed disclosure. (3) Notwithstanding anything contained in section 7, the public information officer shall, within sixty days after receipt of the request under section 6, if the third party has been given an opportunity to make representation under sub-section (2), make a decision as to whether or not to disclose the information or record or part thereof and give in writing the notice of his decision to the third party. (4) A notice given under sub-section (3) shall include a statement that the third party to whom the notice is given is entitled to prefer an appeal against the decision under section 12.	harm or injury to the interests of such party. (2) where a notice is given by the public information officer under sub-section (1) to a third party in respect of any information or record or part thereof, the third party shall, within ten days from the date of issuance of notice, be given the opportunity to make representation against the proposed disclosure. (3) Notwithstanding anything contained in section 7, the public information officer shall, within twenty days after receipt of the request under section 6, if the third party has been given an opportunity to make representation under sub-section (2), make a decision as to whether or not to disclose the information or record or part thereof and give in writing the notice of	sub-section (1) to a third party in respect of any information or record or part thereof, the third party shall, within ten days from the date of receipt of such notice, be given the opportunity to make representation against the proposed disclosure (3) Notwithstanding anything contained in section 7, the public information officer shall, within forty days after receipt of the request under section 6, if the third party has been given an opportunity to make representation under sub-section (2), make a decision as to whether or not to disclose the information or record or part thereof and give in writing the notice of his decision to the third party. (4) A notice given under sub-section (3) shall include a statement that the third party to whom the notice is given is entitled to prefer an appeal under

Contd....

Sl. No.	*Freedom of Information Act, 2002*	*NAC's Right to Information Bill, 2004*	*Right to Information Bill, 2004 as Introduced in Lok Sabha*
1	2	3	4
		his decision to the third party. (4) A notice given under sub-section (3) shall include a statement that the third party to whom the notice is given is entitled to prefer an appeal against the decision under section 12(2).	section 15 against the decision.
			CHAPTER III **THE CENTRAL INFORMATION COMMISSION**
45.	Does not exist in the present Act.	12(1) (i) (a) The President shall appoint or designate a Chief Information Commissioner for all matters pertaining to the Union. Such appointment shall be made on the basis of a recommendation made by an Appointing Committee presided by the Prime Minister, with the Leader of Opposition in the Lok Sabha and the Chief Justice of India as	12 (1) The Central Government shall, by notification in the Official Gazette, constitute a body to be known as the Central Information Commission to exercise the powers conferred on, and to perform the functions assigned to, it under this Act. (2) The Commission shall consist of (a) the Information Commissioner; and (b) such number of Deputy Information Commissioners not exceeding ten as may be deemed necessary.

Contd....

Sl. No.	*Freedom of Information Act, 2002*	*NAC's Right to Information Bill, 2004*	*Right to Information Bill, 2004 as Introduced in Lok Sabha*
1	2	3	4
		members. (i) (b) The Governor shall appoint or designate a State Information Commissioner for all matters pertaining to the State. Such appointment shall be made on the basis of recommendation made by an Appointing Committee presided by the Chief Minister, with the Leader of Opposition in the Legislative Assembly and the Chief Justice of the High Court as members. (ii) Information Commissioners may be appointed by the President or the Governor, as the case may be, in consultation with the appropriate Appointing Committee and the Chief Information	(3) The Information Commissioner and the Deputy Information Commissioners shall be appointed by the President. On the recommendation of a committee consisting of, (i) the Prime Minister, who shall be the Chairperson of me committee; (ii) the Leader of Opposition in the Lok Sabha; and (iii) the Chief Justice of India. *Explanation*:- For the purpose of removal of doubts, it is hereby declared that where the Leader of Opposition in the House of the People has not been recognized as such, the Leader of the single largest group in opposition of the Government in the House of the People shall be deemed to be the Leader of the Opposition. (4) The general superintendence, direction and management of the

Contd....

Sl. No.	Freedom of Information Act, 2002	NAC's Right to Information Bill, 2004	Right to Information Bill, 2004 as Introduced in Lok Sabha
1	2	3	4
		Commissioner or State Information Commissioners, as the case may be. (iii) Every Chief Information Commissioner, State Information Commissioner and Information Commissioner shall be a person with wide knowledge and experience of administration and governance, and/or a person with high public stature. (iv) The Chief Information Commissioners and any Ir.formation Commissioners shall not be members of Parliament or members of the Legislative of any State or Union Territory and shall not hold any other office of profit and	affairs of the Commission shall vest in the Information Commissioner who shall be assisted by the Deputy Information Commissioners and may exercise all such powers and do all such acts and things which may be exercised or done by the Commission autonomously without being subjected to directions by any other authority under this Act. (5) The Information Commissioner and the Deputy Information Commissioners shall be persons of eminence in public life with wide knowledge and experience of administration and governance; (6) The Information Commissioner or a Deputy Information Commissioner shall not be a member of Parliament or Member of the Legislature of any State or Union territory, as the case may be, or hold any other office of profit or connected with

Contd....

Sl. No.	*Freedom of Information Act, 2002*	*NAC's Right to Information Bill, 2004*	*Right to Information Bill, 2004 as Introduced in Lok Sabha*
1	2	3	4
		shall not be connected with any political party or be carrying on any business or practice any profession. (v) The requisite budgetary allocations for the emoluments and expenses, including office expenses, of the Chief Information Commissioner and of other Information Commissioners will be provided by the Government of India through special budgetary provisions made available to the respective states out of the Union Government Budget. (vi) The Chief Information Commissioner and of other Information Commissioners shall function autonomously	any political party or carrying on any business or pursuing any profession. (7) The headquarters of the Commission shall be at Delhi and the Commission may, with the previous approval of the Central Government, establish offices at other places in India. (8) Every Deputy Information Commissioner shall perform his functions within such area as may be specified by the Central Government.

Contd....

Sl. No.	Freedom of Information Act, 2002	NAC's Right to Information Bill, 2004	Right to Information Bill, 2004 as Introduced in Lok Sabha
1	2	3	4
		without being subjected to directions by any other authority and would be under the administrative control of the Government of India, Ministry of Personnel, Administrative Reforms and Public Grievances.	
46.	Does not exist in the present Act.	12 (vii) Every person appointed as a Chief Information Commissioner or an Information Commissioner shall hold office for a term of five years from the date on which he enters upon his office. He/she will not be eligible for reappointment.	13 (1) The Information Commissioner shall hold office for a term of five years from the date on which he enters upon his office or till he attains the age of sixty-five years. Whichever is earlier, and shall not be eligible for reappointment: Provided that the Central Government may extend the term of five years by one more year if recommended by the Committee referred to in sub-section (3) of Section 12. (2) Every Deputy Information Commissioner shall hold office for a term of four years from the date on which he enters upon his office or till be attains the age of

Contd....

Sl. No.	Freedom of Information Act, 2002	NAC's Right to Information Bill, 2004	Right to Information Bill, 2004 as Introduced in Lok Sabha
1	2	3	4
			sixty-five years. Whichever is earlier: Provided that every Deputy Information Commissioner shall, on vacating his office under this sub-section, be eligible for appointment as the Information Commissioner in the manner specified in sub-section (3) of section 12: Provided further that where the Deputy Information Commissioner is appointed as the Information Commissioner, his term of office shall not be more than five years in aggregate as the Deputy Information Commissioner and the Information Commissioner. (3) The Information Commissioner or a Deputy Information Commissioner shall before he enters upon his office make and subscribe before the President or some other person appointed by him in that behalf, an oath or affirmation according to the form

Contd....

Sl. No.	*Freedom of Information Act, 2002*	*NAC's Right to Information Bill, 2004*	*Right to Information Bill, 2004 as Introduced in Lok Sabha*
1	2	3	4
			set out for the purpose in the First Schedule. (4) The Information Commissioner or a Deputy Information Commissioner may, at any time, by writing under his hand addressed to the President, resign from his office: Provided that the Information Commissioner or a Deputy Information Commissioner may be removed in the manner specified under section 14. (5) The Information Commissioner or a Deputy Information Commissioner shall, on cessation of his office, not be eligible for (a) any diplomatic assignment, assignment as administrator of a Union territory or such other assignment or appointment which is required by law to be made by the President by warrant under his hand and seal; (b) further employment to any office of profit under the

Contd....

Sl. No.	Freedom of Information Act, 2002	NAC's Right to Information Bill, 2004	Right to Information Bill, 2004 as Introduced in Lok Sabha
1	2	3	4
			Government of India or the Government cf State. (6) The salaries and allowances payable to and other terms and conditions of service of (a) the Information Commissioner shall be the same as that of a Secretary to the Government of India; (b) the Deputy Information: Provided that if the Information Commissioner or a Deputy Information Commissioner, at the time of his appointment is, in receipt of a pension (other than a disability or wound pension) in respect of any previous service under the Government of India or under the Government of a State, his salary in respect of the service as the Information Commissioner or a Deputy Information Commissioner shall be reduced by the amount of that pension including any portion of pension which was commuted and pension equivalent of other forms

Contd....

Sl. No.	*Freedom of Information Act, 2002*	*NAC's Right to Information Bill, 2004*	*Right to Information Bill, 2004 as Introduced in Lok Sabha*
1	2	3	4
			of retirement benefits excluding pension equivalent of retirement gratuity; Provided further that if the Information Commissioner or a Deputy Information Commissioner, at the time of his appointment is, in receipt of retirement benefits in respect of any previous service rendered in a Corporation established by or under any Central Act or State Act or a Government company owned or controlled by the Central Government or the State Government, his salary in respect of the service as the Information Commissioner or the Deputy Information Commissioner shall be reduced by the amount of pension equivalent to the retirement benefits: Provided also that the salaries, allowances and the other conditions of service of the Information Commissioner and the Deputy Information

Contd....

Sl. No.	*Freedom of Information Act, 2002*	*NAC's Right to Information Bill, 2004*	*Right to Information Bill, 2004 as Introduced in Lok Sabha*
1	2	3	4
			Commissioner shall not be varied to their disadvantage after their appointment. (7) The Central Government shall provide the Information Commissioner and the Deputy Information Commissioners with such officers and employees as may be necessary for the efficient performance of their functions under this Act, and the salaries and allowances payable to and the officers and other employees appointed for the purpose of this Act shall be such as may be prescribed.
47.	Does not exist in the present Act.	Does not exist in the Bill.	14 (1) Subject to the provisions of sub-section (3), the Information Commissioner or any Deputy Information Commissioner shall be removed from his office only by order of the President on the ground of proved misbehaviour or incapacity after the Supreme Court, on a reference made to it by the President, has, on inquiry, reported that the Information

Contd....

Sl. No.	*Freedom of Information Act, 2002*	*NAC's Right to Information Bill, 2004*	*Right to Information Bill, 2004 as Introduced in Lok Sabha*
1	2	3	4
			Commissioner or any Deputy Information Commissioner, as the case may be, ought on such ground be removed. (2) The President may suspend from office, and if deem necessary prohibit also from attending the office during inquiry, the Information Commissioner or Deputy Information Commissioner in respect of whom a reference has been made to the Supreme Court under sub-section (1) until the President has passed orders on receipt of the report of the Supreme Court on such reference. (3) Notwithstanding anything contained in sub-section (1), the President may by order remove from office the Information Commissioner or any Deputy Information Commissioner if the Information commissioner or a Deputy Information Commissioner, as the case may be,

Contd....

Sl. No.	*Freedom of Information Act, 2002*	*NAC's Right to Information Bill, 2004*	*Right to Information Bill, 2004 as Introduced in Lok Sabha*
1	2	3	4
			(a) is adjudged an insolvent; or (b) has been convicted of an offence which, in the opinion of the president, involves moral turpitude; or (c) engages during his term of office in any paid employment outside the duties of his office; or (d) is, in the opinion of the President, unfit to continue in office by reason of infirmity of mind of body; or (e) had acquired such financial or other interest as is likely to affect prejudicially his functions as an Information Commissioner or a Deputy Information Commissioner. (4) If the Information Commissioner or any Deputy Information Commissioner in any way, concerned or interested in any contract or agreement made by or on behalf of the Government of India or participates in any way in the profit thereof or in any

Contd....

Sl. No.	Freedom of Information Act, 2002	NAC's Right to Information Bill, 2004	Right to Information Bill, 2004 as Introduced in Lok Sabha
1	2	3	4
			benefit or emolument arising therefrom otherwise than as a member and in common with the other members of an incorporated company, he shall, for the purposes of sub-section (1), be deemed to be guilty of misbehaviour.
48.	Does not exist in the present Act.	12 (3) Powers of the Chief Information Commissioner/State Information Commissioners/ Information Commissioners: (1) Subject to this Act, the Chief Information Commissioner/ State Information Commissioners/Information Commissioners shall receive and investigate complaints from persons: (a) who have been unable to submit a request to a Public Information Officer, either because none has been appointed as required under the Act or because the Public Information Officer has	15 (1) Subject to the provisions of this Act, it shall be the duty of the Commission to receive and inquire into a complaint from any person: (a) who has been unable to submit a request to a Public Information Officer, either by reason that no such officer has been appointed under this Act, or because the Assistant Public Information Officer has refused to accept his or her application for forwarding the same to the public authority or the appropriate Government; (b) who have been refused

Contd....

Sl. No.	Freedom of Information Act, 2002	NAC's Right to Information Bill, 2004	Right to Information Bill, 2004 as Introduced in Lok Sabha
1	2	3	4
		refused to accept their application; (b) who have been refused access to information requested under this Act; (c) who have not been given a response or access to information within the time limits required under this Act; (d) who have been required to pay an amount under the fees provisions that they consider unreasonable; (e) who believe that they have been given incomplete, misleading or false information under this act; (f) in respect of any other matter relating to requesting or obtaining access to records under this Act. (2) Where a Chief Information Commissioner/State Information Commissioner/	access to any information requested under this Act; (c) who has not been given a response to a request for information or access to information within the time limits specified under this Act; (d) who has been required to pay an amount of fee which he or she considers unreasonable; (e) who believe that he or she has been given incomplete, misleading or false information under this Act; and (f) in respect of any other matter relating to requesting or obtaining access to records under this Act. (2) Where the Commission is satisfied that there are reasonable grounds to inquire into the matter, it may initiate an inquiry in respect thereof. (3) The Commission shall, while inquiring into any matter under

Contd....

Sl. No.	*Freedom of Information Act, 2002*	*NAC's Right to Information Bill, 2004*	*Right to Information Bill, 2004 as Introduced in Lok Sabha*
1	2	3	4
		Information Commissioner is satisfied that there are reasonable grounds to investigate a matter relating to requesting or obtaining access to records under this Act, he/she may initiate a complaint in respect thereof. (3) The Chief Information Commissioner/State Information Commissioners/ Information Commissioners have, in relation to the carrying out of the investigation of any complaint under this Act, power: (a) to summon and enforce the appearance of persons and compel them to give oral or written evidence on oath and to produce such documents and things as the Commissioner deems requisite to the full investigation and	this section, have the same powers as are vested in a civil court while trying a suit under the Code of Civil Procedure, 1908, in respect of the following matters, namely: (a) summoning and enforcing the attendance of persons and compel them to give oral or written evidence on oath and to produce the documents or things; (b) requiring the discovery and inspection of documents; (c) receiving evidence on affidavit; (d) requisitioning any public record or copies thereof from any court or office; (e) issuing summons for examination of witnesses or documents; and (f) any other matter which may be prescribed. (4) Notwithstanding anything consistent contained in any other Act of Parliament, the

Contd....

Sl. No.	*Freedom of Information Act, 2002*	*NAC's Right to Information Bill, 2004*	*Right to Information Bill, 2004 as Introduced in Lok Sabha*
1	2	3	4
		consideration of the complaint, in the same manner and to the same extent as a superior court of record; (b) to administer oaths; (c) to receive and accept such evidence and other information, whether on oath or by affidavit or otherwise, as the relevant Information Commissioner sees fit, whether or not the evidence or information is or would be admissible in a court of law; (d) to enter any premises occupied by any government institution on satisfying any security requirements of the institution relating to the premises; (e) to converse in private with any person in any premises entered	Commission may, during the inquiry of any complaint under this Act, examine any record to which this Act applies which is under the control of the public authority, and no such record may be withheld from any it on any grounds.

Contd....

Sl. No.	*Freedom of Information Act, 2002*	*NAC's Right to Information Bill, 2004*	*Right to Information Bill, 2004 as Introduced in Lok Sabha*
1	2	3	4
		pursuant to paragraph; (d) and otherwise carry out therein such inquiries within the authority of the Chief Information Commissioner under this Act as the Commissioner sees fit; and (f) to examine or obtain copies of or extracts from books or other records found in any premises entered pursuant to paragraph (d) containing any matter relevant to the investigation. (g) To impose the penalties prescribed under this act, after giving due opportunity to the concerned official of being heard.	
		(4) Notwithstanding any other Act of Parliament or any privilege under the law of evidence, an Chief	

Contd....

Sl. No.	*Freedom of Information Act, 2002*	*NAC's Right to Information Bill, 2004*	*Right to Information Bill, 2004 as Introduced in Lok Sabha*
1	2	3	4
		Information Commissioner/ State Information Commissioners/Information Commissioners may, during the investigation of any complaint under this Act, examine any record to which this Act applies that is under the control of a government institution, and no such record may be withheld from any Commissioner on any grounds. (5) All the powers of the Chief Information Commissioner would also be enjoyed by the State Information Commissioners and other Information Commissioners, within their jurisdictions.	
49.	12 (1) Any person aggrieved by a decision of the Public information officer may, within thirty days of receipt of such decision, prefer an appeal to such authority as may be prescribed:	12 (2)(i) Any person who does not receive a decision in the time period specified in Section 7(1) or 7(3)(a) above, or is aggrieved by a decision of the Public Information Officer may, within thirty	12 (2) (i) Any person who does not receive a decision in the time period specified in sub-section (1) or clause (a) of sub-section (3) of section 7, or is aggrieved by a decision of the Public Information

Contd....

Sl. No.	*Freedom of Information Act, 2002*	*NAC's Right to Information Bill, 2004*	*Right to Information Bill, 2004 as Introduced in Lok Sabha*
1	2	3	4
	Provided that such authority may entertain the appeal after the expiry of the said period of thirty days if it is satisfied that the appellant was prevented by sufficient cause from filing the appeal in time. (2) A second appeal against the decision under sub-section (1) shall lie within thirty days of such decision, to the Central Government or the State Government or the competent authority, as the case may be: Provided that the Central Government or the State Government or the competent authority, as the case may be, may entertain the appeal after the expiry of the said period of thirty days if it is satisfied that the appellant was prevented by sufficient cause from filing the appeal in time. (3) The appeals referred to in sub-sections (1) and (2) shall be disposed of within thirty days of	days of the expiry of such a period or of receipt of such a decision, prefer an appeal to an appellate authority prescribed for the purpose in each department and senior in rank to the Public Information Officer: Provided that such authority may entertain the appeal after the expiry of the said period of thirty days if it is satisfied that the appellant was prevented by sufficient cause from filing the appeal in time. (ii) A second appeal against the decision (or lack of it), under sub-section (i), shall lie within 90 days from the time by which the decision should have been made or was actually received, with the relevant Chief/State/ Information Commissioner: Provided that the relevant Chief/State/Information	Officer, may within thirty days from the expiry of such a period or from the receipt of such a decision, prefer an appeal to such officer who is senior in rank to the Public Information Officer in each public authority; Provided that such officer may admit the appeal after the expiry of the period of thirty days if he or she is satisfied that the appellant was prevented by sufficient cause from filing the appeal in time. (2) A second appeal against the decision under sub-section (1) shall lie within 90 days from the date on which the decision should have been made or was actually received, with the Commission: Provided that the Commission may admit the appeal after the expiry of the period of ninety days if is satisfied that the appellant was prevented by

Contd....

Sl. No.	Freedom of Information Act, 2002	NAC's Right to Information Bill, 2004	Right to Information Bill, 2004 as Introduced in Lok Sabha
1	2	3	4
	the receipt of such appeals or within such extended period, as the case may be, for reasons to be recorded in writing. (4) If the decision of the public information officer against which the appeal is preferred under sub-section (1) or (2) also relates to information of third party, the appellate authority shall give a reasonable opportunity of being heard to that third party.	Commissioner may entertain an appeal after the expiry of the said period of ninety days if it is satisfied that the appellant was prevented by sufficient cause from filing the appeal in time. (iii) Where an appeal is being preferred against an order made by the Public Information Officer under Section 11 to disclose third party information, the appeal by the concerned third party must be made within thirty days of the order. (iv) If the decision of the Public Information Officer against which the appeal is preferred relates to information of a third party, the relevant Information Commissioner shall give a reasonable opportunity of being heard to that third party. (v) In any appeal proceedings, the onus to prove that a	sufficient cause from filing the appeal in time. (3) Where an appeal is preferred against an order made by the Public Information Officer under Section 11 to disclose third Party information, the appeal by the concerned third party shall be made within thirty days from the date of the order. (4) If the decision of the Public Information Officer against which an appeal is preferred relates to information of a third party, the relevant Information Commission shall give a reasonable opportunity of being heard to that third party. (5) In any appeal proceedings, the onus to prove that a denial of a request was justified shall be on the public authority which denied the request. (6) An appeals under sub-section (1) or sub-section (2) shall be disposed of within thirty days of the receipt of the appeal or within

Contd....

Sl. No.	*Freedom of Information Act, 2002*	*NAC's Right to Information Bill, 2004*	*Right to Information Bill, 2004 as Introduced in Lok Sabha*
1	2	3	4
		denial of a request was justified will be on the public authority that denied the request. (vi) Appeals to any appellate authority/Information Commissioner shall be disposed of within thirty days of the receipt of the appeals, or within such extended period, not exceeding a total of forty five days from the date of filing of appeal, for reasons to be recorded in writing. (vii) The decision of the Information Commissioner shall be binding. (viii) In his/her decision, the relevant Information Commissioner has the power to: (a) require the public authority to take any such steps as may be necessary to bring it into compliance with the Act,	such extended period not exceeding a total of forty-five days from the date of filing thereof, as the case may be, for reasons to be recorded in writing. (7) The decision of the Commissioner shall be binding. (8) In its decision, the Commissioner has the power to: (a) require the public authority to take any such steps as may be necessary to secure compliance with the provisions of this Act, including – (i) by providing access to information, if so requested, in a particular form; (ii) by appointing a Public Information Officer; (iii) by publishing certain information or categories of information; (iv) by making necessary changes to its practices

Contd....

Sl. No.	*Freedom of Information Act, 2002*	*NAC's Right to Information Bill, 2004*	*Right to Information Bill, 2004 as Introduced in Lok Sabha*
1	2	3	4
		including by: (i) providing access to information, including in a particular form; (ii) appointing an Information Officer; (iii) publishing certain information and/or categories of information; (iv) making certain changes to its practices in relation to the keeping, management and destruction of records; (v) enhancing the provision of training on the right to information for its officials; (vi) providing him or her with an annual report, in compliance with section 4(b);	in relation to the maintenance, management and destruction of records; (v) by enhancing the provision of training on the right to information for its officials; (vi) by providing it with an annual report, in compliance with clause (b) of sub-section (1) section 4; (b) require the public authority to compensate the complainant for any loss or other detriment suffered; (c) impose any of the penalties available under this Act; (d) reject the application. (9) The Commissioner shall serve notice of its decision, including any rights of appeal, to the complainant and the public authority. (10) The Commission shall decide the appeal in accordance with such procedure as may be prescribed.

Contd....

Sl. No.	*Freedom of Information Act, 2002*	*NAC's Right to Information Bill, 2004*	*Right to Information Bill, 2004 as Introduced in Lok Sabha*
1	2	3	4
		(b) require the public body to compensate the complainant for any loss or other detriment suffered; (c) impose any of the penalties available under this Act; (d) reject the application. (ix) The Information Commissioner shall serve notice of his/her decision, including any rights of appeal, on both the complainant and the public authority. (x) A decision of the Information Commissioner may be appealed to the High Court or the Supreme Court, on any point of fact and law.	(11) An appeal against the decision of the Commission shall lie in the High Court on any point of fact and law.
50.	Does not exist in the present Act.	12(4) Penalties (1) Subject to sub-section (3), where any Public Information Officer has, without any reasonable cause, failed to supply the information sought, within the period specified under section 7(1), the relevant	17 (1) Notwithstanding anything contained in the provisions of section 20, where the Commission at the time of deciding any appeal is of the opinion that the Public Information Officer has persistently failed to provide information without any reasonable

Contd....

Sl. No.	*Freedom of Information Act, 2002*	*NAC's Right to Information Bill, 2004*	*Right to Information Bill, 2004 as Introduced in Lok Sabha*
1	2	3	4
		Information Commissioner shall, on appeal, impose a penalty of rupees two hundred and fifty, which amount must be increased by regulation at least once every five years, for each day's delay in furnishing the information, after giving such Public Information Officer a reasonable opportunity of being heard. (2) Subject to sub-section (3), where it is found in appeal that any Public Information Officer has: (i) Refused to receive an application for information; (ii) *Mala fide* denied a request for information; (iii) Knowingly given incorrect or misleading information; (iv) Knowingly given wrong or incomplete information; (v) Destroyed information subject to a request; or (vi) Obstructed the activities of a Public Information Officer, any Information Commissioner or the courts;	cause within the period specified under sub-section (1) of section 7, the Commission may authorize any officer of the Central Government to file a complaint against such Public Information Officer before a Judicial Magistrate of First Class. (2) Any Public Information Officer who is in default under sub-section (1) shall be liable on conviction to fine which may extend to rupees twenty five thousand or a term of imprisonment which may extend to five years, or with both.

Contd....

Sl. No.	Freedom of Information Act, 2002	NAC's Right to Information Bill, 2004	Right to Information Bill, 2004 as Introduced in Lok Sabha
1	2	3	4
		He/she would have committed an offence and will be liable upon summary conviction to a fine of not less than rupees two thousand and imprisonment of up to five years, or both. (3) An officer whose assistance has been sought by the Public Information Officer for the performance of his/her duties under this Act shall be liable for penalty as prescribed in sub-sections (1) and (2) jointly with the Public Information Officer or severally as may be decided by the relevant Information Commissioner.	
		(4) Any fines imposed under sub-sections (1), (2) and (3) shall be recoverable from the salary of the concerned officer, including the Public Information Officer, or if no salary is drawn, as an arrears of land revenue, recoverable within a maximum of six months of the order imposing the fine. (5) The Public Information Officer or	

Contd....

Sl. No.	Freedom of Information Act, 2002	NAC's Right to Information Bill, 2004	Right to Information Bill, 2004 as Introduced in Lok Sabha
1	2	3	4
		any other officer on whom the penalty under sub-sections (1), (2) and (3) is imposed shall also be liable to appropriate disciplinary action under the service rules applicable to him: Provided that in cases where the officer is proved guilty of deliberate denial of information or misinformation, the punishment imposed shall be a major penalty, i.e. dismissal or removal or reduction in rank.	
	CHAPTER IV: MISCELLANEOUS	**CHAPTER IV: MISCELLANEOUS**	**CHAPTER IV: MISCELLANEOUS**
51.	13 No suit, prosecution or other legal proceeding shall lie against any person for anything which is in good faith done or intended to be done under this Act or any rule made thereunder.	13 No suit, prosecution or other legal proceeding shall lie against any person for anything which is in good faith done or intended to be done under this Act or any rule made thereunder.	18 No suit, prosecution or other legal proceeding shall lie against any person for anything which is in good faith done or intended to be done under this Act or any rule made there under.
52.	14 The provisions of this Act shall have effect not withstanding anything inconsistent therewith contained in the Official Secrets Act, 1923, and	14 The provisions of this Act shall have effect not withstanding anything inconsistent therewith contained in the Official Secrets	19 The provisions of this Act shall have effect not withstanding anything inconsistent therewith contained in the Official Secrets Act, 1923, and

Contd....

Sl. No.	*Freedom of Information Act, 2002*	*NAC's Right to Information Bill, 2004*	*Right to Information Bill, 2004 as Introduced in Lok Sabha*
1	2	3	4
	any other law for the time being in force or in any instrument having effect by virtue of any law other than this Act.	Act, 1923, and any other law for the time being in force or in any instrument having effect by virtue of any law other than this Act.	any other law for the time being in force or in any instrument having effect by virtue of any law other than this Act.
53.	15 No court shall entertain any suit, application or other proceeding in respect of any order made under this Act and no such order shall be called in question otherwise than by way of an appeal under this Act.	15 No court shall entertain any suit, application or other proceeding in respect of any order made under this Act and no such order shall be called in question otherwise than by way of an appeal under this Act.	20 No court shall entertain any suit, application or other proceeding in respect of any order made under this Act and no such order shall be called in question otherwise than by way of an appeal under this Act.
54.	16 (1) Nothing contained in this Act shall apply to the intelligence and security organisations, specified in the Schedule being organizations established by the Central Government or any information furnished by such organisations to that Government. (2) The Central Government may, by notification in the official Gazette, amend the Schedule by including therein any other intelligence or security organisation established by that government or omitting therefrom any organisation already specified therein and on the	16 (1) Nothing contained in this Act shall apply to the intelligence and security organisations, specified in the Schedule being organizations established by the Union Government or any information furnished by such organisations to that Government. Provided that information pertaining to alleged violations of human rights, to the life and liberty of human beings and to the allegations of corruption will not be excluded under this clause. (2) The Union Government may, by notification in the official	21 (1) Nothing contained in this Act shall apply to the intelligence and security organisations, specified in the Second Schedule, being organizations established by the Central Government or any information furnished by such organisations to that Government. Provided that the information pertaining to the allegations of corruption shall not be excluded under this sub-section. (2) The Central Government may, by notification in the official Gazette, amend the Schedule by including therein any other intelligence or

Contd....

Sl. No.	*Freedom of Information Act, 2002*	*NAC's Right to Information Bill, 2004*	*Right to Information Bill, 2004 as Introduced in Lok Sabha*
1	2	3	4
	publication of such notification, such organisation shall be deemed to be included in or, as the case may be omitted from the Schedule. (3) Every notification issued under sub-section(2) shall be laid before each house of parliament. (4) Nothing contained in this Act shall apply to such intelligence and security organisations which may be specified, by a notification in the official Gazette, by a state government from time to time. (5) Every notification issued under sub-section (4), shall be laid before the state legislature.	Gazette, amend the Schedule by including therein any other intelligence or security organisation established by that government or omitting therefrom any organisation already specified therein and on the publication of such notification, such organisation shall be deemed to be included in or, as the case may be omitted from the Schedule. (3) Every notification issued under sub-section (2) shall be laid before each house of parliament. (4) Nothing contained in this Act shall apply to such intelligence and security organisations which may be specified, by a notification in the official Gazette, by a state government from time to time: Provided that information pertaining to alleged violations of human rights, to the life and liberty of human beings and to the allegations of corruption will not be excluded under this clause. (5) Every notification issued under	security organisation established by that government or omitting therefrom any organisation already specified therein and on the publication of such notification, such organisation shall be deemed to be included in or, as the case may be, omitted from the Schedule. (3) Every notification issued under sub-section (2) shall be laid before each House of Parliament.

Contd....

Sl. No.	Freedom of Information Act, 2002	NAC's Right to Information Bill, 2004	Right to Information Bill, 2004 as Introduced in Lok Sabha
1	2	3	4
		sub-section (4), shall be laid before the state legislature.	
55.	Does not exist in the present Act.	16A Monitoring and Reporting: 1. The Chief Information Commissioners/State Information Commissioners/ Information Commissioners shall, as soon as practicable after the end of each year, prepare a report on the implementation of this Act during that year and cause a copy of the report to be laid before the legislatures of the concerned state and each House of the Parliament. 2. Each responsible department/ ministry shall, in relation to the public authorities within their jurisdiction, collect and provide such information to the Chief/State/Information Commissioners as is required to prepare the report under this section, and shall comply with any prescribed requirements concerning the	1. The Commission shall, as soon as practicable after the end of each year, prepare a report on the implementation of this provisions of this Act during that year and forward a copy thereof to the Central Government. 2. Each ministry or department shall, in relation to the public authorities within their jurisdiction, collect and provide such information to the Commission as is required to prepare the report under this section, and comply with the requirements concerning the furnishing of that information and the keeping of records for the purposes of this section. 3. Each report shall state in respect of the year to which the report relates: (a) the number of requests made to each public authority; (b) the number of decisions

Contd....

Sl. No.	Freedom of Information Act, 2002	NAC's Right to Information Bill, 2004	Right to Information Bill, 2004 as Introduced in Lok Sabha
1	2	3	4
		furnishing of that information and the keeping of records for the purposes of this section. 3. Each report shall, at a minimum, state in respect of the year to which the report relates: (a) the number of requests made to each public authority; (b) the number of decisions that an applicant was not entitled to access to a document pursuant to a request, the provisions of this Act under which these decisions were made and the number of times each provision was invoked; (c) the number of appeals sent to the Information Commissioners for review, the nature of the complaints and the outcome of the appeals;	where applicant were not entitled to access to the document pursuant to the requests, the provisions of this Act under which these decisions were made and the number of times such provision was invoked; (c) the number of appeals referred to the Commission for review, the nature of the appeals and the outcome of the appeals;. (d) particulars of any disciplinary action taken against any officer in respect of the administration of this Act; (e) the amount of charges collected by each public authority under this Act; (f) any facts which indicate an effort by the public authorities to administer and implement the spirit and intention of this Act; (g) recommendations for reform,

Contd....

Sl. No.	*Freedom of Information Act, 2002*	*NAC's Right to Information Bill, 2004*	*Right to Information Bill, 2004 as Introduced in Lok Sabha*
1	2	3	4
		(d) particulars of any disciplinary action taken against any officer in respect of the administration of this Act; (e) the amount of charges collected by each public authority under this Act; (f) any facts which indicate an effort by public authorities to administer and implement the spirit and intention of this Act; (g) recommendations for reform, including recommendations in respect of particular public authorities, for the development, improvement, modernisation, reform or amendment of this Act or other legislation or common law or any other matter relevant to operationalising the right to access information, as	including recommendations in respect of the particular public authorities, for the development, improvement, modernisation, reform or amendment of this Act or other legislation or common law or any other matter relevant for operationalising the right to access information. 4. The Central Government may, as soon as practicable after the end of each year, cause a copy of the report of the Commission referred to sub-section (1) to be laid before each House of Parliament. 5. If it appears to the Commission that the practice of a public authority in relation to the exercise of its functions under this Act does not conform with the provisions or spirit of the Act, it may give to the authority a recommendation specifying the steps which ought in its opinion to be taken for promoting such conformity.

Contd....

Sl. No.	Freedom of Information Act, 2002	NAC's Right to Information Bill, 2004	Right to Information Bill, 2004 as Introduced in Lok Sabha
1	2	3	4
		appropriate. 4. The Union Government Ministry responsible for the administration of this Act, as soon as practicable after the end of each year, prepare a summary report on the implementation of this Act during that year and cause a copy of the report to be laid before the concerned state legislatures and each House of the Parliament, drawing on the information provided in the reports of the Chief Information Commissioners for each State. 5. If it appears to any Chief Information Commissioner that the practice of a public authority in relation to the exercise of its functions under this Act does not conform with provisions or spirit of the Act, s/he may give to the authority a recommendation specifying the steps which ought in his/her opinion to be taken for promoting such conformity.	
56.	Does not exist in the present Act.	16B (1) The Government must, to the	23. (1) The Central Government may, to

Contd....

Sl. No.	Freedom of Information Act, 2002	NAC's Right to Information Bill, 2004	Right to Information Bill, 2004 as Introduced in Lok Sabha
1	2	3	4
		extent that financial and other resources are available: (a) develop and conduct educational programmes to advance the understanding of the public, in particular of disadvantaged communities, of this Notification and of how to exercise the rights contemplated in this Act; (b) encourage public authorities to participate in the development and conduct of programmes referred to in paragraph (a) and to undertake such programmes themselves; and (c) promote timely and effective dissemination of accurate information by public authorities about their activities. (d) train information officers of public authorities	the extent of availability of financial and other resources,— (a) develop and organize educational programmes to advance the understanding of the public, in particular of disadvantaged communities as to how to exercise the rights contemplated under this Act; (b) encourage public authorities to participate in the development and organisation of programmes referred to in clause (a) and to undertake such programmes themselves; (c) promote timely and effective dissemination of accurate information by public authorities about their activities; and (d) train information officers of public authorities and produce relevant training materials for use by the public authorities

Contd....

Sl. No.	Freedom of Information Act, 2002	NAC's Right to Information Bill, 2004	Right to Information Bill, 2004 as Introduced in Lok Sabha
1	2	3	4
		and/or produce relevant training materials for use by authorities themselves. (2) The Government must, within 18 months of this Act coming into force, compile in each official language a guide containing such information, in an easily comprehensible form and manner, as may reasonably be required by a person who wishes to exercise any right contemplated in this Act. (3) The Government must, if necessary, update and publish the guide at regular intervals. The guide must, without limiting the generality of sub-section (2), include a description of— (a) the objects of this Act; (b) the postal and street address, phone and fax number and, if available, electronic mail address of the Public Information	themselves. (2) The Government must, within 18 months from the commencement of this Act, compile in its official language a guide containing such information, in an easily comprehensible form and manner, as may reasonably be required by a person who wishes to exercise any right specified in this Act. (3) The Government shall, if necessary, update and publish the guidelines referred to in sub-section (2) at regular intervals which shall, in particular and without prejudice to the generality of sub-section (2), include: (a) the objects of this Act; (b) the postal and street address, the phone and fax number and, if available, electronic mail address of the Public Information Officer of every public authority as appointed under sub-section (1) of

Contd....

Sl. No.	Freedom of Information Act, 2002	NAC's Right to Information Bill, 2004	Right to Information Bill, 2004 as Introduced in Lok Sabha
1	2	3	4
		Officer of every public authority as appointed under sub-section (1) of section 5. (c) the manner and form of a request for access to a information of a public authority; (d) the assistance available from and the duties of Public Information Officers of a public authority in terms of this Act; (e) the assistance available from the Information Commissioners in terms of this Act; (f) all remedies in law available regarding an act or failure to act in respect of a right or duty conferred or imposed by this Act, including the manner of lodging an appeal with the appellate authorities/Chief/ State/	section 5; (c) the manner and the form in which request for access to an information shall be made to a public authority; (d) the assistance available from and the duties of the Public Information Officers of a public authority under this Act; (e) the assistance available from the Commission; (f) all remedies in law available regarding an act or failure to act in respect of a right or duty conferred or imposed by this Act, including the manner of filing an appeal to the Commission; (g) the provisions providing for the voluntary, disclosure of categories of records in accordance with section 4; (h) the notices regarding fees to be paid in relation to requests for access to an information; and

Contd....

Sl. No.	Freedom of Information Act, 2002	NAC's Right to Information Bill, 2004	Right to Information Bill, 2094 as Introduced in Lok Sabha
1	2	3	4
		Information Commissioners and a court against a decision by the Public Information Officer of a public authority; (g) the provisions providing for the voluntary disclosure of categories of records in accordance with section 4; (h) the notices regarding fees to be paid in relation to requests for access; and (i) any additional regulations or circulars relevant to obtaining access to information in accordance with this Act. (4) The Government must, if necessary, update and publish the guide at regular intervals.	(i) any additional regulations or circulars made or issued to obtaining access to an information in accordance with this Act. (4) The Government must, if necessary, update and publish the guidelines at regular intervals.
57.	17 (1) The Central Government may by notification in the Official Gazette, make rules	17 (1) The Central Government may by notification in the Official Gazette,	24(1) The Central Government may, by notification in the Official Gazette, make rules

Contd....

Sl. No.	*Freedom of Information Act, 2002*	*NAC's Right to Information Bill, 2004*	*Right to Information Bill, 2004 as Introduced in Lok Sabha*
1	2	3	4
	to carry out the provisions of this Act. (2) In particular, and without prejudice to the generality of the foregoing power, such rules may provide for all or any of the following matters, namely (a) intervals at which matters referred to in sub-clauses (i) to (vi) of clause (b) of section 4 shall be published. (b) The fee payable under sub-section (1) of section 7; (c) The authority before whom an appeal may be preferred under sub-section (1) of section 12; (d) any other matter which is required to be, or may be, prescribed.	make rules to carry out the provisions of this Act. (2) In particular, and without prejudice to the generality of the foregoing power, such rules may provide for all or any of the following matters, namely (a) intervals at which matters referred to in sub-clauses (i) to (vi) of clause (b) of section 4 shall be published. (b) The fee payable under sub-section (1) of section 7; (c) The authority before whom an appeal may be preferred under sub-section (1) of section 12; (d) any other matter which is required to be, or may be, prescribed.	to carry out the provisions of this Act. (2) In particular, and without prejudice to the generality of the foregoing power, such rules may provide for all or any of the following matters, namely (a) intervals at which matters referred to in sub-clauses (i) to (xvii) of clause (b) of sub-section 4 shall be published; (b) the cost of the medium or print cost price of the materials to be disseminated under sub-section (4) of section 4; (c) the fee payable under sub-section (1) of section 6; (d) the fee payable under sub-section (1) of section 7; (e) the salaries and allowances payable to and the terms and conditions of service of the officers and other employees under sub-section (7) of section 13;

Contd....

Sl. No.	*Freedom of Information Act, 2002*	*NAC's Right to Information Bill, 2004*	*Right to Information Bill, 2004 as Introduced in Lok Sabha*
1	2	3	4
			(f) the procedure to be adopted by the Commission in deciding the appeals under sub-section (10) of section 16; and (g) any other matter which is required to be, or may be, prescribed.
58.	18 (1) The State Government may, by notification in the Official Gazette, make rules to carry out the provisions of the Act. (2) In particular, and without prejudice to the generality of the foregoing power, such rules may provide for all or any of the following matters, namely:— (a) the fee payable under subsection (1) of section 7; (b) the authority before whom an appeal may be preferred under sub-section (1) of section 12; (c) any other matter which is required to be, or may be prescribed: Provided that initially the rules	18(1) The State Government may, by notification in the Official Gazette, make rules to carry out the provisions of the Act. (2) In particular, and without prejudice to the generality of the foregoing power, such rules may provide for all or any of the following matters, namely:— (a) the fee payable under sub-section (1) of section 7: (b) the authority before whom an appeal may be preferred under sub-section (1) of section 12: (c) any other matter which	

Contd....

Sl. No.	Freedom of Information Act, 2002	NAC's Right to Information Bill, 2004	Right to Information Bill, 2004 as Introduced in Lok Sabha
1	2	3	4
	shall be made by the Central Government by notification in the official Gazette.	is required to be, or may be prescribed: Provided that initially the rules shall be made by the Central Government by notification in the official Gazette.	
59.	19. (1) The competent authority may, by notification in the official Gazette make rules to carry out the provisions of this Act. (2) In particular, and without prejudice to the generality of the foregoing power such rules may provide for all or any of the following matters, namely:— (a) the fee payable under sub-section (1) of section 7; (b) the authority before whom an appeal may be preferred under sub-section (1) of section 12; (c) any other matter which is required to be, or may be, prescribed.	19. (1) The competent authority may, by notification in the official Gazette make rules to carry out the provisions of this Act. (2) In particular, and without prejudice to the generality of the foregoing power such rules may provide for all or any of the following matters, namely:— (a) the fee payable under sub-section (1) of section 7: (b) the authority before whom an appeal may be preferred under sub-section (1) of section 12; (c) any other matter which	25. (1) The competent authority may, by notification in the official Gazette make rules to carry out the provisions of this Act: (i) intervals at which matters referred to in sub-clauses (i) to (xvii) of clause (b) of sub-section (1) of section 4 shall be published; (ii) the cost of the medium of print cost price of the materials to be disseminated under sub-section (4) of section 4; (iii) the fee payable under sub-section (1) of section 6; (iv) the fee payable under sub-section (1) of section 7; (v) any other matter which is required to be, or may be,

Contd....

Sl. No.	*Freedom of Information Act, 2002*	*NAC's Right to Information Bill, 2004*	*Right to Information Bill, 2004 as Introduced in Lok Sabha*
1	2	3	4
		is required to be, or may be, prescribed.	prescribed.
60.	20. (1) Every rule made by the Central Government under this Act shall be laid, as soon as may be after it is made, before each house of parliament, while it is in session, for a total period of thirty days which may be comprised in one session or in two or more successive sessions, and if, before the expiry of the session immediately following the session or the successive sessions aforesaid, both houses agree in making any modification in the rule or both houses agree that the rule should not be made, the rule shall thereafter have effect only in such modified form or be of no effect, as the case may be, so, however, that any such modification or annulment shall be without prejudice to the validity of anything previously	20. (1) Every rule made by the Central Government under this Act shall be laid, as soon as may be after it is made, before each house of parliament, while it is in session, for a total period of thirty days which may be comprised in one session or in two or more successive sessions, and if, before the expiry of the session immediately following the session or the successive sessions aforesaid, both houses agree in making any modification in the rule or both houses agree that the rule should not be made, the rule shall thereafter have effect only in such modified from or be of no effect, as the case may be, so, however, that any such modification or annulment shall be without	26. (1) Every rule made by the Central Government under this Act shall be laid, as soon as may be after it is made, before each House of Parliament, while it is in session, for a total period of thirty days which may be comprised one session or in two or more successive sessions, and if, before the expiry of the session immediately following the session or the successive sessions aforesaid, both Houses agree in making any modification in the rule or both Houses agree that the rule should not be made, the rule shall thereafter have effect only in such modified form or be of no effect, as the case may be, so, however, that any such modification or annulment shall be without prejudice to the validity of anything previously done under that rule.

Contd....

Sl. No.	*Freedom of Information Act, 2002*	*NAC's Right to Information Bill, 2004*	*Right to Information Bill, 2004 as Introduced in Lok Sabha*
1	2	3	4
	done under that rule.	prejudice to the validity of anything previously done under that rule.	
61.	20 (2) Every rule made under this Act by a State Government shall be laid, as soon as may be after it is notified, before the State Legislature.	20 (2) Every rule made under this Act by a State Government shall be laid, as soon as may be after it is notified, before the State Legislature.	
62.	21 (1) If any difficulty arises in giving effect to the provisions of this Act, the Union Government may, by order published in the official Gazette, make such provision not inconsistent with the provisions of this Act as appear to it to be necessary or expedient for removal of the difficulty: Provided that no such order shall be made after the expiry of a period of two years from the date of commencement of this Act. (2) Every order made under this section shall as soon as may be after it is made, be laid before the houses of parliament.	21 (1) If any difficulty arises in giving effect to the provisions of this Act, the Union Government may, by order published in the official Gazette, make such provision not inconsistent with the provisions of this Act as appear to it to be necessary or expedient for removal of the difficulty: Provided that no such order shall be made after the expiry of a period of two years from the date of commencement of this Act. (2) Every order made under this section shall as soon as may be after it is made, be laid	21 (1) If any difficulty arises in giving effect to the provisions of this Act, the Central Government may, by order published in the official Gazette, make such provision not inconsistent with the provisions of this Act as appear to it to be necessary or expedient for removal of the difficulty: Provided that no such order shall be made after the expiry of a period of two years from the date of commencement of this Act.

Contd....

Sl. No.	*Freedom of Information Act, 2002*	*NAC's Right to Information Bill, 2004*	*Right to Information Bill, 2004 as Introduced in Lok Sabha*
1	2	3	4
		before the houses of parliament.	
63.	Does not exist in the present Act.	Does not exist in the Bill.	(2) Every order made under this section shall as soon as may be after it is made, be laid before the houses of parliament.
64.	Does not exist in the present Act.	Does not exist in the Bill.	28. The Freedom of Information Act, 2002 is hereby repealed.
			The First Schedule **[See Sub-section (3) of section 13]** From of oath or affirmation to be made by the Information Commissioner or the Deputy Information **Commissioner** "I, ……………, having been appointed Information Commissioner/Deputy Information Commissioner swear in the name of God, that I will bear true faith solemnly affirm allegiance to the Constitution of India as by law established, that I will uphold the sovereignty and integrity of India, that I will duly and faithfully and to the best of my ability, knowledge and judgement perform the duties of my office without fear of favour, affection or ill-will and that I will uphold the Constitution and the laws."

Contd....

Sl. No.	*Freedom of Information Act, 2002*	*NAC's Right to Information Bill, 2004*	*Right to Information Bill, 2004 as Introduced in Lok Sabha*
1	2	3	4
65.	**THE SCHEDULE** **[See section 16]** **INTELLIGENCE AND SECURITY ORGANISATIONS ESTABLISHED BY THE CENTRAL GOVERNMENT** 1. Intelligence Bureau. 2. Research and Analysis Wing of the Cabinet Secretariat. 3. Directorate of Revenue Intelligence. 4. Central Economic Intelligence Bureau. 5. Directorate of Enforcement. 6. Narcotics Control Bureau. 7. Aviation Research Centre. 8. Special Frontier Force. 9. Border Security Force. 10. Central Reserve Police Force. 11. Indo Tibetan Border Police. 12. Central Industrial Security Force. 13. National Security Guards. 14. Assam Rifles. 15. Special Service Bureau. 16. Special Branch (CID), Andaman and Nicobar. 17. The Crime Branch—CID, CB, Dadra and Nagar Haveli.	**THE SCHEDULE** **[See section 16 (1)]** **INTELLIGENCE AND SECURITY ORGANISATIONS ESTABLISHED BY THE CENTRAL GOVERNMENT** 1. Intelligence Bureau. 2. Research and Analysis Wing of the Cabinet Secretariat. 3. Directorate of Revenue Intelligence. 4. Central Economic Intelligence Bureau. 5. Directorate of Enforcement. 6. Narcotics Control Bureau. 7. Aviation Research Centre. 8. Special Frontier Force. 9. Border Security Force. 10. Central Reserve Police Force. 11. Indo Tibetan Border Police. 12. Central Industrial Security Force. 13. National Security Guards. 14. Assam Rifles. 15. Special Service Bureau. 16. Special Branch (CID), Andaman and Nicobar.	**THE SECOND SCHEDULE** **[See section 21]** **INTELLIGENCE AND SECURITY ORGANISATIONS ESTABLISHED BY THE CENTRAL GOVERNMENT** 1. Intelligence Bureau. 2. Research and Analysis Wing of the Cabinet Secretariat. 3. Directorate of Revenue Intelligence. 4. Central Economic Intelligence Bureau. 5. Directorate of Enforcement. 6. Narcotics Control Bureau. 7. Aviation Research Centre. 8. Special Frontier Force. 9. Border Security Force. 10. Central Reserve Police Force. 11. Indo Tibetan Border Police. 12. Central Industrial Security Force. 13. National Security Guards. 14. Assam Rifles. 15. Special Service Bureau. 16. Special Branch (CID), Andaman and Nicobar. 17. The Crime Branch—CID, CB, Dadra and Nagar Haveli.

Contd....

Sl. No.	*Freedom of Information Act, 2002*	*NAC's Right to Information Bill, 2004*	*Right to Information Bill, 2004 as Introduced in Lok Sabha*
1	2	3	4
	18. Directorate of Vigilance including Anti-Corruption Branch, National Capital Territory of Delhi. 19. Special Branch, Lakshadweep Police.	17. The Crime Branch-CID, - CB, Dadra and Nagar Haveli. 18. Directorate of Vigilance including Anti-Corruption Branch, National Capital Territory of Delhi. 19. Special Branch, Lakshadweep Police.	18. Special Branch, Lakshadweep Police.

Annexure – II

The Right to Information Act, 2005

No. 22 of 2005

[15th June, 2005]

An Act to provide for setting out the practical regime of right to information for citizens to secure access to information under the control of public authorities, in order to promote transparency and accountability in the working of every public authority, the constitution of a Central Information Commission and State Information Commissions and for matters connected therewith or incidental thereto.

Whereas the Constitution of India has established democratic Republic;

And whereas democracy requires an informed citizenry and transparency of information which are vital to its functioning and also to contain corruption and to hold Governments and their instrumentalities accountable to the governed;

And whereas revelation of information in actual practice is likely to conflict with other public interests including efficient operations of the Governments, optimum use of limited fiscal resources and the preservation of confidentiality of sensitive information;

And whereas it is necessary to harmonise these conflicting interests while preserving the paramountcy of the democratic ideal;

Now, therefore, it is expedient to provide for furnishing certain information to citizens who desire to have it.

Be it enacted by Parliament in the Fifty-sixth Year of the Republic of India as follows:—

CHAPTER I
PRELIMINARY

1 (1) This Act may be called the Right to Information Act, 2005.

(2) It extends to the whole of India except the State of Jammu and Kashmir.

(3) The provisions of sub-section (1) of Section 4, sub-sections (1) and (*2*) of Section 5, sections 12, 13, 15,16, 24, 27 and 28 shall come into force at once, and the remaining provisions of this Act shall come into force on the one hundred and twentieth day of its enactment.

2 In this Act, unless the context otherwise requires,—

(a) "appropriate Government" means in relation to a public authority which is established, constituted, owned, controlled or substantially financed by funds provided directly or indirectly—

(i) by the Central Government or the Union territory administration, the Central Government;

(ii) by the State Government, the State Government;

(b) "Central Information Commission" means the Central Information Commission constituted under sub-section (*1*) of Section 12;

(c) "Central Public Information Officer" means the Central Public Information Officer designated under sub-section (*1*) and includes a Central Assistant Public Information Officer designated as such under sub-section (*2*) of Section 5;

(d) "Chief Information Commissioner" and "Information Commissioner" mean the Chief Information Commissioner and Information Commissioner appointed under sub-section (*3*) of Section 12;

(e) "competent authority" means—

(i) the Speaker in the case of the House of the People or the Legislative Assembly of a State or a Union territory having such Assembly and the Chairman in the case of the Council of States or Legislative Council of a State;

(ii) the Chief Justice of India in the case of the Supreme Court;

(iii) the Chief Justice of the High Court in the case of a High Court;

(iv) the President or the Governor, as the case may be, in the case of other authorities established or constituted by or under the Constitution;

(v) the administrator appointed under Article 239 of the Constitution;

(f) "information" means any material in any form, including records, documents, memos, e-mails, opinions, advices, press releases, circulars, orders, logbooks, contracts, reports, papers, samples, models, data material held in any electronic form and information relating to any private body which can be accessed by a public authority under any other law for the time being in force;

(g) "prescribed" means prescribed by rules made under this Act by the appropriate Government or the competent authority, as the case may be;

(h) "public authority" means any authority or body or institution of self-government established or constituted—

(a) by or under the Constitution;

(b) by any other law made by Parliament;

(c) by any other law made by State Legislature;

(d) by notification issued or order made by the appropriate Government, and includes any—

(i) body owned, controlled or substantially financed;

(ii) non-Government organization substantially financed, directly or indirectly by funds provided by the appropriate Government;

(i) "record" includes—

(a) any document, manuscript and file;

(b) any microfilm, microfiche and facsimile copy of a document;

(c) any reproduction of image or images embodied in such microfilm (whether enlarged or not); and

(d) any other material produced by a computer or any other device;

(j) "right to information" means the right to information accessible under this Act which is held by or under the control of any public authority and includes the right to—

(i) inspection of work, documents, records;

(ii) taking notes, extracts or certified copies of documents or records;

(iii) taking certified samples of material;

(iv) obtaining information in the form of diskettes, floppies, tapes, video cassettes or in any other electronic mode or through printouts where such information is stored in a computer or in any other device;

(k) "State Information Commission" means the State Information Commission constituted under sub-section (*1*) of Section 15;

(l) "State Chief Information Commissioner" and "State Information Commissioner" mean the State Chief Information Commissioner and the State Information Commissioner appointed under sub-section (*3*) of Section 15;

(m) "State Public Information Officer" means the State Public Information Officer designated under sub-section (*1*) and includes a State Assistant Public Information Officer designated as such under sub-section (*2*) of Section 5;

(n) "third party" means a person other than the citizen making a request for information and includes a public authority.

CHAPTER II
RIGHT TO INFORMATION AND OBLIGATIONS OF PUBLIC AUTHORITIES

3 Subject to the provisions of this Act, all citizens shall have the right to information.

4 (1) Every public authority shall—

(a) maintain all its records duly catalogued and indexed in a manner and the form which facilitates the right to information under this Act and ensure that all records that are appropriate to be computerised are, within a reasonable time and subject to availability of resources, computerised and connected through a network all over the country on different systems so that access to such records is facilitated;

(b) publish within one hundred and twenty days from the enactment of this Act,—

(i) the particulars of its organisation, functions and duties;

(ii) the powers and duties of its officers and employees;

(iii) the procedure followed in the decision making process, including channels of supervision and accountability;

(iv) the norms set by it for the discharge of its functions;

(v) the rules, regulations, instructions, manuals and records, held by it or under its control or used by its employees for discharging its functions;

(vi) a statement of the categories of documents that are held by it or under its control;

(vii) the particulars of any arrangement that exists for consultation with, or representation by, the members of the public in relation to the formulation of its policy or implementation thereof;

(viii) a statement of the boards, councils, committees and other bodies consisting of two or more persons constituted as its part or for the purpose of its advice, and as to whether meetings of those boards, councils, committees and other bodies are open to the public, or the minutes of such meetings are accessible for public;

(ix) a directory of its officers and employees;

(x) the monthly remuneration received by each of its officers and employees, including the system of compensation as provided in its regulations;

(xi) the budget allocated to each of its agency, indicating the particulars of all plans, proposed expenditures and reports on disbursements made;

(xii) the manner of execution of subsidy programmes, including the amounts allocated and the details of beneficiaries of such programmes;

(xiii) particulars of recipients of concessions, permits or authorisations granted by it;

(xiv) details in respect of the information, available to or held by it, reduced in an electronic form;

(xv) the particulars of facilities available to citizens for obtaining information, including the working hours of a library or reading room, if maintained for public use;

(xvi) the names, designations and other particulars of the Public Information Officers;

(xvii) such other information as may be prescribed and thereafter update these publications every year;

(c) publish all relevant facts while formulating important policies or announcing the decisions which affect public;

(d) provide reasons for its administrative or quasi-judicial decisions to affected persons.

(2) It shall be a constant endeavour of every public authority to take steps in accordance with the requirements of clause (b) of sub-section (1) to

provide as much information *suo motu* to the public at regular intervals through various means of communications, including internet, so that the public have minimum resort to the use of this Act to obtain information.

(3) For the purposes of sub-section (1), every information shall be disseminated widely and in such form and manner which is easily accessible to the public.

(4) All materials shall be disseminated taking into consideration the cost effectiveness, local language and the most effective method of communication in that local area and the information should be easily accessible, to the extent possible in electronic format with the Central Public Information Officer or State Public Information Officer, as the case may be, available free or at such cost of the medium or the print cost price as may be prescribed.

Explanation.—For the purposes of sub-sections (3) and (4), "disseminated" means making known or communicated the information to the public through notice boards, newspapers, public announcements, media broadcasts, the internet or any other means, including inspection of offices of any public authority.

5 (1) Every public authority shall, within one hundred days of the enactment of this Act, designate as many officers as the Central Public Information Officers or State Public Information Officers, as the case may be, in all administrative units or offices under it as may be necessary to provide information to persons requesting for the information under this Act.

(2) Without prejudice to the provisions of sub-section (1), every public authority shall designate an officer, within one hundred days of the enactment of this Act, at each sub-divisional level or other sub-district level as a Central Assistant Public Information Officer or a State Assistant Public Information Officer, as the case may be, to receive the applications for information or appeals under this Act for forwarding the same forthwith to the Central Public Information Officer or the State Public Information Officer or senior officer specified under sub-section (1) of Section 19 or the Central Information Commission or the State Information Commission, as the case may be:

Provided that where an application for information or appeal is given to a Central Assistant Public Information Officer or a State Assistant Public Information Officer, as the case may be, a period of five days shall be added in computing the period for response specified under sub-section (1) of Section 7.

(3) Every Central Public Information Officer or State Public Information Officer, as the case may be, shall deal with requests from persons seeking information and render reasonable assistance to the persons seeking such information.

(4) The Central Public Information Officer or State Public Information Officer, as the case may be, may seek the assistance of any other officer

as he or she considers it necessary for the proper discharge of his or her duties.

(5) Any officer, whose assistance has been sought under sub-section (4), shall render all assistance to the Central Public Information Officer or State Public Information Officer, as the case may be, seeking his or her assistance and for the purposes of any contravention of the provisions of this Act, such other officer shall be treated as a Central Public Information Officer or State Public Information Officer, as the case may be.

6 (1) A person, who desires to obtain any information under this Act, shall make a request in writing or through electronic means in English or Hindi or in the official language of the area in which the application is being made, accompanying such fee as may be prescribed, to—

(a) the Central Public Information Officer or State Public Information Officer, as the case may be, of the concerned public authority;

(b) the Central Assistant Public Information Officer or State Assistant Public Information Officer, as the case may be,

specifying the particulars of the information sought by him or her:

Provided that where such request cannot be made in writing, the Central Public Information Officer or State Public Information Officer, as the case may be, shall render all reasonable assistance to the person making the request orally to reduce the same in writing.

(2) An applicant making request for information shall not be required to give any reason for requesting the information or any other personal details except those that may be necessary for contacting him.

(3) Where an application is made to a public authority requesting for an information,—

(i) which is held by another public authority; or

(ii) the subject matter of which is more closely connected with the functions of another public authority,

the public authority, to which such application is made, shall transfer the application or such part of it as may be appropriate to that other public authority and inform the applicant immediately about such transfer:

Provided that the transfer of an application pursuant to this sub-section shall be made as soon as practicable but in no case later than five days from the date of receipt of the application.

7 (1) Subject to the proviso to sub-section (2) of Section 5 or the proviso to sub-section (3) of Section 6, the Central Public Information Officer or State Public Information Officer, as the case may be, on receipt of a request under Section 6 shall, as expeditiously as possible, and in any case within thirty days of the receipt of the request, either provide the information on payment of such fee as may be prescribed or reject the request for any of the reasons specified in sections 8 and 9:

Provided that where the information sought for concerns the life or liberty of a person, the same shall be provided within forty-eight hours of the receipt of the request.

(2) If the Central Public Information Officer or State Public Information Officer, as the case may be, fails to give decision on the request for information within the period specified under sub-section (1), the Central Public Information Officer or State Public Information Officer, as the case may be, shall be deemed to have refused the request.

(3) Where a decision is taken to provide the information on payment of any further fee representing the cost of providing the information, the Central Public Information Officer or State Public Information Officer, as the case may be, shall send an intimation to the person making the request, giving—

(a) the details of further fees representing the cost of providing the information as determined by him, together with the calculations made to arrive at the amount in accordance with fee prescribed under sub-section (1), requesting him to deposit that fees, and the period intervening between the despatch of the said intimation and payment of fees shall be excluded for the purpose of calculating the period of thirty days referred to in that sub-section;

(b) information concerning his or her right with respect to review the decision as to the amount of fees charged or the form of access provided, including the particulars of the appellate authority, time limit, process and any other forms.

(4) Where access to the record or a part thereof is required to be provided under this Act and the person to whom access is to be provided is sensorily disabled, the Central Public Information Officer or State Public Information Officer, as the case may be, shall provide assistance to enable access to the information, including providing such assistance as may be appropriate for the inspection.

(5) Where access to information is to be provided in the printed or in any electronic format, the applicant shall, subject to the provisions of sub-section (6), pay such fee as may be prescribed:

Provided that the fee prescribed under sub-section (1) of Section 6 and sub-sections (1) and (5) of Section 7 shall be reasonable and no such fee shall be charged from the persons who are of below poverty line as may be determined by the appropriate Government.

(6) Notwithstanding anything contained in sub-section (5), the person making request for the information shall be provided the information free of charge where a public authority fails to comply with the time limits specified in sub-section (1).

(7) Before taking any decision under sub-section (1), the Central Public Information Officer or State Public Information Officer, as the case may be, shall take into consideration the representation made by a third party under Section 11.

(8) Where a request has been rejected under sub-section (1), the Central

Public Information Officer or State Public Information Officer, as the case may be, shall communicate to the person making the request,—

(i) the reasons for such rejection;

(ii) the period within which an appeal against such rejection may be preferred; and

(iii) the particulars of the appellate authority.

(9) An information shall ordinarily be provided in the form in which it is sought unless it would disproportionately divert the resources of the public authority or would be detrimental to the safety or preservation of the record in question.

8 (1) Notwithstanding anything contained in this Act, there shall be no obligation to give any citizen,—

(a) information, disclosure of which would prejudicially affect the sovereignty and integrity of India, the security, strategic, scientific or economic interests of the State, relation with foreign State or lead to incitement of an offence;

(b) information which has been expressly forbidden to be published by any court of law or tribunal or the disclosure of which may constitute contempt of court;

(c) information, the disclosure of which would cause a breach of privilege of Parliament or the State Legislature;

(d) information including commercial confidence, trade secrets or intellectual property, the disclosure of which would harm the competitive position of a third party, unless the competent authority is satisfied that larger public interest warrants the disclosure of such information;

(e) information available to a person in his fiduciary relationship, unless the competent authority is satisfied that the larger public interest warrants the disclosure of such information;

(f) information received in confidence from foreign Government;

(g) information, the disclosure of which would endanger the life or physical safety of any person or identify the source of information or assistance given in confidence for law enforcement or security purposes;

(h) information which would impede the process of investigation or apprehension or prosecution of offenders;

(i) cabinet papers including records of deliberations of the Council of Ministers, Secretaries and other officers:

Provided that the decisions of Council of Ministers, the reasons thereof, and the material on the basis of which the decisions were taken shall be made public after the decision has been taken, and the matter is complete, or over:

Provided further that those matters which come under the exemptions specified in this Section shall not be disclosed;

(j) information which relates to personal information the disclosure of which has no relationship to any public activity or interest, or which would cause unwarranted invasion of the privacy of the individual unless the Central Public Information Officer or the State Public Information Officer or the appellate authority, as the case may be, is satisfied that the larger public interest justifies the disclosure of such information:

Provided that the information which cannot be denied to the Parliament or a State Legislature shall not be denied to any person.

(2) Notwithstanding anything in the Official Secrets Act, 1923 nor any of the exemptions permissible in accordance with sub-section (1), a public authority may allow access to information, if public interest in disclosure outweighs the harm to the protected interests.

(3) Subject to the provisions of clauses (a), (c) and (i) of sub-section (1), any information relating to any occurrence, event or matter which has taken place, occurred or happened twenty years before the date on which any request is made under secton 6 shall be provided to any person making a request under that section:

Provided that where any question arises as to the date from which the said period of twenty years has to be computed, the decision of the Central Government shall be final, subject to the usual appeals provided for in this Act.

9 Without prejudice to the provisions of Section 8, a Central Public Information Officer or a State Public Information Officer, as the case may be, may reject a request for information where such a request for providing access would involve an infringement of copyright subsisting in a person other than the State.

10 (1) Where a request for access to information is rejected on the ground that it is in relation to information which is exempt from disclosure, then, notwithstanding anything contained in this Act, access may be provided to that part of the record which does not contain any information which is exempt from disclosure under this Act and which can reasonably be severed from any part that contains exempt information.

(2) Where access is granted to a part of the record under sub-section (1), the Central Public Information Officer or State Public Information Officer, as the case may be, shall give a notice to the applicant, informing—

(a) that only part of the record requested, after severance of the record containing information which is exempt from disclosure, is being provided;

(b) the reasons for the decision, including any findings on any material question of fact, referring to the material on which those findings were based;

(c) the name and designation of the person giving the decision;

(d) the details of the fees calculated by him or her and the amount of fee which the applicant is required to deposit; and

(e) his or her rights with respect to review of the decision regarding non-disclosure of part of the information, the amount of fee charged or the form of access provided, including the particulars of the senior officer specified under sub-section (1) of Section 19 or the Central Information Commission or the State Information Commission, as the case may be, time limit, process and any other form of access.

11 (1) Where a Central Public Information Officer or a State Public Information Officer, as the case may be, intends to disclose any information or record, or part thereof on a request made under this Act, which relates to or has been supplied by a third party and has been treated as confidential by that third party, the Central Public Information Officer or State Public Information Officer, as the case may be, shall, within five days from the receipt of the request, give a written notice to such third party of the request and of the fact that the Central Public Information Officer or State Public Information Officer, as the case may be, intends to disclose the information or record, or part thereof, and invite the third party to make a submission in writing or orally, regarding whether the information should be disclosed, and such submission of the third party shall be kept in view while taking a decision about disclosure of information:

Provided that except in the case of trade or commercial secrets protected by law, disclosure may be allowed if the public interest in disclosure outweighs in importance any possible harm or injury to the interests of such third party.

(2) Where a notice is served by the Central Public Information Officer or State Public Information Officer, as the case may be, under sub-section (1) to a third party in respect of any information or record or part thereof, the third party shall, within ten days from the date of receipt of such notice, be given the opportunity to make representation against the proposed disclosure.

(3) Notwithstanding anything contained in Section 7, the Central Public Information Officer or State Public Information Officer, as the case may be, shall, within forty days after receipt of the request under Section 6, if the third party has been given an opportunity to make representation under sub-section (2), make a decision as to whether or not to disclose the information or record or part thereof and give in writing the notice of his decision to the third party.

(4) A notice given under sub-section (3) shall include a statement that the third party to whom the notice is given is entitled to prefer an appeal under Section 19 against the decision.

CHAPTER III
THE CENTRAL INFORMATION COMMISSION

12 (1) The Central Government shall, by notification in the Official Gazette, constitute a body to be known as the Central Information Commission to exercise the powers conferred on, and to perform the functions assigned to, it under this Act.

(2) The Central Information Commission shall consist of—

(a) the Chief Information Commissioner; and

(b) such number of Central Information Commissioners, not exceeding ten, as may be deemed necessary.

(3) The Chief Information Commissioner and Information Commissioners shall be appointed by the President on the recommendation of a committee consisting of—

(i) the Prime Minister, who shall be the Chairperson of the committee;

(ii) the Leader of Opposition in the Lok Sabha; and

(iii) a Union Cabinet Minister to be nominated by the Prime Minister.

Explanation.—For the purposes of removal of doubts, it is hereby declared that where the Leader of Opposition in the House of the People has not been recognised as such, the Leader of the single largest group in opposition of the Government in the House of the People shall be deemed to be the Leader of Opposition.

(4) The general superintendence, direction and management of the affairs of the Central Information Commission shall vest in the Chief Information Commissioner who shall be assisted by the Information Commissioners and may exercise all such powers and do all such acts and things which may be exercised or done by the Central Information Commission autonomously without being subjected to directions by any other authority under this Act.

(5) The Chief Information Commissioner and Information Commissioners shall be persons of eminence in public life with wide knowledge and experience in law, science and technology, social service, management, journalism, mass media or administration and governance.

(6) The Chief Information Commissioner or an Information Commissioner shall not be a Member of Parliament or Member of the Legislature of any State or Union territory, as the case may be, or hold any other office of profit or connected with any political party or carrying on any business or pursuing any profession.

(7) The headquarters of the Central Information Commission shall be at Delhi and the Central Information Commission may, with the previous approval of the Central Government, establish offices at other places in India.

13 (1) The Chief Information Commissioner shall hold office for a term of five years from the date on which he enters upon his office and shall not be eligible for reappointment:

Provided that no Chief Information Commissioner shall hold office as such after he has attained the age of sixty-five years.

(2) Every Information Commissioner shall hold office for a term of five years from the date on which he enters upon his office or till he attains the age

of sixty-five years, whichever is earlier, and shall not be eligible for reappointment as such Information Commissioner:

Provided that every Information Commissioner shall, on vacating his office under this sub-section be eligible for appointment as the Chief Information Commissioner in the manner specified in sub-section (3) of Section 12:

Provided further that where the Information Commissioner is appointed as the Chief Information Commissioner, his term of office shall not be more than five years in aggregate as the Information Commissioner and the Chief Information Commissioner.

(3) The Chief Information Commissioner or an Information Commissioner shall before he enters upon his office make and subscribe before the President or some other person appointed by him in that behalf, an oath or affirmation according to the form set out for the purpose in the First Schedule.

(4) The Chief Information Commissioner or an Information Commissioner may, at any time, by writing under his hand addressed to the President, resign from his office:

Provided that the Chief Information Commissioner or an Information Commissioner may be removed in the manner specified under Section 14.

(5) The salaries and allowances payable to and other terms and conditions of service of —

(a) the Chief Information Commissioner shall be the same as that of the Chief Election Commissioner;

(b) an Information Commissioner shall be the same as that of an Election Commissioner:

Provided that if the Chief Information Commissioner or an Information Commissioner, at the time of his appointment is, in receipt of a pension, other than a disability or wound pension, in respect of any previous service under the Government of India or under the Government of a State, his salary in respect of the service as the Chief Information Commissioner or an Information Commissioner shall be reduced by the amount of that pension including any portion of pension which was commuted and pension equivalent of other forms of retirement benefits excluding pension equivalent of retirement gratuity:

Provided further that if the Chief Information Commissioner or an Information Commissioner if, at the time of his appointment is, in receipt of retirement benefits in respect of any previous service rendered in a Corporation established by or under any Central Act or State Act or a Government company owned or controlled by the Central Government or the State Government, his salary in respect of the service as the Chief Information Commissioner or an

Information Commissioner shall be reduced by the amount of pension equivalent to the retirement benefits:

Provided also that the salaries, allowances and other conditions of service of the Chief Information Commissioner and the Information Commissioners shall not be varied to their disadvantage after their appointment.

(6) The Central Government shall provide the Chief Information Commissioner and the Information Commissioners with such officers and employees as may be necessary for the efficient performance of their functions under this Act, and the salaries and allowances payable to and the terms and conditions of service of the officers and other employees appointed for the purpose of this Act shall be such as may be prescribed.

14 (1) Subject to the provisions of sub-section (3), the Chief Information Commissioner or any Information Commissioner shall be removed from his office only by order of the President on the ground of proved misbehaviour or incapacity after the Supreme Court, on a reference made to it by the President, has, on inquiry, reported that the Chief Information Commissioner or any Information Commissioner, as the case may be, ought on such ground be removed.

(2) The President may suspend from office, and if deem necessary prohibit also from attending the office during inquiry, the Chief Information Commissioner or Information Commissioner in respect of whom a reference has been made to the Supreme Court under sub-section (1) until the President has passed orders on receipt of the report of the Supreme Court on such reference.

(3) Notwithstanding anything contained in sub-section (1), the President may by order remove from office the Chief Information Commissioner or any Information Commissioner if the Chief Information Commissioner or a Information Commissioner, as the case may be,—

(a) is adjudged an insolvent; or

(b) has been convicted of an offence which, in the opinion of the President, involves moral turpitude; or

(c) engages during his term of office in any paid employment outside the duties of his office; or

(d) is, in the opinion of the President, unfit to continue in office by reason of infirmity of mind or body; or

(e) has acquired such financial or other interest as is likely to affect prejudicially his functions as the Chief Information Commissioner or a Information Commissioner.

(4) If the Chief Information Commissioner or a Information Commissioner in any way, concerned or interested in any contract or agreement made by or on behalf of the Government of India or participates in any way in the profit thereof or in any benefit or emolument arising there from otherwise than as a member and in common with the other members of

an incorporated company, he shall, for the purposes of sub-section (1), be deemed to be guilty of misbehaviour.

CHAPTER IV
THE STATE INFORMATION COMMISSION

15 (1) Every State Government shall, by notification in the Official Gazette, constitute a body to be known as the .... (name of the State) Information Commission to exercise the powers conferred on, and to perform the functions assigned to, it under this Act.

(2) The State Information Commission shall consist of—

(a) the State Chief Information Commissioner, and

(b) such number of State Information Commissioners, not exceeding ten, as may be deemed necessary.

(3) The State Chief Information Commissioner and the State Information Commissioners shall be appointed by the Governor on the recommendation of a committee consisting of—

(i) the Chief Minister, who shall be the Chairperson of the committee;

(ii) the Leader of Opposition in the Legislative Assembly; and

(iii) a Cabinet Minister to be nominated by the Chief Minister.

Explanation.—For the purposes of removal of doubts, it is hereby declared that where the Leader of Opposition in the Legislative Assembly has not been recognised as such, the Leader of the single largest group in opposition of the Government in the Legislative Assembly shall be deemed to be the Leader of Opposition.

(4) The general superintendence, direction and management of the affairs of the State Information Commission shall vest in the State Chief Information Commissioner who shall be assisted by the State Information Commissioners and may exercise all such powers and do all such acts and things which may be exercised or done by the State Information Commission autonomously without being subjected to directions by any other authority under this Act.

(5) The State Chief Information Commissioner and the State Information Commissioners shall be persons of eminence in public life with wide knowledge and experience in law, science and technology, social service, management, journalism, mass media or administration and governance.

(6) The State Chief Information Commissioner or a State Information Commissioner shall not be a Member of Parliament or Member of the Legislature of any State or Union territory, as the case may be, or hold any other office of profit or connected with any political party or carrying on any business or pursuing any profession.

(7) The headquarters of the State Information Commission shall be at such place in the State as the State Government may, by notification in the Official Gazette, specify and the State Information Commission may, with

the previous approval of the State Government, establish offices at other places in the State.

16 (1) The State Chief Information Commissioner shall hold office for a term of five years from the date on which he enters upon his office and shall not be eligible for reappointment:

Provided that no State Chief Information Commissioner shall hold office as such after he has attained the age of sixty-five years.

(2) Every State Information Commissioner shall hold office for a term of five years from the date on which he enters upon his office or till he attains the age of sixty-five years, whichever is earlier, and shall not be eligible for reappointment as such State Information Commissioner:

Provided that every State Information Commissioner shall, on vacating his office under this sub-section, be eligible for appointment as the State Chief Information Commissioner in the manner specified in sub-section (3) of Section 15:

Provided further that where the State Information Commissioner is appointed as the State Chief Information Commissioner, his term of office shall not be more than five years in aggregate as the State Information Commissioner and the State Chief Information Commissioner.

(3) The State Chief Information Commissioner or a State Information Commissioner, shall before he enters upon his office make and subscribe before the Governor or some other person appointed by him in that behalf, an oath or affirmation according to the form set out for the purpose in the First Schedule.

(4) The State Chief Information Commissioner or a State Information Commissioner may, at any time, by writing under his hand addressed to the Governor, resign from his office:

Provided that the State Chief Information Commissioner or a State Information Commissioner may be removed in the manner specified under Section 17.

(5) The salaries and allowances payable to and other terms and conditions of service of—

(a) the State Chief Information Commissioner shall be the same as that of an Election Commissioner;

(b) the State Information Commissioner shall be the same as that of the Chief Secretary to the State Government:

Provided that if the State Chief Information Commissioner or a State Information Commissioner, at the time of his appointment is, in receipt of a pension, other than a disability or wound pension, in respect of any previous service under the Government of India or under the Government of a State, his salary in respect of the service as the State Chief Information Commissioner or a State Information Commissioner shall be reduced by the amount of that pension including any portion of pension which was commuted and pension equivalent of other forms of retirement benefits excluding pension equivalent of retirement gratuity:

Provided further that where the State Chief Information Commissioner or a State Information Commissioner if, at the time of his appointment is, in receipt of retirement benefits in respect of any previous service rendered in a Corporation established by or under any Central Act or State Act or a Government company owned or controlled by the Central Government or the State Government, his salary in respect of the service as the State Chief Information Commissioner or the State Information Commissioner shall be reduced by the amount of pension equivalent to the retirement benefits:

Provided also that the salaries, allowances and other conditions of service of the State Chief Information Commissioner and the State Information Commissioners shall not be varied to their disadvantage after their appointment.

(6) The State Government shall provide the State Chief Information Commissioner and the State Information Commissioners with such officers and employees as may be necessary for the efficient performance of their functions under this Act, and the salaries and allowances payable to and the terms and conditions of service of the officers and other employees appointed for the purpose of this Act shall be such as may be prescribed.

17 (1) Subject to the provisions of sub-section (3), the State Chief Information Commissioner or a State Information Commissioner shall be removed from his office only by order of the Governor on the ground of proved misbehaviour or incapacity after the Supreme Court, on a reference made to it by the Governor, has on inquiry, reported that the State Chief Information Commissioner or a State Information Commissioner, as the case may be, ought on such ground be removed.

(2) The Governor may suspend from office, and if deem necessary prohibit also from attending the office during inquiry, the State Chief Information Commissioner or a State Information Commissioner in respect of whom a reference has been made to the Supreme Court under sub-section (1) until the Governor has passed orders on receipt of the report of the Supreme Court on such reference.

(3) Notwithstanding anything contained in sub-section (1), the Governor may by order remove from office the State Chief Information Commissioner or a State Information Commissioner if a State Chief Information Commissioner or a State Information Commissioner, as the case may be,—

(a) is adjudged an insolvent; or

(b) has been convicted of an offence which, in the opinion of the Governor, involves moral turpitude; or

(c) engages during his term of office in any paid employment outside the duties of his office; or

(d) is, in the opinion of the Governor, unfit to continue in office by reason of infirmity of mind or body; or

(e) has acquired such financial or other interest as is likely to affect prejudicially his functions as the State Chief Information Commissioner or a State Information Commissioner.

(4) If the State Chief Information Commissioner or a State Information Commissioner in any way, concerned or interested in any contract or agreement made by or on behalf of the Government of the State or participates in any way in the profit thereof or in any benefit or emoluments arising therefrom otherwise than as a member and in common with the other members of an incorporated company, he shall, for the purposes of sub-section (1), be deemed to be guilty of misbehaviour.

CHAPTER V
POWERS AND FUNCTIONS OF THE INFORMATION COMMISSIONS, APPEAL AND PENALTIES

18 (1) Subject to the provisions of this Act, it shall be the duty of the Central Information Commission or State Information Commission, as the case may be, to receive and inquire into a complaint from any person,—

(a) who has been unable to submit a request to a Central Public Information Officer or State Public Information Officer, as the case may be, either by reason that no such officer has been appointed under this Act, or because the Central Assistant Public Information Officer or State Assistant Public Information Officer, as the case may be, has refused to accept his or her application for information or appeal under this Act for forwarding the same to the Central Public Information Officer or State Public Information Officer or senior officer specified in sub-section (1) of Section 19 or the Central Information Commission or the State Information Commission, as the case may be;

(b) who has been refused access to any information requested under this Act;

(c) who has not been given a response to a request for information or access to information within the time limit specified under this Act;

(d) who has been required to pay an amount of fee which he or she considers unreasonable;

(e) who believes that he or she has been given incomplete, misleading or false information under this Act; and

(f) in respect of any other matter relating to requesting or obtaining access to records under this Act.

(2) Where the Central Information Commission or State Information

Commission, as the case may be, is satisfied that there are reasonable grounds to inquire into the matter, it may initiate an inquiry in respect thereof.

(3) The Central Information Commission or State Information Commission, as the case may be, shall, while inquiring into any matter under this section, have the same powers as are vested in a civil court while trying a suit under the Code of Civil Procedure, 1908, in respect of the following matters, namely:—

(a) summoning and enforcing the attendance of persons and compel them to give oral or written evidence on oath and to produce the documents or things;
(b) requiring the discovery and inspection of documents;
(c) receiving evidence on affidavit;
(d) requisitioning any public record or copies thereof from any court or office;
(e) issuing summons for examination of witnesses or documents; and
(f) any other matter which may be prescribed.

(4) Notwithstanding anything inconsistent contained in any other Act of Parliament or State Legislature, as the case may be, the Central Information Commission or the State Information Commission, as the case may be, may, during the inquiry of any complaint under this Act, examine any record to which this Act applies which is under the control of the public authority, and no such record may be withheld from it on any grounds.

19 (1) Any person who, does not receive a decision within the time specified in sub-section (1) or clause (a) of sub-section (3) of Section 7, or is aggrieved by a decision of the Central Public Information Officer or State Public Information Officer, as the case may be, may within thirty days from the expiry of such period or from the receipt of such a decision prefer an appeal to such officer who is senior in rank to the Central Public Information Officer or State Public Information Officer as the case may be, in each public authority:

Provided that such officer may admit the appeal after the expiry of the period of thirty days if he or she is satisfied that the appellant was prevented by sufficient cause from filing the appeal in time.

(2) Where an appeal is preferred against an order made by a Central Public Information Officer or a State Public Information Officer, as the case may be, under Section 11 to disclose third party information, the appeal by the concerned third party shall be made within thirty days from the date of the order.

(3) A second appeal against the decision under sub-section (1) shall lie within ninety days from the date on which the decision should have been made or was actually received, with the Central Information Commission or the State Information Commission:

Provided that the Central Information Commission or the State Information Commission, as the case may be, may admit the appeal after the expiry of the period of ninety days if it is satisfied that the appellant was prevented by sufficient cause from filing the appeal in time.

(4) If the decision of the Central Public Information Officer or State Public Information Officer, as the case may be, against which an appeal is preferred relates to information of a third party, the Central Information Commission or State Information Commission, as the case may be, shall give a reasonable opportunity of being heard to that third party.

(5) In any appeal proceedings, the onus to prove that a denial of a request was justified shall be on the Central Public Information Officer or State Public Information Officer, as the case may be, who denied the request.

(6) An appeal under sub-section (1) or sub-section (2) shall be disposed of within thirty days of the receipt of the appeal or within such extended period not exceeding a total of forty-five days from the date of filing thereof, as the case may be, for reasons to be recorded in writing.

(7) The decision of the Central Information Commission or State Information Commission, as the case may be, shall be binding.

(8) In its decision, the Central Information Commission or State Information Commission, as the case may be, has the power to—

(a) require the public authority to take any such steps as may be necessary to secure compliance with the provisions of this Act, including—

(i) by providing access to information, if so requested, in a particular form;

(ii) by appointing a Central Public Information Officer or State Public Information Officer, as the case may be;

(iii) by publishing certain information or categories of information;

(iv) by making necessary changes to its practices in relation to the maintenance, management and destruction of records;

(v) by enhancing the provision of training on the right to information for its officials;

(vi) by providing it with an annual report in compliance with clause (b) of sub-section (1) of Section 4;

(b) require the public authority to compensate the complainant for any loss or other detriment suffered;

(c) impose any of the penalties provided under this Act;

(d) reject the application.

(9) The Central Information Commission or State Information Commission, as the case may be, shall give notice of its decision, including any right of appeal, to the complainant and the public authority.

(10) The Central Information Commission or State Information Commission, as the case may be, shall decide the appeal in accordance with such procedure as may be prescribed.

20 (1) Where the Central Information Commission or the State Information Commission, as the case may be, at the time of deciding any complaint or appeal is of the opinion that the Central Public Information Officer or the State Public Information Officer, as the case may be, has, without any reasonable cause, refused to receive an application for information or has not furnished information within the time specified under sub-section (1) of Section 7 or malafidely denied the request for information or knowingly given incorrect, incomplete or misleading information or destroyed information which was the subject of the request or obstructed in any manner in furnishing the information, it shall impose a penalty of two hundred and fifty rupees each day till application is received or information is furnished, so however, the total amount of such penalty shall not exceed twenty-five thousand rupees:

Provided that the Central Public Information Officer or the State Public Information Officer, as the case may be, shall be given a reasonable opportunity of being heard before any penalty is imposed on him:

Provided further that the burden of proving that he acted reasonably and diligently shall be on the Central Public Information Officer or the State Public Information Officer, as the case may be.

(2) Where the Central Information Commission or the State Information Commission, as the case may be, at the time of deciding any complaint or appeal is of the opinion that the Central Public Information Officer or the State Public Information Officer, as the case may be, has, without any reasonable cause and persistently, failed to receive an application for information or has not furnished information within the time specified under sub-section (1) of Section 7 or malafidely denied the request for information or knowingly given incorrect, incomplete or misleading information or destroyed information which was the subject of the request or obstructed in any manner in furnishing the information, it shall recommend for disciplinary action against the Central Public Information Officer or the State Public Information Officer, as the case may be, under the service rules applicable to him.

CHAPTER VI
MISCELLANEOUS

21 No suit, prosecution or other legal proceeding shall lie against any person for anything which is in good faith done or intended to be done under this Act or any rule made thereunder.

22 The provisions of this Act shall have effect notwithstanding anything inconsistent therewith contained in the Official Secrets Act, 1923, and any other law for the time being in force or in any instrument having effect by virtue of any law other than this Act.

23 No court shall entertain any suit, application or other proceeding in respect of any order made under this Act and no such order shall be called in question otherwise than by way of an appeal under this Act.

24 (1) Nothing contained in this Act shall apply to the intelligence and security organisations specified in the Second Schedule, being organisations established by the Central Government or any information furnished by such organisations to that Government:

Provided that the information pertaining to the allegations of corruption and human rights violations shall not be excluded under this sub-section:

Provided further that in the case of information sought for is in respect of allegations of violation of human rights, the information shall only be provided after the approval of the Central Information Commission, and notwithstanding anything contained in Section 7, such information shall be provided within forty-five days from the date of the receipt of request.

(2) The Central Government may, by notification in the Official Gazette, amend the Schedule by including therein any other intelligence or security organisation established by that Government or omitting therefrom any organisation already specified therein and on the publication of such notification, such organisation shall be deemed to be included in or, as the case may be, omitted from the Schedule.

(3) Every notification issued under sub-section (2) shall be laid before each House of Parliament.

(4) Nothing contained in this Act shall apply to such intelligence and security organisation being organisations established by the State Government, as that Government may, from time to time, by notification in the Official Gazette, specify:

Provided that the information pertaining to the allegations of corruption and human rights violations shall not be excluded under this sub-section:

Provided further that in the case of information sought for is in respect of allegations of violation of human rights, the information shall only be provided after the approval of the State Information Commission and, notwithstanding anything contained in Section 7, such information shall be provided within forty-five days from the date of the receipt of request.

(5) Every notification issued under sub-section (4) shall be laid before the State Legislature.

25 (1) The Central Information Commission or State Information Commission, as the case may be, shall, as soon as practicable after the end of each year, prepare a report on the implementation of the provisions of this Act during that year and forward a copy thereof to the appropriate Government.

(2) Each Ministry or Department shall, in relation to the public authorities within their jurisdiction, collect and provide such information to the Central Information Commission or State Information Commission, as the case may be, as is required to prepare the report under this Section and comply with the requirements concerning the furnishing of that information and keeping of records for the purposes of this section.

(3) Each report shall state in respect of the year to which the report relates,—

(a) the number of requests made to each public authority;

(b) the number of decisions where applicants were not entitled to access to the documents pursuant to the requests, the provisions of this Act under which these decisions were made and the number of times such provisions were invoked;

(c) the number of appeals referred to the Central Information Commission or State Information Commission, as the case may be, for review, the nature of the appeals and the outcome of the appeals;

(d) particulars of any disciplinary action taken against any officer in respect of the administration of this Act;

(e) the amount of charges collected by each public authority under this Act;

(f) any facts which indicate an effort by the public authorities to administer and implement the spirit and intention of this Act;

(g) recommendations for reform, including recommendations in respect of the particular public authorities, for the development, improvement, modernisation, reform or amendment to this Act or other legislation or common law or any other matter relevant for operationalising the right to access information.

(4) The Central Government or the State Government, as the case may be, may, as soon as practicable after the end of each year, cause a copy of the report of the Central Information Commission or the State Information Commission, as the case may be, referred to in sub-section (1) to be laid before each House of Parliament or, as the case may be, before each House of the State Legislature, where there are two Houses, and where there is one House of the State Legislature before that House.

(5) If it appears to the Central Information Commission or State Information Commission, as the case may be, that the practice of a public authority in relation to the exercise of its functions under this Act does not conform with the provisions or spirit of this Act, it may give to the authority a recommendation specifying the steps which ought in its opinion to be taken for promoting such conformity.

26 (1) The appropriate Government may, to the extent of availability of financial and other resources,—

(a) develop and organise educational programmes to advance the understanding of the public, in particular of disadvantaged communities as to how to exercise the rights contemplated under this Act;

(b) encourage public authorities to participate in the development and organisation of programmes referred to in clause (a) and to undertake such programmes themselves;

(c) promote timely and effective dissemination of accurate information by public authorities about their activities; and

(d) train Central Public Information Officers or State Public Information Officers, as the case may be, of public authorities and produce relevant training materials for use by the public authorities themselves.

(2) The appropriate Government shall, within eighteen months from the commencement of this Act, compile in its official language a guide containing such information, in an easily comprehensible form and manner, as may reasonably be required by a person who wishes to exercise any right specified in this Act.

(3) The appropriate Government shall, if necessary, update and publish the guidelines referred to in sub-section (2) at regular intervals which shall, in particular and without prejudice to the generality of sub-section (2), include—

(a) the objects of this Act;

(b) the postal and street address, the phone and fax number and, if available, electronic mail address of the Central Public Information Officer or State Public Information Officer, as the case may be, of every public authority appointed under sub-section (1) of section 5;

(c) the manner and the form in which request for access to an information shall be made to a Central Public Information Officer or State Public Information Officer, as the case may be;

(d) the assistance available from and the duties of the Central Public Information Officer or State Public Information Officer, as the case may be, of a public authority under this Act;

(e) the assistance available from the Central Information Commission or State Information Commission, as the case may be;

(f) all remedies in law available regarding an act or failure to act in respect of a right or duty conferred or imposed by this Act including the manner of filing an appeal to the Commission;

(g) the provisions providing for the voluntary disclosure of categories of records in accordance with Section 4;

(h) the notices regarding fees to be paid in relation to requests for access to an information; and

(i) any additional regulations or circulars made or issued in relation to obtaining access to an information in accordance with this Act.

(4) The appropriate Government must, if necessary, update and publish the guidelines at regular intervals.

27 (1) The appropriate Government may, by notification in the Official Gazette, make rules to carry out the provisions of this Act.

(2) In particular, and without prejudice to the generality of the foregoing power, such rules may provide for all or any of the following matters, namely:—

(a) the cost of the medium or print cost price of the materials to be disseminated under sub-section (4) of Section 4;

(b) the fee payable under sub-section (1) of Section 6;

(c) the fee payable under sub-sections (1) and (5) of Section 7;

(d) the salaries and allowances payable to and the terms and conditions of service of the officers and other employees under sub-section (6) of Section 13 and sub-section (6) of Section 16;

(e) the procedure to be adopted by the Central Information Commission or State Information Commission, as the case may be, in deciding the appeals under sub-section (10) of Section 19; and

(f) any other matter which is required to be, or may be, prescribed.

28 (1) The competent authority may, by notification in the Official Gazette, make rules to carry out the provisions of this Act.

(2) In particular, and without prejudice to the generality of the foregoing power, such rules may provide for all or any of the following matters, namely:—

(i) the cost of the medium or print cost price of the materials to be disseminated under sub-section (4) of Section 4;

(ii) the fee payable under sub-section (1) of Section 6;

(iii) the fee payable under sub-section (1) of Section 7; and

(iv) any other matter which is required to be, or may be, prescribed.

29 (1) Every rule made by the Central Government under this Act shall be laid, as soon as may be after it is made, before each House of Parliament, while it is in session, for a total period of thirty days which may be comprised in one session or in two or more successive sessions, and if, before the expiry of the session immediately following the session or the successive sessions aforesaid, both Houses agree in making any modification in the rule or both Houses agree that the rule should not be made, the rule shall thereafter have effect only in such modified form or be of no effect, as the case may be; so, however, that any such modification or annulment shall be without prejudice to the validity of anything previously done under that rule.

(2) Every rule made under this Act by a State Government shall be laid, as soon as may be after it is notified, before the State Legislature.

30 (1) If any difficulty arises in giving effect to the provisions of this Act, the Central Government may, by order published in the Official Gazette, make such provisions not inconsistent with the provisions of this Act as appear to it to be necessary or expedient for removal of the difficulty:

Provided that no such order shall be made after the expiry of a period of two years from the date of the commencement of this Act.

(2) Every order made under this Section shall, as soon as may be after it is made, be laid before each House of Parliament.

31 The Freedom of Information Act, 2002 is hereby repealed.

THE FIRST SCHEDULE
[*See* sections 13(*3*) and 16(*3*)]

Form of oath or affirmation to be made by the Chief Information Commissioner/ the Information Commissioner/the State Chief Information Commissioner/the State Information Commissioner

"I, ..., having been appointed Chief Information Commissioner/ Information Commissioner/State Chief Information Commissioner/State Information Commissioner swear in the name of God solemnly affirm that I will bear true faith and allegiance to the Constitution of India as by law established, that I will uphold the sovereignty and integrity of India, that I will duly and faithfully and to the best of my ability, knowledge and judgment perform the duties of my office without fear or favour, affection or ill-will and that I will uphold the Constitution and the laws."

THE SECOND SCHEDULE
(*See* Section 24)

Intelligence and security organisation established by the Central Government

1. **Intelligence Bureau.**
2. **Research and Analysis Wing of the Cabinet Secretariat.**
3. **Directorate of Revenue Intelligence.**
4. **Central Economic Intelligence Bureau.**
5. **Directorate of Enforcement.**
6. **Narcotics Control Bureau.**
7. **Aviation Research Centre.**
8. **Special Frontier Force.**
9. **Border Security Force.**
10. **Central Reserve Police Force.**
11. **Indo-Tibetan Border Police.**
12. **Central Industrial Security Force.**
13. **National Security Guards.**
14. **Assam Rifles.**
15. **Special Service Bureau.**
16. **Special Branch (CID), Andaman and Nicobar.**
17. **The Crime Branch-C.I.D.- CB, Dadra and Nagar Haveli.**
18. **Special Branch, Lakshadweep Police.**

LOK SABHA

A BILL to amend the Right to Information Act, 2005.
(Shri V. Narayanasamy, Minister of State in the Ministry of Personnel, Public Grievances and Pensions)

As Introduced in Lok Sabha
Bill No. 112 of 2013

THE RIGHT TO INFORMATION (AMENDMENT) BILL, 2013

A BILL *to amend the Right to Information Act,* 2005. BE it enacted by Parliament in the Sixty-fourth Year of the Republic of India as follows:

1. Short title and commencement—
   (1) This Act may be called the Right to Information (Amendment) Act, 2013.
   (2) It shall be deemed to have come into force on the 3rd day of June, 2013.
2. Amendment of Section 2—
   In Section 2 of the Right to Information Act, 2005 (hereinafter referred to as the principal Act), in clause (*h*), the following *Explanation* shall be inserted, namely:–
   '*Explanation.*—The expression "authority or body or institution of self-government established or constituted" by any law made by Parliament shall not include any association or body of individuals registered or recognised as political party under the Representation of the People Act, 1951.'.
3. Insertion of new Section 32—After Section 31 of the principal Act, the following Section shall be inserted, namely:—
   "32. Notwithstanding anything contained in any judgment, decree or order of any court or commission, the provisions of this Act, as amended by the Right to Information (Amendment) Act, 2013, shall have effect and shall be deemed always to have effect, in the case of any association or body of individuals registered or recognised as political party under the Representation of the People Act, 1951 or any other law for the time being in force and the rules made or notifications issued thereunder.".

Statement of Objects and Reasons

The Right to Information Act, 2005 was enacted by the Government for setting out a framework for effectuating the right to information for citizens and to secure access to information under the control of public authorities, in order to promote transparency and accountability in the working of every public authority.

2. The Central Information Commission in one of its decision dated 03.06.2013 has held that the political parties namely AICC/INC, BJP, CPI (M), CPI, NCP and BSP are public authorities under Section 2(*h*) of the said Act. The Government considers that the CIC has made a liberal interpretation of Section 2(*h*) of the said Act in its decision. The political parties are neither established nor constituted by or under the Constitution or by any other law made by Parliament. Rather, they are registered or recognised under the Representation of the People Act, 1951 and the rules/orders made or issued thereunder.

3. It has also been observed that there are already provisions in the Representation of the People Act, 1951 as well as in the Income-tax Act, 1961 which deals with the transparency in the financial aspects of political parties and their candidates.

4. Declaring a political party as public authority under the RTI Act would hamper its smooth internal working, which is not the objective of the said Act and was not envisaged by Parliament under the RTI Act. Further, the political rivals may misuse the provisions of RTI Act, thereby adversely affecting the functioning of the political parties.

5. In view of above, the Government has decided to amend the RTI Act to keep the political parties out of the purview of the RTI Act, with a view to remove the adverse effects of the said decision of the CIC. It is also necessary to give retrospective effect to the proposed amendment with effect from the date of the said decision of CIC, that is, 3rd day of June, 2013.

6. The Bill seeks to achieve the above objects.

V. NARAYANASAMY

NEW DELHI;
The 5th August, 2013.

ANNEXURE

Extract from the Right to Information Act, 2005
(22 of 2005)

* * * * *

2. *Definition:* In this Act, unless the context otherwise requires, —

* * * * *

(*h*) "public authority" means any authority or body or institution or self-government established or constituted—

(a) by or under the Constitution;

(b) by any other law made by Parliament;

(c) by any other law made by State Legislature;

(d) by notification issued or order made by the appropriate Government, and includes any—

(*i*) body owned, controlled or substantially financed;

(*ii*) non-Government organisation substantially financed, directly or indirectly by funds provided by the appropriate Government;

* * * * *

Annexure – III

Central Information Commission

AUGUST KRANTI BHAWAN, BHIKAJI CAMA PLACE, NEW DELHI-110066

FILE NO. CIC/SM/C/2011/001386
FILE NO. CIC/SM/C/2011/000838

Complainants

1. Shri Subhash Chandra Agrawal
2. Shri Anil Bairwal

Respondents

1. Indian National Congress/All India Congress Committee (AICC);
2. Bhartiya Janata Party (BJP);
3. Communist Party of India (Marxist) (CPM);
4. Communist Party of India (CPI);
5. Nationalist Congress Party (NCP); and
6. Bahujan Samaj Party (BSP)

Dates of hearing: 26th September & 1st November, 2012.
Date of Decision: 3rd June 2013.

Facts

Complainant Subhash Chandra Agrawal (Shri S.C.Agrawal) has filed Complaint No. CIC/SM/C/2011/001386 and Complainant Shri Anil Bairwal, Complaint No. CIC/SM/C/2011/000838. In both the complaints, the common issue relating to the disclosure of the accounts and funding of Political Parties has been raised. Hence, it has been decided to dispose of these matters through a common order.

File No. CIC/SM/C/001386

2. By his RTI application dated 16.5.2011, complainant S.C. Agrawal has sought the following information from the Presidents/Secretaries of the Indian National Congress (INC/AICC) and the Bhartiya Janata Party (BJP):

"1. Copies of Election Menifestoes by BJP for Lok Sabha elections in the years it formed NDA govenment with Shri Atal Bihari Vajpayee as Prime Minister.
2. Were all the promises made in these election manifestoes fulfilled after BJP having formed government at the Centre.
3. If not, list of promises highlighted in BJP election manifestoes but remained unfulfilled after BJP came to power.
4. Outline of receipts (separately by cash/online/cheque etc.) by BJP in last two years separately for each year for which updated account information may be there.
5. Outline of payments (separately by cash/online/cheque etc.) made by BJP in last three years separately for each year for which updated account information may be there.
6. Is it compulsory for every BJP legislature either at Centre or in States or in civic bodies etc. to contribute towards party funds?
7. If yes, please provide complete and detailed information including also defaulters in making such contributions to party fund in last three years.
8. Is BJP aware of any of its legislatures (both at Centre and in States)/civic body member etc. involved in corrupt and other malpractices in last three years?
9. If yes, please provide complete details including action taken by party and others against such persons.
10. Has B.J.P. suggested any proposals to Union Government/Election Commission towards electoral reforms?
11. If yes, please provide complete details including reply received from concerned ones if any.
12. Any other related information.
13. File notings on movement of this RTI petition and on all aspects mentioned in this RTI petition."

3. Shri Moti Lal Vora, Treasurer, AICC, in his letter dated 20th May, 2011, had informed the complainant that AICC did not come under the purview of the RTI Act.

4. Shri Shanti Prasad Aggarwal, Rashtriya Prabhari of BJP, in his letter dated 28th May, 2011, had informed the complainant that BJP was not a public authority and, therefore, the Party was not obliged to provide the requisite information.

5. Complainant Anil Bairwal, in his RTI application dated 29.10.2010 had sought the following information from the undermentioned Political Parties:

- INC/AICC
- BJP
- NCP
- CPI(M)
- CPI
- BSP

"1. (a) Sources of the 10 maximum voluntary contributions received by your party from Financial Year 2004-05 to Financial Year 2009-10?

(b) The modes of these donations (Cheque, cash, DD etc.)?

(c) The amounts of these donations?

(d) The Financial Years in which these contributions were made?

You may provide this information in the following format:

S. No.	*Source/Name of Contributor*	*Mode of Contribution*	*Amount of Contribution*	*Financial year in which contribution was made*
1				
2				
3				
4				
5				

2. Sources/Names of all Voluntary Contributors along with their addresses who have made single contributions of more than Rs. 1 lakh to your party from Financial Year 2004-05 to Financial Year 2009-10?

You may provide this information in the following format:

S.No	*Source/Name of Contributor*	*Address of Contributor*
1		
2		
3		
4		

6. By his letter dated 15th November, 2010, Shri Moti Lal Vora, Treasurer, AICC, had informed the complainant that AICC did not come under the purview of the RTI Act.

7. Shri Chandan Bose, PRO, Nationalist Congress Party, in his letter dated 27th November, 2010, had informed the complainant as under:

"It is very important to mention here that NCP is a non-government organization. Hence, we do not have much more resources nor surplus staff to expedite unusual work, which is not in our routine job.

We generate funds from the membership drive and through other resources also, i.e. voluntary contributions from the well-wishers, and followers etc. State units of NCP have major role in membership drive from which we are getting funds in lakhs. State units of NCP at district level, block level and panchayat level organize membership camps frequently and every two years, we file the details regarding our membership and all necessary requisites in Election Commission and other government authorities.

However, I would like to inform you that ours is a National Party duly recognized by Election Commission of India and that from the day of

inception of our Party, we have been regularly filing our returns to the Income Tax authorities and also to the Election Commission of India along with whatever voluntary contributions received. It is pertinent to mention here that our all obligation towards authorities are up to date. If you feel like, you may collect all the information you desired, from the above said authorities.

In case you want any clarification, please feel free to contact us."

8. Shri K.C. Bansal of CPI, in his letter dated 6th November, 2010, had informed the complainant of the sources of ten maximum voluntary contributions received by the Party for the financial years 2004-05 to 2009-10.

9. Importantly, other Political Parties chose not to respond to the RTI application.

10. Shri Subhash Chandra Agrawal had filed a complaint dated 6th September, 2011, before this Commission in which he had mentioned that All India Congress Committee and Bhartiya Janata Party, being national parties, had got premium land in Delhi/New Delhi at zonal **variant institutional rate which was much less than** the prevailing market rate and, therefore, it was not correct on their part to plead that they did not fall under the purview of the RTI Act. It was his contention that both AICC/INC and BJP fell under the ambit of Section 2(h) of the RTI Act.

11. Likewise, Shri Anil Bairwal had filed a complaint dated the 14th March, 2011, before the Commission against the responses received from INC/AICC, NCP & CPI, contending therein that the Political Parties, being beneficiaries of the Government, fell under the ambit of Section 2(h) of the RTI Act and, therefore, they were mandated to disclose full and complete information to him.

12. As the matters in hand raised complex issues of law, the Chief Information Commissioner in his Order dated 31st July, 2012 had constituted a Full Bench comprising of the following:

- Shri Satyananda Mishra, Chief Information Commissioner;
- Smt. Annapurna Dixit, Information Commissioner; and
- Shri M.L. Sharma, Information Commissioner

13. The Full Bench held the first hearing **on 26th September, 2012**. The following were present:

Complainants

1. Shri S.C. Agrawal, along with Shri Prashant Bhushan and Pranav Sachdeva.
2. Shri Anil Bairwal, along with Shri Jagdeep S. Chhokar, Shri Trilochan Sastry, Ms. Shivani Kapoor, Shri Manoj Kumar & A.K. Aneja.

Respondents

1. Shri Chandan Bose, PRO, NCP.

2. Shri D. Raja, CPI

Election Commission

1. Shri K.F. Wilfred, Principal Secretary, Election Commission.

14. The Full Bench held its second hearing on 1st November, 2012. The following were present:

Complainants

1. Shri S.C. Agrawal.
2. Shri Anil Bairwal, along with Shri Jagdeep S. Chhokar, Ms. Shivani Kapoor, Shri Manoj Kumar and Shri A.K. Aneja.

Respondents

1. Advocate Shubhashis R. Soren for BJP.
2. Shri S. Ramachandran Pillai of CPI(M).
3. Advocates Shail Kumar Dwivedi & G.V. Rao for BSP.
4. Shri Chandan Bose, PRO, NCP and Advocate Amit Anand Tiwari for NCP.

15. Shri S.C. Agrawal has filed a written representation before the Commission in which he has vehemently pleaded for declaring Political Parties as public authorities under Section 2(h) of the RTI Act. The salient points made in his representation are enumerated hereinbelow :

(i) The Political Parties hold constitutional status and wield constitutional powers under the Tenth Schedule of the Constitution in as much as they have the power to —
   "(a) disqualify legislators from Parliament and State Assemblies;
   (b) bind legislators in their speeches and voting inside the house;
   (c) decide what laws are made;
   (d) decide whether Government remains in power or which Government should come to power;
   (e) decide public policies that affect lives of millions of people."

(ii) As per Article 102 (2) of the Constitution, a person can be disqualified from being a member of either House of Parliament under the Tenth Schedule and that a similar provision exists for the State Legislators under Article 191(2) of the Constitution. Furthermore, as per Article 102(2), if a member of a House belonging to a Political Party votes or abstains from voting in the House contrary to the directions issued by the Political Party, he is liable to be disqualified from being a Member of the House.

(iii) The Political Parties have been given statutory status under Section 29A of the Representation of the People Act, 1951.

(iv) Under Section 29A (5) of the Representation of People Act, 1951, the Political Parties are required to bear true faith and allegiance to the Constitution of India as by law established.

(v) The Political Parties give tickets to the candidates and the people vote on party symbols and, thus, the Political Parties are important instrumentalities of democratic governance.

(vi) The Political Parties are substantially financed by the 'appropriate Government' in multiple ways and are exempt from Income Tax.

16. To canvass his case, Shri Agrawal has furnished a copy of letter dated 2.9.2011 of the CPIO of the Land and Development Office (L&DO), Ministry of Urban Development, addressed to him providing information regarding allotment of land by Land and Development Office to various Political Parties. The details of the land allotment to various Political Parties as furnished by the L&DO are extracted below:

"LIST OF POLITICAL PARTIES WHICH HAVE BEEN ALLOTTED LAND BY LAND & DEVELOPMENT OFFICE FOR THEIR OFFICE BUILDINGS

S. No.	*Name of Party*	*Location, Area & Date of allotment*
1.	All India Congress Committee of Indian National Congress	Plot at Dr. Rajinder Prasad Road, New Delhi (also known as Jawahar Bhawan), Area = 9518.42 sq. yds. allotted on 8.9.75. Pocket-9A, Kotla Road, Area = 8092 sq. m. Allotted on 19.11.2007
2.	Rashtriya Janata Dal	Plot Nos. 34, 57, 58 & 59 at Kotla Road, New Delhi Area = 1904 sq. m. allotted on 3.7.2007.
3.	Communist Party of India (Marxist)	Plot Nos. 27, 28 & 29 at Market Road Institutional Area, New Delhi Area = 1197 sq. m. allotted on 24.11.1967 Plot Nos. 10, 11, 12 & 13 at Kotla Road Area = 2535 sq. m. allotted on 11.12.2008.
4.	Samajwadi Party	Plot No. 1, Vasant Kunj Institutional Area, New Delhi Area = 1 acre, Allotted on 21.1.2009.
5.	Communist Party of India	Plot No. 15, Kotla Marg, New Delhi Area = 0.3 acres. Allotted on 2.12.1967
6.	Bharatiya Janata Party (National Level)	Between Dr. Rajendra Prasad Road and Raisina Road,New Delhi. Area = 1.87 acres. Allotted on 8.3.2001.
7.	Janata Dal (United)	Plot No.4, Vasant Vihar Institutional Area, New Delhi Area = 2000 sq. m. allotted on 27.4.2010
8.	Bharatiya Janata Party (Delhi State)	Alternative allotment at Plot No.4 & 5, Kotla Road, New Delhi Area = 1060.80 sq. m. allotted on 12.5.2010
9.	All India Anna Dravida Munnetra Kazhakham	Plot No. 13 & 25, Pushp Vihar, M.B. Road, Saket, New Delhi, Area = 1008 Sq. m. Allotted on 30.7.2010
10.	Delhi Pradesh Congress Committee	Plot No. 2, Rouse Avenue Institutional Area Area = 1127 sq. yds. Allotted on 15.5.1987
11.	All India Trinamool Congress	Plot Nos. 2 and 3, at DDU Marg, New Delhi Area = 1000 sq. m. allotted on 01.03.2011.

17. In addition to the above, Shri Agrawal has also furnished information regarding the allotment of accommodation to various Political Parties on rental basis and the

outstanding dues against them, as received by him from the Directorate of Estates vide their letter dated 24.8.2011. The relevant information is extracted below:

S. No.	*Name of the Party*	*Accommodation*	*Monthly rent charged*
1.	Indian National Congress Committee (I)	26, Akbar Road	3015 + Furniture charges
2.	Indian National Congress	24, Akbar Road	42817 + Furniture charges
3.	Indian National Congress	5, Raisina Road	34189 + Furniture charges
4.	Indian National Congress	CII/109, Chanakyapuri	8078
5.	Bharatiya Janata Party	11, Ashoka Road	66896 + Furniture charges
6.	Bharatiya Janata Party	14, Pandit Pant Marg	15077 + Furniture charges
7.	C.P.I.	AB-4, Purana Quila Road	1550
8.	Nationalist Congress Party	10, Dr. B.D. Marg	1320
9.	President Bahujan Samaj Party	4, G.R.G. Road	1320
10.	Samajwadi Party	18, Copernicus Road	12138
11.	Shri Prakash Karat, General Secretary, CPI(M)	8, Teen Murti Lane	1550

18. Shri Anil Bairwal has also filed a detailed representation before this Commission to contend that Political Parties fall in the ambit of Section 2(h) of the RTI Act. In his representation, Shri Bairwal has made the following salient points :

(i) All the Political Parties have been claiming tax exemption under Section 13A of the Income Tax Act. As per his representation, various Political Parties claimed Income Tax exemption as given in the following Table:

Party	*Tax Payable exempted in FY 2006-07 (Rs. crores)*	*Tax payable exempted in FY 2007-08 (Rs. crores)*	*Tax payable exempted in FY 2008-09 (Rs. crores)*	*Tax payable exempted in 3 years (Rs. crores)*
BJP	26.86	40.68	73.71	141.25
INC	57.00	75.05	168.87	300.92
BSP	15.44	23.60	0.80	39.84
CPI(M)	6.98	4.62	6.53	18.13
CPI	0.01	0.21	0.02	0.24
NCP	0.90	0.68	8.06	9.64

Source : Compilation from copies of Income Tax Returns received from Income Tax Department under RTI Act.

(ii) State has been indirectly financing various Political Parties by way of free air time on All India Radio. As per his calculation, the amount spent by the State on the Political Parties under this Head is as follows:

S. No.	Name of the party	Time allotted for broadcast at the AIR during LS'09 (Min) for Political Parties	Rate charged by AIR in time category-3 for every 10 seconds	Amount spent by the State for AIR (Rs. lakhs)
1.	BJP	140	800	6.72
2.	BSP	70	800	3.36
3.	CPI	50	800	2.40
4.	CPI(M)	70	800	3.36
5.	INC	160	800	7.68
6.	NCP	50	800	2.40
7.	RJD	55	800	2.64
	Total	595	800	28.56

Source: Compilation from Spot Buy Rates and Time Allocated to various Political Parties received from All India Radio and Election Commission of India under various RTI applications.

(iii) The complainant has also argued that the State has spent huge amounts on the Political Parties in the matter of free air time on Doordarshan. The table given by him is reproduced below:

S. No.	Name of the Party	Time allotted for telecast at the national network of DD during Lok Sabha'09 (Min)	Rate charged by national network of DD at non prime time every 10 seconds	Amount spent by the state for the national network during LS'09 (Rs. Crores)	Time allotted for telecast at the regional network during LS'09 (Min.)	Rate Charged by regional network at non prime time every 10 seconds	Amount spent by State for the regional network during LS'09 (Rs. crores)	Total Amount spent by the state on political parties for both the national and regional network during LS'09 (Rs.crores)
1	BJP	140	15,000	**1.26**	215	10,000	**1.25**	**2.51**
2	INC	160	15,000	**1.44**	240	10,000	**1.44**	**2.88**
3	BSP	70	15,000	**0.63**	100	10,000	**0.60**	**1.23**
4	CPI	50	15,000	**0.45**	75	10,000	**0.45**	**0.90**
5	CPI(M)	70	15,000	**0.63**	105	10,000	**0.63**	**1.26**
6	NCP	50	15,000	**0.45**	80	10,000	**0.48**	**0.93**
7	RJD	55	15,000	**0.49**	85	10,000	**0.51**	**1.00**
	Total	**595**		**5.35**	**900**		**5.40**	**10.75**

Source: Compilation from Spot Buy Rates and Time Allocated to various Political Parties received from Doordarshan and Election Commission of India under the RTI Act).

(iv) The valuation of the properties allotted by the Government, as estimated by the complainant Shri Bairwal, as given in his representation, is as follows:

Party	Office and address (with allotment dates)	Area (A)	Area in Sq.Fts. (1 sq.m.=10.76 Sq. fts, 1 sq. yd.= 9 sq.fts., 1 Acre= 4840 sq.yds.) (B)	Current Market Value of the Allotteed Plots Land (based on Real Estate Consulting Reports @ Rs. 60,000 per sq. ft (Rs.in Crores) (C=B*60,000)	Current Market Value of these of allotted plots (Party-wise) (Rs. In crores)
INC	1. Plot at Dr. Rajinder Prasad Road, New Delhi (Allotted on 08.09.1975)	9518.42 sq yds.	85665.78	513.99	1036.41
	2. Pocket 9A, Kotla Road, New Delhi (allotted on 19.11.2007	8092 sq. m	87069.92	522.42	
BJP	1. Between Dr. Rajendra Prasad Road and Raisiua Road (allotted on 08.03.2001)	1.87 acres	81457.20	488.74	557.23
	2. Plot No. 4 & 5 Kotla Road New Delhi (allotted on 12.05.2010)	1060.80 sq.m	11414.21	68.49	
CPI(M)	Plots No. 27, 28 & 29 at Market Road Institutional Area, New Delhi (allotted on 11.04.1967)	1197 sq.m.	12879.72	77.28	240.94
	Plot No. 10, 11, 12 & 13 Kotla Road, New Delhi (allotted on 11.12.2008)	2535 sq.m.	27276.60	163.66	
CPI	Plot No. 15 Kotla Marg, New Delhi (allotted on 2.12.1967)	.3 acres	13068.00	78.41	78.41
RJD	Plots No. 34,57,58 & 59 at Kotla Road, New Delhi (allotted on 03.07.2007)	1904 sq.m.	20487.04	122.92	122.92
SP	Plot No. 1, Vasant Kunj Institutional Area, New Delhi (Allotted on 21.01.2009)	1 Acre	43560.00	261.36	261.36
JD	Plot No. 4, Vasant Vihar Institutional Area, New Delhi (allotted on 24.10.2010)	2000 sq.m.	21520.00	129.12	129.12
AIADMK	Plot Nos. 2 and 3 at DDU Marg New Delhi (Allotted on 01.03.2011)	1008 sq.m.	846.08	65.08	65.08
AITC	Plot Nos. 2 and 3 at DDU Marg, New Delhi (Allotted on 01.03.2011)	1000 sq. m	10760.00	64.56	64.56
Total of current Market Values of the plots of land allotted to the Political Parties (Rs. In Crores)				2556.02	2556.02

(v) Under Rules 11 and 12 of the Registration of Electors Rules, 1960, two copies of the Electoral Rolls are supplied to the recognized Political Parties, free of cost. This is another instance of indirect financing of the Political Parties by the State.

(vi) The Central Government and the State Governments have allotted various houses/buildings/other types of accommodation to various Political Parties either free of cost or at concessional rates. This also amounts to indirect financing of Political Parties by the respective Governments.

(vii) The Political Parties are continuously engaged in the performance of public duty and it is, therefore, important that they become accountable to the public. Transparency in the working and financial operations of the Political Parties is essential in the larger public interest.

19. Senior Advocate, Shri Prashant Bhushan addressed the Commission on 26th September, 2012 on behalf of complainant Shri S.C. Agrawal. He vehemently contended that the entire political system in India revolved around the Political Parties. They perform a public function and, therefore, warrant to be declared 'public authority' under Section 2(h) of the RTI Act. In amplification of his above broad submission, he has advanced the following arguments:

(i) Tenth Schedule to the Constitution vests tremendous powers with the Political Parties in as much as they can oust an elected member – whether MP or MLA — from out of the Party if he steps out of the party line. The vast power of the Political Parties has been recognised in this Schedule and, therefore, if purposive interpretation of the Tenth Schedule is made, then the Political Parties can be deemed to be covered under Section 2(h) of the RTI Act.

(ii) As per Section 29C of the Representation of People Act, 1951, all donations of and above Rs. 20,000/- made to Political Parties are required to be reported to the Income Tax Department. This obligation cast on the Political Parties points towards their public character.

(iii) By virtue of powers conferred on it under Article 324 of the Constitution read with Section 29A of the Representation of People Act, 1951, and Rules 5 and 10 of the Conduct of Election Rules, 1961, and other powers vested in it, the Election Commission of India made and promulgated the Election Symbols (Reservation and Allotment) Order, 1968. Under this Order, Election Commission allots symbols to various Political Parties. The Election Commission is an instrumentality of the State. Allotment of election symbols by the Election Commission to various Political Parties is suggestive of the public character of the Political Parties.

(iv) The Political Parties get huge tax exemptions under Section 13 A of the Income Tax Act, 1961, which amounts to indirect financing of the Political Parties in terms of Section 2(h)(d)(i) of the RTI Act.

(v) The Central Government and the State Governments have allotted huge plots of land/buildings/other accommodation in prime locations to all Political

Parties all-over the country either, free of cost, or on hugely concessional rates. This also amounts to indirect financing of the Political Parties.

(vi) Doordarshan of India allots free air time to the Political Parties during the elections. This is another instance of indirect financing of the Political Parties.

(vii) As the Political Parties are the life blood of the entire constitutional scheme in a democratic polity and as they are indirectly financed by the Central Government and the State Governments in various ways, as discussed hereinabove, the Political Parties need to be declared public authority under Section 2(h) of the RTI Act.

20. Shri A.K. Aneja, appearing on behalf of the complainants, in his brief submission has drawn the Commission's attention to Section 80 GGB of the Income Tax Act which provides that contribution made by an individual or Company to a Political Party is deductible from the total income of the assesee. This provision is exclusively applicable to the Political Parties and is suggestive of indirect financing of the Political Parties by the State.

21. Complainant Shri Anil Bairwal has also filed detailed extra submissions before the Commission arguing that the Political Parties need to be declared Public Authority under Section 2(h) of the RTI Act. His first and foremost submission is that Political Parties have a 'binding nexus with the populace'. He goes on to say that "As the Central Institution of democracy, they embody the will of the people and carry all their expectations that democracy will be truly responsive to their needs and help solve the most pressing problems that confront them in the daily lives".

22. His second submission is that there is need for accountability and transparency in the functioning of the Political Parties. It is his contention that transparency in the functioning of Political Parties was recommended by the Law Commission of India in their 170th Report on "Reform of Electoral Laws (1999)". The relevant para of the Law Commission's report as extracted by him is given below :

> **"On the parity of the above reasoning,** ***it must be said that if democracy and accountability constitute the core of our constitutional system, the same concepts must also apply to and bind the Political Parties which are integral to parliamentary democracy.*** **It is the Political Parties that form the Government, man the Parliament and run the governance of the country.** ***It is therefore, necessary to introduce internal democracy, financial transparency and accountability in the working of the Political Parties. A political party which does not respect democratic principles in its internal working cannot be expected to respect those principles in the governance of the country. It cannot be dictatorship internally and democratic in its functioning outside".*****(emphasis added by the complainant)**

23. Shri Bairwal has also relied on this Commissions decision dated 29.04.2008 in File No. CIC/AT/A/2007/01029 & 01263-01270 wherein transparency in the functioning of Political Parties has been underlined. He particularly draws our attention to para 28 of the decision extracted below :

"28. Political Parties are a unique institution of the modern constitutional State. These are essentially civil society institutions and are, therefore, non-governmental. Their uniqueness lies in the fact that in spite of being non-governmental, Political Parties come to wield or directly or indirectly influence, exercise of governmental power. It is this link between State power and Political Parties that has assumed critical significance in the context of the Right of Information—an Act which has brought into focus the imperatives of transparency in the functioning of State institutions. ***It would be facetious to argue that transparency is good for all State organs, but not so good for the Political Parties which control the most important of those organs.*** **For example, it will be a fallacy to hold that transparency is good for the bureaucracy but not good enough for the Political Parties which control those bureaucracies through political executives".**

24. The Commission has further observed :

"38. The laws of the land do not make it mandatory for Political Parties to disclose the sources of their funding, and even less so the manner of expending those funds. In the absence of such laws, the only way a citizen can gain access to the details of funding of Political Parties is through their Income Tax Returns filed annually with Income Tax authorities. This is about the closest the Political Parties get to accounting for the sources and the extent of their funding and their expenditure. There is unmistakable public interest in knowing these funding details which would enable the citizen to make an informed choice about the Political Parties to vote for. The RTI Act emphasizes that "democracy requires an informed citizenry", and that transparency of information is vital to flawless functioning of constitutional democracy. It is nobody's case that while all organs of the State must exhibit maximum transparency, no such obligation attaches to Political Parties. ***Given that Political Parties influence the exercise of political power, transparency in their organization, functions and, more particularly, their means of funding is a democratic imperative, and, therefore, is in public interest*"****.**

25. Another strand of his submissions is that the Public Authority, as defined under Section 2(h) of the RTI Act, is a broader term than the 'State' as defined under Article 12 of the Constitution. In other words, it is possible that an entity may fall short of being 'State' and yet may be a 'Public Authority' under the RTI Act. In fact, 'Public Authority' and the 'State' are different and distinct from each other. Shri Bairwal has relied on para 25 of the judgment of Punjab and Haryana High Court in WP(C) No. 19224/2006 along with 23 other cases as extracted below:

"25. Above-all, the deep and pervasive control as required under Article 12, is not required and essential ingredient for invoking the

provisions of RTI Act. The primary purpose of instrumentality of the State is in relation to enforcement of the fundamental rights through Courts, *whereas the RTI Act is intended to achieve, access to information and to provide an effective framework for effecting the right to information recognized under Article 19 of the Constitution.* The complainants are not claiming any kind of monetary benefits or property from the empire of the petitioner-institutions. To my mind, the enforcement of fundamental rights through Courts and the question of applicability of writ jurisdiction on an instrumentality of the State for the purpose of determination of substantive rights and liabilities of the parties are *altogether (entirely) different than that of the field of RTI Act, only meant to impart the information.* Hence, in my view, the ambit and scope of phrase of instrumentality of the State under Article 12 of the Constitution is entirely different and distinct than that of the regime of RTI Act. *If the intention of the Legislature was to so restrict the meaning to the expression of public authority, straightjacketing the same within the four corners of the State, as defined under Article 12, then there was no need/occasion to assign a specific broader definition of public authority under Section 2(h) of RTI Act in this relevant connection*".

26. The complainant has also argued that while determining whether a particular entity is a Public Authority or not, narrow interpretation of the words used in the statute would frustrate the object of the Act. The purpose of this Act is transparency and accountability in the functioning of entities which impact citizens' daily lives. The Political Parties are such entities. He has relied on para 41 of the Delhi High Court judgment delivered by Justice Ravindra Bhat in Indian Olympic Association Vs. Veerish Malik and others(WP)(C) No. 876/2007 as extracted below:

"The Act marks a legislative milestone in the post-independence era to further democracy. It empowers citizens and information applicants to demand and be supplied with information about public records. *Parliamentary endeavour is to extend it also to public authorities which impact citizens daily lives.* The Act mandates disclosure of all manner of information and abolishes the concept of locus standi of the information applicant; no justification for applying (for information) is necessary; decisions and decision making processes, which affect lives of individuals and groups of citizens are now open to examination. *Parliamentary intention apparently was to empower people with the means to scrutinize government and public processes, and ensure transparency.* At the same time, the need of society at large, and Governments as well as individuals in particular, to ensure that sensitive information is kept out of bounds have also been accommodated under the Act."

27. Yet another submission of the complainant is that the Political Parties are

being indirectly financed by the State in various ways viz. allotment of land, free of cost, or at nominal rates and exemptions from the Income Tax etc. Paras 3.1 to 3.7 of his representation are extracted below:

"3.1 All Political Parties claim to work for the people and in the national interest. Income tax returns of Political Parties obtained by ADR using the RTI Act reveal that on an average only about 20 per cent of the income of Political Parties comes from donations that they disclose to the Election Commission under Section 29C of the Representation of People Act. The sources of the remaining 80 per cent of the income are shrouded in mystery. This is what gives rise to all kinds of speculation about the pernicious influence of illegal money.

3.2 After various RTI applications filed to the central agencies, it was discovered that Political Parties enjoy a number of "facilities" provided to them by the government. This is a clear instance of being "financed indirectly by funds provided by the appropriate government" which puts Political Parties squarely under the definition of 'public authority' as provided for in Section 2(h)(d)(ii) of the RTI Act.

3.3 In addition to the 100% exemption on income under Section 13A of the Income Tax Act, all the major Political Parties have been provided "facilities" for residential and official use by Directorate of Estates (DOE), Government of India, in New Delhi. They have been given offices and residential accommodations at prime locations in New Delhi (Lutyen's Delhi) such as Akbar Road, Raisina Road, Chanakyapuri. The rentals charged are a fraction of the market rent. These facilities are not just provided to them at nominal rates but their maintenance, upgradation, modernization, renovation, etc. are also done at State expense. *Similar "facilities" are also provided at various State capitals, details of which are extremely difficult to obtain.*

3.4 Money is also spent by Election Commission of India on Political Parties for providing "facilities" to Political Parties such as free electoral rolls, Doordarshan and All India Radio also provide free broadcast facilities to the Political Parties at election time which results in loss of revenue in terms of *air time which has a market value.*

3.5 If closely monitored and totalled, the total of public funds spent on Political Parties would possibly amount to hundreds of crores.

3.6 There have been several Judicial pronouncements and also decisions by the Central Information Commission that have held that allotment of real estate, rental on subsidized rated, exemption from tax of various types including income tax amount to "indirect financing" in terms of Section 2(h)(d)(ii) of the RTI Act. A few of the more useful citations are given below.

3.6.1 Land : The case that is relevant here is Civil Writ Petition No. 16750 of 2010, The Sutlej Club Vs. State Information Commission and another decided on 09.05.2011, commonly referred to as CWP No.

19224 of 2006 along with 23 connected cases. The Punjab and Haryana High Court held as follows :

"72. Now adverting to the financial help of petitioner-Sutlej Club, Ludhiana (at Sr. No.15) is concerned, the SIC mentioned that as per revenue record, the land owned by the Provincial Government is given to the Club which amounts to substantial financial assistance by the State Government. *The fact that the valuable land upon which the Club was constructed, belongs to the Government and no rent/lease is paid by it to the Government shows that there is a substantial financial assistance by the State* to the Club. The cost of prime land provided to the club would be much more than its normal revenue expenditure. Apart from land provided for construction of the club building, the Government has also incurred a part of expenditure on its construction.... In my view, the SIC has recorded the correct finding of fact based on the material on record, by virtue of impugned order dated 8.7.2010.

3.6.2 Land and Income Tax concessions : A directly relevant case here, dealing with both, land and income tax, was decided by the Central Information Commission on 11.01.2012. It was Mr. Tilak Raj Tanwar Vs. Government of NCT of Delhi, File No. : CIC/AD/A/2011/001699. After considering all aspects of the issue, the Commission decided as follows :

"12. The Commission while relying upon the various decisions given hereinabove is convinced that the Mount St. Mary's School *may be considered as being "substantially financed" by the appropriate Governmen, in view of the 5 acres of prime land granted to it at subsidized rates and income tax concessions being enjoyed by the school and that, therefore, it can be declared as a Public authority*".

3.6.3 Exemption from Tax : The case that is relevant here is Civil Writ Petition No. 16086 of 2008, Punjab Cricket Association, SAS Nagar (Mohali) Vs. State Information Commission, Punjab and another, decided on 09.05.2011, commonly referred to as CWP No. 19224 of 2006 along with 23 connected cases. The Punjab and Haryana High Court held as follows:

"68. Now adverting to the case of petitioner –PCA (at Sr. No.12), it is *admitted position that it is enjoying tax exemption from entertainment tax which is an direct financial aid by the State to it.* Although the SIC has negatived the plea of the complainant-information seeker, but to my mind, the SIC has slipped into deep legal error in this regard because *the PCA is saving heavy amount from exemption of entertainment tax which naturally is an incidence of financial aid by the Government*.

3.6.4 <u>Tax exemption and nominal rent</u> : Another case relevant here is Board of Control for Cricket India and another Vs. Netaji Cricket Club and others [2005 AIR (SC) 5921]. The Supreme Court observed as follows :

"80. The Board is a society registered under the Tamil Nadu Societies Registration Act. It enjoys a monopoly status as regard regulation of the sport of cricket in terms of its Memorandum of Association and Articles of Association. It controls the sport of cricket and lays down the law therefor. It, *inter alia, enjoys benefits by way of <u>tax exemption</u> and right to use stadia at nominal annual rent.*

3.7 While it may well be argued that the above quoted decisions refer to institutions such as schools, clubs which, in some characteristics, are different from Political Parties but *these decisions do recognize, accept and establish the principle that exemption from tax and allotment or permission to use land and other real estate is an accepted form of "financing", though it may be considered "indirect" as it is not in the physical form of money.* And this principle is one of the factors that makes Political Parties come under the definition of "public authority" as given in Section 2(h) of the RTI Act."

28. More importantly, the complainant has contended that Political Parties have constitutional and statutory status. It is his contention that incorporation of Articles 102(2) and 191(2) through the 42nd Amendment and the 10th Schedule to the Constitution has given constitutional status to the Political Parties. According to him, it is a fallacy to say that any individual can form a political party. A body or entity does not become a political party in the legal sense until it is registered by the Election Commission of India under Section 29A of the Representation of the People Act, 1951, and this registration **lends it the colour** of Public Authority.

29. Lastly, the complainant has also contended that in exercise of its powers, the Election Commission of India under Elections Symbols (Reservation and Allotment) Order, 1968, promulgated under Article 324 of the Constitution and Rules 5 & 10 of the Conduct of Election Rules, 1961, grants symbols to various Political Parties for election purposes for the recognition of Political Parties and can suspend or withdraw recognition of recognized Political Parties on their failure to observe model code of conduct or not following the lawful directions and instructions of the Commission. It is indicative of the public character of the Political Parties.

30. It may be further mentioned that Shri S. Sudhakar Reddy, General Secretary, Communist Party of India, sent a letter dated 24.9.2012 to the Commission stating therein that the Political Parties do not come under the ambit of Section 2(h) of the RTI Act. The relevant paragraphs of his letter are extracted below:

"Com. A.B. Bardhan, the then General Secretary has written a letter expressing willingness to keep the accounts of our Party transparent. In our view, Political

Parties do not come under Section 2(h)(d)(ii) of the RTI Act. Notwithstanding this, we have always been prepared to be transparent in our accounts. We submit our accounts to Election Commission of India every year and every year we submit our accounts to the Income Tax Department also. The accounts of our Party are audited by internal audit committee and also by the Chartered Accountant. It is then submitted to our Party National Council for obtaining their approval. We are prepared to make all the income and expenditure of our Party transparent."

31. On the other hand, Shri A.B. Bardhan, General Secretary, CPI, in letter dated 21.3.2011 addressed to Shri Anil Bairwal has stated that CPI is a Public Authority under Section 2(h) of the RTI Act. The relevant portion of his letter is extracted below:

"(a) Yes, we are Public Authority under Section 2(h)(d)(ii) "non-governmental organizations" substantially financed, directly or indirectly, by funds provided by the appropriate Government.

(b) We have our internal Appellate Authority 'Central Control Commission'."

32. It would, thus, appear that CPI has a contradictory stand in the matter, even while vouching for transparency in their accounts.

33. Shri Ambeth Rajan has filed a counter affidavit dated 31.10.2012 on behalf of Bahujan Samaj Party (BSP) in which he has taken the plea that the Political Parties are not public authorities under Section 2(h) of the RTI Act. Taking his argument further, he would submit that BSP is a political party that has not been notified as public authority by means of any Notification of the appropriate government to the effect that BSP is under control of or substantially financed by the appropriate government. He has also contended that State funding on the electoral rolls during elections is done merely to meet statutory obligations under the Registration of Electoral Rules, 1960. Similarly, tax exemption under Section 13A of the IT Act is subject to the compliance of the provisions of Income Tax Act. Furthermore, allotment of government/public land to the Political Parties on concessional rates does not cloth the party into a public authority within the meaning of Section 2(h) of the RTI Act. Paras 04, 08 & 10 of his representation are extracted below:

"4. That at the outset, I submit that the complainant has had no legal right to file application under Section 6(1) of the Right to Information Act, 2005, against the answering respondent for the reason that the Political Parties are not the public authorities under Section 2(h) of the Right to Information Act, 2005. The Bahujan Samaj Party being one of the six national Political Parties duly recognized by the Election Commission of India is, therefore, not a 'Public Authority' within the meaning of Section 2(h) of Right to Information Act, 2005. Therefore, the present complaint petition is liable to be dismissed.

- That I hereby submit that the BSP is a political party. It has not been notified as a public authority by means of any notification of appropriate government to the effect that BSP is owned, controlled or substantially financed by the appropriate government. Merely because some concessions, rebate and subsidy has been granted like it has been granted to any other political party, the BSP does not automatically become a body owned, controlled or substantially financed by the appropriate government.

10. That in view of the above, the present complaint petition against the answering respondent is legally not maintainable only on the ground that there is a State funding on free air time during elections on Doordarshan and All India Radio. The State funding on the electoral roll during elections is done to meet statutory obligations under Registration of Electoral Rules, 1960, which mandates that two copies of the electoral roll, one printed copy and another in CD is supplied to recognized Political Parties, free of cost. Further Tax exemption u/s 13A of the Income Tax Act is again subject to the compliance of the provisions of the Income Tax Act. The allotment of Government/public offices of Political Parties on concessional rent does not clothe the political party into a public authority within the meaning of Section 2(h) of Right to Information Act, 2005."

34. Shri Amit Anand Tiwari, counsel for Nationalist Congress Party (NCP), has argued at length to canvass that NCP is not a public authority. He has also filed a detailed representation in this regard. It is his contention that the NCP does not fall within the ambit of Section 2(h) of the RTI Act. He has refuted the arguments advanced by the complainants that the Political Parties are substantially financed by the Government. His contention is that free airtime granted to NCP during the election time on national television and national radio is not suggestive of government financing in as much as during elections, it is a popular practice in most of the democracies. He has referred to the case of Canada in this context. Further, according to him, supply of free electoral rolls during elections to NCP, again, is not indicative of financing by the Government. It is his contention that under rule 11(C) of the Registration of Electoral Rolls, 1960, the Registration Officer is mandated to provide two copies of Electoral Rolls, free of cost, to Political Parties registered under Section 29A of the Representation of People Act. This is a statutory requirement and cannot be construed as substantially financing. Similarly, allotment of party office to NCP at economical rates cannot be construed as substantial financing in as much as the Government makes this facility available not only to Political Parties recognized by the Election Commission but also to other segments of population such as journalists etc. Furthermore, it is Shri Tiwari's contention that exemption from Income Tax granted under Section 13A of the Income Tax Act also does not mean that the NCP is substantially financed by the Government.

He has given the example of Income Tax exemption to the farmers but by virtue of this, the farmers cannot be designated as public authority under Section 2(h) of the RTI Act.

35. Without prejudice to the above arguments, Adv. Tiwari has argued that even if it is admitted that the Government is funding the Political Parties in the manner mentioned hereinabove, it cannot be said to be 'substantial financing'. It is his contention that the NCP receives less than 1.55% of its total funding from the Government and, therefore, cannot be construed as public authority. Paragraphss 13.1 and 13.2 of his representation are extracted below:

> **"13.1 In *Mohd. Safdar Iman* Vs. *Indian Institute of Welfare* (dated 5.1.2008), this Hon'ble Commission held that the respondent institute was not a public authority mainly because it received not more than 20% of grant-in-aid from the government, which cannot be deemed to be substantial financing. In *Sh. Shanmuga Patro* Vs. *Rajiv Gandhi Foundation* (Decision No. 6010/ IC(A)/2010), THIS Hon'ble Commission has considered DAV *College case* and its own decision *in Mohd. Safdar Imam* and held that since the respondent body received a very nominal amount of grants from the Government amounting to barely 4 per cent, it cannot be said to be a public authority on account of being substantially financed by the Government. In *DAV College & Trust and Management Society* Vs. *Director of Public Institutions & Ors.* (AIR 2008 P&H 117), the Punjab & Haryana High Court held that where the appellant society was receiving 45 per cent of grant-in-aid from Government, it was being substantially financed by the Government, thus a *'public authority'* under Section 2(h) of the RTI Act.**
>
> **13.2 From the above stated judicial precedents and definitions, it becomes clear that every financing would not bring a person within the purview of Section 2(h). Such financing must be apparently considerable and done through subscribing of shares or advancing of loans etc. In cases where financing has been less than 20 per cent of the total finance of the authority or body or organization, same was held not to be substantial financing within the meaning of Section 2(h)."**

36. Adv. Tiwari has filed additional submissions dated 1.11.2012 for NCP in which he has made the following salient points:

(i) The power exercised by the Political Parties under the 10th Schedule of the Constitution cannot be construed to mean that the Political Parties are public authorities under Section 2(h) in as much as these powers can be exercised only when an elected Member has voted or abstained from voting against the whip of the political party or he has voluntarily given up the membership of such political party. Even in such cases, the political party cannot disqualify a Member of Legislature. All that it can do is to move an application seeking disqualification of such elected Member before the Chairman/Speaker of the House who has exclusive authority to declare such elected Member to be disqualified or otherwise.

(ii) No doubt, Political Parties have played a significant role in public life but public interest is not the criterion for declaring a body or institution as public authority under Section 2(h) of the RTI Act.

(iii) If Political Parties are declared to be public authorities,, then they will be flooded with applications by pseudo information seekers to maliciously engage the party workers only in responding to the RTI applications thereby causing detriment to their political functioning. The law laid down by the High Court in the Indian Olympic Association case, Commonwealth Games Committee case and Sanskriti School case is not applicable to the Political Parties in as much as there was evidence of huge direct financing by the Government to these bodies/entities which is not true in case of Political Parties.

(iv) Public interest argument is not valid in case of Political Parties under Section 11 of the RTI Act. If this argument is accepted, then the identities of the contributors would have to be disclosed and the contributors may not like this to happen. Such disclosure may expose them to harassment and threats by other Political Parties.

(v) In decision dated 8.7.2009 of a Single Bench of this Commission in Complaint No. CIC/MISC/2009/0001 and CIC/MISC/2009/0002, it was held that Political Parties are not covered under Section 2(h) of the RTI Act.

(vi) In the decision dated 5.2.2010 of Goa State Information Commission (*Shri Pandu Ram* Vs. *the President, Maharashtrabadi Gomantak Party*), it was held that MGP was not established or constituted under any enactment of State Legislature or by any Notification or order by the Government. Nor was it owned or substantially financed by the State Government and, therefore, was not a public authority.

37. Shri Shanti Prasad Aggarwal of the BJP, in his letter dated 28.5.2011, addressed to the complainant S.C. Agrawal has taken the stand that the BJP is not a public authority under the RTI Act.

38. Similarly, Shri Moti Lal Vora, Treasurer, AICC, in letter dated 20.5.2011 addressed to complainant S.C. Agrawal has taken the stand that the INC/AICC does not come under the purview of public office and, hence, is not liable to provide information under the RTI Act.

39. After hearing the arguments, the Commission decided to address a letter dated 8.11.2012 to the following Political Parties:

- Nationalist Congress Party
- Bahujan Samaj Party
- Bharatiya Janata Party
- Communist Party of India
- Communist Party of India (Marxist)
- INC/All India Congress Committee

seeking from them the following information:

"(A) Details of lands/buildings allotted by Govt. and its instrumentalities to your Party:
(a) in Delhi
(b) in State Capital(s)
(c) at Distt; HQrs;
In the following format, category wise :
(i) Year of allotment
(ii) Postal address of plots/buildings.
(iii) Size of plots/buildings.
(iv) Whether any consideration paid to Central or State Govt. If yes, amount thereof.
(v) Whether the lands/buildings were allotted at market rate or at concessional rate.
(vi) The estimated value of plots/buildings at present (property-wise).

(B) Amount of contributions received by your Party during the last five financial years i.e. 2007-08 to 2011-12, year-wise.

(C) Incomes received by your Party from any other sources during the last five financial years i.e. 2007-08 to 2011-12."

40. Only two parties viz. NCP and CPI(M) chose to respond to the Commission's notice. The other Political Parties simply ignored it.

41. Shri S.R. Kohli, Parliamentary Secretary, NCP, in letter dated 22.11.2012 informed the Commission that his party was not covered under Section 2(h) of the RTI Act and, therefore, it was not bound to supply any information.

42. However, Shri Prakash Karat, General Secretary, CPI(M) wrote a detailed letter dated 21.11.2012 to the Commission in which he gave details of the two buildings allotted to CPI(M) viz., A.K. Gopalan Bhawan – Plot Nos. 27, 28 and 29 at Market Road, measuring 1197.33 sq mts. allotted on 22.11.1983 and Kotla Road Plot Nos. 10, 11, 12 and 13, measuring 2534.46 sq. mts., allotted on 11.12.2008. As regards A.K. Gopalan Bhawan plot, he informed the Commission that the Party had deposited security amount of Rs. 31.42 lacs with licence fee of Rs. 78,574/-. As regards Kotla Road plot, the Party had paid premium of Rs.53.80 lacs with ground rent of Rs. 1,34,512/- per annum. Shri Karat has also clarified that the Party has only lease-hold rights on the plots under reference. Shri Karat has also given details of the income of the party from 2007-08 to 2011-12. But as regards the question of the quantum of tax exemption availed by the Party, he took the following stand:

> "Parliament took the decision to exempt the income of the Political Parties from Income Tax liabilities with the aim to strengthen the democratic polity in the country as Political Parties and their activities are its important components."

He also added that it is not a fact that all persons making contributions enjoy full tax exemption on the amounts contributed to Political Parties.

43. It needs to be underlined that it has been the tenor of the arguments advanced by the complainants herein that the Political Parties are substantially financed, albeit indirectly, by the appropriate Government (Central Government in this case) by way of :

- Allotment of large tracts of land in prime areas of Delhi either free of cost or at concessional rates;
- Allotment of houses on rental basis on concessional rates;
- Exemption from Income Tax u/s 13-A of the I.T. Act;
- Free air time on All India Radio;
- Free air time on Door Darshan; and
- Provisioning of free electoral rolls etc.

44. The Commission had written to the Secretary, Ministry of Urban Development, Government of India, New Delhi, to confirm the position regarding the allotment of plots to various Political Parties, as claimed by the complainants. The Deputy Land & Development Officer, in his letter dated 21.5.2013, has written to the Secretary of the Commission regarding the allotment of land to various Political Parties. The operative portion of his letter is reproduced below:

"I am directed to refer to your letter No. Secy/CIC/2013/Misc./02 dated 7th March, 2013 and 16th April, 2013 on the above mentioned subject and to provide information available in this office in respect of Table-1 as under :

S. No.	*Name of party*	*Location*	*Area*
1.	All India Committee of Indian National Congress	Dr. Rajender Prasad Road (also known as Jawahar Bhawan Trust), Kotla Road, Pkt.9A.	4736.1 sq. yds. 4583.32 sq.yds. 8093 sq. mts.
2.	Rashtriya Janata Dal	Kotla Road Plot Nos. 34, 57, 58 & 59	1904 sq.mts.
3.	Communist Party of India (Marxist)	Market Road, Plot Nos. 27, 28 & 29	1197.33 sq. mts.
4.	Samajwadi Party	Vasant Kunj, Plot No.1	1 acre
5.	Communist Party of India	Kotla Road, Plot No.15	0.3 acre
6.	Bharatiya Janata Party (National Level)	Between Dr. Rajinder Prasad Road-Raisina Road	1.87 acre
7.	Janata Dal (United)	Vasant Vihar, Plot No.4	2000 sq. mts.
8.	Bharatiya Janata Party (Delhi State)	Kotla Road, Plot No.4 & 5, alternative	1060.80 sq. mts.
9.	All India Anna Dravida Munnetra Kazhakham	Pushp Vihar, M.B. Road, Saket Plot No. 15 & 22	1008 sq.mts.
10.	Delhi Pradesh Congress Committee	Rouse Avenue, Plot No.2	1127.78 sq.mts.
11.	All India Trinamool Congress	DDU Marg, Plot No.2 & 3	1000 sq. mts.

It is informed that the information provided in the Table-1 is factually correct and the allotments were made to these Political Parties on **institutional land rates of this office**. Copies of allotment letters in respect of above mentioned Political Parties are enclosed herewith."

45. The terms and conditions of allotment to AICC/INC are contained in the DL&DO's letter dated 19.7.2007. Para 2(i) of the said letter is reproduced below:

"(i) The allottee will pay the premium of land @ **Rs. 88 Lakh per acre provisionally** plus **2.5%** thereof as **annual ground rent.** This rate was valid up to 31.3.2000. The allottee shall have to pay difference of premium in case the land rates are revised retrospectively by the Government. w.e.f. 1.4.2000. The allottee shall submit an undertaking to this effect on a non-judicial stamp paper worth Rs. 10/-."

46. The land has been allotted to other Political Parties also more or less on the same terms and conditions. However, the earlier allotments made to various Political parties were at lower rates.

47. The Commission has received another letter dated 15.5.2013 from the Director of Estates enclosing therewith allotment of government accommodation to various Political Parties on monthly rental as extracted below:

Sl. No.	*Name of parties*	*Address of Govt. Accommodation*	*Allotment Letter*	*License deed*	*Current monthly rent charged from parties*
1.	Indian National Congress Committee	26, Akbar Road	Enclosed	—	Rs.8,632/- + Furniture charges
2.	Indian National Congress	24, Akbar Road	Enclosed	Enclosed	Rs.68,571/- + Furniture charges
3.	Indian National Congress	5, Raisina Road	Enclosed	—	Rs.47,665/- Furniture charges
4.	Indian National Congress	C-II/109, Chanakya puri	Enclosed	—	Rs.15,137/- + Furniture charges
5.	Bharatiya Janata Party	11, Ashoka Road	—	—	Rs.86,832/- + Furniture charges
6.	Bharatiya Janata Party	14, Pandit Pant Marg	Enclosed	Enclosed	Rs.24,788/- + Furniture charges
7.	C.P.I.	AB-4, Purana Quila Road	—	—	Rs.1,550/-
8.	Nationalist Congress Party	10, Dr. B.D. Marg	—	—	Rs.1,320/-
9.	President Bahujan Samaj Party	4, G.R.G. Road	Enclosed	Enclosed	Rs.1,320/-
10.	Samajwadi Party	18, Coper Nicus Road	Enclosed	Enclosed	Rs.20,352/-
11.	Shri Prakash Karat, General Secretary, CPI(M)	8, Teen Murti Lane	—	—	Rs.1,550/-

48. Before proceeding further in this matter, it would be pertinent to have a look at the registration, recognition and functioning of Political Parties as per the existing law/rules. The following salient points need to be underlined:

- The Political Parties are registered with the Election Commission of India (ECI) under Section 29A of the Representation of People Act, 1951.
- For the purposes of R.P. Act and elections, an association/body gets the status of political party only on its registration with the ECI under Section 29A.
- Para 16A of the Election Symbols (Reservation & Allotment) Order, 1968, empowers ECI to suspend or withdraw the recognition of a political party if it refuses to follow the lawful directions and instructions of the Commission or if it refuses to observe the provisions of the Model Code of Conduct.
- As per Supreme Court judgment in Common Cause Vs. Union of India (AIR 1996 SC-3081), ECI is empowered under Article 324 of the Constitution to require the Political Parties to submit details of expenditure incurred by them in connection with elections.
- ECI has directed the Political Parties to submit their accounts within 90 days after general elections in case of Lok Sabha and within 75 days in the case of Assembly elections.
- Under Section 29C of the R.P. Act, a Political Party is required to report to the ECI in respect of contributions received by it in excess of Rs. 20,000/- from any person or Company.
- The contributions made to the Political Parties are exempt from the Income Tax, both for the donor and the donee.
- Recognition of Political Parties is governed by the provisions of Election Symbols (Reservation and Allotment), 1968, which is an order issued by ECI under Article 324 of the Constitution read with Rules 5 & 10 of the Conduct of Election Rules, 1961, to provide for specification, reservation & allotment of symbols and recognition of Political Parties and matters related thereto.

DECISION NOTICE AND REASONS

49. The Political Parties constitute one of the most important institutions in a constitutional democracy. Prof. Harold J Laski in his classic text "Grammar of Politics" has termed them 'natural', though not 'perfect'. According to him, the life of a democratic State is built upon the party system. Without Political Parties, there would be no means available of enlisting the popular decisions in a politically satisfactory manner. To quote him

> **"The life of the democratic State is built upon the party-system and it is important at the outset to discuss the part played by party in the arrangement of affairs. Briefly, that part may be best described by saying that parties arrange the issues upon which people are to vote. It is obvious that in the confused welter of the modern State, there must be some**

selection of problems as more urgent than others. It is necessary to select them as urgent and to present solutions of them which may be acceptable to the citizen-body. It is that task of selection, the party undertakes.
It acts, in Mr. Lowell's phrase, as the broker of ideas. From the mass of opinions, sentiments, beliefs, by which the electorate moves, it chooses out those it judges most likely to meet with general acceptance. It organizes persons to advocate its own view of their meaning. It states that view as the issue upon which the voter has to make up his mind. Its power enables it to put forward for election candidates who are willing to identify themselves with its view. Since its opponents will do the same, the electorate, thereby, is enabled to vote as a mass and decision that would otherwise be chaotic, assumes some coherency and direction.
What, at least, is certain, is that without parties there would be no means available to us of enlisting the popular decision in such a way as to secure solutions capable of being interpreted as politically satisfactory."

50. All modern democracies operate on a party system, some with two as in the USA and some others with multiple Political Parties like in India. The Political Parties mobilize public opinion around their ideologies and beliefs and contest elections to form government. No democracy can exist today without Political Parties. An ordinary citizen does not have direct access to the government except through his elected representative and cannot hope to be part of the government without being a member of a Political Party. His membership of a legislature depends on his membership of a Political Party to begin with. It is, thus, through the Political Parties that the citizens of a democracy operationalise the democratic state. This is precisely what Prof. Laski has meant when he says that the existence of Political Parties gives the citizens of a country a viable means to give shape to their political aspirations and beliefs by forming a government of their choice. It will, therefore, not be an exaggeration to say that no Political Party, no democracy. In view of this central importance that they enjoy that the Political Parties have been given in our country such enormous powers and benefits, through both constitutional and statutory arrangements so that they can fulfill their just roles in representing their constituents.

51. The Political Parties, for example, play a critical role in the disqualification of legislators on ground of defection. As per paragraph 02 of the Tenth Schedule, a Member of a House belonging to any Political Party can be disqualified in certain circumstances. Paragraphs 01, 02 & 03 of Article 02 are extracted below:

"2. Disqualification on ground of defection. – (1) Subject to the provisions of paragraphs 3, 4 and 5, a member of a House belonging to any political party shall be disqualified for being a member of the House—
(a) if he has voluntarily given up his membership of such political party; or
(b) if he votes or abstains from voting in such House contrary to any direction issued by the political party to which he belongs or by any

person or authority authorized by it in this behalf, without obtaining, in either case, the prior permission of such political party, person or authority and such voting or abstention has not been condoned by such political party, person or authority within fifteen days from the date of such voting or abstention.

Explanation – **For the purposes of this sub-paragraph,—**

(a) an elected member of a House shall be deemed to belong to the political party, if any, by which he was set up as a candidate for election as such member;

(b) a nominated member of a House shall, —

(i) where he is a member of any political party on the date of his nomination as such member, be deemed to belong to such political party;

(ii) in any other case, be deemed to belong to the political party of which he becomes, or, as the case may be, first becomes, a member before the expiry of six months from the date on which he takes his seat after complying with the requirements of article 99 or, as the case may be, article 188.

(2) An elected member of a House who has been elected as such otherwise than as a candidate set up by any political party, shall be disqualified for being a member of the House if he joins any political party after such election.

(3) A nominated member of a House shall be disqualified for being a member of the House if he joins any political party after the expiry of six months from the date on which he takes his seat after complying with the requirements of Article 99 or, as the case may be, Article 188."

52. We may also take notice of certain statutory provisions in this regard. Section 29A of the Representation of People (RP) Act, 1951, empowers the Election Commission of India (ECI) to register Political Parties for the purposes of this Act. **In other words, without such registration, a Political Party cannot participate in the electoral process**. Sub-section (1) of 29-A is extracted below :

> **"(1) Any association or body of individual citizens of India calling itself a political party and intending to avail itself of the provisions of this Part shall make an application to the Election Commission for its registration as a political party for the purposes of this Act."**

53. Further, in exercise of its powers under Article 324 of the Constitution read with Section 29A of the RP Act, 1951, and rules 05 and 10 of the Conduct of Election Rules, 1961, the Election Commission has issued the Election Symbols (Reservation & Allotment) Order, 1968. This Order has been issued for the purity of the elections in the Lok Sabha and the Legislative Assemblies of States and in the interest of conduct of such elections in a fair and efficient manner and for "the specification, reservation,

choice and allotment of symbols for the recognition of Political Parties". This order lays down conditions for recognition of the National Parties and the State Parties. The Election Commission allots symbols to National and State Political Parties under para 08 of the Order. This order also provides for allotment of symbols to unrecognized Political Parties. Para 16-A of the order empowers the Commission to suspend or withdraw permission of a recognized political party for its failure to observe the model code of conduct or follow lawful directions and instructions of the Commission. Importantly, as per para 07 of the order, the Election Commission can issue Notifications in the Gazette of India publishing therein the list specifying the National Parties/State parties and the symbols respectively reserved for them. It can also issue Gazette Notifications in respect of unrecognized Political Parties and addresses of their Headquarters etc.

54. At this stage, it would be useful to crystalise the outcome of discussion held herein-before. In our view, the following facts clearly emerge:

(A) Legal/General

(a) that the Political Parties are the building blocks of a constitutional democracy;
(b) that under Tenth Schedule of the Constitution, a Political Party can have a Member of the House disqualified in certain circumstances;
(c) that a Political Party is required to be registered by the Election Commission of India under Section 29A of the Representation of People Act, 1951;
(d) that under Section 29C of the RP Act, 1951, a Political Party is required to submit a report for each Financial Year to the Election Commission of India in respect of contributions received by it in excess of 20,000/- rupees from any person as also contributions in excess of 20,000/- rupees received from non-Government companies;
(e) that in exercise of its powers under Article 324 read with Section 29A of the RP Act, 1951, and rules 5 & 10 of the Conduct of Election Rules, 1961, the Election Commission has issued Election Symbols (Reservation & Allotment) Order, 1968, under which election symbols are allotted to various National/ State Political Parties;
(f) that Election Commission can suspend or withdraw recognition of a recognized political party in the event of violation of provisions of Election Symbol (Reservation & Allotment) Order, 1968;
(g) that Central Information Commission's order dated 29.4.2008 directing the Political Parties to disclose their Income Tax Returns holds the field and is being complied with.

(B) Financial

(a) that the Land & Development Office of the Ministry of Urban Development has allotted large tracts of land in Delhi to various Political Parties either free of cost or at concessional rates;

(b) that the Directorate of Estates, Ministry of Urban Development, has allotted accommodation in Delhi to various Political Parties on rental basis at concessional rates;
(c) that Political Parties have been claiming and granted total tax exemption under Section 13A of the Income Tax Act for all their income;
(d) that the State has been indirectly financing Political Parties by way of free air time on All India Radio and Doordarshan of India during the elections; and
(e) that recognized Political Parties are issued copies of electoral rolls by the Election Commission, free of cost, at the time of elections.

55. Section 2(h) of the RTI Act defines 'public authority' as follows :

(h) "public authority" means any authority or body or institution of self-Government established or constituted,—
(a) by or under the Constitution;
(b) by any other law made by Parliament;
(c) by any other law made by State Legislature;
(d) by notification issued or made by the appropriate Government, and includes any –
(i) body owned, controlled or substantially financed;
(ii) non-Government Organisation substantially financed, directly or indirectly by funds provided by the appropriate Government;"

56. The issue to be determined is whether these six political parties have the ingredients which would qualify them to be public authorities within the meaning of Section 2(h) of the Right to Information (RTI) Act.

57. It is quite obvious that out of the many ways a public authority can be established or constituted, those provided in (a), (b), (c) and (d) above would not apply to these political parties. They have not been established or constituted by and under the Constitution; nor by any other law made by Parliament or the State Legislature; nor are these bodies owned or controlled by any appropriate government. We have to examine if these political parties would qualify under the remaining provisions. It is also true that these political parties have not been established or constituted by any specific notification issued or order made by an appropriate government as provided in (d) of this particular section. However, it is pertinent to remember that they have been brought into existence first as political parties and then as national level political parties by the Election Commission of India thereby entitling them to a host of benefits, the principal among them being the right to accept contribution from both individual citizens and private companies and also to get complete income tax exemption on all their incomes. The other important benefit that accrues to these political parties on account of their recognition by the Election Commission of India as national level political parties is the common symbol on which their candidates can contest elections. Thus, if not strictly within the letter of this particular provision (d), but at least, in

spirit, these political parties can be said to have been constituted by their registration by the Election Commission of India, a fact akin to the establishment or constitution of a body or institution by an appropriate government.

58. Having said this, the next classification under which these political parties can be placed is what is provided in Section 2(h)(ii). According to this provision, any non-governmental organisation which is substantially financed, directly or indirectly, by funds provided by the appropriate government would become a public authority for the purpose of the Right to Information Act. Now, the question is whether these political parties are being substantially financed, directly or indirectly, by funds provided by the appropriate government. Both the parties in this case have placed considerable importance in favour of and against this position. While the complainants have submitted that the land and buildings provided to these political parties in the national capital at Delhi and probably elsewhere in the States and the complete income tax exemption provided to them would amount to substantial financing, the political parties themselves have strongly argued that whatever benefits they might have received from the Central Government would hardly amount to any substantial financing. While it is true that the expression "substantial" has not been defined in the Right to Information Act, in a number of decisions, the superior courts have held that "substantial financing" need not be "majority financing". In other words, there must be evidence of state funding which is not "insubstantial" of such non-governmental bodies to bring them within the ambit of this particular provision. Keeping this in view, let us see if the tangible and intangible financial benefits extended to these political parties would amount to substantial financing.

59. The Delhi High Court in its decision dated 14.5.2010 in Krishak Bharati Cooperative Ltd. Vs. Ramesh Chand Bawa [W.P. (C) 6129/2007 and W.P.(C) 7770/2008] has interpreted the words "and includes" as follows :

> **"13.________________________________**
>
> **The expression "and includes" [Ref : Sec.2(d)]connotes that those entities which answer the description following those words need not fall within the definition of entities that precedes those words. The word "includes" is generally understood in statutory interpretation as enlarging meaning of the phrases in the body of the statute".**

60. In the said decision (supra), the High Court has also observed

> "19.________________________________
>
> **In the context of the RTI Act it may well be that a body which is neither a "state' for the purposes of Article 12 nor a body discharging public functions for the purpose of Article 226 of the Constitution might still be a 'public authority' within the meaning of Section 2(h)(d)(i) of the RTI Act. To state differently, while a 'body' which is either a 'State' for the purposes of Article 12 or a 'body' discharging public functions for the purpose of Article 226 is likely to answer the description of 'public**

authority' in terms of Section 2(h)(d)(i) of the RTI Act, the mere fact that such body is neither, will not take it out of the definition of 'public authority' under Section 2(h)(d)(i) of the RTI Act. _____________"

61. It may now be pertinent to allude to certain decisions of the High Courts and this Commission in this regard:

(i) In Indian Olympic Association and others Vs. Veeresh Malik & others (WP)(C) No. 876/2007 the Delhi High Court in its decision dated 7th January 2010, held that Indian Olympic Association is a public authority under Section 2(h). The relevant paragraph is extracted below:

"Having regard to the pre-eminent position enjoyed by the IOA, as the sole representative of the IOC, as the regulator for affiliating national bodies in respect of all Olympic sports, armed with the power to impose sanctions against institutions – even individuals, the circumstance that it is funded for the limited purpose of air fare, and other such activities of sports persons, who travel for events, is not a material factor. The IOA is the national representative of the country in the IOC; it has the right to give its nod for inclusion of an affiliating body, who, in turn, select and coach sportsmen, emphasizes that it is an Olympic sports regulator in this country, in respect of all international and national level sports. The annual reports placed by it on the record also reveal that though the IOA is autonomous from the Central Government, in its affairs and management, it is not discharging any public functions. On the contrary, the funding by the government consistently is part of its balance sheet, and IOA depends on such amounts to aid and assist travel, transportation of sportsmen and sports managers alike, serves to underline its public, or predominant position. Without such funding, the IOA would perhaps not be able to work effectively. Taking into consideration all these factors, it is held that the IOA is "public authority" under the meaning of that expression under the Act."

(ii) In the same judgment, the Delhi High Court also held the Sanskriti School to be public authority. The relevant paragraph is extracted below:

"As discussed earlier, grants by the Government retain their character as public funds, even if given to private organizations, unless it is proven to be part of general public policy of some sort. Here, by all accounts, the grants – to the tune of Rs. 24 crores were given to the school, without any obligation to return it. A truly private school would have been under an obligation to return the amount, with some interest. The conditionality of having to admit children of employees of the Central Government can hardly be characterized as a legitimate public end; it certainly would not

muster any permissible classification test under Article 14 of the Constitution. The benefit to the school is recurring; even if a return of 10% (which is far less than a commercial bank's lending rate) is assumed for 6 years, the benefit to the school is to the tune of Rs. 14.88 crores. This is apart from the aggregate grant of Rs. 24.8 crores, and the nominal concessional rate at which the school was allotted land for construction.

On a consideration of all the above factors, this court holds that the school fulfils the essential elements of being a non-government organization, under Section 2(h) of the Act, which is substantially financed by the Central Government, through various departments, and agencies. It is therefore, covered by the regime of the Act."

(iv) In decision dated 22.4.2010 in Amardeep Walia Vs. Chandigarh Lawn Tennis Association (File No. CIC/LS/C/2009/900377), the Central Information Commission held Chandigarh Lawn Tennis Association to be public authority. Para 19 of the order is extracted below:

"19. The gravamen of the above judgments is that for a private entity to qualify to be a public authority, substantive financing does not mean 'majority' financing. What is important is that the funding by the appropriate Government is achieving a "felt need of a Section of the public or to secure larger societal goals." The ratio of the above judgments, particularly of Delhi High Court, applies to the present case on all the fours. A huge property has been placed at the disposal of CLTA by the Chandigarh Administration at a notional rental of Rs.100/- per annum. Besides, grant of one lakh rupees was also given to CLTA in FY 2008-09. Concededly, CLTA fulfils the felt need of a Section of the society by way of imparting training to the budding tennis players. It is, therefore, held that CLTA is a Public Authority."

(v) In another decision dated 21.1.2011 in Pradeep Bhanot Vs. Chandigarh Club, Chandigarh (File No. CIC/LS/A/2010/001184), the Central Information Commission held that the Chandigarh Club was a public authority. The broad facts in this case were that a plot of land measuring 3.85 lacs sq.ft. was leased out to the Club at the rent of Rs. 1,08,208/- per month w.e.f. 20.7.2005 to 19.7.2010 with annual increase of 5 per cent. The Finance Department of Chandigarh Administration had submitted before the Commission that the aforesaid rent was not at par with the market rent. Considering the totality of circumstances, the Commission had concluded that Chandigarh Club was public authority under Section 2(h). Paras 3 and 4 of the order are extracted below :

"3. We have now received a response from the Finance Department of the Chandigarh Administration under the signatures of the Joint Secretary, Finance. Paras 2 & 3 thereof are extracted below :

"2. In this regard it is informed that the bodies like Chandigarh Club etc. are providing the public service and while fixing the rate of rent in such bodies, this aspect is taken into consideration. In view of the public services being provided by these bodies, the said bodies cannot be termed as commercial sites. Due to this reason, the rent of Chandigarh Club was fixed as Rs. 1,08,208/- per month with effect from 20.7.2000 with annual increase of 5%. It is not out of place to mention here that other similarly situated bodies like Chandigarh Golf Club and Chandigarh Golf Association which are also providing the public services have been kept at par with Chandigarh Club while determining the rate of rent. In case we consider the Chandigarh Club as commercial site, then the rent comes out to be Rs. 31,57,400 per month. Keeping in view the urban character of the city, rent being charged from the Chandigarh Club is not at par with the market rent. Further, by charging the rent at a lower rate, it will make amply clear that the Chandigarh Administration is indirectly financing the promotion of services being rendered by the Chandigarh Club.

3. In view of the aforesaid circumstances and in view of the fact that said club is being indirectly financed for promotion of public services by the Chandigarh Administration the same is squarely covered under the definition of 'public authority' as defined under Section 2 (h) (ii) of the RTI Act, 2005."

4. In view of the categorical position taken by the Chandigarh Administration extracted above and the fact that there is vast differential between the monthly rental being paid by the Chandigarh Club and the commercial rent that the premises could fetch in the open market (as estimated by the Finance Deptt.), we are of the opinion that the Chandigarh Club is being indirectly financed by the Chandigarh Administration. In this view of the matter, we hold that the Chandigarh Club is 'public authority' u/s 2 (h) (ii) of the RTI Act. Hence, the club management is hereby directed to put in place a mechanism for servicing the RTI Act."

(vii) Furthermore, in Amrit Mehta Vs. India International Centre (File No. CIC/WB/A/2009/000965/LS) decided on 1.2.2011, the Commission held that India International Centre is a public authority under Section 2(h). The broad facts in this case were that 4.69 acres of prime land was given on perpetual lease to IIC against deposition of Rs. 1,68,840/- as per agreement signed on 22.4.1960 between the President of India and IIC. The yearly rent payable by IIC to the Central Government was Rs. 8,442/- which has remained unchanged during the last five decades. In the facts of the case, the Commission had held as follows:

"XVIII. In view of the above discussion, it clearly emerges that a huge

chunk of land measuring 4.69 acres was allotted to IIC in 1968 at a premium of Rs. 1,68,840/- only, obviously, at a concessional rate. The agreement between the parties expressly speaks of concessional allotment of land. Further, IIC was required to pay rent of Rs. 8,442/- per year to the Central Government and this amount has remained unchanged during the last 52 years. This is also clearly indicative of the rent being nominal/ concessional in nature. These facts clearly establish that the Central Government has indirectly financed IIC. The RTI Act does not define 'substantial financing'. The expression 'substantial financing' has to be interpreted in the context of a specific case. This has been so held by the Punjab and Haryana High Court in Civil Writ Petition No. 19224/ 2006(The Hindu Urban Cooperative Bank Ltd. Vs. State Information Commission, Punjab) extracted above. Considering the fact that a huge chunk of land was allotted to IIC in 1960 in the very heart of the capital city of Delhi at a premium of Rs.1,68,840/- only and also considering the fact that IIC is paying rent of only Rs. 8,442/- per year to the Central Government over all these years, in our opinion, amounts to indirect substantial financing of IIC by the Central Government. In this view of the matter, we hold that IIC is a Public Authority under Section 2(h) of the RTI Act."

(vii) Yet another decision of this Commission needs to be adverted to in this connection. 6,000 sq. mts. of land was allotted to Delhi Public School, Rohini, by DDA at a highly subsidised rate of Rs. 65 lacs per acre in February, 1997. Another plot of land measuring 10,000 sq. mtrs. was also allotted to DPS, Rohini, for a play ground on temporary basis on payment of nominal ground rent of only Rs. 10/- per annum. The question before the Commission was whether DPS, Rohini, can be deemed to be a Public Authority in terms of Section 2(h) of the RTI Act. Vide decision dated 23.8.2011 in File No. CIC/ SG/C/2010/001036/AD, this Commission held that in the facts and circumstances of the case, DPS, Rohini, is a Public Authority under Section 2(h). The reasoning given by the Commission is encapsulated in the para extracted hereinafter:

"Considering the above factual matrix of the case at hand, one can sum up that 6000 sq. mts of land has been given to the school at a concessional rate of Rs. 65 lacs per acre and 10,000 sq. mts of land at a highly subsidised nominal ground rent of Rs. 10/- per Annum by DDA. The School is under the governance, control and regulation of the Delhi Schools Education Act 1973, Rule 50 whereof mandates disclosure of information in the form of reports etc. to the Director of the Directorate of Education, the Administrator and concerned authority from the Central Government, as already discussed above. The Directorate of Education has appointed two nominees in the key Managing Committee of the School thereby ensuring position of power of managing affairs of the School and having control over the Respondent School."

62. The question before the Commission is whether INC/AICC, BJP, CPI(M), CPI, NCP and BSP can be held to be Public Authorities under Section 2(h) of the RTI Act. The complainants have adduced the following three principal grounds to persuade the Commission to hold that the aforesaid Political Parties are Public Authorities viz.:

(i) Indirect substantial financing by the Central Government;
(ii) Performance of public duty by the Political Parties; and
(iii) Constitutional/legal provisions vesting Political Parties with rights and liabilities.

63. Now we will take these facets one by one.

SUBSTANTIAL FINANCING OF POLITICAL PARTIES BY THE CENTRAL GOVT.

64. The complainant has vehemently pleaded that Political Parties are substantially financed by the Central Government in multiple ways. The first and foremost method of indirect financing is allotment of large tracts of land in prime areas of Delhi either, free of cost, or at concessional rates. Information supplied by complainant Shri Anil Bairwal is depicted in a tabular form at para 18(iv) of this order. This information has been confirmed to the Commission by L&DO as per details given in para 43 of this order.

65. Even allowing for the margin of error in the estimation of the value of land allotted to various political parties by complainant Shri Bairwal, we have reasons to believe that this land has been allotted at hugely concessional rates. The lease value of these properties in the open market has not been placed before us. Even so, we strongly believe that the premium and the lease rent being charged from the Political Parties does not reflect the true value of these properties. This, in our considered opinion, amounts to indirect financing and when added to the income tax exemption enjoyed by these political parties, it would amount to substantial financing.

66. We may also like to add that the complainants have proffered information before the Commission in regard to the lands allotted at Delhi by the Central Government. We are informed that such allotments have also been made at the State capitals by the State Governments. If so, this only reinforces the complainants' contention that the appropriate Governments have indirectly financed Political Parties in a big way.

67. Another method of financing of Political Parties by the Central Government is allotment of houses on rental basis on concessional rates. Information given by the complainant, Shri Bairwal in this regard is mentioned at para 17 of this order which need not be repeated. The Directorate of the Estates, Ministry of Urban Development has also corroborated allotment of various properties to these political parties on rental basis. The rent being charged from the Political Parties is shown in the last column of the said table. The rental value of these properties in the open market has not been placed before us. Even so, we strongly believe that the rent being charged from the

Political Parties does not reflect the true rental value of these properties. This arrangement also contributes to the indirect financing of Political Parties.

68. Of the various benefits that the central government extends to these political parties, the total exemption from payment of income tax on their incomes, very obviously, constitutes the most important benefit. Section 13 A of the Income Tax Act reads as follows:

> **"Any income of a political party which is chargeable under the head income from house property or income from other sources or capital gains or any income by way of voluntary contributions received by a political party from any person shall not be included in the total income of the previous year of such political party:**
> **Provided that —**
> **(a) such political party keeps and maintains such books of account and other documents as would enable the assessing officer to properly deduce its income therefrom;**
> **(b) in respect of each such voluntary contribution in excess of Rs. 20,000, such political party keeps and maintains a record of such contribution and the name and address of the person who has made such contribution; and**
> **(c) the accounts of such a political party are audited by an accountant as defined in the explanation below sub-section 2 of Section 288:**
> **Provided further that if the treasurer of such political party or any other person authorised by that political party in this behalf fails to submit a report under sub-section 3 of Section 29C of the Representation of the People Act, 1951 for the financial year, no exemption under this Section shall be available for that political party for such financial year."**

69. Since these political parties have not paid any income tax, the exact quantum of money that the Central Government has forgone in the process has not been worked out specifically. However, since the level of income of all these political parties would place them in the highest slab of income tax, at least 30% of their total income would have been collected as income tax but for the total exemption given to them by law. By a simple calculation, this would show that the Central Government has bestowed financial benefits on the six political parties to the extent of the amount shown against each as per the following table:

Party	*Tax Payable exempted in FY 2006-07 (Rs. crores)*	*Tax payable exempted in FY 2007-08 (Rs. crores)*	*Tax payable exempted in FY 2008-09 (Rs. crores)*	*Tax payable exempted in 3 years (Rs. crores)*
BJP	26.86	40.68	73.71	141.25
INC	57.00	75.05	168.87	300.92
BSP	15.44	23.60	0.80	39.84
CPI(M)	6.98	4.62	6.53	18.13
CPI	0.01	0.21	0.02	0.24
NCP	0.90	0.68	8.06	9.64

70. Thirty per cent of their income which these political parties would have otherwise paid by way of income tax has been given up in their favour by the Central Government. No one can dispute that this is substantial financing, though indirectly. Added to this the concessional allotment of land and buildings in prime locations in the national capital and, probably, in several state headquarters, if not at district level also, the total amount of direct and indirect financing/funding of these political parties is considerable. On behalf of the political parties, it has been argued that the income tax exemption cannot be said to be a form of financing. In support of this argument, they have submitted that such concessions and exemptions are routinely extended to many charitable and non-profit non-governmental organisations across the country. Therefore, according to them, if those numerous non-governmental organisations are not considered to be public authorities, there is no reason why the political parties should be considered so. We cannot accept this argument. There is a great difference between the tax exemption given to charitable and non-profit non-governmental organisations and that given to the political parties. The exemption given to the former is strictly conditional: full or part exemption is given to these organisations only if they pursue the objectives outlined in their respective charters, be it the memorandum of association and bye-laws in case they are societies or the trust deeds, in case they are private trusts. There are other strict conditions laid down in the Income Tax Act which the assessee must comply with. In other words, if any of these non-governmental organisations are found not to be pursuing their objectives or spending the tax exempt amount on activities other than what is enshrined in their respective charters or not comply with the conditions, their entire income becomes subject to taxation, sometimes with penalty. On the other hand, the tax exemption given to the political parties is complete, the only condition being that they must report to the Election Commission of India, every year, the details of all the contributors who contribute Rs. 20,000 or more to the political party concerned. Thus, the political parties enjoy an almost unfettered exemption from payment of income tax, a benefit not enjoyed by any other charitable or non-profit non-governmental organisations.

71. It has been also argued before us that Political Parties are beneficiaries of free air time on All India Radio. The amounts spent by the State in this regard on AIR for Lok Sabha Elections – 2009 in respect of various Political Parties is depicted in para 18(ii) of this order. Similarly, the amounts spent by the State on free air time on Doordarshan on various Political Parties is depicted in para 18(iii). These amounts may be small but they contribute to the kitty of Political Parties at the Government cost.

72. In view of the above, we are of the considered opinion that Central Government has contributed significantly to the indirect financing of Political Parties in-question.

73. However, the question remains whether the aforesaid financing can be held to be 'substantial financing' in terms of Section 2(h)(d)(i) of the RTI Act. Justice Ravindra Bhat of Delhi High Court in judgment dated 7.1.2010 in Indian Olympic Association Vs. Veeresh Malik and Ors. (WP)(C) No. 876/2007 has observed that the expression 'Public Authority' has to be interpreted liberally and not restrictively. Paras 45 & 46 of his order are extracted below :

"45. Now, if the parliamentary intention was to expand the scope of the definition "public authority" and not restrict it to the four categories mentioned in the first part, but to comprehend other bodies or institutions, the next question is whether that intention is coloured by the use of the specific terms, to be read along with the controlling clause 'authority ... of self government" and "established or constituted by or under" a notification. A facial interpretation would indicate that even the bodies brought in by the extended definition : (i) "Body owned, controlled or substantially financed; (ii) Non-Government organization substantially financed, directly or indirectly by funds provided by the appropriate Government." are to be constituted under, or established by a notification, issued by the appropriate government. If, indeed, such were the intention, sub-clause (i) is a surplusage, since the body would have to be one of self-government, substantially financed, and constituted by a notification, issued by the appropriate government. Secondly – perhaps more importantly, it would be highly anomalous to expect a "non-governmental organization" to be constituted or established by or under a notification issued by the government. These two internal indications actually have the effect of extending the scope of the definition "public authority"; it is, thus, not necessary that the institutions falling under the inclusive part have to be constituted, or established under a notification issued in that regard. Another significant aspect here is that even in the inclusive part, Parliament has nuanced the term; sub-clause (i) talks of a "body, owned, controlled or substantially financed" by the appropriate government [the subject object relationship ending with sub-clause (ii)]. In the case of control, or ownership, the intention here was that irrespective of the constitution (i.e. it might not be under or by a notification), if there was substantial financing, by the appropriate government, and ownership or control, the body is deemed to be a public authority. This definition would comprehend societies, co-operative societies, trusts, and other institutions where there is control, ownership, (of the appropriate government) or substantial financing. The second class, i.e. non-government organization, by its description, is such as cannot be "constituted" or "established" by or under a statute or notification.

46. The term "non-governmental organization" has not been used in the Act. It is a commonly accepted expression. Apparently, the expression was used the first time, in the definition of "international NGO" (INGO) in Resolution 288(X) of ECOSOC on February 27, 1950 as "any international organization that is not founded by an international treaty". According to Wikipedia "...Non-governmental organization (NGO) is a term that has become widely accepted as referring to a legally constituted, non-governmental organization created by natural or legal persons with no participation or representation of any-government. In the cases in

which NGOs are funded totally or partially by governments, the NGO maintains its non-governmental status and excludes government representatives from membership in the organization. Unlike the term intergovernmental organization, "non-governmental organization" is termed in general use but is not a legal definition. In many jurisdictions these types of organizations are defined as "civil society organizations" or referred to by other names..." Therefore, inherent in the context of a "non-government" Organization is that it is independent of government control in its affairs, and is not connected with it. Naturally, its existence being as a non-state actor, the question of its establishment or constitution through a government or official notification would not arise. The only issue in its case would be whether it fulfils the "substantial financing" criteria, spelt out in Section 2(h). Non-governmental organizations could be of any kind: registered societies, co-operative societies, trusts, companies limited by guarantee or other juristic or legal entities, but not established or controlled in their management, or administration by state or public agencies."

74. As to the question of 'substantial financing', the Delhi High Court in the said judgment has held that 'majority' test is not appropriate to decide whether or not an Organisation is substantially financed, directly or indirectly, by the appropriate Government. It has been observed that financing in percentage terms in relation to the total budget of the body is not important. To quote:

"60. This court therefore, concludes that what amounts to "substantial" financing cannot be straight-jacketed into rigid formulae, of universal application. Of necessity, each case would have to be examined on its own facts. That the percentage of funding is not "majority" financing, or that the body is an impermanent one, are not material. Equally, that the institution or organization is not controlled, and is autonomous is irrelevant; indeed, the concept of non-governmental organization means that it is independent of any manner of government control in its establishment, or management. That the organization does not perform – or pre-dominantly performs – "public" duties, too, may not be material, as long as the object for funding is achieving a felt need of a Section of the public, or to secure larger societal goals. To the extent of such funding, indeed, the organization may be a tool, or vehicle for the executive government's policy fulfilment plan. This view, about coverage of the enactment, without any limitation, so long as there is public financing."

75. A similar view has been taken by the Karnataka High Court in Bangalore International Airport Limited Vs. Karnataka Information Commission (WP 12076/2008). The operative para of the order dated 9.2.2010 is extracted below :

"It is to be noticed that as observed earlier, wording, "non-government organisation substantially financed, directly or indirectly" is required to be split into two. Whether the non-government organisation is substantially financed directly that is the cash flow would come from the Government agency or indirectly which would necessarily mean that the exemptions are granted to the non-government organisation. In the case on hand, it is to be noticed that a perusal of the agreements would conclusively go to show that the petitioner-BIAL is a beneficiary of innumerable exemptions which, if one were to translate into cash flow would certainly cascade into a substantial amount. Another factor which is required to be taken note of is large chunk of land to the extent of 4000 acres of prime agricultural land is acquired by paying enormous amounts as compensation to the farmers who owned the lands. It is estimated that this amount would run into hundred of crores."

The Learned Judge further held that :

"Let us now consider what are the implications of the words 'substantially financed'. It is obvious that as per Section 2(h)(i) "body substantially financed" would be a body where the ownership may not lie with the Government, nor the control. Hence clearly the wording 'substantially financed' would have to be given meaning at less than 50% holding. The company law gives significant rights to those who own 26% of the shares in a company. Perhaps this could be taken to define *the criterion of 'substantial finance'. The finance could be as equity or subsidies in land or concession in taxation*".

76. The gravamen of the above judgments is that for a private entity to qualify to be a public authority, substantial financing does not mean majority financing. What is important is that the funding by the appropriate Government is achieving a "felt need of a Section of the public or to secure larger societal goals". The ratio of the above judgments, particularly of Delhi High Court, applies to the present case. Large tracts of land in prime areas of Delhi have been placed at the disposal of the Political Parties in-question at exceptionally low rates. Besides, huge Government accommodations have been placed at the disposal of Political Parties at hugely cheap rates thereby bestowing financial benefits on them. The Income Tax exemptions granted and the free air time at AIR and Doordarshan at the time of elections also has substantially contributed to the financing of the Political Parties by the Central Government. We have, therefore, no hesitation in concluding that INC/AICC, BJP, CPI(M), CPI, NCP and BSP have been substantially financed by the Central Government and, therefore, they are held to be public authorities under Section 2(h) of the RTI Act.

PERFORMANCE OF PUBLIC DUTY

77. The Political Parties are the life blood of our polity. As observed by Laski "The life

of the democratic state is built upon the party system". Elections are contested on party basis. The Political Parties select some problems as more urgent than others and present solutions to them which may be acceptable to the citizens. The ruling party draws its development programmes on the basis of its political agenda. It is responsible for the growth and development of the society and the nation. Political Parties affect the lives of citizens, directly or indirectly, in every conceivable way and are continuously engaged in performing public duty. It is, therefore, important that they became accountable to the public.

78. Political Parties are the unique institution of the modern constitutional State. These are essentially political institutions and are non-governmental. Their uniqueness lies in the fact that in spite of being non-governmental, they come to wield or directly or indirectly influence exercise of governmental power. It would be odd to argue that transparency is good for all State organs but not so good for Political Parties, which, in reality, control all the vital organs of the State.

79. In the W.P. No.12076 of 2008 dated 9.2.2010 in the case of Bangalore International Airport Limited Vs. Karnataka Information Commission, the Karnataka High Court has held that:

> ***"A public authority may be described as a person or administrative body entrusted with functions to perform for the benefit of the public and not for private profit. Not every such person or body is expressly defined as a public authority or body, and the meaning of a public authority or body may vary according to the statutory context; one of the distinguishing features of an authority not being a public authority, is profit making. It is not incumbent that a body in order to be a public body must always be constituted by a statute; for an authority to be a 'public authority' it must be an authority exercised or capable of being exercised for the benefit of the public".***

80. The purity of elections assumes critical significance in this context. In Union of India Vs. Association of Democratic Reforms & Anr (AIR 2002 SC 2112), the Supreme Court has laid emphasis on the purity of elections in the following words:

> **"To maintain the purity of elections and in particular to bring transparency in the process of election, the Commission can ask the candidates about the expenditure incurred by the Political Parties and this transparency in the process of election would include transparency of a candidate who seeks election or re-election. In a democracy, the electoral process has a strategic role. The little man of this country would have basic elementary right to know full particulars of a candidate who is to represent him in Parliament where laws to bind his liberty and property may be enacted."**

81. The National Commission to Review the Working of the Constitution in its report submitted in March 2002 has recommended that Political Parties as well as

individual candidates be made subject to a proper statutory audit of the amounts they spend. In Common Cause (A Registered Society Vs. Union of India) (AIR 1996 SC 3081), the Supreme Court has dealt with the income and expenditure incurred by the Political Parties and has laid emphasis on transparency on election funding.

82. The people of India must know the source of expenditure incurred by Political Parties and by the candidates in the process of election. These judicial pronouncements unmistakably commend progressively higher level of transparency in the functioning of Political Parties in general and their funding in particular.

83. We may also add that the preamble to the Constitution of India aims at securing to all its citizens: JUSTICE, social, economic and political; LIBERTY of thought, expression, belief, faith and worship; and, EQUALITY of status and of opportunity. Coincidentally, the preamble of RTI Act also aims to promote these principles in the form of transparency and accountability in the working of the every public authority. It also aims to create an 'informed citizenry' and to contain corruption and to hold government and their instrumentalities accountable to the governed. Needless to say, Political Parties are important political institutions and can play a critical role in heralding transparency in public life. Political Parties continuously perform public functions which define parameters of governance and socio-economic development in the country.

84. In view of the nature of public functions performed by Political Parties and the dicta of the High Court extracted above, we conclude that Political Parties in question are Public Authorities under Section 2(h) of the RTI Act.

Constitutional/Legal Provisions Vesting Political Parties with Rights and Liabilities

85. The appellants have also contended that Political Parties have constitutional and legal rights and liabilities and, therefore, need to be held to be Public Authorities. The argument runs thus. Political Parties are required to be registered with the ECI under Section 29A of the R.P. Act, 1951—a Central Legislation. An association or body gets the status of a political party on its registration. ECI awards symbols to Political Parties under the Election Symbols (Reservation and Allotment) Order, 1968, only after registration. The ECI calls for details of expenses made by the Political Parties in the elections. Contributions of the value of Rs. 20,000/- and above received from any person or a Company by a Political Party are required to be intimated to ECI under Section 29C of the R.P. Act. ECI is vested with the superintendence, direction and control of elections under Article 324 of the Constitution. ECI is also vested with the authority to suspend or withdraw recognition of a political party in certain contingencies. More importantly, Political Parties can recommend disqualification of Members of the House in certain contingencies under the Tenth Schedule. The contention is that the aforesaid constitutional/statutory powers of Political Parties bring them in the ambit of Section 2(h).

86. We find the above submissions quite compelling and unerringly pointing towards their character as public authority.

Stand of Political Parties

87. It may be recalled that the INC/AICC and the BJP have made a bland assertion that they are not Public Authorities under the RTI Act. CPI(M) has disclosed some information to the Commission regarding allotment of land to it by the Central Government on certain terms and conditions but has not conceded that it is Public Authority under Section 2(h) of the RTI Act. The contentions of the above parties have to be rejected in the light of findings recorded hereinabove.

88. Interestingly, the CPI office bearers have taken a contradictory stand. While Shri A.B. Bardhan in his letter dated 21.3.2011 addressed to Shri Anil Bairwal has stated that CPI is a Public Authority under Section 2(h), on the other hand Shri Sudhakar Reddy, vide letter dated 24.9.2012 sent to the Commission, has taken the stand that Political Parties do not fall in the ambit of Section 2(h). As the stand of CPI is confusing, it does not call for any comments.

89. However, the submissions made by Shri A.A. Tiwari, counsel for Nationalist Congress Party need to be dealt with at some length. It is his contention that free air time granted to the NCP during the elections on National Television and National Radio does not amount to government financing of NCP as it is a popular practice in other democracies of the world. According to him, free provisioning of electoral rolls of Political Parties is a statutory requirement and cannot be construed as substantial financing. Similarly, allotment of plots of land/Government accommodation to Political Parties at economical rates cannot be construed as substantial financing. Similarly, tax exemption under Section 13A given to Political Parties under the provisions of the statute also cannot be construed as financing of Political Parties by the Central Government.

90. The arguments of Shri Tiwari cannot be accepted by us in the light of statutory provisions and the case law referred to hereinabove and they have to be rejected. We may further add that his contention that NCP has received less than 1.55% of its total funding from the Government also cannot be accepted by us as he has not produced any figures before us to substantiate this claim. Further, assuming that these figures are true, this contention is liable to be rejected on the ground that NCP, being a Political Party, performs public functions, which along with other reasons mentioned above, qualifies it to be Public Authority under Section 2(h).

91. Yet another contention of Shri Tiwari is that if Political Parties are held to be Public Authorities, then the political rivals would maliciously flood their CPIOs with numerous RTI applications at the time of elections thereby wasting their time and energy and, thus, causing detriment to their political functioning. In our view, the validity of a statute cannot be questioned only on the basis of presumption of its possible misuse. On the contrary, we are of the opinion that bringing the Political Parties in the ambit of RTI Act is likely to usher an era of transparency in their functioning. Besides it would result in strengthening of democracy and democratice institutions in the country. In view of the above discussion, we do not find any merit in the submissions of Adv. Tiwari and reject the same.

92. In view of the above discussion, we hold that INC, BJP, CPI(M), CPIO, NCP and BSP have been substantially financed by the Central Government under Section 2(h)(ii) of the RTI Act. The criticality of the role being played by these Political Parties in our democratic set up and the nature of duties performed by them also point towards their public character, bringing them in the ambit of Section 2(h). The constitutional and legal provisions discussed hereinabove also point towards their character as public authorities. The order of the Single Bench of this Commission in Complaint No. CIC/MISC/2009/0001 and CIC/MISC/2009/0002 is hereby set aside and it is held that AICC/INC, BJP, CPI(M), CPI, NCP and BSP are public authorities under Section 2(h) of the RTI Act.

93. The Presidents, General Secretaries of these Political Parties are hereby directed to designate CPIOs and the Appellate Authorities at their headquarters in 6 weeks time. The CPIOs so appointed will respond to the RTI applications extracted in this order in 4 weeks time. Besides, the Presidents/General Secretaries of the above mentioned Political Parties are also directed to comply with the provisions of Section 4(1) (b) of the RTI Act by way of making voluntary disclosures on the subjects mentioned in the said clause.

94. The complaints are disposed of as per the above directions.

(Mrs. Annapurna Dixit)
Information Commissioner

(M. L. Sharma)
Information Commissioner

(Satyananda Mishra)
Chief Information Commissioner

Authenticated true copy. Additional copies of orders shall be supplied against application and payment of the charges, prescribed under the Act, to the Additional Registrar of this Commission.

(Aakash Deep Chakravarti)
Joint Secretary (Law) & Additional Registrar

Reportable

IN THE SUPREME COURT OF INDIA
CIVIL ORIGINAL JURISDICTION

Review Petition [C] No. 2309 of 2012
in Writ Petition [C] No. 210 of 2012

Union of India ... Petitioner

Versus

Namit Sharma ...Respondent

WITH

Review Petition [C] No. 2675 of 2012
in Writ Petition [C] No. 210 of 2012

State of Rajasthan & Anr. ... Petitioners

Versus

Namit Sharma ... Respondent

Judgment

A. K. Patnaik, J.

These are petitions filed under Article 137 of the Constitution of India for review of the judgment dated 13.09.2012 of this Court in Writ Petition (C) No. 210 of 2012 (hereinafter referred to as 'the judgment under review').

Background Facts

2. In Writ Petition (C) No. 210 of 2012 filed under Article 32 of the Constitution of India, Namit Sharma, the respondent herein, had prayed for declaring the provisions of Sections 12(5), 12(6), 15(5) and 15(6) of the Right to Information Act, 2005 (for short 'the Act') as *ultra vires* the Constitution. Sections 12(5), 12(6), 15(5) and 15(6) of the Act are extracted hereinbelow:

> "12(5) The Chief Information Commissioner and Information Commissioners shall be persons of eminence in public life with wide knowledge and experience in law, science and technology, social service, management, journalism, mass media or administration and governance."

"12(6) The Chief Information Commissioner or an Information Commissioner shall not be a Member of Parliament or Member of the Legislature of any State or Union Territory, as the case may be, or hold any other office of profit or connected with any political party or carrying on any business or pursuing any profession."

"15(5) The State Chief Information Commissioner and State Information Commissioners shall be persons of eminence in public life with wide knowledge and experience in law, science and technology, social service, management, journalism, mass media or administration and governance."

"15(6) The State Chief Information Commissioner or a State Information Commissioner shall not be a Member of Parliament or Member of the Legislature of any State or Union Territory, as the case may be, or hold any other office of profit or connected with any political party or carrying on any business or pursuing any profession."

The grounds taken in the writ petition were that the provisions of Sections 12(5), 12(6), 15(5) and 15(6) of the Act laying down the eligibility criteria for appointment of Central Information Commissioners and State Information Commissioners were vague and had no nexus with the object of the Act and were violative of Article 14 of the Constitution of India and while enacting these provisions, Parliament had not exercised legislative power in consonance with the constitutional principles and guarantees.

3. After hearing the learned counsel for the respondent-writ petitioner and the learned Additional Solicitor General for Union of India, this Court held in the judgment under review that the provisions of Sections 12(5) and 15(5) of the Act did not specify the basic qualifications of the persons to be appointed as Information Commissioners and only mentioned that the Chief Information Commissioner and Information Commissioners shall be persons of eminence in public life with wide knowledge and experience in law, science and technology, social service, management, journalism, mass media or administration and governance. This Court held that the knowledge and experience in the different fields mentioned in Section 12(5) and Section 15(5) of the Act would presuppose a graduate who possesses basic qualification in the concerned field. This Court also held that Sections 12(6) and 15(6) of the Act, which provide that the Chief Information Commissioner or an Information Commissioner shall not be a Member of Parliament or Member of the Legislature of any State or Union Territory or hold any other office of profit or be connected with any political party or carry on any business or pursue any profession, do not disqualify such persons for consideration for appointment as Chief Information Commissioner or Information Commissioner, but these disqualifications will come into play after a person is appointed as Chief Election Commissioner or Information Commissioner. In other words, after a Chief Election Commissioner or Information Commissioner is appointed, he cannot continue to be a Member of Parliament or Member of the Legislature of any State or hold any other office of profit or remain connected with any political party or carry on any business or pursue any profession.

4. In the judgment under review, this Court also held that the Information Commission, as a body, performs functions of wide magnitude, through its members,

including adjudicatory, supervisory as well as penal functions. This Court held that access to information is a statutory right, subject to certain constitutional and statutory limitations and the Information Commissioners have been vested with the power to decline furnishing of information under certain circumstances and in the specified situations. This Court held that disclosure of information under the Act may also involve the question of prejudice to a third party, unlike in some countries where information involving a third party cannot be disclosed without the consent of that party. This Court held that considering all these functions to be performed by the Information Commission, the exercise of powers and passing of the orders by the Information Commission cannot be arbitrary and have to be in consonance with the principles of natural justice, namely, notice to a party, grant of hearing and passing of reasoned orders, and, therefore, the Information Commission is a Tribunal discharging quasi-judicial functions. This Court held that there is a *lis* to be decided by the Information Commission inasmuch as the request of a party seeking information is to be allowed or to be disallowed and the decisions rendered by the Information Commission on such a *lis* may prejudicially affect a third party. For these reasons, this Court further held that the Information Commission possesses the essential attributes and trappings of a Court as the adjudicatory powers performed by the Information Commission are akin to the Court system and the adjudicatory matters that they decide can have serious consequences on various rights including the right to privacy protected under Article 21 of the Constitution.

5. In the judgment under review, this Court also expressed the opinion that for effectively performing the functions and exercising the powers of the Information Commission, there is a requirement of a judicial mind. For holding this opinion, the Court relied on the judgments of this Court in *Bharat Bank Ltd., Delhi* Vs. *Employees of Bharat Bank & Ors.* [AIR 1950 SC 188], *S.P. Sampath Kumar* Vs. *Union of India and Others* [(1987) 1 SCC 124], *Union of India* Vs. *R. Gandhi, President Madras Bar Association* [(2010) 11 SCC 1] and *L. Chandra Kumar* Vs. *Union of India and Others* [(1997) 3 SCC 261]. This Court also held that separation of powers and the independence of judiciary are fundamental constitutional values in the structure of our Constitution as without these two constitutional values, impartiality cannot thrive as has been held by this Court in *Union of India* Vs. *R. Gandhi, President, Madras Bar Association* (supra). This Court, thus, held that though the independence of judiciary *stricto sensu* applied to the Court system, by necessary implication, it would also apply to Tribunals whose functioning is quasi-judicial and akin to the Court system and the entire administration of justice has to be so independent and managed by persons of legal acumen, expertise and experience that persons demanding justice must not only receive justice, but should also have the faith that justice would be done. This Court accordingly held that the persons eligible for appointment should be of public eminence, with knowledge and experience in the specified fields and should preferably have some judicial background and they should possess judicial acumen and experience to fairly and effectively deal with the intricate questions of law that would come up for determination before the Information Commission in its day-to-day working. This Court held that the Information Commission is a judicial tribunal having the essential trappings of a Court and, as an irresistible corollary, it will follow that the appointments to the

Information Commission are made in consultation with the judiciary. The Court, however, observed that in the event, the Government is of the opinion and desires to appoint not only judicial members but also experts from other fields to the Commission in terms of Section 12(5) of the Act, to ensure judicial independence, effective adjudicatory process and public confidence in the administration of justice by the Commission, it would be necessary that the Commission is required to work in Benches comprising one judicial member and one other member from the specified fields mentioned in Sections 12(5) and 15(5) of the Act.

6. On the appointment procedure, this Court also held in the judgment under review that the appointments to the post of judicial member has to be made in consultation with the Chief Justice of India in case of Chief Information Commissioner and members of the Central Information Commission, and the Chief Justices of the High Courts of the respective States, in the case of State Chief Information Commissioner and State Information Commissioners of that State Commission. This Court further held that in the case of appointment of members to the respective Commissions from other specified fields, the DoPT in the Centre and the concerned Ministry in the States should prepare a panel, after due publicity.

Empanelling the names proposed should be at least three times the number of vacancies existing in the Commission and the names so empanelled, with the relevant record should be placed before the High Powered Committee mentioned in Section 12(3) and 15(3) of the Act and in furtherance of the recommendations of the High Powered Committee, appointments to the Central and State Information Commissions should be made by the competent authority.

7. For the reasons recorded in the judgment under review, this Court disposed of the writ petition of the respondent-writ petitioner with the following directions/ declarations:

> "1. The writ petition is partly allowed.
>
> 2. The provisions of Sections 12(5) and 15(5) of the Act of 2005 are held to be constitutionally valid, but with the rider that, to give it a meaningful and purposive interpretation, it is necessary for the Court to 'read into' these provisions some aspects without which these provisions are bound to offend the doctrine of equality. Thus, we hold and declare that the expression 'knowledge and experience' appearing in these provisions would mean and include a basic degree in the respective field and the experience gained thereafter. Further, without any peradventure and veritably, we state that appointments of legally qualified, judicially trained and experienced persons would certainly manifest in more effective serving of the ends of justice as well as ensuring better administration of justice by the Commission. It would render the adjudicatory process which involves critical legal questions and nuances of law, more adherent to justice and shall enhance the public confidence in the working of the Commission. This is the obvious interpretation of the language of these provisions and, in fact, is the essence thereof.
>
> 3. As opposed to declaring the provisions of Section 12(6) and 15(6) unconstitutional, we would prefer to read these provisions as having effect

'post-appointment'. In other words, cessation/termination of holding of office of profit, pursuing any profession or carrying any business is a condition precedent to the appointment of a person as Chief Information Commissioner or Information Commissioner at the Centre or State levels.

4. There is an absolute necessity for the legislature to reword or amend the provisions of Sections 12(5), 12(6) and 15(5), 15(6) of the Act. We observe and hope that these provisions would be amended at the earliest by the legislature to avoid any ambiguity or impracticability and to make it in consonance with the constitutional mandates.

5. We also direct that the Central Government and/or the competent authority shall frame all practice and procedure related rules to make working of the Information Commissions effective and in consonance with the basic rule of law. Such rules should be framed with particular reference to Section 27 and 28 of the Act within a period of six months from today.

6. We are of the considered view that it is an unquestionable proposition of law that the Commission is a 'judicial tribunal' performing functions of 'judicial' as well as 'quasi-judicial' nature and having the trappings of a Court. It is an important cog and is part of the court attached system of administration of justice, unlike a ministerial tribunal which is more influenced and controlled and performs functions akin to the machinery of administration.

7. It will be just, fair and proper that the first appellate authority (i.e. the senior officers to be nominated in terms of Section 5 of the Act of 2005) preferably should be the persons possessing a degree in law or having adequate knowledge and experience in the field of law.

8. The Information Commissions at the respective levels shall henceforth work in Benches of two members each. One of them being a 'judicial member', while the other an 'expert member'. The judicial member should be a person possessing a degree in law, having a judicially trained mind and experience in performing judicial functions. A law officer or a lawyer may also be eligible provided he is a person who has practiced law at least for a period of twenty years as on the date of the advertisement. Such lawyer should also have experience in social work. We are of the considered view that the competent authority should prefer a person who is or has been a Judge of the High Court for appointment as Information Commissioners. The Chief Information Commissioner at the Centre or State level shall only be a person who is or has been a Chief Justice of the High Court or a Judge of the Supreme Court of India.

9. The appointment of the judicial members to any of these posts shall be made 'in consultation' with the Chief Justice of India and Chief Justices of the High Courts of the respective States, as the case may be.

10. The appointment of the Information Commissioners at both levels should be made from amongst the persons empanelled by the DoPT in the case of Centre and the concerned Ministry in the case of a State. The panel has to be prepared upon due advertisement and on a rational basis as afore-recorded.

11. The panel so prepared by the DoPT or the concerned Ministry ought to be placed before the High-powered Committee in terms of Section 12(3), for final recommendation to the President of India. Needless to repeat that the High Powered Committee at the Centre and the State levels is expected to adopt a fair and transparent method of recommending the names for appointment to the competent authority.

12. The selection process should be commenced at least three months prior to the occurrence of vacancy.

13. This judgment shall have effect only prospectively.

14. Under the scheme of the Act of 2005, it is clear that the orders of the Commissions are subject to judicial review before the High Court and then before the Supreme Court of India. In terms of Article 141 of the Constitution, the judgments of the Supreme Court are law of the land and are binding on all courts and tribunals. Thus, it is abundantly clear that the Information Commission is bound by the law of precedent, i.e., judgments of the High Court and the Supreme Court of India. In order to maintain judicial discipline and consistency in the functioning of the Commission, we direct that the Commission shall give appropriate attention to the doctrine of precedent and shall not overlook the judgments of the courts dealing with the subject and principles applicable, in a given case.

It is not only the higher court's judgments that are binding precedents for the Information Commission, but even those of the larger Benches of the Commission should be given due acceptance and enforcement by the smaller Benches of the Commission. The rule of precedence is equally applicable to intra-court appeals or references in the hierarchy of the Commission."

Contentions of the Learned Counsel for the Parties

8 Mr. A.S. Chandhiok, learned ASG appearing for the Union of India, submitted that under the Constitution it is only the Legislature which has the power to make law and amend the law and the Court cannot in exercise of its judicial power encroach into the field of legislation. In support of this submission, he relied on the decision of a seven-Judge Bench of this Court in <u>P. Ramachandra Rao</u> Vs. <u>State of Karnataka</u> [(2002) 4 SCC 578] in which this Court has recognised the limits of judicial power in a constitutional democracy. He also cited the decision of a three-Judge Bench in <u>Union of India and Another Vs. Deoki Nandan Aggarwal</u> [1992 Supp. (1) SCC 323] for the proposition that courts cannot rewrite, recast or reframe the legislation for the very good reason that it has no power to legislate. He submitted that this being the position of law, this Court could not have held in the judgment under review that the knowledge and experience in different fields mentioned in Sections 12(5) and 15(5) of the Act would presuppose a graduate or basic degree in the concerned field when Parliament has not provided in Sections 12(5) and 15(5) of the Act that only persons with basic degree in law, science and technology, social science, management, journalism, mass media, etc. would be eligible for appointment as Chief Information Commissioner and Information Commissioners. He submitted that directions nos. 2 and 7 of the judgment

under review that persons possessing basic degree in the respective fields can be Information Commissioners amount to amendment of Sections 12(5) and 15(5) of the Act.

9. Mr. Chandhiok next submitted that the view taken by this Court in the judgment under review that the Information Commissioners should possess the essential attributes of a court and that for effectively performing the functions and powers of the Information Commission there is requirement of a judicial mind and hence persons eligible for appointment as Information Commissioners should preferably have some judicial background and possess judicial acumen, is a patent error of law. He submitted that Information Commissioners have a duty to act judicially and perform quasi-judicial functions, but this does not mean that they must have the experience and acumen of judicial officers. In support of this submission, he cited the observations of Hidayatullah, J in *Harinagar Sugar Mills Ltd.* Vs. *Shyam Sunder Jhunjhunwala and Others* (AIR 1961 SC 1669) that an officer who is required to decide the matters judicially does not make him a Court or even a Tribunal because that only establishes that he is following the standards of conduct and is free from bias and interest. He submitted that as Information Commissions are not really exercising judicial powers, and are not courts, Parliament has not provided in Sections 12(5) and 15(5) of the Act that Information Commissioners have to have judicial experience and acumen. He argued that direction no. 8 that Information Commissions at the respective levels shall work in Benches of two members each and one of them has to be a judicial member possessing a degree in law and having judicially trained mind and experience in performing judicial functions and the direction that competent authority should prefer a person who is or has been a Judge of the High Court for appointment as Information Commissioners and that the Chief Information Commissioner shall only be a person who is or has been a Chief Justice of a High Court or a Judge of the Supreme Court of India is a palpable error which needs to be corrected in this review. He further submitted that consequently direction no. 9 in the judgment under review that the appointment of judicial members as Information Commissioners shall be in consultation with the Chief Justice of India and Chief Justice of High Court of the respective States, as the case may be, should be deleted.

10. Mr. Chandhiok finally submitted that in direction no. 5 of the judgment under review, this Court has further directed the Central Government to frame all practice and procedure related rules to make working of the Information Commissions effective and in consonance with the basic rule of law under Sections 27 and 28 of the Act within a period of 6 months but law is well settled that the Court cannot direct a rule making authority to make rules in a particular fashion. He relied on the decision of this Court in *Mallikarjuna Rao and Others* Vs. *State of Andhra Pradesh and Others* [(1990) 2 SCC 707] in support of this submission. He argued that direction no. 5 of the judgment under review is, therefore, a patent error which needs to be corrected in this review.

11. Dr. Manish Singhvi, Additional Advocate General for the State of Rajasthan, submitted that the Information Commissioners do not perform functions which prior to the Act were vested in courts and therefore they need not be persons having judicial background/judicial training/judicial experience. He submitted that in *Union of India* Vs. *R. Gandhi, Madras Bar Association* (supra), this Court took the view that only if

functions which have been dealt with by civil courts are transferred to tribunals, such tribunals should be manned by persons having judicial background/judicial training/ judicial experience. He submitted that the view taken by this Court in the judgment under review that persons having judicial background/judicial training/judicial experience should be preferred while appointing Information Commissioners is an apparent error which should be corrected in this review.

12. Mr. M.S. Ganesh, learned senior counsel appearing for the intervener, Commonwealth Human Rights Initiative, submitted that the Information Commission is not vested with sovereign judicial powers and discharges only administrative functions under the provisions of the Act and the view taken by this Court in the judgment under review that Information Commissioners should be persons having judicial background, judicial experience and judicial acumen is not a correct view. He cited the opinion of Lord Greene, M.R. in B. Johnson & Co. (Builders), Ltd. Vs. Minister of Health [(1947) 2 All England Law Reports 395] as well as the opinion of Lord Diplock in Bushell Vs. Secretary of State for the Environment [(1980) 2 All ER 608 HL] that Information Commissioners arrive at administrative decisions and do not decide litigations and therefore they need not have judicial background, judicial experience and judicial acumen. Mr. Ganesh next submitted that persons who have been appointed as Chief Information Commissioners and Information Commissioners under Sections 12(5) and 15(5) of the Act, have been persons without any eminence in public life. He submitted that mostly retired IAS Officers and IPS Officers without any experience in public life but only experience in administration have been appointed as Information Commissioners. He submitted that in this review, the Court should issue appropriate directions to ensure that appointment of Chief Information Commissioners and Information Commissioners are made in accordance with Sections 12(5) and 15(5) of the Act.

13. Mr. Prashant Bhushan, learned senior counsel appearing for the interveners, Mr. Shailesh Gandhi and Mrs. Aruna Roy, submitted that as the Information Commissions do not perform judicial work, they need not be manned by judicial officers and Justices of High Courts and Supreme Court and, therefore, directions No. 8 and 9 of the judgment under review need to be deleted. He further submitted that directions No. 10 and 11 of the judgment under review regarding the procedure to be followed for appointment of Information Commissioners may not ensure transparency in the matter of appointment of Information Commissioners. He submitted that this Court in Centre for PIL and Another Vs. Union of India & Another [(2011) 4 SCC] has laid down a procedure in para 88 for selecting and appointing the Central Vigilance Commissioner and Vigilance Commissioners under Section 3 (3) of the Central Vigilance Commission Act, 2003 and has laid down therein that the empanelment of persons to be considered for appointment of Central Vigilance Commissioner and Vigilance Commissioner shall be carried out on the basis of rational criteria, which is to be reflected by recording of reasons and/or noting akin to reasons by the empanelling authority. He submitted that similar procedure should be followed for shortlisting persons for appointment as Information Commissioners and some reasons should be indicated as to why the person has been empanelled for appointment as Information

Commissioner. He further submitted that the direction No. 8 in the judgment under review that Information Commissioners at the respective levels shall henceforth work in benches of two members and one of them should be a judicial member would result in very few Division Benches of the Information Commission taking up matters and the working of the Information Commission in dealing with matters will slow down. He submitted that instead legal training can be given to Information Commissioners to decide matters involving intricate questions of law.

14. Learned counsel for the respondent-writ petitioner Mr. Amit Sharma, on the other hand, supported the judgment under review. According to him, this Court has rightly held that the Information Commission functions as an adjudicatory authority and decides issues relating to the fundamental right of a citizen to be informed about the Government policies and information. He submitted that to ensure proper adjudication of the fundamental right to information of every citizen, it is absolutely necessary that an independent person who does not have a political agenda is appointed as Information Commissioner. He further submitted that Information Commissioners also have to adjudicate issues relating to right of privacy of the citizens of India, which is part of their personal liberty under Article 21 of the Constitution and for this reason also a person with judicial experience and training is best suited and therefore this Court has rightly held that persons with judicial experience and training and judicial acumen should be preferred for appointment as Information Commissioners. He finally submitted that it will be evident from Sections 7, 8, 9 and 11 of the Act that a *lis* between the parties will have to be decided by the Central Public Information Officer or State Public Information Officer and this Court has rightly held in judgment under review that Information Commissions which decide appeals under Section 20 of the Act against the decisions of the Central Public Information Officer or State Public Information Officer are akin to courts. He referred to Section 18 of the Act to show that Information Commissions have been vested with the powers of a civil court and, therefore, are in the nature of courts which have to be manned by judicial officers.

15. Mr. Sharma vehemently argued that in the event this Court holds in this review that the persons with judicial experience and training need not be appointed as Information Commissioners, then the provisions of Section 12(5) and 15(5) of the Act have to be struck down as *ultra vires* Article 14 of the Constitution. He cited the decision of this Court in *Indra Das* Vs. *State of Assam* [(2011) 3 SCC 380] in which it has been held that ordinarily the literal rule of interpretation while construing a statutory provision should be followed, but where such interpretation makes the provision unconstitutional it can be departed from and the statute should be read down to make it constitutional. He submitted that in the judgment under review, this Court has saved the provisions of Section 12(5) and 15(5) of the Act by reading down the said provisions.

16. Mr. Sharma referred to the chart at page 40 of the writ petition to show qualifications of persons appointed equivalent to Information Commissioners in Australia, Canada, Scotland, England and United States and argued that they are required to obtain a degree in the field of law. He cited the observations of this Court in the case of *Union of India* Vs. *R. Gandhi, President, Madras Bar Association* (supra) that the assumption that members of the civil services will have the judicial experience or expertise in company law to be appointed either as judicial member or technical member

is an erroneous assumption. He submitted that in that case, this Court therefore issued directions that only High Court Judges or District Judges of 5 years experience or lawyers having practice of 10 years can be considered for appointment as judicial members of the National Company Law Tribunal. He also relied on the decision of this Court in *Pareena Swarup* Vs. *Union of India* [(2008) 14 SCC 107] in which this Court observed that while creating new avenue of judicial forums, it is the duty of the Government to see that they are not in breach of basic constitutional scheme of separation of powers and independence of judiciary and held that the provisions of the Prevention of Money-Laundering Act, 2002 as enacted may not ensure an independent judiciary to decide the cases under the Act and accordingly directed the Union of India to incorporate the proposed provisions to ensure independence of judiciary.

Findings of the Court

17. Review of a judgment or order of this Court under Article 137 of the Constitution is confined to only errors apparent on the face of the record as provided in Order XL Rule 1 of the Supreme Court Rules, 1966. A three Judge Bench of this Court has held in *Commissioner of Sales Tax, J & K and Others* Vs. *Pine Chemicals Ltd. and Others* [(1995) 1 SCC 58] that if a reasoning in the judgment under review is at variance with the clear and simple language in a statute, the judgment under review suffers from a manifest error of law, an error apparent on the face of the record, and is liable to be rectified. Hence, in these Review Petitions, we have to decide whether the reasoning and directions in the judgment under review is at variance with the clear and simple language employed in the different provisions of the Act and accordingly whether the judgment under review suffers from manifest errors of law apparent on the face of the record.

18. As we have noticed, Sections 12(5) and 15(5) of the Act provide that Chief Information Commissioner and Information Commissioners shall be persons of eminence in public life with wide knowledge and experience in law, science and technology, social service, management, journalism, mass media or administration and governance. These provisions of the Act do not provide that the Chief Information Commissioner and Information Commissioners shall be persons having judicial experience, training and acumen and yet this Court has held in the judgment under review that for effectively performing the functions and exercising the powers of the Information Commission, there is a requirement of a judicial mind and therefore persons eligible for appointment should preferably have judicial background and possess judicial acumen and experience. We may now examine the bare provisions of the Act, whether this finding that there is requirement of a judicial mind to discharge the functions of Information Commission is an error apparent on the face of the record.

19. Sections 18, 19 and 20 of the Act, which confer powers on the Information Commission, are extracted hereinbelow:

> **"18. Powers and 'Functions of Information Commissions.**—(1) Subject to the provisions of this Act, it shall be the duty of the Central Information

Commission or State Information Commission, as the case may be, to receive and inquire into a complaint from any person,—

(a) who has been unable to submit a request to a Central Public Information Officer or State Public Information Officer, as the case may be, either by reason that no such officer has been appointed under this Act, or because the Central Assistant Public Information Officer or State Assistant Public Information Officer, as the case may be, has refused to accept his or her application for information or appeal under this Act for forwarding the same to the Central Public Information Officer or State Public Information Officer or senior officer specified in sub-section (1) of Section 19 or the Central Information Commission or the State Information Commission, as the case may be;

(b) who has been refused access to any information requested under this Act;

(c) who has not been given a response to a request for information or access to information within the time limit specified under this Act;

(d) who has been required to pay an amount of fee which he or she considers unreasonable;

(e) who believes that he or she has been given incomplete, misleading or false information under this Act; and

(f) in respect of any other matter relating to requesting or obtaining access to records under this Act.

(2) Where the Central Information Commission or State Information Commission, as the case may be, is satisfied that there are reasonable grounds to inquire into the matter, it may initiate an inquiry in respect thereof.

(3) The Central Information Commission or State Information Commission, as the case may be, shall, while inquiring into any matter under this section, have the same powers as are vested in a civil court while trying a suit under the Code of Civil Procedure, 1908, in respect of the following matters, namely:—

(a) summoning and enforcing the attendance of persons and compel them to give oral or written evidence on oath and to produce the documents or things;

(b) requiring the discovery and inspection of documents;

(c) receiving evidence on affidavit;

(d) requisitioning any public record or copies thereof from any court or office;

(e) issuing summons for examination of witnesses or documents; and

(f) any other matter which may be prescribed.

(4) Notwithstanding anything inconsistent contained in any other Act of Parliament or State Legislature, as the case may be, the Central Information Commission or the State Information Commission, as the case may be, may, during the inquiry of any complaint under this Act, examine any record to which this Act applies which is under the control of the public authority, and no such record may be withheld from it on any grounds.

19. Appeal.—(1) Any person who, does not receive a decision within the time specified in sub-section (1) or clause (a) of sub-section (3) of Section 7, or is aggrieved by a decision of the Central Public Information Officer or State Public Information Officer, as the case may be, may within thirty days from the expiry of such period or from the receipt of such a decision prefer an appeal to such officer who is senior in rank to the Central Public Information Officer or State Public Information Officer as the case may be, in each public authority:

Provided that such officer may admit the appeal after the expiry of the period of thirty days if he or she is satisfied that the appellant was prevented by sufficient cause from filing the appeal in time.

(2) Where an appeal is preferred against an order made by a Central Public Information Officer or a State Public Information Officer, as the case may be, under Section 11 to disclose third party information, the appeal by the concerned third party shall be made within thirty days from the date of the order.

(3) A second appeal against the decision under sub-section (1) shall lie within ninety days from the date on which the decision should have been made or was actually received, with the Central Information Commission or the State Information Commission:

Provided that the Central Information Commission or the State Information Commission, as the case may be, may admit the appeal after the expiry of the period of ninety days if it is satisfied that the appellant was prevented by sufficient cause from filing the appeal in time.

(4) If the decision of the Central Public Information Officer or State Public Information Officer, as the case may be, against which an appeal is preferred relates to information of a third party, the Central Information Commission or State Information Commission, as the case may be, shall give a reasonable opportunity of being heard to that third party.

(5) In any appeal proceedings, the onus to prove that a denial of a request was justified shall be on the Central Public Information Officer or State Public Information Officer, as the case may be, who denied the request.

(6) An appeal under sub-section (1) or sub-section (2) shall be disposed of within thirty days of the receipt of the appeal or within such extended period not exceeding a total of forty-five days from the date of filing thereof, as the case may be, for reasons to be recorded in writing.

(7) The decision of the Central Information Commission or State Information Commission, as the case may be, shall be binding.

(8) In its decision, the Central Information Commission or State Information Commission, as the case may be, has the power to—

(a) require the public authority to take any such steps as may be necessary to secure compliance with the provisions of this Act, including—

   (i) by providing access to information, if so requested, in a particular form;

(ii) by appointing a Central Public Information Officer or State Public Information Officer, as the case may be;
(iii) by publishing certain information or categories of information;
(iv) by making necessary changes to its practices in relation to the maintenance, management and destruction of records;
(v) by enhancing the provision of training on the right to information for its officials;
(vi) by providing it with an annual report in compliance with clause (b) of sub-section (1) of Section 4;

(b) require the public authority to compensate the complainant for any loss or other detriment suffered;
(c) impose any of the penalties provided under this Act;
(d) reject the application.

(9) The Central Information Commission or State Information Commission, as the case may be, shall give notice of its decision, including any right of appeal, to the complainant and the public authority.

(10) The Central Information Commission or State Information Commission, as the case may be, shall decide the appeal in accordance with such procedure as may be prescribed.

20. Penalties.—(1) Where the Central Information Commission or the State Information Commission, as the case may be, at the time of deciding any complaint or appeal is of the opinion that the Central Public Information Officer or the State Public Information Officer, as the case may be, has, without any reasonable cause, refused to receive an application for information or has not furnished information within the time specified under sub-section (1) of Section 7 or malafidely denied the request for information or knowingly given incorrect, incomplete or misleading information or destroyed information which was the subject of the request or, obstructed in any manner in furnishing the information, it shall impose a penalty of two hundred and fifty rupees each day till application is received or information is furnished, so however, the total amount of such penalty shall not exceed twenty-five thousand rupees:
Provided that the Central Public Information Officer or the State Public Information Officer, as the case may be, shall be given a reasonable opportunity of being heard before any penalty is imposed on him:
Provided further that the burden of proving that he acted reasonably and diligently shall be on the Central Public Information Officer or the State Public Information Officer, as the case may be.

(2) Where the Central Information Commission or the State Information Commission, as the case may be, at the time of deciding any complaint or appeal is of the opinion that the Central Public Information Officer or the State Public Information Officer, as the case may be, has, without any reasonable cause and persistently, failed to receive an application for

information or has not furnished information within the time specified under sub-section (1) of Section 7 or malafidely denied the request for information or knowingly given incorrect, incomplete or misleading information or destroyed information which was the subject of the request or obstructed in any manner in furnishing the information, it shall recommend for disciplinary action against the Central Public Information Officer or the State Public Information Officer, as the case may be, under the service rules applicable to him.

20. It will be clear from the plain and simple language of Sections 18, 19 and 20 of the Act that, under Section 18 the Information Commission has the power and function to receive and inquire into a complaint from any person who is not able to secure information from a public authority, under Section 19 it decides appeals against the decisions of the Central Public Information Officer or the State Public Information Officer relating to information sought by a person, and under Section 20 it can impose a penalty only for the purpose of ensuring that the correct information is furnished to a person seeking information from a public authority. Hence, the functions of the Information Commissions are limited to ensuring that a person who has sought information from a public authority in accordance with his right to information conferred under Section 3 of the Act is not denied such information except in accordance with the provisions of the Act. Section 2(j) defines "Right to Information" conferred on all citizens under Section 3 of the Act to mean the right to information accessible under the Act, "which is held by or under the control of any public authority". While deciding whether a citizen should or should not get a particular information "which is held by or under the control of any public authority", the Information Commission does not decide a dispute between two or more parties concerning their legal rights other than their right to get information in possession of a public authority. This function obviously is not a judicial function, but an administrative function conferred by the Act on the Information Commissions.

21. In the judgment under review, this Court after examining the provisions of the Act, however, has held that there is a *lis* to be decided by the Information Commission inasmuch as the request of a party seeking information is to be allowed or to be disallowed and hence requires a judicial mind. But we find that the *lis* that the Information Commission has to decide was only with regard to the information in possession of a public authority and the Information Commission was required to decide whether the information could be given to the person asking for it or should be withheld in public interest or any other interest protected by the provisions of the Act. The Information Commission, therefore, while deciding this *lis* does not really perform a judicial function, but performs an administrative function in accordance with the provisions of the Act. As has been held by Lord Greene, M.R. in <u>B. Johnson & Co. (Builders), Ltd.</u> Vs. <u>Minister of Health</u> (supra):

> "*Lis*, of course, implies the conception of an issue joined between two parties. The decision of a *lis*, in the ordinary use of legal language, is the decision of that issue. The What is described here as a *lis* – the raising of the objections to

> the order, the consideration of the matters so raised and the representations of the local authority and the objectors – is merely a stage in the process of arriving at an administrative decision. It is a stage which the courts have always said requires a certain method of approach and method of conduct, but it is not a *lis inter partes*, and for the simple reason that the local authority and the objectors are not parties to anything that resembles litigation."

22. In the judgment under review, this Court has also held after examining the provisions of the Act that the Information Commission decides matters which may affect the rights of third parties and hence there is requirement of judicial mind. For example, under Section 8(1)(d) of the Act, there is no obligation to furnish information including commercial confidence, trade secrets, or intellectual property, the disclosure of which would harm the competitive position of the third party, unless the competent authority is satisfied that the larger public interest warrants the disclosure of such information. Similarly, the right to privacy of a third party, which is part of his personal liberty under Article 21 of the Constitution, may be breached if a particular kind of information, purely of personal nature may be directed to be furnished by the concerned authority. To protect the rights of third parties, Section 11 of the Act provides that where a Central Public Information Officer or a State Public Information Officer, as the case may be, intends to disclose any information or record or part thereof, may on a request made under the Act, which relates to or has been supplied by a third party and has been treated as confidential by that third party, a written notice will have to be given to such third party inviting such party to make a submission in writing or orally, regarding whether the information should be disclosed, and such submission of the third party can be kept in view while taking a decision about disclosure of the information. The decision taken by the Central Public Information Officer or the State Public Information Officer, as the case may be, under Section 11 of the Act is appealable under Section 19 of the Act before the Information Commission and when the Information Commission decides such an appeal, it decides only whether or not the information should be furnished to the citizen in view of the objection of the third party. Here also the Information Commission does not decide the rights of a third party but only whether the information which is held by or under the control of a public authority in relation to or supplied by that third party could be furnished to a citizen under the provisions of the Act. Hence, the Information Commission discharges administrative functions, not judicial functions.

23. While performing these administrative functions, however, the Information Commissions are required to act in a fair and just manner following the procedure laid down in Sections 18, 19 and 20 of the Act. But this does not mean that the Information Commissioners are like Judges or Justices who must have judicial experience, training and acumen. In <u>Harinagar Sugar Mills Ltd.</u> Vs. <u>Shyam Sunder Jhunjhunwala and Others</u> (supra), Hidayatullah, J, explained:

> "33. In my opinion, a Court in 'the strict sense is a tribunal which is a part of the ordinary hierarchy of Courts of Civil Judicature maintained by the State under its constitution to exercise the judicial power of the State. These Courts

perform all the judicial functions of the State except those that are excluded by law from their jurisdiction. The word "judicial", be it noted, is itself capable of two meanings. They were admirably stated by Lopes, L.J. in *Royal Aquarium and Summer and Winter Garden Society* Vs. *Parkinson* (1892) 1 QB 431(452) in these words:

> "The word 'judicial' has two meanings. It may refer to the discharge of duties exercisable by a judge or by justices in court, or to administrative duties which need not be performed in court, but in respect of which it is necessary to bring to bear a judicial mind — that is, a mind to determine what is fair and just in respect of the matters under consideration."

That an officer is required to decide matters before him "judicially" in the second sense does not make him a Court or even a tribunal, because that only establishes that he is following a standard of conduct, and is free from bias or interest."

24. Once the Court is clear that Information Commissions do not exercise judicial powers and actually discharge administrative functions, the Court cannot rely on the constitutional principles of separation of powers and independence of judiciary to direct that Information Commissions must be manned by persons with judicial training, experience and acumen or former Judges of the High Court or the Supreme Court. The principles of separation of powers and independence of judiciary embodied in our Constitution no doubt require that judicial power should be exercised by persons with judicial experience, training and acumen. For this reason, when judicial powers vested in the High Court were sought to be transferred to tribunals or judicial powers are vested in tribunals by an Act of the legislature, this Court has insisted that such tribunals be manned by persons with judicial experience and training, such as High Court Judges and District Judges of some experience. Accordingly, when the powers of the High Court under Companies Act, 1956 were sought to be transferred to Tribunals by the Companies (Amendment) Act, 2002, a Constitution Bench of this Court has held in *Union of India* Vs. *R. Gandhi, President Madras Bar Association* (supra):

> "When the legislature proposes to substitute a tribunal in place of the High Court to exercise the jurisdiction which the High Court is exercising, it goes without saying that the standards expected from the judicial members of the Tribunal and standards applied for appointing such members, should be as nearly as possible as applicable to High Court Judges, which are apart from a basic degree in law, rich experience in the practice of law, independent outlook, integrity, character and good reputation. It is also implied that only men of standing who have special expertise in the field to which the Tribunal relates, will be eligible for appointment as technical members. Therefore, only persons with a judicial background, that is, those who have been or are Judges of the High Court and lawyers with the prescribed experience, who are eligible for appointment as High Court Judges, can be considered for appointment as judicial members."

In *Pareena Swarup* Vs. *Union of India* (supra), having found that judicial powers were to be exercised by the Appellate Tribunals under the Prevention of Money-Laundering Act, 2002 this Court held that to protect the constitutional guarantee of independence of judiciary, persons who are qualified to be judges be appointed as members of the Appellate Tribunal. But, as we have seen, the powers exercised by the Information Commissions under the Act were not earlier vested in the High Court or subordinate court or any other court and are not in any case judicial powers and therefore the Legislature need not provide for appointment of judicial members in the Information Commissions.

25. Perhaps for this reason, Parliament has not provided in Sections 12(5) and 15(5) of the Act for appointment of persons with judicial experience and acumen and retired Judges of the High Court as Information Commissioners and retired Judges of the Supreme Court and Chief Justice of the High Court as Chief Information Commissioner and any direction by this Court for appointment of persons with judicial experience, training and acumen and Judges as Information Commissioners and Chief Information Commissioner would amount to encroachment in the field of legislation. To quote from the judgment of the seven-Judge Bench in *P. Ramachandra Rao* Vs. *State of Karnataka* (supra):

> "Courts can declare the law, they can interpret the law, they can remove obvious lacunae and fill the gaps but they cannot entrench upon in the field of legislation properly meant for the legislature."

26. Moreover, Sections 12(5) and 15(5) of the Act while providing that Chief Information Commissioner and Information Commissioners shall be persons with eminence in public life with wide knowledge and experience in law, science and technology, social service, management, journalism, mass media or administration and governance, also does not prescribe any basic qualification which such persons must have in the respective fields in which they work. In the judgment under review, however, this Court has "read into" Sections 12(5) and 15(5) of the Act missing words and held that such persons must have a basic degree in the respective field as otherwise Sections 12(5) and 15(5) of the Act are bound to offend the doctrine of equality. This "reading into" the provisions of Sections 12(5) and 15(5) of the Act, words which Parliament has not intended is contrary to the principles of statutory interpretation recognised by this Court. In *Union of India and Another* Vs. *Deoki Nandan Aggarwal* (supra) this Court has held that the court could not correct or make up for any deficiencies or omissions in the language of the statute. V. Ramaswami, J. writing the judgment on behalf of a three-Judge Bench says:

> "It is not the duty of the Court either to enlarge the scope of the legislation or the intention of the legislature when the language of the provision is plain and unambiguous. The Court cannot rewrite, recast or reframe the legislation for the very good reason that it has no power to legislate. The power to legislate has not been conferred on the courts. The Court cannot add words to a statute

> or read words into it which are not there. Assuming there is a defect or an omission in the words used by the legislature the Court could not go to its aid to correct or make up the deficiency. Courts shall decide what the law is and not what it should be. The Court of course adopts a construction which will carry out the obvious intention of the legislature but could not legislate itself. But to invoke judicial activism to set at naught legislative judgment is subversive of the constitutional harmony and comity of instrumentalities."

27. In the judgment under review, this Court has also held that if Sections 12(5) and 15(5) of the Act are not read in the manner suggested in the judgment, these Sections would offend the doctrine of equality. But on reading Sections 12(5) and 15(5) of the Act, we find that it does not discriminate against any person in the matter of appointment as Chief Information Commissioner and Information Commissioners and so long as one is a person of eminence in public life with wide knowledge and experience in law, science and technology, social service, management, journalism, mass media or administration and governance, he is eligible to be considered for appointment as Chief Information Commissioner or Information Commissioner. However, to ensure that the equality clause in Article 14 is not offended, the persons to be considered for appointment as Chief Information Commissioner or Information Commissioner should be from different fields, namely, law, science and technology, social service, management, journalism, mass media or administration and governance and not just from one field.

28. Sections 12(6) and 15(6) of the Act, however, provide that the Chief Information Commissioner or an Information Commissioner shall not be a Member of Parliament or Member of the Legislature of any State or Union Territory, as the case may be, or hold any other office of profit or connected with any political party or carry on any business or pursue any profession. There could be two interpretations of Sections 12(6) and 15(6) of the Act. One interpretation could be that a Member of Parliament or Member of the Legislature of any State or Union Territory, as the case may be, or a person holding any other office of profit or connected with any political party or carrying on any business or pursuing any profession will not be eligible to be considered for appointment as a Chief Information Commissioner and Information Commissioner. If this interpretation is given to Sections 12(6) and 15(6) of the Act, then it will obviously offend the equality clause in Article 14 of the Constitution as it debars such persons from being considered for appointment as Chief Information Commissioner and Information Commissioners. The second interpretation of Sections 12(6) and 15(6) of the Act could be that once a person is appointed as a Chief Information Commissioner or Information Commissioner, he cannot continue to be a Member of Parliament or Member of the Legislature of any State or Union Territory, as the case may be, or hold any other office of profit or remain connected with any political party or carry on any business or pursue any profession. If this interpretation is given to Sections 12(6) and 15(6) of the Act then the interpretation would effectuate the object of the Act inasmuch as Chief Information Commissioner and Information Commissioners would be able to perform their functions in the Information Commission without being influenced by

their political, business, professional or other interests. It is this second interpretation of Sections 12(6) and 15(6) of the Act which has been rightly given in the judgment under review and Sections 12(6) and 15(6) of the Act have been held as not to be violative of Article 14 of the Constitution. Therefore, the argument of Mr. Sharma, learned counsel for the respondent-writ petitioner, that if we do not read Sections 12(5) and 15(5) of the Act in the manner suggested in the judgment under review, the provisions of Sections 12(5) and 15(5) of the Act would be *ultra vires* the Article 14 of the Constitution, is misconceived.

29. In the judgment under review, in direction no. 5, the Central Government and/or the competent authority have been directed to frame all practice and procedure related rules to make working of the Information Commissions effective and in consonance with the basic rule of law and with particular reference to Sections 27 and 28 of the Act within a period of six months. Sections 27(1) and 28(1) of the Act are extracted hereinbelow:

> "**27. Power to make rules by appropriate Government.**—(1) The appropriate Government may, by notification in the Official Gazette, make rules to carry out the provisions of this Act.
>
> **28. Power to make rules by competent authority**.—(1) The competent authority may, by notification in the Official Gazette, make rules to carry out the provisions of this Act."

The use of word "may" in Sections 27 and 28 of the Act make it clear that Parliament has left it to the discretion of the rule making authority to make rules to carry out the provisions of the Act. Hence, no *mandamus* can be issued to the rule making authority to make the rules either within a specific time or in a particular manner. If, however, the rules are made by the rule making authority and the rules are not in accordance with the provisions of the Act, the Court can strike down such rules as *ultra vires* the Act, but the Court cannot direct the rule making authority to make the rules where the Legislature confers discretion on the rule making authority to make rules. In the judgment under review, therefore, this Court made a patent error in directing the rule making authority to make rules within a period of six months.

30. Nonetheless, the selection and appointment of Chief Information Commissioner and Information Commissioners has not been left entirely to the discretion of the Central Government and the State Government under Sections 12 and 15 of the Act. Sections 12(3) and 15(3) provide that the Chief Information Commissioner and Information Commissioners shall be appointed by the President or the Governor, as the case may be, on the recommendation of the Committee named therein. Sections 12(5) and 15(5) provide that Chief Information Commissioner and Information Commissioners have to be persons of eminence in public life with wide knowledge and experience in the different fields mentioned therein, namely, law, science and technology, social service, management, journalism, mass media or administration and governance. Thus, the basic requirement for a person to be appointed as a Chief Information Commissioner or Information Commissioner is that he should be a person of eminence in public life

with wide knowledge and experience in a particular field. Parliament has insisted on this basic requirement having regard to the functions that the Chief Information Commissioner and Information Commissioners are required to perform under the Act. As the preamble of the Act states, democracy requires an informed citizenry and transparency of information which are vital to its functioning and also requires that corruption is contained and Governments and their instrumentalities are held accountable to the governed. The preamble of the Act, however, cautions that revelation of information in actual practice is likely to conflict with other public interests including efficient operations of the Governments, optimum use of limited fiscal resources and the preservation of confidentiality of sensitive information. Moreover, under the Act, a citizen has the right to information held or under the control of public authority and hence Information Commissioners are to ensure that the right to privacy of person protected under Article 21 of the Constitution is not affected by furnishing any particular information.

31. Unfortunately, experience over the years has shown that the orders passed by Information Commissions have at times gone beyond the provisions of the Act and that Information Commissions have not been able to harmonise the conflicting interests indicated in the preamble and other provisions of the Act. The reasons for this experience about the functioning of the Information Commissions could be either that persons who do not answer the criteria mentioned in Sections 12(5) and 15(5) have been appointed as Chief Information Commissioner or Information Commissioners or that the persons appointed answer the criteria laid down in Sections 12(5) and 15(5) of the Act but they do not have the required mind to balance the interests indicated in the Act and to restrain themselves from acting beyond the provisions of the Act. This experience of the functioning of the Information Commissions prompted this Court to issue the directions in the judgment under review to appoint judicial members in the Information Commissions. But it is for Parliament to consider whether appointment of judicial members in the Information Commissions will improve the functioning of the Information Commissions and as Sections 12(5) and 15(5) of the Act do not provide for appointment of judicial members in the Information Commissions, this direction was an apparent error. Sections 12(5) and 15(5) of the Act, however, provide for appointment of persons with wide knowledge and experience in law. We hope that persons with wide knowledge and experience in law will be appointed in the Information Commissions at the Centre and the States. Accordingly, wherever Chief Information Commissioner is of the opinion that intricate questions of law will have to be decided in a matter coming before the Information Commissions, he will ensure that the matter is heard by an Information Commissioner who has such knowledge and experience in law.

32. Under Order XL of the Supreme Court Rules, 1966 this Court can review its judgment or order on the ground of error apparent on the face of record and on an application for review can reverse or modify its decision on the ground of mistake of law or fact. As the judgment under review suffers from mistake of law, we allow the Review Petitions, recall the directions and declarations in the judgment under review and dispose of Writ Petition (C) No. 210 of 2012 with the following declarations and directions:

(i) We declare that Sections 12(5) and 15(5) of the Act are not *ultra vires* the Constitution.

(ii) We declare that Sections 12(6) and 15(6) of the Act do not debar a Member of Parliament or Member of the Legislature of any State or Union Territory, as the case may be, or a person holding any other office of profit or connected with any political party or carrying on any business or pursuing any profession from being considered for appointment as Chief Information Commissioner or Information Commissioner, but after such person is appointed as Chief Information Commissioner or Information Commissioner, he has to discontinue as Member of Parliament or Member of the Legislature of any State or Union Territory, or discontinue to hold any other office of profit or remain connected with any political party or carry on any business or pursue any profession during the period he functions as Chief Information Commissioner or Information Commissioner.

(iii) We direct that only persons of eminence in public life with wide knowledge and experience in the fields mentioned in Sections 12(5) and 15(5) of the Act be considered for appointment as Information Commissioner and Chief Information Commissioner.

(iv) We further direct that persons of eminence in public life with wide knowledge and experience in all the fields mentioned in Sections 12(5) and 15(5) of the Act, namely, law, science and technology, social service, management, journalism, mass media or administration and governance, be considered by the Committees under Sections 12(3) and 15(3) of the Act for appointment as Chief Information Commissioner or Information Commissioners.

(v) We further direct that the Committees under Sections 12(3) and 15(3) of the Act while making recommendations to the President or to the Governor, as the case may be, for appointment of Chief Information Commissioner and Information Commissioners must mention against the name of each candidate recommended, the facts to indicate his eminence in public life, his knowledge in the particular field and his experience in the particular field and these facts must be accessible to the citizens as part of their right to information under the Act after the appointment is made.

(vi) We also direct that wherever Chief Information Commissioner is of the opinion that intricate questions of law will have to be decided in a matter coming up before the Information Commission, he will ensure that the matter is heard by an Information Commissioner who has wide knowledge and experience in the field of law.

33. There shall be no order as to costs.

……………………… J.
(A. K. Patnaik)
……………………… J.
(A. K. Sikri)

New Delhi,
September 03, 2013.

Annexure – IV

The Department Related Parliamentary Standing Committee on Personnel, Public Grievances, Law and Justice met at 3 p.m. on 1.2.2005 in Committee Room 'A', Parliament House Annexe, New Delhi.

(CHAIRMAN : SHRI E.M. SUDARSANA NATCHIAPPAN)

CHAIRMAN: Before we call the witnesses for making their presentation on the Right to Information Bill, I would like to put on record one thing. It is a very important Bill. From 1997 onwards, a lot of discussion took place on this Bill. There was the Chief Ministers' Conference where this issue was discussed. Finally, this Bill was passed in 2002. There was some discussion whether the Parliament has got the right to make these types of institutions so that our citizens could get information through these Institutions. We have come to know that, at that time also, the opinion of the Attorney General was sought. He was of the opinion that under Schedule 7, Part 1, item No. 97, the Parliament has got the right to go into it. Now, according to the preliminary study, a lot of provisions of this law are being watered down. I would like to know from the hon. Members whether we should seek the opinion of the present Attorney General in this regard. If the Committee feels that we should call the Attorney General, we can summon him to depose before the Committee. The point is whether we have got the right to have a legislation which is binding on the State Governments also. Now I leave it to the Members. What is your view?

SHRI HARIN PATHAK: We can summon him. It is a sensitive issue.

CHAIRMAN: Okay, we will call him.

Secondly, in the last sitting, we had asked the Ministry to present the report of the Justice Sharrof Committee on Arbitration. At that time, the hon. Members felt that when this particular legislation was being discussed here, then why the Government was having some other Committee to go into it. Therefore, we had directed the Law Secretary to present the report before 30th January, 2005. Accordingly, they have submitted this report. We feel that there is need for some more discussion within the Secretariat on this issue. We also want that they should come forward with what is the position of the Government in this regard. We want to give them some time. in the meantime, we will go on with other Bills. I just wanted to inform you and bring it on record. Now we can call the witnesses. (Followed by 1B)

RG/3.10/1B

LIST OF WITNESSES

Shri A.N. Tiwari, Secretary
Ministry of Personnel, Public Grievances and Pensions
Shri T.K. Viswanathan, Secretary
Legislative Department, Ministry of Law and Justice.
Shri R.L. Meena, Secretary
Department of Legal Affairs, Ministry of Law and Justice

CHAIRMAN: Good Afternoon to all of you. This Committee is presently considering this very important Bill which is attracting the attention of the entire population of India, more especially, the fourth pillar of democracy, that is, the media. This Bill is attracting a lot of attention of all intellectuals not only in India but also throughout the world. We wanted to go into the legal aspects of this Bill also in connection with certain provisions. That is why we requested the Legislative Department as well as the Department of Legal Affairs to participate in this discussion.

First of all we would like to know the reason for repealing of the Act of 2002 and coming forward with a new Bill. On the face of it we find that a lot of main provisions have been watered down, and the recommendations of the previous Committee of Home Affairs, which submitted its Report No. 78 on Freedom of Information Bill, 2000, have also, in certain parts, not implemented. We would like to have clarifications on these two points also when the Secretary, Ministry of Personnel, Public Grievances and Pensions, make his presentation. After his presentation, the other two Secretaries, Shri R.L. Meena and Shri T.K. Viswanathan, can make their presentation on the legal points. After this, the hon. Members will raise certain queries and clarifications. You may reply to them immediately or you. can also give your views in writing and send them to the Committee.

Whatever discussions take place here have to be kept confidential till the Report is placed before Parliament. Now, Shri A.N. Tiwari to make his presentation.

SHRI V. RADHAKRISHNAN: Madam, before the Secretary starts his presentation, with your permission, I would like to say something.

As you are all aware, Parliament had passed the Freedom of Information Act 2002, and it was formally notified in the Gazette. Normally, the practice is that when a legislation is passed and some amendments are required, an Amendment Bill is brought. Here is a new case altogether than you are claiming yourself of having brought a new statute, but the objective of both appears to be the same. Now it is also a fact that we are going to repeal the Act of 2002. This was passed after scrutiny by the Standing Committee and after an elaborate discussion and debate in both the Houses of Parliament. I would like to know what is the reason behind bringing a new legislation instead of making some changes in the already existing law. Basically, we find that there is only a change in nomenclature. Another thing, is, that we did not have penal provisions in the earlier Act. But here you are bringing in penal provisions. But this could have been included by way of an amendment.

What is the purpose? What is the thinking in the Government? Why this amendment is being brought forward? This means all the labour put in by the 13th Lok Sabha has gone waste. You must give us convincing reasons for coming forward with such an unusual procedure. It is really very unusual. You are repealing an Act that was passed by Parliament. Of course, no law is an end in itself. No law can be there for perpetuity. Any law must change according to the changes taking place in the society. I could understand if you wanted to change the nomenclature of the Bill. Now, here, more or less all the provisions are the same. Of course, some cosmetic changes have been made, for example, about penalising.

My friend, we are poor people. We are not experts in such matters. We presume that you are great experts and you have the specialised knowledge about these things. We are representatives of poor people. We are innocent people. Please give us convincing reasons why you have brought this new legislation.

CHAIRMAN: Let me tell you he is not so innocent and so poor.

SHRI HARIN PATHAK: I humbly endorse the views expressed by Shri Radhakrishnan. I am also surprised at the fact that when there was this earlier enactment, which had been gazetted and published, this new amendment has been brought and that too, without any major changes. Let me put it on record that there is no major change. This is unprecedented that a Bill is passed, it is assented to by the hon. President, it is published in the Gazette and a new Bill is brought. The Committee would like to know the major changes that you have brought. What was the reason for repealing the earlier Act?

SHRIMATI KIRAN MAHESHWARI: Yes, we just want to know why the earlier law has not been amended and why a fresh Bill is being brought forward.

SHRI A. N. TIWARI: Sir, I express my thanks to you for having given to me and my colleagues this opportunity to be present here and to give our position about this Right to Information Bill which has been introduced in Parliament.

As you are aware, Sir, this Bill seeks to replace the Freedom of Information Act of 2002. That Act was devised largely to give to the people of India the right to access information held by Government, both the Central Government and the State Governments, except that information which was held by Government in its proprietary right. The citizens of India have the right to access that information regardless of the fact whether it is the State Government or the Central Government. So, that Act of 2002 had an all-India applicability. It, in effect, meant that it superseded the Acts which the State Governments might have planned or promulgated. As you know, eight State Governments in this country have already had their Right to Information Acts, which preceded both this Bill and the Act of 2002. After that, the CMP passed a resolution which was communicated to the Department of Personnel through the Prime Minister's Office which said that there shall be an attempt made to make the Right to Information Bill more progressive, participatory and meaningful. In pursuance of that, we started working on the measures which needed to be amended so as to make the Bill more progressive. The Department held the view that a few amendments could be carried out in the existing Act and it could be brought before the Parliament. At that time, we received from the National Advisory Council 35 amendments including the one about the nomenclature of the Act. When we examined the range of these amendments, it turned out that we would have to carry out a very large number of amendments in the existing Act—both cosmetic and substantive. Therefore, in consultation with our colleagues in the Department of Law and Legal Affairs, we decided that perhaps a better alternative would be to bring in a new Bill which will incorporate all those amendments, rather than to amend it comprehensively. That was the sole reason. There was no complex thinking that went behind it. It was decided that perhaps a new Bill will meet the requirement better than a comprehensively amendment of the existing Act. That was all to it. I say with all humility and transparency that there was no complex thinking that went behind taking this decision of brining a new bill rather than amending the existing Act.

SHRI HARIN PATHAK: Could you tell us the major changes that you have proposed here?

SHRI V. RADHAKRISHNAN: You see, the Act passed by the House was not given effect to. How did you know that the amendments would be required? Once an Act is gazetted and published, it becomes operative. But it has not been notified by the Government because there is a clause in the original Act that it will become operative from the date on which the Government notifies it. That was not done. And that is what I cannot understand.

CHAIRMAN: Mr. Secretary, First you make your presentation and after that, you can clarify these points. (Followed by 1D)

TDB/1D/3.30

SHRI A.N. TIWARI: Sir, the Right to Information Bill, 2004 which we have brought before you, has incorporated the amendments which were suggested to us— copies of which have already been submitted to you— by the National Advisory Council. A majority of them were incorporated in the Bill; some of them could not be incorporated, as I said earlier, because they were not of much significance.

Sir, the title of the Bill has been changed from 'Freedom of Information Act' to 'Right to Information Act'. The reason behind that was that it was believed that the word 'right' will position it very correctly within the ambit of fundamental right of speech and expression. Therefore, the Right to Information Bill was thought to be a better alternative to the 'Freedom of Information Act'. The Bill provides for a very definitive day for its commencement, i.e., 120 days from its enactment. It was not so in the case of the previous Act. It excludes the State Government bodies and applies only to public authorities under the Central Government, Constitutional bodies and bodies established by Parliament. It is a debatable Constitutional point whether the Central Government has the authority to enact a legislation which will have effect over the State subjects. Therefore, this point was also very extensively debated that the State Governments should have the authority to enact their own laws whereas the Right to Information Act enacted by the Central Government would apply only in respect of subjects administered by the Central Government.

Sir, the Bill provides that each Department and Ministry will have a Public Information Officer who will be in place within 120 days of the enactment of the Act. So, there is a definitiveness as to when the action will be taken to create the required infrastructure for the implementation of this Act. The Bill provides for transfer of a request by a public authority to another public authority wherein the subject matter/information is held by the latter. As per the Bill, the exemptions provided are not absolute and withholding of information must be balanced against disclosure in the public Interest. All the exemptions are conditional exemptions. All exemptions are weighed against disclosure in public interest. Information is to be released even if harm is shown to the public authority, if the public benefit in knowing the information outweighs the harm that may be caused by disclosure. The Bill envisages creation of an independent non-judicial machinery. This is a major difference. It says that there shall be a non-judicial machinery, i.e., the Central Information Commission comprising of an Information Commissioner and Deputy Information Commissioners to decide second appeals. There is a new right to information hierarchy which has been created under this Bill. The legal framework of exercise of powers by the Commission are defined in the Bill.

SHRI V. RADHAKRISHNAN: The Bill provides for an Information Commissioner. The Prime Minister, the Leader of Opposition in the Lok Sabha and the Chief Justice of India will form a Committee, and the President would appoint the Information Commissioner in consultation with that Committee.

SHRI A.N. TIWARI: The first appeal would lie to the departmental officer senior to the PIO. The second appeal is to be made to the Commission. There is even a provision for imposition of penalty up to Rs. 25,000/- or an imprisonment up to five years or both may be imposed on a Public Information Officer or anybody who is withholding the information, if convicted for persistent failure to provide information without any reasonable cause within the specified time period. As per the Bill, exemption of specified intelligence/security agencies is not absolute; agencies shall have the obligation to provide information in matters relating to corruption. In all integrity matters, security related exemptions are not absolute.

Sir, as far as monitoring and reporting is concerned, the Bill makes a provision to produce statistics to assess the implementation of the Act so that improvements could be effected, wherever requirement is perceived. The Central Information Commission is to monitor the implementation of the Act and prepare an Annual Report to be laid before Parliament. The Central Government is to prepare programmes for development of 'information' regime, and this will be followed by the repeal of the Freedom of Information Act, 2002. So, these are the main clauses of the Bill which I have paraphrased before the Committee. The number of amendments suggested to the Freedom of Information Act, 2002 was quite elaborate. It was becoming very difficult for us to incorporate so many amendments in the Freedom of Information Act, 2002. Because of those amendments, framing of the new Bill became essential. That is why a decision was taken to repeal the previous Act and bring in a new Bill.

SHRI V. RADHAKRISHNAN: I have a doubt in my mind. The first appeal will be made to the immediate superior officer in the very office. You are not specifying him in the Bill. Only in the second appeal, the appeal would go to the Commissioner. The first appeal will go to the officer above him in the same office.

SHRI A.N. TIWARI: There is one point about which the hon. Chairman made a mention, and that was about the legislative competence. This matter has generated quite an elaborate debate at the moment. As I submitted, the Freedom of Information Act, 2002 really provided a single common Act for the entire country. It was silent as to what would happen, after that Act came into being to the State Acts which were already in place. Our presumption, perhaps is, it will supersede those Acts and they will become redundant. We were not quite sure how this process shall be taken forward. But, assuming for a moment that, that Act was an all-India Act and other State Acts did not have currency in the presence of that Act, some doubts were raised in certain quarters whether the Central Act could be used for accessing information held by the State Governments. So, there were two options before us. One was...

SHRI V. RADHAKRISHNAN: There are some States which have got the Freedom of Information Act on their statute books. For example, Karnataka has got one such Act. In case of a dispute between the Central Act and a State Act, I think, the Central Act will prevail. What is your stand on that?

SHRI A.N. TIWARI: The Central Act, as it was passed by Parliament did not mention that it would supersede the State Acts. It just said that the Central Act would be there. Now, there was a question of competency about our enacting a Central legislation to provide for accessing information held by the State Governments by their citizens. There were two viewpoints. One was, we allow the Central Act and the State Acts to remain present concurrently and leave the option to the citizen to decide how to access information held by the State Governments, they can do it either through the Central Act or through the State Acts. The information held by the Central Government would be accessed through the Central Act. There was dual option in respect of the information held by the State Governments. This was contested by some legal experts and it was said, perhaps, this position would not be defensible in law. So, in order to prevent any further litigation on this point, we introduced this provision in the Bill that the Central information shall be accessed only through the Central Act and the State information by the State Acts. That is the position, at the moment. If there are any further queries I would be very glad to clarify them. (Followed by 1e)

kgg/1e/3.40/PPG/1.2.05

SHRI RAM NATH KOVIND: Mr. Secretary, my hon. colleague, Shri Radhakrishnan asked you to give a convincing reply, but even after your reply, we are not satisfied yet. When we go through the Gazette of India, this Freedom of Information Act was notified after its passage on 7th January, 2003. It is said, "It shall come into force as and when the Central Government notifies it in the Official Gazette for bringing this Act into force." We are not yet convinced.

SHRI HARIN PATHAK: I am sorry to say this about the fault of the Department. It is a pity that both Ministries, Ministry of Law and Ministry of Personnel, could not be competent enough to bring forward a comprehensive Bill in the Parliament. In a span of just six months, the new Bill has been set into motion. I have nothing to say except that I feel sorry. It is not fair in democracy. Efficiency has taken a beating. That is all. I am not personally satisfied with the reasons given.

SHRI V. RADHAKRISHNAN: When this Bill was taken up in the House, we discussed the amendments. I have a question with regard to exemptions. Exceptions are also enumerated in that. A change in situation may effect a change in exceptions also. Today it may be an exception, and in future, it may not be so. It is evident that you are bound to give the information that is sought. Because of exceptions, you may give today and you may not give it in future. Even the 'exceptions' may be changed. The question is, who is the competent person to decide on the question of exceptions? Otherwise, it becomes meaningless.

DR. P.C. ALEXANDER: I just have to make a comment in favour of officers. We should not think that officers have come up with the suggestions on their own. Left to themselves, they were happy that it was introduced in the Parliament, was discussed and was passed and became a law. But for certain other reasons, which I don't have to mention, they have been asked to bring about a new Bill. They are not in a position to tell us what we seek. We are asking them to explain something for which they are really not responsible. I am telling this to Mr. Radhakrishnan, that we have to take a different look at this matter.

Now I have a question to the Secretaries present here. You have not taken all the recommendations of the National Advisory Council into account. They made 34 recommendations. You have simply refused some and modified some. Then, you have differed on certain matters. You have accepted totally whatever they have said on some. Then, you have been asked to bring forward a new Bill. I want to ask the legal experts who are here, supposing this Committee comes to a conclusion that instead of bringing in a new Bill some provisions should be modified, what would you say? If the Committee asks you to take into account some of the things which you have placed before us, and the recommendations of the National Advisory Council, and some which have been changed by the Cabinet Committee concerned, what would be the best way of doing it from your point of view?

Suppose we come to a decision on some provisions of the Act, without accepting the new legislation, how will the Government look at that? We may say that such and such amendments are not necessary and we ask you to consider that, and we even say that we would consider it at a later stage, what would be the format of making those amendments? How will the Government look at that?

SHRI A.N. TIWARI: Sir, this matter has already received the approval of the Cabinet. Now it is before the Standing Committee. And your views will certainly be taken into account. We will again go back to the Cabinet.

SHRI V. RADHAKRISHNAN: In the Common Minimum Programme, the right to information is an item. So, they wanted to bring this Bill adding 'right' to this law.

DR. P.C. ALEXANDER: My submission is, it is a matter which should be discussed amongst ourselves. We should arrive at a conclusion. We may agree with the new suggestions or we may not.

CHAIRMAN: The Secretary also says that there is a suspicion in the minds of media as also in the public, that with a change in Government, or, maybe, there is a change of mindset in six months. They say, "Here is a National Advisory Council which has recommended on certain things to strengthen the law which is prevailing now but it was not implemented. That means, the bureaucracy is dragging its feet to see that this law should not be there. It is a harassment of the democracy."

That is the mind of certain sections of the media. This is the main reason why hon. Members have raised certain doubts. It is not for blaming the bureaucracy, nor is it a comment on the political mileage.

(Contd. by 1f)

KLS/1F-3.50/PPG/1.2.2005

CHAIRMAN (CONTD): This particular subject was discussed from 1997 onwards throughout India. It was discussed in the Chief Ministers' Conference. There was a consensus and on that basis this Bill was drafted. Then it has gone to different Committees, Group of Ministers, Group of Secretaries, etc., Finally, a law was made in 2002. That was about to be implemented. It was not implemented for one year. Then there was a change of Government. After that Advisory Council suggested 34 amendments. This is the feeling of the public and also of the media. That is why we are asking these questions. It is not either to blame this side or that side. If you have any explanation, please give it to us.

श्री शैलेन्द्र कुमार: चेयरमैन साहब, अभी जैसा माननीय सदस्यों, श्री अलेक्जेन्डर जी, श्री पाठक जी व श्री राधाकृष्णन जी ने इस बिल के बारे में चिन्ता व्यक्त की कि 7 जनवरी, 2003 को जब यह पारित हो गया था, तब फिर क्यों एक वर्ष तक यह यूं ही पड़ा रहा। एक सरकार गई तो दूसरी सरकार आने का इंतजार था, इसकी सफाई के तौर पर यह कहा गया। इसका क्या कारण था? हम ब्यूरोक्रेसी के ऊपर इल्जाम नहीं लगाते, लेकिन फिर भी एक वर्ष तक रोके रखना कितना उचित था। इस पर राष्ट्रीय सलाहकार समिति ने 34 सुझाव भी भेज दिए, फिर भी यह एक वर्ष तक रुका रहा। इस पर कार्मिक विभाग ने कुछ न कुछ टिप्पणी तो अवश्य की होगी। मेरे ख्याल से इससे सम्बन्धित फाइल को मंगवाया जाए क्योंकि विलम्ब बहुत अधिक हुआ है। इस प्रकार से जो भी तथ्य इसके पीछे हैं, वे सामने आ जाएंगे। यही सुझाव अपनी ओर से मैं जानकारी के तौर पर देना चाहूंगा।

श्रीमती किरण माहेश्वरी: हम यही तो आपसे पूछना चाहेंगे कि क्या आप संतुष्ट हैं या इस बात से सहमत हैं कि नया बिल आना चाहिए।

CHAIRMAN: We would also like to know from the Law Secretary whether the opinion of Attorney-General was taken in this regard. It was discussed in the previous report which was about the powers of the Central Government because right to information is a fundamental right. There is a residuary power given. All these things were itemised in Schedule Seven and in other Schedules Eleven and Twelve. Then all the powers will come under the Central List, that is, the Union List. Therefore, that was already discussed in item 97 of List I. The Government of India has got the right which is not specifically mentioned in any of the items. When that is the thing, it is only that you are giving power for the citizens which were already available in the Constitution of India. But now this power is going to be given in a different version by a statutory support. That is the only reason why we are making it a law. It is not the end of it. You have the writ jurisdiction of the court where the Government can be asked and the Government's decisions can be told to the citizens when there are any sort of writs. They have got the right to information from the Government or any Government agency or Government funded agency. That is the comment made by the Supreme

Court of India. Therefore, we are enacting a law, which gives more power to the citizens. We are having only single citizenship, We do not have any dual citizenship like America. As has been rightly mentioned by the hon. Member, if there is a contradiction between a State law and the Central law, then the Central law would prevail. In 1997, Chief Ministers decided that they are ready for this law. This is history. Therefore, why are you creating a doubt that this enactment will go against the States' interests and there will be litigation and things like that. We do not find that reason. We would like to know whether you are supported by the Attorney General or not.

SHRI V. RADHAKRISHNAN: This is a fundamental right in the Central list. Some States, for example Karnataka, have passed a statute regarding right to information. Some States have already passed legislation. What is the status of those statutes? How States can enact on a subject pertaining to Union List? If it is in the Concurrent List, States can legislate on this topic. You please consider that aspect. So far, this is in the Union List. Only Parliament can legislate on it. If it is included in the Concurrent List, both State Governments and the Union Government can legislate. Here how the States can legislate on a subject which is in the Union List? What is the legal status of the State statutes which they have already passed. I do not question the intelligence of the people from the States. They are fully advised about the legal opinion. We do not say that they are not competent people. But the point is the State Assemblies have passed such statutes and there is a confusion.

SHRI T.K. VISWANATHAN: Sir, it is a very complicated matter. We are treating information as norm and we relate it to one of the entries which are there in the three lists. All things are itemised, public order, police, etc. You have public order, police, etc. You cannot segregate information separately. We cannot say that you can legislate on this and you cannot legislate on this. It is very risky. It will raise the question of Centre-State relations. This is one area where we are not clear. It cannot be said under this pretext that information is my subject, so I will legislate on information. This will lead to a very complex situation. That is what we foresee when we are trying to draft this legislation. This is something on which we will be guided by the Committee. Nobody is clear on this area. We cannot say that State legislations are null and void. The States legislate on matters, which are in the State List, and the Central Government legislates on the subjects, which are in the Central List. We have to keep in view the Centre-State relations. This is where we have to be conscious. We are before the Committee. We will go by the Committee's recommendations. (Contd. by 1G)

<u>SSS/1G/4.00/PPG/1.2.05</u>

SHRI T.K. VISWANATHAN (CONTD.): We have no problem in extending it to the States also.

CHAIRMAN: As you have said, you are specifying certain exemptions. For example, you have exempted CBI or Intelligence. Information could not be called for. At the same time, law and order problem, a local subject, can be called for by anybody. Even the media is calling and the court is allowing it. That cannot be the reason. The reason is whether the citizen has got a right to know about the working of the

Government. That is the main reason on the basis of which we have enacted the law. What is the transparency? What is the thing you have made in the aims and objectives in the Bill? But you started telling in the first part of the Statement of Objects and Reasons, "In order to ensure greater and more effective access to information, the Government resolved that the Freedom of Information Act, 2002 enacted by the Parliament needs to be made more progressive, participatory and meaningful. The National Advisory Council deliberated on the issue and suggested certain important changes to be incorporated in the existing Act to ensure smoother and greater access to information." But nothing has been followed. You have clubbed with Objects and Reasons but the advice has not been properly taken. If you have got any legal doubt, the Attorney General was telling that the State cannot be interfered or this Bill 2002 is not giving anything out of it. It is only supporting the Fundamental Rights of the citizen to know the day-to-day affairs of the Government decision. They want to have a transparency in democratic system.

SHRI A. N. TIWARI: In fairness let me submit that Attorney General's advice was: this act will have an over-riding effect on the State laws. 2002 Act will have transparency. That is one advice of the Attorney General. Attorney General had no legal adviser. They said that both the laws will co-exist and the citizens will have the option to have laws through a Central legislation or a State Legislation. That is the only point, which needs light on at this moment. Law Secretary says, since we are enacting the law, it cannot extend to State subject. So, if today, we take a decision that, yes, whatever law we pass today will have transparency all-over the country, then we have the Attorney General's view. The matter at the moment before us is, these laws and the State laws co-exist. Therefore, a decision was taken that they can co-exist. That is the position we have taken at this moment. I cannot say that yes, the position he has taken is quite truly correct. The only provision which he has said is that this is the power which extends to the Central laws, the Concurrent List and the State List. That is the position at the moment. I am quite certain that the moment this Act comes into force when it is made applicable with the State Government, there is bound to be enormous amount of administrative problems in making the law applicable. A man can ask for some information through the State law and another man can ask some information through the Central Law. The infrastructure is there for collecting this information. There is no convergence between them. Apart from that, if we just look at the administrative problem from a totally legal form we find that enormous amount of litigation would be generated if we take up this decision.

DR. P. C. ALEXANDER: If the Secretary is able to do, let him do with the material available this type of comparative Statement which they have made. They have made a Statement for specific issues mentioned there. The Committee and I would like to have a comparative statement about the financial powers, the decision of the Cabinet on them and what is expected by the Cabinet and what is incorporated in the 2004 Bill. In the same way, what are the things which differentiate between the new Bill and the old Bill. Then we should make a decision among ourselves which we can support and we can come to a conclusion that only 10 or 7 or 6 of these changes are needed. We can take a view on this. These things can be brought out by an amendment.

CHAIRMAN: Already they have given a comparative statement.

DR. P. C. ALEXANDER: That is not sufficient.

CHAIRMAN: You have to make it in 2002 Act. Another thing is the Advisory Committee's recommendations and the third is, the present Bill. If you make it clause-by-clause it would be better.

DR. P. C. ALEXANDER: If that is done, it is for the Standing Committee to take a view about the changes.

CHAIRMAN: We started taking public evidence from I4th onwards.. We are sitting on the 14th and 15th for evidence. Before that we can get it. During the evidence we can seek clarifications. Mr. Meena, what is your opinion? What is the actual opinion of the previous Attorney-General and the present Attorney General?

SHRI R. L. MEENA: Sir, right from the beginning, the view of the Department of Legal Affairs has been that as regards public records pending with the Central Government or Central Government undertakings or agencies, Parliament, no doubt, has a jurisdiction. As regards records maintained by the State Government, Parliament does not have any jurisdiction. As regards records maintained by the State Government Parliament does not have any jurisdiction even from 1997. That has been the view of the Department of Legal Affairs. This was again agitated. Then we ultimately sought opinion of Mr. Soli Sorabjee. Then he said it could be covered. That was the view. We recorded this. Our opinion was sent to the Department of Personnel. Even now we hold that as regards the records maintained by the State Government, Central Government does not have any jurisdiction.

CHAIRMAN: On what basis are you making this opinion? Have you got any statutory support or Constitutional support?

SHRI R. L. MEENA: Basis is very simple. There are certain entries up to 1996. Specific entries are given. So, for the thing which is not covered by either the Concurrent List or State List or Union List, we resort to residuary powers. According to me, when we maintain record for administration, this information is part of that subject. That is our view. If that is so, then 1997 is not attractive. That is the view that we have taken.

<u>(FOLLOWED BY 1H)</u>

NBR/1H/4.10.

CHAIRMAN: In the academic interest, I would like to know from you a point. You know there is the Water Act. You have enacted this in Parliament. And, you are also very well aware that 'Water' is a State Subject. So, under what powers have you enacted this legislation? Under this, certain Committees were also constituted, certain powers were given to those Committees, you also want to impose tax on certain industries/polluting units, etc. And, it is governed by the Government of India.

SHRI R.L MEENA: Sir, so far as my information goes, Water Cess Act has been enacted in pursuance of a resolution passed by the States.

CHAIRMAN: I am not talking about the Water Cess Act. I am talking about the Water Act.

SHRI R.L. MEENA: Even that we have acquired jurisdiction because of certain provisions of Constitution...

CHAIRMAN: Then, have any suggestions been made in the Chief Ministers' Conference. Or, have you called for the views of any experts? We have indicated in the note that since 1997 onwards, at every stage, you are asked to get the information from all the States. We would like to know from you as to how many States have said, 'we will look into it and...

SHRI T.K. VISWANATHAN: Sir, jurisdiction is something which the States cannot confer. We have to read the Constitution because the States cannot confer jurisdiction and I don't think that may be relevant. That is what I feel.

CHAIRMAN: You are enacting a number of laws. You have legislated many laws as model laws. You are making the States obligatory; and, when they need they can make legislation. Even in the proposed Bill, you are giving delegated legislation. They can never, at any particular time, have examined whether they can exclude or include. When you look at the Concurrent List or the State List, you are allowing them to change their position. You have never said that citizens right to information cannot be taken away from the State Governments. We do not have the Federal Government like USA. We are a unitary form of Government. At the same time, the entire jurisdiction comes under the Central Government when it is a subject of residuary and you are saying that the Right to Information cannot be covered under Entry 97 of the Seventh Schedule. Kindly support it with any provisions of the Constitution or decisions of the apex court or High Courts. Without that how do you justify your argument?

For example— it may be out of context— the nationalised banks want to compete with the market and in that process, the banks wish to lend money to Tsunami victims in re-establishing or reopening of their businesses or to buy boats, nets, etc. In such a situation, how can the State Government say, 'you do not have the authority or power to do that.' Nobody can say that. It is a commercial need. If the nationalised banks wish to give money to Tsunami victims by way of loans, how can you say, 'no.' If you ask the State Governments, the State Governments object to all legislation enacted by the Union.

SHRI T.K. VISWANATHAN: Sir, I am reading Entry 97 of the Seventh Schedule. It says, "Any other matter not enumerated in List II or List III including any tax not mentioned in either of those Lists. And if you come to the State List, Entry 12 of the State List says, "Libraries, museums and other similar institutions controlled or financed by the State; ancient and historical monuments and records other than those declared by or under law made by Parliament to be of national importance." Under this, they have enacted the Right to Information Act. Entry 97 is not very broad. And it is not something which is left where all the other fields have been occupied. You cannot use this to encroach upon the other things covered by an Entry of the State List. Entry 97 cannot operate like this. This is what we feel.

CHAIRMAN: The point is not about the mention in the List alone. When the nation is growing, new subjects are coming in. Is there any reference in the Constitution about the electronic data? So, we have to grow up with the evolution. Many new things are coming up. When such things come before us, then the Central Government or the Union Government will have the right to legislate. We want to be very frank. We would like to know as to what made the Department of Legai Affairs to be afraid of touching this particular aspect when you are enforcing the Fundamental Rights. It is the fundamental right of any citizen to know the information as to how the Government is working, how the executive is working, how the taxpayers' money is being spent, or, whether it is with regard to Panchayati Raj or any body for that matter.

SHRI T.K. VISWANATHAN: It is not merely a platonic declaration of the right to information. The Supreme Court has interpreted the Constitution many times. The problem comes in when you try to operationalise the right by providing for a regime to enforce those rights. It is not merely a declaration. We are thinking of following it up. When we had enacted earlier, at that time, we did not have the wherewithal, especially the machinery. It makes us reluctant. I would also like to say that under the previous Act there was no machinery or punishment to enforce. In the proposed legislation, both enforcement as well as machinery is available. At the same time, in the earlier Act, there was no punishment. So, there was no friction. But, in the proposed legislation, there is a scope for friction as per the proposed provisions. The result is, the relations between the Central and the State Governments get affected. So, what I wish to say is that when we concretise this, then we will have problem and it is where we have to strike.

CHAIRMAN: I am sorry that this enactment or any advice given by anybody or the Advisory Committee or even the earlier Committee, does not mean that you have to do it. We are proposing to enact a model law which will be applicable for the entire country. And, the Union Government has got specific institutions created and it gives powers which can be followed by the State Governments. If the State Governments have so much secrecy on a piece of information which ought to be revealed for the citizens of this country and if it does not want to reveal, what do you do? I am afraid we are not convinced with your submissions that we are interfering into the subjects of the State.

SHRI RAM NATH KOVIND: You are now changing your stand.

CHAIRMAN: We are implementing the Fundamental Rights.

SHRI RAM NATH KOVIND: So, the Central Government has a right to legislate upon the State Governments.

SHRI V. RADHAKRISHNAN: Sir, the simple question is: Right to Information is a Fundamental Right and the Union Government alone is the competent authority to enforce the Fundamental Rights. How could it come within the purview of the State Governments?

CHAIRMAN: We have to protect the interests of the Constitution.

SHRI V. RADHAKRISHNAN: Right to Information is a Fundamental Right arid it is for the Union or the Parliament to legislate, not the States. At the same time, it can be a Central Act. The Central Government can make laws and the States will have to follow suit. For that, a Commissioner has to be appointed in the State. The Governor has to appoint him in consultation with the Chief Minister as has been done at the Centre. (Followed by "1J")

USY/1 J/4.20

CHAIRMAN: Let us come to the conclusion. According to the Law Secretary and the Secretary, Legal Affairs, in Attorney General's view we have got the power under item No. 97. Secondly, even, then the Law Department feels that we should not encroach upon the State powers.

SHRI A.N. TIWARI: Sir, there are two legal opinions before us. In Attorney General's opinion either this Act could have all-India consideration or the Central Act can confine itself only to the Centre. The point is whether we can concurrently have two Acts – the Central Act and the State Act. There is no light on this point.

DR. P.C. ALEXANDER: Why are you concerned about that? I think we need not raise this issue. We should try to confine ourselves to find a solution. We should go by the advice. If you get into it, you will get into more controversies.

CHAIRMAN: Okay. Kindly give us the notes on the points that are under your domain. And, if necessary, we will call you again. Kindly join us for a cup of tea.

(The witnesses then withdrew and the Committee adjourned)

TDB/1A/11.00/PPG/14.2.2005

The Department Related Parliamentary Standing Committee on Personnel, Public Grievances, Law and Justice held at 11.00 A.M. on Monday, the 14th February, 2005 in Committee Room 'A', Parliament House Annexe, New Delhi.

(SHRI E.M. SUDARSANA NATCHIAPPAN - CHAIRMAN)

List of Witnesses:

1. Shrimati Aruna Roy, Representative of Mazdoor Kisan Shakti Sangathan (MKSS);
2. Dr. Jean Dreze, Profession, Centre for Development Economics, Delhi School of Economics; and
3. Ms. Angela Rangad, Representative of National Campaign for People's Right to Information (NCPRI) & others.

CHAIRMAN: Good morning to everybody. I welcome you all to this historic occasion of considering the Right to Information Bill. I hope, the Right to Information Bill, 2004 is acceptable to you. We are happy to get the evidence of Shrimati Aruna Roy, a well-known international personality who has won the Magsaysay Award for her commitment to work at the level of Panchayat, for the rural people. She is also a well-known personality in the field of Right to Information. She is leading a very famous institution, namely, the Mazdoor Kisan Shakti Sangathan. The Committee is very happy that today she has got an opportunity to present her views before it. She has got with her very committed persons who have fought for the right to information of the common man.

SHRIMATI ARUNA ROY: I think, you are going to make a power-point presentation of half-an-hour duration. We have already got your Memorandum. After your presentation, Members would seek certain clarifications from you. If you are able to reply to them immediately, it is okay; otherwise, you can send the replies in writing to the Committee within a week's time. If you want to make some additional points, in addition to the points which have been given in the Memorandum, before the Committee, you can do so. (Contd. by 1b)

kgg/1b/11.10/PPG/14.2.05

CHAIRMAN: We are very happy to hear all of you. Smt. Aruna Roy, you may proceed.

SMT. ARUNA ROY: Thank you Chairman and Members of the Standing Committee for your words. We are very happy to be here to present our case. It has been a major preoccupation of many of us in the country to see a corruption-free and just India. This dream of just and corruption-free India requires the right to know for all people and it also needs transparency at the Government. These two are the imperatives. The move is necessary but not sufficient. But, without this right to information and transparency at Government, there can be no development, there can be no justice, there can be no progress too.

We feel, this is extremely important and fundamental to all of us. I remember, when we had launched initial operations of the campaign, Nikhil Chakravarty had given a statement saying, "This should be a part of the Constitution and specified under article I9(1)(a). It is very important and it is extremely beneficial for the people of this country." I will just read out a small paragraph. It is S.P. Gupta Versus the Union of India. It is a Constitutional Bench judgment:

"Now it is obvious from the Constitution that we have adopted a democratic form of Government where a society has chosen to accept democracy as its creed and faith; it is elementary that citizens ought to know what the Government is doing. The citizens have a right to decide by whom and by what rules they shall be governed and they are entitled to call on those who govern on their behalf, to account for their conduct. No democratic government can survive without accountability and the basic postulate of accountability is that people should have information about the functioning of the Government. It is only if people know how the Government is functioning that they can fulfil the role which democracy assigns to them and make democracy really an effective participatory democracy."

To make better India, it is crucially important that we have the right to information. So, its success and strength depends on the collective understanding; the need is right to information. Actually, if we want to implement any of the programmes of Government, if we want the poor should cease to be poor, then it is extremely important to have the right to know. When the initial campaign was launched, we called the right to know as right to live. The right to live hinges on the basic benefits we have got. It becomes important for them to exist.

Sir, very briefly, I will show a thirteen-minute film which encapsulates the grassroots activities and how important the right to information is for the people. We will go one by one.

(A film was shown) (Contd. by 1c)

KLS/1C-11.20/PPG/14.2.2005

CHAIRMAN: It is a very useful film. It shows how the grass-root people are not getting information, how they are reacting and how they are changing their attitude. I would request you to kindly supply one hard copy of the film's titles. (Followed by 1D)

SSS/11.30/1D/PPJ/14.2.05

SHRIMATI ARUNA ROY: This film is made by the Lal Bahadur Academy of Administration. They made this film so that they will be clubbed with the right kind of background. What we want in this Act today is, this. The National Advisory Council had a mandate for Freedom of Information Act, we looked at it, redrafted it and sent amendments to the Government of India. They suggested since there were many amendments, they would give a new Bill. This was under the Chairperson of Smt. Sonia Gandhi. What are the residuary issues? I will quickly run through. They will all speak. The first contention is the Act should be wide in scope because it really concerns very ordinary people. We are not really hitting at large things. The main thing is, ordinary lives should be better. It should be applicable to all public authorities. Any money, which goes to the States, is going to be funded by the State Governments. There should be strong penalties for non-compliance. So, there should be strong penalty. It is a deterrent. It is not to punish officers but they should be able to give information. We do not make mechanisms within the State but outside, so that there is an appeal outside the Government. There is a normal chain of officers who look at the applications. The fourth point is, fees procedure should be made easy. These are the four issues what we are bringing today. After the Government of India made a Bill and tabled this in Parliament, the Chairperson has written to the Prime Minister and Group of Ministers and that attention should be looked at again. This Bill can be amended. I would like to say that the copy of this film is given to Mr. Pathak. You can have a copy of it if you like.

SHRI PRASHANT BHUSHAN: Thank you Mr. Chairman and hon. Members of this Committee. I am sure all of you understand the importance of this Right to Information Act. Of course, the Supreme Court has now held at least six major Constitutional bench institutions. The Right to Information Bill is part of the Right to Freedom of Speech because you cannot expect a person to exercise his Right to Freedom of Speech unless he knows what is really happening in the Government which is governing him and his people on their behalf. So it is not merely a question of Fundamental Right, it is also an issue of deepening democracy in this country. The Supreme Court has rightly said you cannot have proper democracy unless the people, on whose behalf any representative democracy is there in this country, when the representatives are governing on behalf of the people, have the right to know why the representatives are taking the decisions that they are taking on their behalf. That is another major reason why it is important in a democracy. This new Bill which has been tabled in the Parliament is, of course, much better than the previous Information Act 2002. 2002 Act firstly had a large number of exemptions, which this Bill does not have. Secondly, the previous Act did not have any penalty for non-compliance. But this Bill has. Firstly, the previous Bill did not have any independent appeal mechanism but this Bill does have independent appeal mechanism which makes it better. But still there are weaknesses in the Bill. The first is, the Bill has been made applicable only to the Centre and to the Government officers under the Central Government and it is not applicable to the States or to the local bodies. So, under this Act people cannot access under bodies controlled by the State Government or by the local bodies. I believe that this has been done on the basis of some advice given by Law Ministry which thought that perhaps the Parliament cannot legislate for Right to Information in respect of authorities under the State Governments or under the local bodies. But in my view that is clearly not the correct position in law because as you all know there is residuary entry in the Union List, the last entry which gives 'any other matter not mentioned in either of the State List or the Union List'. Apart from the fact that it has been deleted under Article 1.9(1) A, Right to Information is not specifically mentioned in either the Union List or the State List. Therefore, it would clearly be covered by the residuary entry of the Union List under which the Union has the power, that is, the Parliament has to bring to power to legislate on this issue and once the Parliament legislates it can certainly legislate in respect of officers under the State Government and under local bodies. That is the critical weakness of this Bill. In fact, the draft was sent. Unfortunately, because of some legal advice it has been deleted. NFC draft is perfectly correct. While there are State legislations in about ten States right now, since this Bill will cover or should cover all public authorities including 'under the States' and that under local bodies the Bill should further have a clause saying that the right providing this Act is in addition to not interaction but any right which may have been provided to State Act. So if there is some particular State Act which has more liberty than the Central Act, the people should have the option to seek information under the State Act also. The second issue is, the issue of penalties. While the previous Bill did not have any provision for penalties, this Bill has provision for penalties but unfortunately, due to hurry in drafting the penalty provision which is in Change 17 of this Bill, it has been very clumsily drafted. Unfortunately, because the draft which was sent by the NAC provided for penalties for two kinds of things, penalties for not providing information within the time prescribed and secondly, penalties for destroying information, *mala fide* refusing to supply information or supplying wrong information, wilfully supplying incorrect information. So, we have suggested in the representation that has been given on behalf of NLPRI, we have suggested that Section 17 should be amended. Penalties for two separate kinds of things: one is penalty for not giving information within the time prescribed. That penalty can be imposed by the Information Commissioner and the right prescribed.

NBR/1E/11.40.

SHRI PRASHANT BHUSHAN (CONTD.): The second point is, *mala fide* refusal to supply information, destruction of information, or, providing wrong information, should be made into an offence for which the penalty should not merely be a monetary penalty but it should be imprisonment as well. For that, the Information Commissioner should be authorised to prosecute the offender involved. He should be given power to file a complaint or if it is found that an officer has destroyed information which was sought or has wilfully supplied wrong information, etc., then, he can order for prosecution of that officer and the prosecution should be conducted before the courts. That change needs to be made in Clause relating to Penalties.

Sir, the third point is with regard to fee. The Bill, which has been tabled, does not prescribe any fee, even though the National Advisory Council draft sent to the Government of India did have a clause saying that the fee shall not be unreasonable and in a sense not more than the cost of supplying that piece of information has to be charged. That has been deleted from the present Bill. It is quite important because we have seen from our experience that some of the States impose fee so high that it makes impossible for the common man even to get information.

So, these are the three main points on which there is a need to amend the provisions of the Bill.

There are some other things which we have mentioned in the representation submitted to the hon. Committee. The first one is: The Bill that has been tabled in Parliament exempt the security agencies from the application of this legislation. The exception is that information regarding corruption in the security agencies will be accessible. We have suggested—the National Advisory Council also recommended this—that there should be two exceptions to the exemption given to the security agencies. The first one is regarding corruption and other one is human rights violations. There is no reason why information regarding human rights violations by the security agencies should not be made accessible by the people. This amendment needs to be made in the Bill that is before the Committee for its consideration.

So, Mr. Chairman, Sir, these are the main points I wanted to mention before the august body. Thank you.

SHRI NIKHIL DEY: Thank you Mr. Chairman, for giving me this opportunity to express some of my views on the subject. I will just add to what Mr. Arundhati Roy and Shri Prashant Bhusan has said in practical terms. I come from Rajasthan. I have been working in Rajasthan at the field level for the last ten years. When we talk of participatory democracy, people actually helped us with the whole task of governance. In our experience— I have worked for twenty years— when the Right to Information became a tool in the hands of the people; they are able to access information as their right and it became very clear. The ordinary people were not getting the information which they had been asking for continuously, since there was no Act relating to the right to information. I will give you the example of drought relief works which take place year-after-year in Rajasthan. It is a traditional notion in the 'heart-belt' of Rajasthan. But, as soon as the provisions of the Right to Information Act getting enforced, there has been a dramatic difference which both the political parties on the ruling side and in the opposition have came to know that the right to information gave people a right to ask what is in the muster roll, who is there in the muster roll, what is the amount that they are getting, etc. Sir, if you look at the works that were undertaken under last year's drought in Rajasthan, the amount of corruption came down dramatically and that continues even today. It is not something which affected either one party or one ideology but it is helping the democratic values of the State.

The second point is it brings out many anomalies in policies to the forefront. For instance, there is 60:40 ratio on rural development. Since the Right to Information has come into being, the officials and the elected representatives have said that you have to remove this impracticable ratio of requiring 60 per cent to be spent on labour and 40 per cent needs to be spent on material side. You are actually spending much more on material. So, you must remove this wrong kind of rule that allows corruption. As a result that kind of a thing has been removed.

For instance, in Panchayat elections, Sarpanches are elected and each Sarpanch will get Rs. 400 a month. How can he work for Rs. 400? Sarpanch is supposed to be a full-time worker. How can they survive with Rs. 400 per month? Earlier they were managing and getting money through other means. Now, when the Right to Information Act came into being, if any Sarpanch or any official passes a wrong bill, then he gets caught. And, now, it forces them to say that these are the problems in the policy *or* legislation, you should change this now. And at the same time, earlier we did not have honest ration dealers, you did not have honest Sarpanches, honest officials, etc., till the Right to Information Act came into force. What I am trying to say is that the Right to Information Act is helping the people to get information. At the same time, you cannot have inspectors at every place. And then, the whole concept of social audit has been brought in Panchayat and it is supposed to look after all works that took place in a ward.

To a point about the coexistence of the Central and the State Acts, I would submit that in the State of Rajasthan, the first change in the right to information has been made in the Panchayat Raj Act, According to this, they required to provide information within four days. This was passed in 1997. In the year 2000, the Right to Information Act was passed for the whole of the State of Rajasthan. Now, we have both the Acts existing together for the citizens. If we want to ask information relating to Panchayat they ask under the Panchayat Act because it provides information within four days. If they want information that comes under the State Government, they would seek information with the help of the Right to Information Act which is the State Act. Here, the people can choose under which Act they wish to seek information from the officials. Similarly, the same example should be used if the State Act and the Central Act are in existence. Then, the people will have a choice to choose.

One of the points which did not come is this. It is there under the Constitution. The Right to Information is there under Article 19 (1)(a) of the Constitution. The Right to Information Bill, placed before Parliament, allows access information to its citizens. One of our biggest fears is that if the public information officer or the public authorities who are supposed to supply the information demands for proving the citizenship of the person who sought information, then, it defeats the very purpose of this legislation. Any public information officer should not deny anyone of supplying the information sought on the ground that he fails to prove his citizenship. But, when you look at the Fundamental Rights of the Constitution, they clearly say about the right to information. Therefore, our submission is this. Information should be made accessible to all persons and no official should ask first to prove the citizenship.

Similarly, there has to be a clear-cut and specific mention about the fee which should be low for supplying the information, reason for refusing should be specifically mentioned in very narrow terms and penalties should be stringent in a way that actually helps the Government and governance and helps our collective reasons to try and get a better Act.

Sir, with your permission, there is one last thing that I would like to say. This Act, in our experience, in Rajasthan, helps to align people. It helps to align the ethical people within the Government, outside the Government, within the press, within the civil society and within the ordinary people. The Act is actually aligning the people against the vested interests that exist.

Therefore, it is not that spirit of cooperation and experience. But from the State Acts it becomes very clear that a strong law is what allows people to really have access to information, otherwise it is only in the name.

SHRIMATI ARUNA ROY: Our fear is that it would be very difficult for the poor people to prove their citizenship. So, it should not be an issue on which information is denied to the people.

Now, Ms. Angela Rangad, who is from Meghalaya, would present her viewpoint.

MS. ANGELA RANGAD: Sir, thank you very much for providing me this opportunity. I hail from the State of Meghalaya. And, I think, I am here to represent the Right to Information Movement in the State of Meghalaya. So, I would like to stress on a few viewpoints.

First of all, the Right to Information Act needs to cover the States and local authorities. We have had a Right to Information Movement since 2001, which, in our experience, came up as a result of people coming together against certain scams that had taken place over a period of time. Despite all this pressure our Government has not made any attempt to have a Right to Information Act. We need to have this Act also because our experience has shown that in the States which have very weak and ineffective Opposition, there is a tendency to legislate through Ordinances. Even where there are such Acts, they are not very effective. For example, the State of Assam has an Act. But it is very weak. In fact, even the rules have not been framed. In the absence of any penalty provision, it is nothing. That is why we should make sure that this Act also covers the States and local bodies.

Now, I come to the point of giving blanket exemption to the security and intelligence agencies. Sir, I come from a region, which is a militarilized zone. The intelligence and security agencies impinge upon our daily lives. There are already safeguards for our country's integrity and sovereignty. Therefore, we do not need to give this blanket exemption to the security and intelligence agencies. Then, we have other laws also, like, the Armed Forces Special Power Act. So, it is more important for the people to have the Right to Information to access information from the intelligence and security agencies too. That will serve as a check on these agencies that they do not abuse their powers. It is a reality that human rights' abuses take place in the region. And, a move on the part of the Government in this regard would help in bridging the gap between the people and these agencies. So, I appeal that this Act should also apply to the States as well as the local bodies. We should also rethink about giving blanket exemption to the security and intelligence agencies. Thank you very much.

SHRIMATI ARUNA ROY: Sir, 'corruption' has been included in the present Act. Ms. Angela has rightly pointed out that 'human rights violation' should also be included in this Bill.

Now, Shri Harsh Mander, who had been an IAS officer, would present his viewpoint.

SHRI HARSH MANDER: Thank you very much, Sir. I want to say that as a serving civil servant I found that when you try to fight corruption, you find that the system does not deliver a way where the people are free of corruption. It seems that for the first time people would have a power in their hands to have access to information through the Right to Information Act. But within the civil services too some apprehensions had been expressed about the right to information. There had been apprehensions that a lot of blackmail and harassment of honest officers would be there; and, sometimes it will increase the workload because there will be a lot of demand from the people to have information. But gradually it was found that the reality was quite opposite. In fact, the honest officers would feel more fearless because everything would be available to the people. They know that you cannot just make allegations in the air. Therefore, far from the apprehensions that it would act against the honest officers, it would rather be the strength of the honest officers. It would also not add to workload because it is just not about the right to information, but we are talking about a transparent system. And, if the system starts functioning in a transparent manner, then, by its very nature, the workload will not increase. But the workload would actually reduce. I would also like to state that it is not necessary that you are going to have thousands of people lining up and seeking information. But it is really pre-emptive power of the law. People will know that it is possible for them to get any information. Therefore, it would act as a check against corruption. It is not just a control on a corrupt government, but I think we need to emphasise that it is not only about corrupt exercises of the States— that will be controlled—but also about the arbitrary exercises. Though the decision may not be taken with any financial motivation, it could be an arbitrary decision. It could be an anti-people decision. So. the right to information law will make the system more transparent. We are happy to note that even noting on files will also be accessible to the people. Therefore, not just the decision, but the reasons for arriving at that decision will also be known to the people. It will require more responsible and accountable administration. I will give you two examples. The worst human right violations take place in custodial institutions where children who are picked up for begging etc. are kept. This is, probably, an example of the most non-transparent form of things. The other example is Tsunami itself. I am very happy to note that realising the importance of the right to information, the survivors of Tsunami tragedy and the organisations working there have expressed that a lot of corruption as well as the waste that is associated with reconstruction after such a huge disaster will be prevented if the people are armed with the power of seeking information as to how much money has been provided; what are the plans; and how is it being utilised? Over the last 10-15 years, we have observed that accountability within the system has gone down a great deal. So, this right to information law will actually strengthen the governance and hands of those who are honest and ethically working in this system.

SHRIMATI ARUNA ROY: Sir, actually, disclosure, transparency and the right to know are two sides of a coin. Now, I will invite Dr. Jean Dreze to express his views.

DR. JEAN DREZE: Sir, I think most of the important points have been made. I will, briefly, make just four or five points. Firstly, I think it is important to see the importance of this law not just from the point of view of eradicating corruption— it is an important goal— but in the larger context of the need to strengthen democratic institutions and restore accountability in public life, because democracy is fundamentally about accountability to the public and it will not be possible if information is hidden from the public.

My second point is, in many ways, the right to information law is fundamental to the realisation of the Common Minimum Programme of this Government.

Thirdly, the right to information is relevant to the CMP not because a promise had been made in the CMP to implement a strong right to information law but also because the realisation of the other items on the CMP is highly contingent on eradication of corruption. I will just give you one example and, that is, adoption and implementation of an effective employment guarantee scheme. It is one of the fundamental pledges of the Common Minimum Programme and it can be implemented effectively if we have a strong right to information law. Then, fourthly, right to information law is good not from the point of view of ethics but it will also save huge amount of money to the Government. Just to give you a small example, I have brought with me some figures on the extent of corruption in the public distribution system. I do not want to go into the details, but very briefly, I will explain to you. These figures show that about half of the grains which are released by the FCI for PDS ends up being stolen by dealers and others. And, since the total offtake at the moment is about 15 million tonnes per year, that means, about seven-and-a-half million tons of foodgrains are embezzled from the Public Distribution System every year. The value of that is about Rs. 5,000 crores. So, from PDS alone, Rs. 5,000 crores disappear every year. This remark applies to some other developmental programmes also. What I mean to express is, savings that can be made through the right to information law could be substantial. Then, the next point is, this law is not extendable to the whole country. This kind of a law already exists in various forms in several States. The State of Maharashtra has very strong right to information law. Finally, I just want to reiterate the importance of a strong law because the whole purpose of this law is to empower citizens and to give power to those who have a stake in eradicating corruption. It may not feel good to give sweeping powers to citizens but the history of all social legislations is inspite of having such legislations the people have to work very hard to realise their entitlement. Therefore, I think it would be a big mistake if the people are not given power that they need to eradicate corruption and especially to restore accountability in the system.

SHRIMATI ARUNA ROY: I would like to say that Dr. Jean Dreze, who apart from being an economist, has travelled widely in India. He speaks Hindi well and has communicated with people of this country. So, his words are very important. What we really want to present is that this is not a single voice of a human being, but a voice from different areas and parts of the country. We want transparency in the system. We also want accountability of the Government to its people. It will help vigilance associations and regulatory mechanisms of this country to function effectively. We want to see that each and every grain or help that is provided for the people should reach the really needy people.

We want to look at it. Thank you very much for listening us so patiently in detail. Thank you very much.

CHAIRMAN: It seems that you are in a hurry. We have to ask you certain questions.

SHRIMATI ARUNA ROY: Sir, we have absolutely no problem in clarifying anything which the Committee wants us to clarify. But I stood up because I thought that the Committee would now hear Shri Anna Hazare who is sitting here to tender his evidence before the Committee. That is why I stood.

CHAIRMAN: We will hear him after we finish our deliberations with you.

SHRIMATI ARUNA ROY: Sorry, Sir; I did not. quite understand the procedure.

CHAIRMAN: No problem. Now, we can break for tea. We will come back in five minutes. The hon. Members would then like to seek certain clarifications from you.

SHRIMATI ARUNA ROY: Sure; Sir.

(The Committee then adjourned for Tea)

1J/12.20/SKC PPG - 'A' 14.02.2005

(The Committee re-assembled and the meeting continued after tea-break.)

CHAIRMAN: Now hon. Members of the Committee would raise certain questions, which you could answer. If you feel that you could provide us with some more inputs that are different from what you have already circulated to us, you could do so within a week's time, so that we could send them to the concerned departments of the Government and obtain their remarks. In the meantime— I would observe the usual formality— whatever we discuss here should not be revealed to the media or anybody else until we place the report in the Parliament. The deliberations of the meeting have to be kept confidential; you cannot invoke 'the right to information' here!

DR. P. C. ALEXANDER: Thank you, Mr. Chairman. I should say we have been benefited a great deal by the presentations made by all the witnesses this morning. I am very happy to see Shri Anna Hazare in our midst today, as one who had been closely associated with the Government of Maharashtra for a decade, I know how valuable his views are in shaping policies on reforms in our country, and, I am sure, he will intervene at the appropriate time and give us the benefit of his views. On this question of the right of the Central Government to legislate on this subject, we had a preliminary discussion amongst ourselves on the issues, which you have raised today and solved in your own way. This issue was raised by some of us and we are still in a bit of hesitation on certain aspects of it. While we all believe that the Centre has the right under the residuary powers, the question I would like to pose to you, Mr. Prashant Bhushan particularly, is: can we have a set of words from you which will make the intentions clear that the Central legislation will, to quote your words, be applicable to all public authorities in India, whether they are under the Centre or States or under local bodies. These are the words. So, that one set of words, which can be incorporated somewhere, will make it very clear that whatever is contained in the new Bill, will be applicable to all bodies—Central, State and local bodies. If we do that, then, is it necessary to allow the State legislations to continue because eight or nine States have the legislation? If the Central legislation comes into practice, is it necessary to continue the State legislations also because even as you have put it in your draft proposal, where the State legislation exists, the person will have the right to seek information under the State law as well as under this Act, if the information pertains to a subject under the State List under the Schedule VII? Can we not have another set of words by which everybody will have the right to use the Central legislation for getting information from the State relating to the subjects exclusively within the jurisdiction of the State? I am only asking you whether it is necessary to keep a sort of concurrent legislation for both, the States and the Centre. Will it not create confusion in the minds of the people? Will it not become an excuse for officers at the State level? He may say that this falls under the jurisdiction of the Central Government or the information can be readily supplied by the Central Government officers working in the State at the local level. So, those, who ask for the information, can be sent from pillar to post. Can you give your advice whether one legislation by the Centre covering, to use again Shashi Bhushan's words, all public authorities in India whether under the Centre, States or local bodies? Now, I come to my second question. In the presentation, that you made, you said that the penalty clause should be strong enough to also become a deterrent not as a punishment and it will have value as a deterrent also. Now, in the new Bill, in the clause 17(2), there is a provision for a very strong penalty, that is, imprisonment up to five years. It was not there in the original Bill. In fact, there had been total absence of any penalty provisions in the original Act. Do you think that it still needs more teeth or this is adequate to begin with, and it will not get the impression that we are going to enforce the right to information with only *danda* and to remove that type of feeling? Can we not just leave it like that, that this is good enough? The third question is about the Schedule. Now, in the original Bill, there is an insertion as item 17 on bringing the Directorate of Vigilance, including Anti-Corruption Branch, into the so-called provision list. You had also accepted that Directorate of Vigilance, including Anti-Corruption Branch, should be in the Provision List and you have also proposed in the Schedule. But, the Bill does not refer to the Directorate of Vigilance. What is your view on this? I may refer to your opinion, which is conspicuously absent, but you did not make any comment on it. Do you agree that Directorate of Vigilance should also be in the Schedule?

SHRI PRASHANT BHUSHAN: The first issue, that you raised, was whether the Central Act could legislate regarding the bodies under the States. On that, I think, the answer is very clear and does not admit of any other opinion whatsoever because the residuary clause in the Union List says that anything, which is not mentioned in the State List or the Union List, is covered under it. Clearly, right to information is not specifically mentioned in the State List. So, Parliament, certainly, has the right to legislate on the right to information. Once, Parliament legislates on that, it is applicable on everybody. But, if that is the case, in fact, the previous Attorney General, Shri Soli Sorabjee, at once—I understand when the Madhya Pradesh Government passed the Bill relating to right to information and sent it to the President for assent—had given an opinion that the States, have no authority on right to information, and only Parliament has the authority. Because it is not mentioned in the State List, it can only be legislated in the residuary entry. At that time, my father's opinion was sought on this issue. His opinion was that right to information is also an incidental power. On every subject, for example, if there is a legislation on a particular subject by a State, let us assume, on a subject covered by the State List, but then, the State has an incidental power to say that on this subject, to which this legislation pertains, there shall be right to information. People will have the right to information. There is an incidental power of the States on all the matters covered by the State List. However, as a subject, right to information is not mentioned in any of the Lists. Therefore, as a subject, it will be covered under the residuary clause, on which, Parliament has the right and once, Parliament has the right, it can legislate on this subject. Then, the other question is regarding the use of both the Acts simultaneously and allowing a State Act to remain once the Central Act comes into practice. On that, our view has been that firstly, it can remain; that it is already there for the States, under the Panchayati Raj Act, there is a right to information in some of the States.

There would not be two bureaucracies for this. Bureaucracy can remain the same. According to the rules, the same bureaucracy, which has been created by the States for the State subject, that can deal with the request for the right to information whether they are under the Central Act or under the State Act. However, the Central Act can provide that these are the minimum standards, which everybody has to comply with. The Central Act lays down the minimum standards, and, it further says that there can be a clause mentioning—as my father also said—that, however, if the State Act is more liberal in respect of any subject covered by the State List, then the right conferred by the Central Act will not be in derogation to the right conferred by the Right to Information Act of the State.

For example, the State of Maharashtra has a liberal Act, and, if it allows information on something in the State List, and, the Central Act does not allow that, then the person should have the right to say that under the State Act, this matter is covered by the State List as this is a State subject, and, accordingly, the State Act allows me to access this information, and, he may also say that even though the Central Act may not allow, let me access this information under the State Act.

This will be taken care of by one residuary clause in the Bill, which says that the rights created by this Act will be in addition, and, not in derogation to any right created by the State Acts. So, the bureaucracy will remain the same.

As far as the issue of 'penalties' is concerned, I would submit that Section 17 has two problems. One is that the Information Commissioner cannot directly impose the penalty. He has to make a complaint. It says that the Commission may authorise any officer of the Central Government to file a complaint against such public information officer before a Judicial Magistrate of the First Class. It will be a prosecution before the Judicial Magistrate. What we have suggested is that we can separate the penalties into two parts. One is a monetary penalty alone for not providing information within the time prescribed. For that, there will be a modest monetary penalty that can be straightway imposed by the Information Commissioner.

However, if the information officer destroys the information, or, wilfully provides false information then it shall be treated as an offence for which he can be prosecuted before a Magistrate. If you see our suggestions, we have actually provided the amended version of this Act. Instead of Section 17, we can substitute that by the following:

1. Subject to Sub-section 3, where any public information officer or any other officer who holds or is responsible for holding the information, as the case may be, has, without any reasonable cause failed to supply the information sought, within the period specified under section 7(1), the Information Commissioner shall, on an appeal, impose a penalty of two hundred fifty rupees for each day's delay in furnishing the information after giving such public information officer, or, the other officer, as the case may be, a reasonable opportunity of being heard.

2. Where it is found in appeal that any public information officer has
   – refused to receive an application for information,
   – malafide denied a request for information,
   – knowingly given incorrect or misleading information,
   – knowingly given wrong or incomplete information,
   – destroyed information subject to a request, or,
   – obstructed the activities of a public information officer, any information Commission or the courts,

   he/she would have committed an offence and will be liable upon summary conviction to a fine of not less than rupees two thousand, and, imprisonment of up to five years, or, both.
3. where the Commission comes to the prima facie conclusion that an offence under sub-section (2) has been committed, the Commission shall through an officer of the Commission file charges against the offending officer in a court of competent jurisdiction.

For this category of offences, that is, destroying the information, he is liable to be prosecuted in the court, but for the delay in providing information, same penalty can be imposed straightway by the Information Commissioner. According to the present Section, it does not even talk about destroying of information etc. In fact, it makes even the delay in supplying information an offence, which is punishable up to five years. There has to be a monetary penalty for delay, which the Information Commissioner can impose straightway. But for more serious things, it should be prosecution.

As far as the issue relating to security agencies is concerned, there should not be a blanket exemption for the security agencies. Section 8, clause of exemptions mentions, 'any information of any public body including security agencies', or, 'in so far as national security is concerned'. So, even the security agencies are covered under that. Therefore, there should not be a blanket exemption for the security agencies merely because they are security agencies. However, since there is a lot of sensitivity in the Government about the security agencies, we agreed to it but we suggested for providing information at least about two things. One is about 'corruption', and, second is about 'human rights'. So, that is why, 'corruption' has been included, but, unfortunately, 'human rights' has not been included. Regarding this particular issue about Directorate of Vigilance including anti-corruption branch etc., we have not taken any special view on it, and, if it has to be included, it can be, but, however, unless it says that the Directorate of Vigilance is a security agency, probably, it should not be included.

SHRI V. RADHAKRISHNAN: Mr. Chairman, Sir, regarding the question raised by my hon. friend Dr. Alexander, there is another aspect on which I would like to seek clarification. The 13th Lok Sabha of which I was also a Member discussed the Freedom of Information Bill, and, the Bill was passed. There the issue of jurisdiction, the State jurisdiction as well as the Central jurisdiction, was discussed in detail. I would like to submit that the Right to Information is a fundamental right. It is the prerogative of the Parliament to legislate on matters of fundamental rights, and, it is applicable to all the States. So, we took the stand that it is for the Parliament of India to legislate on the issue of Right to Information, as it is a fundamental right, and, that is why, the previous Parliament discussed it and passed it. But due to some reasons better known to the authorities, it was not notified. That Act is still in the Statute Books, and, now here is a new Bill to replace the Act, which was passed by the Parliament.

Since there were so many amendments to be carried out, it was found appropriate to have a new Bill. Most of the sections in these two Bills are more or less the same. The intention is also more or less the same. But it was found very convenient or feasible to have a new Bill. That is why, this new Bill was introduced in the Parliament repealing the previous one.

The stand taken is that this being a central subject, the State cannot legislate on this matter. I do not question the wisdom of the State Legislature. I was also the Speaker of the Kerala Legislative Assembly for a long time.

SK/1M/12.50/PPG/14.02.2005

They had their own business. In Kerala, it was not passed. It was passed in some other State. It was passed on the basis of Directive Principles of State Policy where it was provided that the States can also pass such a thing. I presume, that may be the reason for the State Legislation to encroach upon this particular topic. But, the Indian Parliament has taken a different view on this issue, and that is why this Act was passed. Anyhow, the matter has come up again as an encroachment in the federal structure of our Constitution has taken place. That also will have to be looked into because if it is an encroachment of the States, definitely, it has to be curtailed. If you have any different view, please enlighten us.

Now, another question is regarding Official Secretes Act. It is still there and there are certain documents which are classified as classified documents. I would like to know, by passing this statute, would it be possible to get information, because so many officials in bureaucracy can easily escape their transparency by claiming a document as a classified document, or by claiming that it is under the Official Secrets Act. So, what should be done in this respect? The Act should be repealed and the term 'classified document' will also have to go. Otherwise, you will not be able to get information on a large number of Government documents. Any officer in the Government of India or any top bureaucrat can claim official secrecy. This may save him from certain misdeeds. So considering this aspect, I would like to have your views on this. I would like to know who is to decide as to which are the secret documents. We will have to take a decision on who is the authority to take a decision whether it is a classified document or not. That matter will have to be provided in the Statute Book. Otherwise, the purpose for which this Act was passed, will become futile. You may look into that matter also.

Then there is a question of delay. That is the most important thing. As far as possible, delay should be prevented and avoided. In case of prosecution, if it is a minor court, it means delay. The purpose is not served. So, what are your views in this regard? Shall we have some special courts or some agency to deal with these cases? Otherwise, if we leave it to the normal course, it will not be good. So, all these aspects will have to be looked into. I would welcome you if you enlighten us with your views on this.

Now, the question comes how far we are justified in passing a new statue when already there is a previous one with same status, with same aims and ambitions and all that. Fortunately, we are now discussing the new statute replacing the previous one. There is a lot of criticism for bringing in a new legislation. That aspect may also be looked into. I expect your expert opinion on all these matters. Thank you.

CHAIRMAN: I would also like to raise some questions. We can very much appreciate that clause 17 is not having the required strength and also the powers of the Commission should be somewhat strengthened. I hope you have got the Bill. If you go to Chapter 3, clause 12 (4), this is regarding the Constitution of Central Information Commission. There, if you see clause 4, it says, "The general superintendence, direction and management of the affairs of the Commission shall vest in the Information Commissioner who shall be assisted by the Deputy Information Commissioners and may exercise all such powers". Now, the powers are mentioned in clause 15 (1) (a) which says, "Who has been unable to submit a request to a Public Information Officer, either by reason that no such officer has been appointed under this Act, or because the Assistance Public Information Commissioner has refused to accept his or her application: for forwarding the same to the public authority or the Government". But, as you said, we could also find out that it is not having a very strong power to interfere when there is a rejection of the request of the citizen to get the accessibility of the information. So, even if the information is not partly given or it is not fully given, but when you go to the condition of the person who will be appointed, we will see how much that Commission becomes powerless. I want to show it, whether you agree or not with that. You come back to clause 12 (6) which says, "The Information Commissioner or a Deputy Information Commissioner shall not be a Member of Parliament or a Member of the Legislature of any State or Union Territory, as the case may be, or hold any other office of profit or connected with any political party or carrying on any business or pursuing any profession". What is this? Should he be a jobless fellow? They are giving another disqualification in clause 13 (5), which says, "The Information Commissioner or a Deputy Information Commissioner shall, on cessation of his office, not be eligible for (a) any diplomatic assignment, assignment as administrator of a Union Territory or such other assignment or appointment which is required by law to be made by the President by warrant under his hand and seal; (b) further employment to any office of profit under the Government of India or the Government of a State". Simply for finding out whether the petition is properly accepted by the subordinate officer, you lose your job.

YSR/1.00/1N/PPG/14.02.2005

Now, I come to the proviso regarding removal of Information Commissioner or Deputy Information Commissioner. It says, "14.(1) Subject to the provisions of sub-section (3), the Information Commissioner or any Deputy Information Commissioner shall be removed from his office only by order of the President on the ground of proved misbehaviour or incapacity after the Supreme Court, on a reference made to it by the President, has, on inquiry, reported that the Information Commissioner or any Deputy

Information Commissioner, as the case may be, ought on such ground be removed." It means only the President can refer the matter to the Supreme Court.

> "(2) The President may suspend from office, and if deem necessary prohibit also from attending the office during inquiry, the Information Commissioner or Deputy Information Commissioner in respect of whom a reference has been made to the Supreme Court under sub-section (1) until the President has passed orders on receipt of the report of the Supreme Court on such reference."

Then nobody will come to do this job because the President here means the Executive who is giving an order.

Now, please look at the bottom of page 9. It says, "Provided further that if the Information Commissioner or a Deputy Information Commissioner if, at the time of his appointment is, in receipt of retirement benefits in respect of any previous service rendered in a Corporation established by or under any Central Act or State Act or a Government company owned or controlled by the Central Government or the State Government, his salary in respect of the service as the Information Commissioner or the Deputy Information Commissioner shall be reduced by the amount of pension equivalent to the retirement benefits."

This shows that only Government servants, who are very meek and just obey orders of the Government, should be appointed as the Information Commissioner. It is my personal opinion. All of you are working in some NGOs or the other, and you have the experience, that is why we would like to seek information on this from you. How do you view this? Why I am saying this is because the entire Bill rests upon this Commission. Here we are just trying to explain the fundamental rights, which are already interpreted by the Supreme Court of India, namely, right to freedom of speech and right to information. Now, the activists like you are saying that our democracy should be strengthened by making people aware of the information and how they are going to get benefits out of it. This work can be done by the Government; this work can be done by the Parliament; and this work can be done by the judiciary. But here we are going to create an organisation, which is a commission. The Commission has to see to it that this right to information is properly implemented. If it is not properly implemented, then the Commission has to enforce it. It will be its constitutional obligation. If this organisation is not going to function properly, then what is the purpose of bringing this enactment? We are not enacting this law just to become a part of the Statute Book. I think you have to focus upon this particular aspect and give us your valuable suggestions. Shri Anna Hazare, social activist, is also here. He can share his practical experiences with this Committee.

Now, it is my suggestion; it is not the suggestion of the Committee. This Commission should perform its duties more than the Central Vigilance Commission. Its job is to see whether corruption cases are properly handled or not. We have got the Election Commission, which works independently. We have the office of the Comptroller and Auditor-General. Both are constitutional offices. Do you think that type of body should be created then only this can be enforced? Are you of the view that Members of Parliament should not be excluded; Members of Legislative Assemblies should not be excluded; or a judge should not be excluded? Or if a person who is a Member of Parliament may be appointed as a Commissioner and on that day onwards his membership should be ceased. I request you to consider about it and give us some inputs.

My colleague, Dr. P.C. Alexander, has already asked about legal implications. We are happy that you have chosen appropriate persons to represent before us. Regarding human rights issue, we need some input from you. It is contained in the Criminal Procedure Code that the information should be given to the complainant and a constitutional protection is also there, that is, the accused should be produced before a judicial magistrate within 24 hours. Even then we are not getting the clear information as to why somebody was arrested, or how some custodial deaths or harassment of women took place. I do not want very extreme comments because now the Human Rights Commission is also being summoned by the High Court. You have to tell us whether the right to information should be made enforceable one or not.

Another aspect is about enforcement of fundamental rights. It is the constitutional obligation on the Government of India to enact a law and that law is meant only for the protection of citizens and not against any State Government or any local body. That is why the fundamental rights have not been mentioned in the three lists, namely, Union List, State List and Concurrent List. These are not mentioned because these are fundamental rights. We can even say none of the things in the fundamental rights were mentioned as powers of the Union Government. These are not powers, but rights for all citizens. It will be power only when you get fundamental rights enforced by the State.

V.VKK/10/1.10/14.2.2005 PPG

Only those powers will be mentioned in the different Lists. Therefore, the best way we can say is that it is residuary power, Item 97 of Para 1. That we accept. But my conception is that you enforce a Fundamental Right constitutionally. Constitutional obligation is on Parliament. Parliament knows how best we can protect the Constitution and also the Indian necessity. Therefore, I feel that the powers, sovereign powers, are also enshrined. On that also, if you consider, you can make recommendations to us. The third point is that you have given very good things from public distribution system. I hope this does not include falsely recorded statistics. The grains are sold, but the actual beneficiaries do not receive them. If you have got a stock in a particular shop, you will distribute according to the cardholders. Many of the people are having no purchasing power. They could not purchase the food materials. That food material is sold to the black-market, showing that it has also been sold. I think you have included the stolen part only. I think you have not taken the full thing into consideration. If you can do that, we can find out how we are losing it. Thank you very much.

SHRIMATI ARUNA ROY: Most of these questions, we would reply in writing. Mr. Prashant would reply to a few here.

SHRI PRASHANT BHUSHAN: You are right about the Official Secrets Act which says that any information which comes to a Government servant in his official capacity, is an official secret and if he parts with that information with any unauthorised person, it is an offence. It is this section alone in the Official Secrets Act which is very objectionable. Ideally, that section of the Official Secrets Act should be repealed simultaneously with the passage of the Right to Information Act. Even if that is not repealed, if it is made clear that the Right to Information Act shall have effect notwithstanding anything contained in the Official Secrets Act, then that will take care of most of the problem. However, I do feel that, that provision in the Official Secrets Act is very detrimental to the functioning of democracy. How can you say that any information which comes to a Government servant in his official capacity, is an official secret, even though it may have no detrimental effect on the public interest? That needs to be deleted. That is one of our recommendations.

SHRIMATI ARUNA ROY: Although we must end now, I would like to submit that we have not been able to get BPL lists from anywhere. Of course, it is impossible because of the existence of the Official Secrets Act. We will look into it and write to you.

CHAIRMAN: You told about the identity of the citizens. It is not mentioned in the law. It is not mentioned in the Bill. That means you want to say 'any person'. 'Any person' means people may think that the sovereignty of the country will be totally gone and anybody will get the information.

SHRIMATI ARUNA ROY: Perhaps we could ensure that we can access the information despite being called citizens.

CHAIRMAN: You mean to say there should not be any qualification for identity of the citizens. It should be allowed.

Thank you very much. Kindly join us for lunch.

(The witnesses then withdrew)

WITNESS

1. Shri Anna Hazare
2. Shri Prakash Kardaley

CHAIRMAN: Welcome to Shri Anna Hazare, the famous social activist who is a living Gandhian. You can give lot of boost to us. We are very happy that you have implemented the Gandhian principles in the area in which you are active and have revolutionised that area. Even our hon. Dr. Alexander, who was the Governor of Maharashtra, holds you in high respect for your Gandhian movement and Shri Prakash Kardaley. We are happy that we would get inputs from both of you so that we can make this Right to Information Bill useful for the public and the citizens of India.

Our hon. Members will raise certain queries after your presentation. You may avoid those things in your presentation which you have already submitted. You can highlight the points which have not been highlighted.

The discussion in the Committee is confidential and has not to be divulged outside till the report is filed before the Parliament. If you want to write over the queries of hon. Members, you can do so within one week. Afterwards, we are going to the next stage of clause-by-clause consideration. Now, I request both of you to present your submissions.

SHRI PRAKASH KARDALEY: Sir, I would submit for a few minutes, then I would hand over to Shri Anna Hazareji who wants to make oral submissions. I have already submitted my written submissions. I would highlight only two or three points. I come from Maharashtra. Thanks to the initiatives of Shri Annaji, who is present with us and thanks to the positive support given by the Maharashtra Government, we have the best legislations on the right to information in our State. I am very happy to tell you, Sir, that hundreds of citizens of Maharashtra, which is a large State, are using it right now. People are using it. (Contd. by 1P)

RSS/1.10/1P

SHRI PRAKASH KARDALEY (CONTD.): They were getting information as well. Our recent survey has shown that even in the first go, after having filed a requisition, 25 per cent of the people have got the information, and after following the appellate mechanism, the percentage has gone up to 40 per cent. It means three out of four people are not getting the information. Even after appeals, 60 per cent people are not getting the information. The success rate in some of the advanced countries like Canada and South America has not been to that extent which we are having in Maharashtra. In that way, we are very lucky. We are progressing ahead. Shri Anna Hazareji is monitoring the progress. We have been successful in such a short span of time in Maharashtra mainly because of certain provisions in the Act. The first is, the penalty on default. Any public information officer, who does not respect the provisions of this Act, who does not give the information in a stipulated period, is penalised. Annaji pursued this matter with the Government, and the Government, after issuing various circulars, is actually penalising the concerned persons. According to our Act, the first appellate officer is supposed to penalise the PIO. Eye-brows were raised against the appellate authority. They were told that a departmental action will be taken against them. At the moment, in our State, nearly 40 per cent of the public information officers have already been penalised and the amount recovered on this score is something like Rs. 25,000/-. It has an electrifying effect, and ail the public information officers, who were not respecting the provisions of the Act, have fallen in line and giving information. We were looking forward for having a Central legislation which would be better than the best. As a State, we are all one country. We want that one legislation should be applicable not only in respect of public bodies and its agencies, but also to the entire country. Yes, we wanted it in that way. I was very happy to read that a National Advisory Council had prepared a dream piece of legislation. Unfortunately, when it came back from the Law Ministry, certain pruning was done, and a few recommendations of the National Advisory Council were removed and that made it totally ineffective. Those few points were, firstly, a penal clause. Simple penalty for delay which involves the monetary penalty. I am penalised for filing my return with a delay. The moment there is a delay, there is a penalty on me. This power is vested in middle level officers, and even the lower middle level functionaries of the Government. The Information Commissioner will be appointed by the panel, comprising of the Prime Minister, the Leader of the Opposition and the Chief Justice of India. Such senior functionaries are not having simple powers of penalising for delay. What has remained is only the prosecution for giving the false information. But the penal clause has worked in Maharashtra. It is because of this penal provision that information is forthcoming. It was only after the PIOs started getting penalised that the information started coming, and the success rate has gone up tremendously. In most State laws, the penal provision is there which is missing from the Central law, and I cannot understand why it is so.

Secondly, if this information is for the common man, this information should also be made available at an affordable price. I am not talking of subsidy. But, at the same time, I am asking for insertion of a simple provision, which is there in the State law of Maharashtra, that the cost of information prescribed to be levied, shall not exceed the actual cost of copying. In Maharashtra, it is called the zeroxing cost of 50 paisa. We pay 50 paisa per page, and if the document consists of 500 pages, I shall have to give Rs. 250/-. If that prerogative is given to some functionary, and if he charges Rs. ten per page, I will have to pay accordingly, and the common man may not be in a position to afford that. So, the cost of information should be affordable. The National Advisory Council had recommended that the cost shall not exceed the actual cost of copying, and it also involves the cost of inspection of material, which is missing. Suppose, certain work has been done in accordance with the Maharashtra Act. Suppose, I want to take that material, give it to the laboratory and have it examined to ensure that the work has been done according to the specification of the Government. That clause is missing here. In the absence of that clause, a very prohibitive cost will be levied. Even if the right to information is called the fundamental right, we will not be in a position to apply it to the common man in view of the cost involved. If it is applied by a few elitists, then it is not a law for the common man.

Thirdly, I come to the question of a third party. There is an unreasonable protection given to the third party, which is not there in any of the State laws. I am not a legal person. Suppose, I want to construct a building in Pune, and it is governed by the Municipal Corporation laws of Pune. Suppose, Annaji wants to know what kind of building permission I have obtained from the Municipal Corporation, Pune. He has a suspicion that, in league with the officers of the Pune Municipal Corporation, I might have violated certain rules. Under this Act, the public information officer will refer the matter to me as a third party. I will raise an objection whether the information should be given, whether the copy of the sanction plan should be given to Annaji. I will take an objection. He will take a decision, and then only, the information shall be passed on to Annaji. This will create a problem. This clause apparently looks innocuous as if the reasonable opportunity is being granted to the person, but it is going to destroy the content of the Act. The third party is supposed to get back the information in ten days from the Public Information Officer. Suppose, I write a letter to the third party on receiving the information, it is doubtful whether the public information officer will send this letter in five days. In a scenario where courts summons are not served for months together, I really do not know whether the PIO letter ever reaches the third party within that period.

(Contd. by 1Q)

TMV-AKG/1Q/1.30/PPG/14.02.2005

Suppose I ask for the information—in fact, Mr. Shailesh Gandhi of Ahmedabad, who is going to depose before you in the afternoon, had asked for this information from the Director-General of Police—from the Director-General of Police as to how many Ministers, MPs and MLAs had recommended transfers of police officers. If it involves 100 persons, the Public Information Officer and the Director-General of Police will write to 100 different people.

DR. P.C. ALEXANDER: Do not exaggerate. That is not the intention of this Bill. These are regarding simple information. Whatever information is available, that should be provided.

SHRI PRAKASH KARDALEY: I am talking about the practical difficulty that we may face.

DR. P.C. ALEXANDER: You are stretching it too much. You are considering them as a third party. Your point is well taken that the third party resort should be very minimal and it should be done only in a legitimate case. The third party has also a right. You don't forget that. Your own note on the Draft Bill has recognised the third party right.

SHRI PRAKASH KARDALEY: Sir, may I now come straightaway to the third party? If the principle, in an open democracy, is that there is no distinction between the people and the Government and the Government functionaries are functioning on my behalf or on behalf of the people, I have a right to information how he is functioning on my behalf. If there is no duality between the Government and I, there is no question of anyone claiming a third party right. The third party comes when they are two distinct entities, the person requiring the information and the Government. If they are not two different entities, there is no question of a third party. Anyway, I leave it to you.

Now, I come to the last point which relates to the Deputy Information Commissioner. I am skipping the Information Commission, etc., because Smt. Aruna Roy and her team dealt with them. It is mentioned that the number of Deputy Information Commissioners should be restricted to ten and that they should be appointed as and when necessary. Now, for a vast sub-continental country like ours, this is not enough. If the first Appellate Authority does not have powers under this Bill for penalising an officer, it essentially has to go to the Information Commissioner. The Information Commissioner is going to sit in Delhi. Suppose there are no Deputy Information Commissioners suitably located, once again, this is not going to work for the common man. Therefore, instead of the words "such number of Deputy Information Commissioners not exceeding ten as may be deemed necessary", let there be a mandate that there will be minimum 10 Deputy Information Commissioners to be appointed along with the Information Commissioner and suitably located in the entire country so that they are accessible to the common man. Otherwise, a person from Kerala or Nagaland has to come all the way to Delhi for a second appeal. These are my humble submissions.

श्री अन्ना हजारे: 'राइट टू इनफॉरमेशन' एक्ट आजादी के 56 साल बाद बनने जा रहा है। मुझे इस पर संतोष है। हम लोगों ने महाराष्ट्र में भी 'राइट टू इनफॉरमेशन' के ऊपर एक कानून बनाया है। वास्तव में यह जनता का मूलभूत हक है। 26 जनवरी 1950 को जब यह देश प्रजासत्तात्मक बना था, उस दिन इस देश में सत्ता प्रजा के हाथ में आ गई और सरकार की तिजोरी जनता की तिजोरी हो गई। उस तिजोरी का व्यवस्थापन करने के लिए जनता ने लोकशाही को स्वीकार किया और अपने प्रतिनिधि, एमएलए, एमपी चुन कर भेजे। राष्ट्रपति ने जो आईएएस, आईपीएस आदि ऑफिसर नियुक्त

किए हैं, वे गवर्नमेंट सर्वेंट हैं। जनता मालिक है। सरकार की तिजोरी जनता की तिजोरी है। हमारी तिजोरी का क्या हो रहा है, यह जानना जनता का हक है। यह मूलभूत हक है। वास्तव में 26 जनवरी 1950 को, जिस दिन हमने अपने देश को प्रजासत्तात्मक बनाया, उसी दिन यह कानून बन जाना चाहिए था, लेकिन ऑफिशियल सीक्रेट् एक्ट इसके बीच आ गया। वास्तव में 26 जनवरी 1950 को ही इसे खत्म करना चाहिए था या इसमें सुधार लाना चाहिए था। जब जनता मालिक हो गई, आप सब सेवक हैं, तो जनता से सब छिपा कर रखा जाए, यह क्या लोकशाही है? उसी दिन इसे या तो निकाल देना चाहिए था, या इसमें सुधार लाना चाहिए था, परन्तु यह नहीं हुआ। इसके कारण आजादी के 56 साल बाद तक जनता को कभी भी जानकारी नहीं मिल पाई। इसके कारण करप्शन बढ़ा, और काम की क्वालिटी, गरीबों के पास जो कुछ सुविधाएँ पहुँचनी चाहिए, इसमें डिफिकल्टी आई। यह छिपा कर रखने के कारण पैदा हुई।

हम इस कानून में यह सजेशन रखना चाहते हैं कि यह जनता का मूलभूत हक है, इसलिए हक समझ कर यह कानून बनाना जरूरी है। जो गवर्नमेंट के और पालिसी आदि हैं, वे अलग बात हैं, लेकिन यह जनता का राइट है। चूँकि जनता मालिक है, और ये सब सेवक हैं, इसलिए मालिक जब जानकारी मांगता है, जो जानकारी देना उनका कर्त्तव्य है। इसमें इन बातों पर ध्यान दे कर यह कानून बनाना जरूरी है।

अब इसमें दण्डात्मक कार्रवाई पर ध्यान दें। गोवा, तमिलनाडु, राजस्थान ने भी इसके ऊपर कानून बनाया, लेकिन अपील अथॉरिटी के पास दण्डात्मक कार्रवाई का अधिकार नहीं होने के कारण एक्शन नहीं हो पा रहा है। इसलिए इसमें लोगों का जो इनवाल्वमेंट होना चाहिए था, वह नहीं हुआ और उनकी संख्या उतनी नहीं बढ़ी। महाराष्ट्र में अभी-अभी यह कानून बना है। इसमें अपील अथॉरिटी को दण्डात्मक कार्रवाई का अधिकार दिया गया है। इससे लोग जागृत हो गए। इसके कारण जनता आगे आ गई। अब लोग तहसीलदार से जवाब मांग रहे हैं कि अपने तहसील में कितना काम हुआ, कितना डिस्ट्रीब्यूशन हुआ, इसके बारे में जानकारी दो। अब उन्हें जानकारी देनी पड रही है।

हमने अन्नपूर्णा योजना बनाई। अभी हमारे पास यह जानकारी आई कि अन्नपूर्णा योजना में लाभकारों को पता ही नहीं है कि इस योजना में वे लाभधारकों में हैं, और इसका अनाज निकाल कर बाहर भेजा जा रहा है। इस राइट टू इनफॉरमेशन के कारण लोगों में जागृति आ गई। एक एप्लिकेशन दे कर वे तहसीलदार से अन्नपूर्णा योजना में लाभधारकों के बारे में जानकारी मांग रहे हैं, तो इस पर ब्रेक लग गया। मेरे कहने का मतलब यह है कि इस राइट टू इनफॉरमेशन में यह जनता का हक है, इस पर हमारा ज्यादा नजरिया होना चाहिए। कोई बोर्ड, योजना या पॉलिसी बनना एक अलग बात है, लेकिन इसमें यह बात हो गई तो इसमें पारदर्शिता आ जाएगी। इसमें जितनी पारदर्शिता आएगी, करप्शन पर उतना ब्रेक लगेगा।

दूसरी बात यह है कि हमारे गरीब लोग इम्प्लायमेंट एक्सचेंज जाते हैं, उनका दस-दस साल तक नंबर नहीं आता है। अब इस राइट टू इनफॉरमेशन के अन्दर वह इम्प्लायमेंट एक्सचेंज के ऑफिसर से पूछ रहा है कि उसके आगे कितने लोग हैं? तो यह जानकारी उन्हें देनी पड रही है। इससे गरीब आदमी को न्याय मिलेगा। इन बातों से इसमें पारदर्शिता आ रही है। यह मुझे बहुत महत्वपूर्ण लग रही है। इसमें दण्डात्मक कार्रवाई सबसे महत्वपूर्ण है। इसमें अपील अथॉरिटी अपने नीचे इनफॉरमेशन ऑफिसर से कह रहा है कि वह जानकारी दे दे। अगर वह जानकारी नहीं दे तो क्या होगा, इसमें कोई तरदुत नहीं है। ('1आर' पर जारी)

RG/HMS/1.40/1R

श्री अन्ना हजारे (क्रमागत): अपील अथॉरिटी और कमीशन को दंडात्मक कार्यवाही की पावर नहीं है। फिर वह कोर्ट में जाएंगे और उससे बहुत डिले हो जाएगा। इसलिए दंडात्मक कार्यवाही होना बहुत जरूरी है। इसके लिए एक तो अपील अथॉरिटी और दूसरे कमीशन दोनों को पावर मिलना बहुत जरूरी है। तभी इस कानून में गति आ पाएगी। इससे एक तो पारदर्शिता आएगी और दूसरे सुदृढ़ व नेक-लोकशाही का निर्माण होगा। आज की परिस्थिति में जो 10 स्टेट्स हैं उनमें और सेंटर में आर्थिक स्थिति को बदलने में भी यह कानून लाभदायक हो सकता है। साथ ही इससे हमारी अर्थ-व्यवस्था भी बदल सकती है। दूसरे, बड़े-बड़े राज्यों की आर्थिक स्थिति को सुधारने में भी इस कानून से मदद मिलेगी। इस नजरिए से भी इस कानून को देखना जरूरी है।

अभी दक्षिण कोरिया गवर्नमेंट को जब इस कानून के बारे में पता लगा कि हमारे महाराष्ट्र राज्य में ऐसा कानून है तो उन्होंने 5 लोगों की एक टीम हमारे यहां भेजी और उन्होंने उसका चित्रीकरण किया। अब वे दक्षिण कोरिया में देशवासियों को बताएंगे कि महाराष्ट्र में एक ऐसा कानून बना है। ऐसे कानून बनाने के बारे में कई देशों का लक्ष्य है और वे कानून बनाने जा रहे हैं। इसलिए हमारे देश में जो यह कानून बनने जा रहा है, वह एक ऐसा कानून हो जोकि कई देशों के लिए मिसाल बने, उदाहरण हो कि भारत में एक ऐसा कानून बना है। इससे जिन देशों में अभी कानून नहीं बना है, वे भी अपने यहां बना सकेंगे या वहां की कमियों को सुधार लेंगे।

मैं तो पिछले 45 दिन से महाराष्ट्र में इस "राइट टू इनफॉरमेशन" की लोक शिक्षा और लोक जागृति के लिए टूर पर हूं। परसों मुझें यहां आने के लिए मैसेज मिला तो मैं अचानक आ गया। मैं इस कानून के बारें में कॉलेज स्टुडेंट्स को जगा रहा हूँ। मैं पिछले 45 दिनों में 85 कॉलेजों में गया और उन्हें जगा रहा हूँ कि "राइट टू इनफॉरमेशन" क्या है। इसमें ट्रेनिंग और मॉनीटरिंग की भी बहुत जरूरत है।

मैं यहां इतना ही कहूंगा कि इसमें दंडात्मक कार्यवाही का होना बहुत जरूरी है। दूसरे जब हम जानकारी मांगते हैं तो एक कॉपी के लिए कितना पैसा देना है, वह तय होना चाहिए। इसमें लिखा है कि ऑफिसर बताएगा कि कितना देना है। हमने हमारे यहां उसमें लिखा है कि 50 पैसे पर कॉपी यानि जीरोक्स की कॉपी के पैसे लेने हैं। यह कानून में डालना बहुत जरूरी है। अभी हमारे सामने एक उदाहरण आया कि गवर्नमेंट ट्रेजरी में एक ऑफिसर ने 1 लाख 60 हजार रुपया मांगा। मैं चीफ मिनिस्टर को मिला और बताया कि क्या 1 लाख 60 हजार रुपया उसकी कीमत हो सकती है। तो उसकी जांच शुरु हुई है। मेरे कहने का मतलब यह है कि यह हमारे कानून में आना चाहिए कि जितनी कॉपी देंगे यानि उस पर जितना खर्चा आएगा वह उस को देना होगा। अगर आप उसे ऑफिसर पर छोड़ देंगे तो उसका नाजायज उपयोग होगा और उससे लोगों को काफी नुकसान होगा, लोगों को सही जानकारी नहीं मिलेगी और वे हताश हो जाएंगे।

ये दो-तीन बातें मैं आपके सामने रखना चाहता हूँ। मैंने विस्तार से ड्राफ्ट नहीं देखा है क्योंकि पिछले डेढ़ महीने से मैं इसी काम के लिए सफर पर हूं। बाद में और बातें बता दूंगा।

CHAIRMAN: I would like to get one, two pieces of information from you. If you know it, you tell us. Otherwise, we will get it through other sources. When the Maharashtra law was applied, there were several cases of complaints. How many such cases were filed? How many cases ended with penalty and how much was collected through this?

SHRI PRAKASH KARDALEY: At this stage I don't think even the Maharashtra Government has compiled this information.

CHAIRMAN: How did you say that around 2,000 cases are already there...

SHRI PRAKASH KARDALEY: As for how many requisitions have been filed under the Act, I can say, it would be around 3,000 to 4,000...

CHAIRMAN: We will try to get authenticated information because when you go for penal provision, we would like to know how effectively the Maharashtra law has been enforced, how much benefit people have got and whether it is working properly or not. Also, we are aware of how e-govemance is being implemented in Tamil Nadu. Even in villages, people who have got internet facilities can get information regarding shares, rent and other things. Is it available in Maharashtra also?

SHRI PRAKASH KARDALEY: Not to the extent of Tamil Nadu, yet it is building up. But, in that case, you are referring to the transparency provision, the information which the Government *suo motu* has to give when I seek information under the Right to Information. That itself is part of this Act. But most of our requests go beyond this.

CHAIRMAN: What type of information are you seeking?

SHRI PRAKASH KARDALEY: For example, I have a building sanction. Anna Saheb can demand a copy of the plan consent of the Municipal Corporation of Pune because he might feel that there is something hanky panky in it. I suppose that is within his right.

श्री अन्ना हजारे: अभी हमारी महाराष्ट्र में चीफ मिनिस्टर व चीफ सेक्रेटरी के साथ एक सप्ताह पहले अभी तक हुए फाइन के बारे में मीटिंग हुई थी। हर डिस्ट्रिक्ट में कितने लोगों को फाइन हुए हैं, उसकी लिस्ट बन गयी है। अभी तक ज्यादा-से-ज्यादा 35-37 हजार रुपये फाइन हुआ है।

CHAIRMAN: When you get it, kindly pass it on to us for our perusal. Thank you very much for coming over here and making your presentation. Kindly join us for lunch.

The witnesses then withdrew.

The Committee then adjourned at 1.48 p.m.

1S/2.40/KS

(The Committee reassembled after Lunch)

Witnesses

1. Shri Shekhar Singh Convenor, National Campaign for People's Right to Information.
2. Shri Shailesh Gandhi, Fellow, IIM, Ahmedabad.

CHAIRMAN: We are happy, Mr. Shekhar Singh, that NCPRI has come forward with many suggestions. We got your submission through e-mail. You can highlight the points on which you want to lay stress. If you want to make more suggestions, you can do that. Thereafter, the hon. Members will seek clarifications, which, if you can reply immediately, you can do so; otherwise, you can send your response to those questions in writing within a week's time, because we have to take up the Clause-by-Clause consideration of this Bill. As you are aware, the deliberations of the Committee are confidential and should not be disclosed to anyone before the Committee presents its report to the Parliament. You can proceed now.

SHRI SHEKHAR SINGH: It is a great privilege to have this opportunity. I will briefly cover the points that I have already submitted to the Committee. Sir, we feel that there is a test of four principles, which must be applied to any right to information or transparency Bill to determine how good or bad the Bill is.

The first principle is: How much does it disclose and how much does it keep back? The second is whether there is an independent appeal mechanism and, if so, how independent that appeal mechanism is. Thirdly, what are the penalties and how severe are those penalties? Fourthly, how easily accessible the information to the people is? These are the four principles that we have applied while looking at this Bill.

Take the first principle of maximum disclosure. There are a few points, which could be highlighted. There is a blanket exemption so far as the security and intelligence agencies are concerned. The Bill has removed the obligation of the security and intelligence agencies to provide information in relation to human rights violations and threats to the life and liberty of persons, though it has retained this proviso in cases of corruption. First of all, we thought that there ought not to be this blanket exclusion. Surely the violation of human rights and the threat to life and liberty is no less important than corruption, and requires no less public scrutiny. This is the first point.

The second point is about exemptions. The NAC draft gave citizens the right to access all documents after a 25 year period. It had said that after 25 years all information should become public. In the Bill, that clause has been dropped. Our plea is that you could still have some screening, but it is an unacceptable principle that some information will never be made public. People must know how certain things happened. It is very important to have that clause back into this Bill.

The third point, of course, is about exclusion of States. There are two points. I believe there is, first of all, some debate on whether we can have both a national Act and the State Acts. The NAC draft— and why I refer to it is because NCPRI had actually given a draft to the NAC and the NAC draft of the Bill had included many of the suggestions that we had given. We had said that as States also have certain very specific characteristics, for example, certain States in the North-Eastern Region do not have Panchayats, they have District Councils, they would have to have specific provisions under their individual Acts. So, we could have the Central and, additionally, the State Acts. If it is found to be problematic, to my mind, having a national Act covering all States, would be preferable; it would be better than the other proposition. Now, it is thought by all that the Maharashtra Act is the best of all that we have. If the Central Act is better than the Maharashtra Act, then there is no problem in having a Central Act. But I would prefer if both could work together so that the specific characteristics of States could be taken care of.

The fourth point on exclusions is about restrictions on third party information. I have a very simple submission to make. Third party information can be restricted only when it is about some ongoing investigation and so on. Otherwise, it will become discretionary matter on what basis the third party information can be kept out. I think that discretion will lead to a lot of differences. There will be no universality in how the Act is being exercised.

The second principle is about appeal mechanisms. I have two submissions to make. First of all, the level at which the Bill proposes to have Information Commissioner, to my mind, is too low. They have said that the Information Commissioner would be of the level of Secretary of the Government of India and the Deputy Information Commissioners of the level of Additional Secretary or Joint Secretary to the Government of India. This, to my mind, is too low a level. The Information Commission is not only the appellate authority for the executive, judiciary and the legislature but it would also be responsible to oversee the implementation of the RTI law. We feel that they must be of the status of the Chief Election Commissioner and Election Commissioners because they have to have a sort of status where they can discharge the sort of responsibility given to them. The second point is that they have limited the number of Deputy Information Commissioners to 10 only. Our feeling was that each State must have at least one Deputy Information Commissioner and in larger States, perhaps, more than one so that people who want to file appeals do not have to go to Delhi from Kerala. I feel, therefore, no restriction should be put. Of course, initially if you want you can have a few of them. This restriction, I feel, should be dropped. (Contd. by 1T)

TDB/1T/2.50

The third thing is about penalties. There are, again, certain issues which need to be discussed about the penalties. The first thing is about the process of imposition of penalty— I am sure this point has been raised before. The NAC draft says that the Information Commissioner will impose the penalties. Bit, this Bill takes away that power from the Information Commissioner and says that the Information Commissioner shall authorise a Central Government officer to file a complaint. There is no mandatoriness on the part of the Central Government, but they can file a case. We feel that this will finish the whole clause. Our submission is, as far as fines are concerned, they should be imposable by the Information Commissioner. Where it comes to criminal procedure, the Information Commissioner should be authorised to file a case in the court so that, at least, there is no further break. As per the current provision, they have to ask the Central Government, who then has to decide whether to do it or not.

There is a strange anomaly in the Bill. If you read the Bill, you will find that offences have been described very strangely. In fact, the Bill, as it reads today, seems to recognise only one offence, i.e., persistent delay in giving the information. This creates a very absurd situation, where destruction of information is not an offence, giving false information is not an offence, refusal to accept an application for requisition of information is not an offence, even coming in the way of functioning of the Information Commissioner is not an offence. Only persistent delay in providing information is an offence. This obviously is something which has been over- looked. If destruction of information is not an offence, as an officer, I would destroy the information rather than making persistent delay in giving it. So, in order to escape from this absurdity, it is important that the following be recognised as offences: (A) Refusal to accept an application for information, because this is a common problem. (B) Delay in providing information—which is already there in the Bill. (C) *Mala fide* denial of a request for information. (D) Knowingly giving incorrect or misleading information. (E) Knowingly giving wrong or incomplete information. (F) Destroying information subject to a request. (G) Obstructing the activities of a Public Information Officer, any of the Information Commissioner. So, all these should be made offences under this Bill. For (A) and (B) above, the penalty can be fine, and in the case of (B) above, the fine must be imposed for each day of delay. If you have a blanket fine, then, what will happen is this. Once you have delay, there is no incentive for giving the information quickly, and there will be more delay in giving the information. So, our suggestion is, there should be a provision for per day fine which will work as an incentive. In this way, the information will come as quickly as possible. For (C), (D), (E) and (F), it should be both fine and also criminal prosecution, as in the Bill, except the Information Commissioner should be authorised.

Sir, as far as my fourth point is concerned, I have two-three submissions to make. There is a provision in the NAC draft Bill that the fees must not exceed the cost price. We have found in Delhi, for example, that the fees for one page information was put at fifty five rupees— five rupees as photocopy fee and fifty rupees for asking for the information. A lot of people who are using the Right to Information are the poor people, who are living below the poverty line or who come under the Antodaya Scheme, who have to get their ration through their ration cards from the ration shops. If a person wants to know from the Government whether last month ration has been issued in his name, he has to spend fifty five rupees, five rupees for photocopy and fifty rupees as fee. That fifty five rupees would give him 20 kilograms of wheat. Imagine a person who has sacrificed his twenty kilograms of wheat for one page of information! So, we think that it should be at the cost price. In any case, it is the function of the Government to provide that information. If need be, charge the minimum possible cost, not the maximum cost. It must be provided in the Bill; otherwise, it would become a major impediment in people's access to information.

The second point is about people versus citizens. The NAC draft gave all persons the right to information. However, the Right to Information Bill of 2004 restricts the right to information to citizens alone. Just a month back, in the Delhi High Court, a case was filed by the ration shop owners, who wanted the records of ration shops in Delhi. They were not given the required information because it was argued that information could not be given to them, as the applicant was not an Indian citizen, but an NGO. This Bill puts the onus on the applicant to first prove that he or she is a citizen. The Bill is applicable only to the citizens of India. It is something like the Government or the court asking a person first prove your citizenship, then only the Bill will be applicable to you. What are the risks, if any, involved in it? Why do we want our information to be made available to the citizens of India only? If a non-citizen wants to have some information, he can surely get it through a citizen. By allowing this right to information to all persons, we are not compromising our security. Suppose, an accused Bangladeshi national wants to access some information, he should not be denied that information because he is not an Indian citizen. Unless, I think, there are many risks, I don't see any reason why it is not open to all the persons.

Sir, my last point is about certified copy and photocopies. In chapter 1, section 2(j), the right to information accessible under the Act should include the right to certified copies and photocopies of the kind of information listed as accessible. If it is not there, then, people will have problem in it. The other Right to Information Acts are having this problem. Please ensure that this problem is not there in this Bill.

SHRI JUSTICE (RETIRED) N.Y. HANUMANTHAPPA: Why can't the judges be appointed as Information Commissioners?

CHAIRMAN: You have suggested that the Information Commissioner should be independent like the Election Commissioner. The hon. Member wants to know whether the judges should be appointed as the Information Commissioners.

SHRI SHEKHAR SINGH: I personally have no problem with the judges being appointed as the Information Commissioners. We discussed it among ourselves and felt that the job of the Information Commissioner is a full time job. As the Judiciary is already short of judges and we don't want to tax the system further.

CHAIRMAN: The Government has to bear the expenditure on that count. The Government cannot say that it cannot bear the expenditure incurred on the judges when they are appointed as chairmen of Commissions. The retired judges are being appointed to various Commissions. A former Chief Justice of India is the Chairman of the National Human Rights Commission. One day, a High Court simply calls him, and asks as to why he has not issued a particular notice.

SHRI SHEKHAR SINGH: Sir, there are two things. There is problem with the retired judges in the Human Rights Commission because the institution itself has no teeth. If the law provides them teeth, then, I think, it will be all right. Here, we are trying that the Information Commissioner should, at least, have the right to impose penalty and initiate legal proceedings. The moment they could do it, we will be providing them the necessary teeth. Then, it won't matter whether they are sitting judges or retired judges. I personally have no problem with the retired judges or the sitting judges. I just feel that we should open up this field to other types of people so that we have certain diversity in this.

DR. P.C. ALEXANDER: When you have a Central Act — already nine States are having their own legislations—and if some more come, there will be as many legislations as there are States, will it not create complications as somebody will have to first make a distinction as to where he should go? If it is a State subject, then he can go to the Commission under the State Act, and there can be even confusion at the receiving end. (Contd. by 1u)

kgg/1 U/3.00/PPG/14.2.05

DR. P.C. ALEXANDER: If a person applies to the State's Commissioner and doesn't want to go to the Centre's, what happens? The Act provides that one can apply under both the Acts and that it depends on one's judgment. If we have a Central Act which has a complete jurisdiction overall—whether State or local Governments—will it not be a better and smoother one instead of having two legislations?

SHRI SHEKHAR SINGH: There was a strong point of view in our discussion. We debated on what happens if you have multiple Acts. It would create confusion at the field, maybe, to the disadvantage of the Act itself. The way we envisaged it—the Central Act for Central matters, and State Act or the Central Act for State matters—here may be some confusion in the mind of an application as to which Act he should use; by and large, which Act would be more favourable to the information to him. He may wonder like that. The confusion may be in terms of response in the Government, in terms of the forms that he would be filling up for information; they may contain clearly the specification, under section such and such and under such and such Act. Whether this clause or this column is the right option for the applicant? That is given to the applicant to decide. But one thing is certain, for Central matters it should be the Central Act—and people would fill up forms accordingly. You ask me what are the advantages? Getting a law by itself doesn't achieve much, you know it.

As compared to the Central law the State laws may evoke more interest because that would have been debated in the Legislative Assembly and that would have been printed or published in the media. Even today, people, by and large, are aware of the State Government Acts and it is mainly because of the local press. This is one concern as far as the State Act is concerned.

The second concern is, if we are not able to get the Central Act, which is as good as some of the State Government's Act; and if the Central Government repeals the State Act by a way. Perhaps, Karnataka, Delhi and Maharashtra are the States which are doing it better. This is our second concern.

The third concern is, it is difficult for the National Act to take into account all the specificities of the States because the Central Act doesn't see local things as clearly as the State Government can. This particular thing will become a grey area. This Act, in some States, can be in addition to the Act prevailing ever there, which is specifically applicable as in the North Eastern States. It may affect them. There is some potential for that confusion.

DR. P.C. ALEXANDER: Are you recommending that the rules should be altogether dispensed with?

SHRI SHEKHAR SINGH: My own recommendation is that if you are going to exclude any third party 'open ended', then we are inviting problems. We found this problem when we drafted. The same problem was later found in the NAC. In fact, some friends from Maharashtra brought this newer version. Every information which pertains to any Government Department, if anybody takes it up, technically, he becomes a third party. Any time they can give a notice. It will make things worse. This is my own personal view. There is something that is called national justice. I am going to argue that this must be so critically defined that it can't be misused. It must see that the third party clause should be referred to individual *quay* individual and not to State. That information which pertains to A, B, C, D, could be covered under the clauses of privacy.

Somebody may seek information as to how many roads have been built as a third party, from an officer of the MCD. This is where the problem arises.

DR. P.C. ALEXANDER: In this case, nobody will ask about the MCD. It will be directly asked. What I say is that, just as an information seeker is exercising the right, the third party has an inherent right. There are so many rights, human right, and privacy right... You can't rule out the third party. Here, some concession is called for. Otherwise, it will be doing justice to the information seeker but an injustice to somebody.

SHRI SHEKHAR SINGH: I agree with you. We faced a problem. We wanted the list of ration shops in Delhi, of a certain area. They have not been able to supply it.

They went to the High Court for a stay. They got 7 months. They said, "This is our private information." Finally, the High Court vacated that stay. Suppose I ask details of contracts given to somebody. The contractor can say, "This is a third party!" You get into the whole problem. I totally agree with you. But let us make third party rights very specific. Let us not leave it general. The legitimate rights of third party are protected without keeping it open-ended.

SHRI V. RADHAKRISHNAN: You are aware about the Public Interest Litigations. That is being used by citizens every now and then. That is a right and should be used. But it is being misused also. How can you prevent it? Though it is a very good idea and a noble gesture, once this law is implemented, what is the guarantee that it would not be misused and what should be the provisions for preventing that misuse?

SHRI SHEKHAR SINGH: In fact, the whole debate on transparency is a very important one. What is the guarantee that the information that is got under the right to information is not misused? My own answer is, truth can never be misused. In fact, the potential of blackmail is more prevalent when there is a curb on the truth. Under the right to information, you can't get lies. Only the truth. Today, I can make an allegation against a public figure; and people will believe it because of doubt, "Though he is a big figure, who knows?" Tomorrow, if you have the Right to Information Act, a question can be put to you: Why don't you access the information and find it out for yourself?

Actually, it is impossible for me to conceive of a situation where truth can be misused. I can, in fact, argue that people who are susceptible to blackmail will get protected. Even civil servants get protected because today people can pass comments against them. Tomorrow, a civil servant can defend himself seeking the right information. Today he is in danger because the files are kept secret. Under the right to information, the civil servant can ask for information and can say that his name is being maligned.

Frankly speaking, I can't see how truth can be misused.

SHRI V. RADHAKRISHNAN: Then, for personal things, information can be gathered to express vengeance. So many cases may arise.

(Contd. by 1W)

KLS/1 W-3.10/PPG/14.2.2005

SHRI V. RADHAKRISHNAN (CONTD): Suppose, he has not done justice to him and he may feel aggrieved, then he will ask for information to put him into the box.

SHRI SHEKHAR SINGH: Today what is happening is that if you are powerful, if you are rich, you can get information about anybody because government leaks information, and every other organization leaks information. Tomorrow it will be equal for all. In fact, some of the people who have right to information are powerful people. Powerful journalists get access to the information. Other journalists do not have access to the information. Now, CBI has access to information. At the moment, you have to have clout or money to get information. Now without power, with this Act, people can get information. We would equalise.

SHRI V. RADHAKRISHNAN: There are such instances. Should we not make some provision to prevent the misuse of this Act? You are free to get information.

People may even misuse it. It is quite natural. Should we not make a provision for preventing its misuse? I will tell you that there are certain official secrets. I do not stand for them, is another matter. In public interest certain things may not be good for giving information. A person for personal vengeance may ask for information. We should have prevention of misuse of this Act. This right is a very exhaustive right. This right is available to citizens in all walks of life. You can seek information either on State or Central or local authority. It has such a wide range. There should be a measure to check misuse of this provision.

SHRI SHEKHAR SINGH: Sir, it is very difficult to define misuse.

SHRI V. RADHAKRISHNAN: That prevention should not be a curtailment.

SHRI SHEKHAR SINGH: Sir, I was in Indonesia. They have a draft Bill or Act, which provides that if a person misuses the information, he is liable to 10 years imprisonment.

Once you have given somebody the truth, how can he misuse it, I cannot understand that. If truth starts being misused, that is something not comprehensive. You can use lies or half lies.

SHRI V. RADHAKRISHNAN: I will tell you that in my State Kerala, there was Nawab Rajenderan who misused the process of law. His successors also misused the process of law with some ulterior motives. The law is being misused. That is quite common in our country. We want a check on that. But that does not mean that we should curtail the rights of the people. Rights of a citizen must be protected. Everything should be done to protect his rights. There is no doubt about that. But that right should not be taken as a licence. For that purpose, should we not make some measures to prevent the misuse of such a right? A person may not seek information for his own use. He can seek information, which is not beneficial to him. He may give it to somebody else. He may give to some other person who is not prepared to come forward. He will do it for somebody else to please him. He can do it for money also. So, right to information can be misused. It can be used for making money. It can be sought for some other somebody else. That man is behind the curtain. He is not prepared to come forward. Such misuse may take place.

CHAIRMAN: But there are some exceptions. Clause 8 (f), (g), (h) and all these things are there. It is covered under that.

SHRI SHEKHAR SINGH: Once it goes into public domain, you cannot blackmail that person. Suppose, somebody takes a sample of environment related thing and that sample is not up to the standard, he can ask the industrialist to pay him, say, Rs.5000 and would tell him not to take any action. But then somebody else comes with that sample, the industrialist would think of putting a treatment plant instead of paying money again and again. As long as information is selectively available, you can misuse it. You can blackmail people. Once it becomes universal and it is available to all, then it cannot be misused. (Followed by 1X)

NBR/1X/3.20.

CHAIRMAN: I am happy to welcome you Mr. Gandhi to this meeting. Now, you can make your views on the Bill known to the Committee. You have already submitted a Memorandum before the Committee. If you want to add something to the one that has been supplied to us, you can do so. Or, if you want to say something that has not been covered in the Memorandum, you can say so.

Now, you can start your presentation. Thank you.

SHRI SHAILESH GANDHI: Good afternoon and I thank you all for providing me an opportunity to express my views on the Bill. I think this brings me to know as to why this Act has become extremely important. Somewhere along the line, as the hon. Chairman mentioned, we have created institutions like NHRC and institutions of that nature, which are ineffective. The fact is that we do not really have a democracy in the functioning sense. Therefore, today, we have a doubt whether the citizens have a right to information. The fact remains that for more citizens in India there are no worthwhile rights, except the right to vote. Beyond this, they can exercise no right. With this submission, I would like to tell you, as a user and practitioner of the Right to Information Act in Maharashtra, I found that even if you look at every comma and every Section, it is the best Act available in the country. But, this has been completely misused and subverted the spirit of the Act itself. Therefore, we plead with you that this is a momentary opportunity that you have to really really bring back freedom into India. I do not think there would be another opportunity that the citizens of this country will get.

Coming to the specific submissions that I have made, I submit that I have suggested that the Preamble of the Bill itself is wishy-washy. It does not recognise. It flows out of the fundamental rights to the citizens. If you do not regard that, you will find that a lot of cases will go to court. So, this proposed legislation should be used effectively. I would also like to tell you that wherever the word 'public interest' has been used, the PIOs and others always use it against the 'public interest' because a citizen coming and asking for information is considered as absolutely unacceptable.

The second point I wish to place is this. I think there is a need to define which public authorities are going to be covered. It is again a grey area where people will say that I am not covered or somebody else is covered.

The third point is about the State Act and the Central Act. Why is there such a discussion on this? I think he has also mentioned about it. The primary concern of some of us is that we do not have adequate faith today that we will be getting a Central Act which is better than the Maharashtra Act. If we really have that faith, I think, most of us would be prepared to say that one Act is adequate. But, there is a worry. There is a genuine worry. As far as we know, until December 15, we believe that the Bill presented before Parliament containing the same provisions recommended by the National Advisory Council. But it was not so. Therefore, this worry is there between the Union and the States. Since the issue of right to information flows from the Fundamental Rights, there is no reason why the Central Act cannot prevail all over the country, provided we believe in sincerity that you have an Act which is better than the Maharashtra Act.

Now, I come to Clause 2(j). Sir, the two words 'Xerox copies' are extremely important. It sounds like two simple words. In Maharashtra Act we have these words. Maharashtra Act insists that they will have to give the certified copies. For this, they were charging between Rs. 50 and Rs. 150. For example, if a person wants to get some information which contains 100 pages and if this is the cost that we have to bear, then it is impossible for the citizens. Therefore, those two simple words — Xerox copies or certified copies — have to be explained and charges should be clearly mentioned in the Act itself. You have also proposed in the Bill that not only the Information Commissioner but also the appellate authority should have the right. Otherwise, it will mean that all the cases will go to the Information Commissioner and the Information Commissioner will get overloaded.

Now, I come to the next Clause which is extremely contentious. I would come back and say what Mr. Sekhar has said. Why are we worried about truth? If truth can be misused, it means, we are afraid of truth. If this is so, it is a sad end. Today we are worried that truth can be misused. If a nation, which has got its independence from truth, is afraid of truth then it is very unfortunate. A nation which was born on 'Satyameva Jayate' is afraid of truth, then we can do nothing. Sir, truth cannot be misused and even if there is one instance in one thousand cases where we believe that we can genuinely prove that truth has been misused, I think, that risk we, as a society, must be prepared to take. We have compromised on everything but not on truth. Going back to the Fundamental Rights, I would say that truth is what we held in honour. It cannot be misused. In the overall context — this is what recognised for generations — if you recognise this as a fundamental fact that becomes the basis to provide right to information.

Coming to the Clause relating to penalty, I would say that why it again required is because we know that our governance structure is not what it supposed to be. We are aware that citizens' right of any nature is not respected and this can be brought back if you impose penalty. Even in Maharashtra, we have the penalty clause. Sir, for the information of the Committee, I would like to submit that in the last one-and-a-half years there have been numerous cases of blocking information. The total penalty is less than Rs. 1 lakh. And, we are getting the information as to how much actually realised. But, the recovery is not more than Rs. 20,000. The only thing is that threat remains. There is some threat of punishment. When there is a threat that there is a provision for punishment, it works as deterrent. If we do not implement the provision of the Act effectively, we can just write off this Act. Then, we will have one more Act and the entire exercise would be a futile exercise.

On fee, again, the problem, I think, is this. We found that it is very difficult to trust that the fee, even for application, would be reasonable. I would like to bring to the notice of the august Committee that the Freedom of Information Act has been made about two years ago and the rules specified thereunder shows that there is an exorbitant charge for the information to be provided. That is the reason why we are submitting our plea that please specify the cost so that the citizens can make use of it.

At the end, I would say that let us recognise the truth that we do not have a good structure for governance. We do not have a structure that is really responsive to citizens' rights and information. That is the reason why we plead with you that please don't think unnecessarily what would happen after one year or after five years. Look at the future of India. This one single legislation has the potential to meet the requirements of our citizens as far as providing information is concerned.

So, please do the needful of changing the entire governance structure in India. Thank you.

DR. P.C. ALEXANDER: Mr. Gandhi, you have started by saying that the Preamble is weak. Does is really matters?

SHRI SHAILESH GANDHI: Sir, the Preamble is the spirit of the legislation. If the spirit of the legislation is so weak, obviously, it is not of much use.

DR. P.C. ALEXANDER: Have you seen the wording of what was proposed by the National Advisory Council and the Maharashtra Right to Information Act?

SHRI SHAILESH GANDHI: Sir, twice the Lokayukta was not willing to give favourable judgment because he was going on debating on coma, full stop and all that. I pleaded by saying, 'look at the preamble' and all I can submit is that we have got a favourable judgment. It is not that we have got favourable judgment because of anything. But because we argued well on points, including preamble, we have got a favourable judgment.

DR. P.C. ALEXANDER: Will you say that this - Preamble - will give greater credibility to the whole legislation? (Followed by "1Y")

PK/1Y/3.30

SHRI SHAILESH GANDHI: I would say, 'yes', particularly because, in future, some of these cases will go to courts. At that time, Preamble will help the citizens.

CHAIRMAN: I would like to seek some more clarifications regarding the cases of corruption as also human rights. As regards the corruption, the CVC is already putting the matters on the website. Do you feel that that type of thing should come down to the level of States, districts and panchayats?

SHRI SHEKHAR SINGH: Sir, the CVC has very limited jurisdiction, but this Bill has much wider scope. The CVC looks at only Central Government and Public; Sectors. Here, we are bothered about the security aspect also. For example, let us take the North-East. I have spent five years there where the people got disappeared. I was teaching in a university. Now, 25 years down, I don't know what happened to them. We must have some mechanism by which we can ask some information, Let them answer. Today, under this Act, you cannot ask any information. I cannot ask Assam Rifles any question about human rights. So, the idea behind this is to empower the citizens; otherwise, the CVC has a lot of powers we, probably, need under RTI. At the same time, they have their own restrictions also.

CHAIRMAN: Already we are having writ jurisdiction. One of the hon. Members has also mentioned that PIL has been misused. It may be misused but it is one of the parts of the RTI. The people do not know how the environment is looked after by the Government or whether the Forest Act is properly implemented or not. To know these things, people go for PIL But the problem comes when the courts take up the role of executive. In that case, PIL becomes something diverted. From your presentation what we could find out is, you want that the people should have a right to know what is happening within the machinery of the Government, public sector enterprises and other relevant bodies where tax payers' money is spent for their welfare. Now e-governance is going down to the level of villages. If you put everything on the website, won't it be considered as a way of giving information to the people? Won't it be a single mode of finding out the truth, instead of asking each and every person from the village to the top level? If we ask each and every person from the village to the top level, we know that they will say, "we are feeling tired, or we are having some other urgent work;

therefore, we will make it after three days." They want to escape from that route. The same thing will not happen in e-governance. If all the decisions, datas or transactions are put on the website, won't it be easy? Can't we stress by this Act itself that every information should be put on the website? The information, whatever it is, should be available, should be accessible. There should not be any secret clause. Why don't we make this type of a thing at a stroke? Certain States are doing it like Karnataka is doing it, Delhi Government is doing it, Tamil Nadu is doing it. Why don't we make a particular clause in this Act itself? Make it mandatory that whatever decisions are made by any organisation should be put on the website. It will help in overcoming the cost problem. Then, the problem of penalty clause will also be over. Harassment of people at the lower level of bureaucracy will be over. Just think about it. If possible, you can make a comparison with other advanced countries where this kind of a legislation exists. We would like to have your opinion on this aspect. You just ponder over this.

As regards the human rights issue, we have found that at the State level, Chairman of the Committee has not been appointed, and Members also have not been appointed. And, even if they are appointed, their orders are not carried out by the Home Ministry. Same is the case at the all-India level. We keep on creating Commissions after Commissions, Commission on Women, Minorities Commission, OBC Commission etc. but nothing is acted upon. What is the point in creating so many commissions clashing with each other? Now, are we going to add one new Commission or to have vibrant institutions where if you touch it, you will get the information? It is only information that you are asking for. You are not asking for any relief. To get any relief, you have to collect datas, hear the other parties and come with a solution. But here it should be like this, just push the button and get the information. That is why Justice Hanumanthappa asked whether you are not thinking on the lines of having an institution where the Commissioner should have all the powers. Only courts can do it. At the Supreme Court level they can do it. The Commission which is created should be very vibrant. It should be just like electricity, that is, if you touch it, it will give you a shock. Please think over the point as to who should man it, I have put these questions to you. Kindly go through these. See you are intellectuals, You can unite together and think about it and suggest some ways away from it. You have rightly suggested and I had also said in the morning that it should be at the level of Chief Election Commission or the Election Commissioner. That is the correct suggestion. How can it be applied? The Election Commission attracted the attention of the people only after Shri T.N. Sheshan became the Commissioner. He made so many reforms, (Contd. by 1Z)

1Z2A/3.40/SKC-GSP

CHAIRMAN: It happened only then. Therefore, it is only when the person sits there, when that person implements certain laws, that the office becomes powerful. Therefore, kindly think about it.

While going through the Bill, one feels the need for some dynamism, some vibrancy. The soul of the entire Bill rests on Clause 12. If that clause were taken away, whatever other rights may be conferred would be meaningless. But the Commission has not been conferred the same powers by the clause as are conferred by clauses relating to other independent commissions. Therefore, I want both of you to find a way out and suggest measures. If you could send your suggestions and recommendations within a week's time it would be very useful for us. If you make a comparative study of other countries where they are working on it, that would be helpful, too. When you go through Clauses 12, 13 and 14, you would be disgusted to find that they are creating a nonsensical rather than a sensible institution.

SHRI SHEKHAR SINGH: Sir, we shall give the suggestions in writing later. Your first point was about *suo motu* disclosure. I totally agree with it. The same clause is there in the Bill; it needs to be strengthened. There are three additions that you have mentioned. One is, of course, that it saves the time of the Government. The Government does have this complaint that they have to spend so much time in processing requests because everything is up there on the net and people can access it. Secondly, that it takes away the temptation to fiddle with information because once it is out, you can keep getting back and fiddling with it. So, it should be organized in a better way. The third point, which is most important, is to see that it protects the people who ask for information. You would find that if a person tries to seek some information, he is asked to take back his request for information, and threatened to be killed if he fails to do so. Once the information is sought on the web, they won't know who is seeking the information and hence, there is no risk involved. I had personally requested the hon. Chief Minister of Delhi—I was in the State Council of the Right to Information at Delhi to put all the relevant records on the web so that we do not have to face this day-to-day conflict. I am totally with you that it should be put on the web. The only thing is that it has to be done over a period of time. In a country like India, access to the net is urban based, and it would be difficult till we can actually have the web accessible to everyone.

CHAIRMAN: You are also talking like a bureaucrat. We have to see that we make our best efforts to make it possible. Otherwise, we would remain backward. Many of the States have become competent: they have come out with innovative ideas. We are spending huge amounts of money. Our department, our Committee, is looking after the computerisation scheme. We want to make it available even at the block level, at the taluk level, to the courts and magistrates up to Supreme Court level.

Everything should be based on e-governance. We are spending huge amounts of money in every Budget; the Central Government is spending money even for a small court in a small village. We are funding it. We are trying to implement it. The pace may be slow but if you could make it a statutory provision, then somebody might go to the courts saying that such and such information is not available on the web. Then the courts might take a view and give instructions. My point is, can you suggest some way of making the data available on the web that would solve the regular problems? For instance, the problems like bureaucrats complaining that people are bothering them, or asking people not to ask certain questions because their regular work is being disturbed, and so on. Such problems would be solved. They would not be bothered and we would also be equipped with the information. Why don't you suggest some such thing?

SHRI SHEKHAR SINGH: Sir, the Right to Information has one backward linkage and one forward linkage. The backward linkage is record management, that is, the office management of records. Unless you manage your records well, you cannot service right to information. In today's world, it has to be done in a computerised manner. The forward linkage is the prosecution agencies who get the information and who will act.

If courts were the sole prosecution agencies, then there would be a huge backlog of cases. But we totally agree with you and we shall certainly look into how the mechanism could be strengthened.

As far as the commissions go, as you have mentioned, there are so many commissions which are not functioning properly. But there is a slight difference here: this is going to be a people-fuelled act. Many commissions have their own agencies and they have their own working. The Information Commission is going to be a responsive body, which means that if the citizens want to take it up, if the people of India take it up, it would really work in their favour.

In our country, nine States have the Act. Look at the experience in Rajasthan, Delhi and Maharashtra. People are really using the Right to information Act. It has become something that is empowering people. I would say that they don't bother whether they get the information or not. The fact that they have the right to information makes them feel empowered. That is why I feel that this Commission would help because it is going to be pushed by the people to act, rather than by their own agendas. Of course, we will have some problems such as how could a person get on to this Commission. All of you are hon. Members of the Parliament and you could decide as to who could be the best possible person.

Then, you were talking about this Commission functioning in a particular way. I would just say that when governance starts becoming a problem, the last resort is to go back to the people. So, when commissions don't work, when CVCs don't work, what we are trying to do is to get the common person involved in governance more directly, who could say, 'look, this is my relief, I want it; this is my account, I want it.' That will empower and energise our country. In other countries, as also in India, there has been a principle of regulation by disclosure. That is to say, if you disclose information, that disclosure itself acts as a regulatory process. People involved in some lapse become embarrassed. This is going on. In Europe and the US, they are using this in the case of commercial airlines. There was a law in some countries saying that every airline has to show on record the flying time and punctuality of airlines. So, people would know about the punctuality or otherwise of airlines. Hence, nothing more was needed to be done to improve their functioning! I feel that if a lot of information is just put up on the web, it will embarrass the people involved and that itself will act as a regulator. Nobody will have to do anything. Thank you very much for this question.

CHAIRMAN: You have to give your suggestions to us. We cannot go on our own. We have got a certain role to play and if you could give your suggestions and inputs that could be incorporated in the report, that would be helpful.

SHRI SHEKHAR SINGH: Yes, Sir. We understand that, Sir.

SHRI SHAILESH GANDHI: Sir, I have a point to make. You have stressed on making *suo motu* disclosures on the web. The fact is, if I talk of Bombay, which is very well-governed, the authorities there don't know how much land they have given to whom. They have no obvious record immediately available, such as how much land is on lease and for how long, etc. In some cases, the lease would have expired for decades. What I am submitting is that in this scenario, *suo motu* disclosure is some way away.

CHAIRMAN: When you come up with the facts, there will not be any problem. I am saying the same thing that if you put the information on the website, everything will be accessible to the people. A record needs to be created and put on the website. Suppose it is mandatory under an Act to display information on the website, automatically the department concerned will have to search for the records and put it on the website. If they do not do so, there should be a punishment under the relevant provisions to be prepared under the Act. The Commissioner can proceed against the department and take action against the person responsible for this. The next day, various organizations or activists, or NGOs or journalists would publish the same.

So many commissions have come and gone. So, let us have this concrete structure, let us have a perfect structure where all information is made available on the web by every department. That will be good for us as also for them. When we have come out with so many things, why not apply this too? We are spending huge amounts of the tax-payers' money on them.

Thank you very much. We are expecting your reply within a week's time. Kindly join us for a cup of tea.

(The witnesses then withdrew and Committee adjourned for tea.)

(Contd. by 2B)

YSR/4.00/2B/PPG/14.02.2005

(The Committee re-assembled after tea-break)

List of Witnesses:

1. Mrs. Maja Daruwala, Director, Commonwealth Human Rights Initiative (CHRI), Delhi.
2. Ms. Charmaine Rodrigues.
3. Mr. Venkatesh Nayak.
4. Mr. Jayaprakash, Convenor, Lok Satta

CHAIRMAN: I welcome you all to this meeting of the Committee. We are happy to see you here. I hope you will finish your presentation in about 15 minutes or so.

MRS. MAJA DARUWALA: It is up to you, Sir. (Contd. by 2c)

2C/4.10/KS

SHRIMATI MAJA DARUWALA (CONTD.): We can quickly make some points and then respond to your questions.

CHAIRMAN: That will be better. You can highlight certain points. The hon. Members will then put questions. We will take up both the groups together. I request you, Mrs. Maja Daruwala, to start. After that, Mr. Jayaprakash, Convenor of Lok Satta, will make his presentation. We know that both of your groups are well-informed. So, we need a lot of inputs from you. Before you start, let me say that the deliberations of the Committee are confidential and nothing should be divulged outside before we present our Report to Parliament.

After your presentations, you can either respond to questions put by hon. Members immediately, or otherwise, you can send your written responses within a week's time. You can proceed now, Mrs. Daruwala.

SHRIMATI MAJA DARUWALA: We have done a great deal of work and carried out a detailed analysis of the Right to Information Bill, 2004 which is in front of you.

When I came here in the afternoon, you had mentioned that you wanted some basis for the recommendations that we are making in terms of a comparative law. We have done that in like-minded jurisdictions like Mexico or South Africa and so on. We have particularly paid attention to them because they are developing country jurisdictions. So, first of all, what I would like to address myself to is the legislative competence which I know that you are very concerned about, then the Information Commissioners, increasing of penalties, exemptions and then about training and dissemination if I have some time.

Sir, I am at a disadvantage because I do not know what went on in the morning in the Committee. So, I apologise if there is any repetition.

Now, in terms of legislative competence, there remains a lack of clarity in the Government about the constitutional provisions under which this Bill is coming into being. The earlier law was applicable to the whole of the country and, presumably, it was enacted under the exclusive Residuary Powers under Entry 97, coupled with article 248. But now, Clause 2, pertaining to Definitions, seems to suggest that it does not permit this, but allows the 2004 Bill to apply only to Central matters. Nevertheless, I believe that the 2004 Bill should apply to all the people of the country. In its present form, it leaves too many people out. We would argue that the 2004 Bill, if it is brought under Entry 12 of the Concurrent List, it would permit the State laws to stand, along with the Central law. Where there is no law, where there are States, which have not yet enacted any law, the Central law would apply until such time as the State chooses to enact its own law. Otherwise, in its present form, it defeats its very purpose by keeping too many people out of the Act because there are now only nine Acts in place. This way of doing things also removes the possibility of any conflict, because we have been concerned about the fact that if we apply for information under one Act, how it will be sorted out to remove this possibility of the conflict, though it will create a parallel system for enforcement and adjudication. So, I see no problem in the functioning of two laws provided that the person who is requesting is not put to the test of answering 'which law' and 'how', and provided it is simplified for him to access whatever information he wants to access. The issue is that it should be easy for that information to be given to him. Now, would you like to put your questions on this aspect now, or, shall I continue?

CHAIRMAN: You mentioned Entry 12 of the Concurrent List. As I understand it, you want to say that we can enact a law under it.

SHRI VENKATESH NAYAK: Sir, Entry 12 of the Concurrent List is: *Evidence and oaths; recognition of laws, public acts and records, and judicial proceedings,* meaning thereby that the Parliament at the Central level and the State Legislatures at the State level can legislate on this subject. So, since it is the Fundamental Right, the right to information, there should be no conflict of interest. It has also been recognised by the Supreme Court that unless there is a conflict, both the laws can apply.

SHRIMATI MAJA DARUWALA: I want to know on which of the constitutional provisions they are enacting this law under. Usually, the purpose of the Act, which is written on the first page, does have that clarification.

CHAIRMAN: Residuary Powers.

SHRIMATI MAJA DARUWALA: Yes, and once the Centre has enacted this law, then the State laws would go, and that is not necessary to have. If it is done under the Concurrent List, then both the Centre and the State have the jurisdiction to enact laws and there are provisions for repugnancy and conflict, which take care of the matter. At the same time, the citizen is also in no way deprived.

CHAIRMAN: Now, article 248 talks about the residuary powers. Then you mention about Entry 12 of the Concurrent List. As I understand it, you want to say that it can be done both ways.

MS. CHARMAINE RODRIGUES: Sir, as we understand the term 'residuary', where in the Constitution the power is being given to no one, it is residuary power because that means that everything not mentioned in the three Lists becomes part of the residuary power. But, effectively, it means that the States have no power. What I am saying is that if you really talk about the residuary powers, then the States have no legislative competence. It was because of that reason we had tried and we found out from the Ministry. (Contd. by 2D)

TDB/2D/4.20

MS. CHARMAINE RODRIGUES (CONTD.): That is why we thought, possibly, it is entry 12 in List III.

SHRIMATI MAJA DARUWALA: Doing that way, reconcile the fact that there have been Acts which are already there in the States, they get Presidential assent, it does not prevent the Centre from passing laws that would go all across. That is how we made adjustments.

The next thing I would like to point out is about the Information Commissioners. We would like to say that we really commend the Government having put this idea of Information Commissioners. We have been fighting very hard for it. The Information Commissioner should be as strong as he can be. The challenge here is that it should not go the way other Commissions have gone. We have seen these weaknesses in the working of other Commissions that have been set up, most notably in the State Human Rights Commissions. They fall into certain pattern of weakness which we would not like this Commission to fall into. How to safeguard it? It must be autonomous and independent. We wanted to give better criteria for appointment and wanted the Act to state quite clearly that it would have operational independence and budgetary independence so that the budget should be out of the Consolidated Fund of India. I would like to say that let them have its own cadre; it should make its own rules and own procedures and it should report directly to Parliament. It should not be like the State Human Rights Commissions and National Human Rights Commission which give their reports to the Central Ministry.

CHAIRMAN: Normally, all the Commissions place their reports in Parliament.

SHRI VENKATESH NAYAK: The report of this Commission is routed through the Government. It is not directly tabled in the Parliament.

SHRIMATI MAJA DARUWALA: It should have its own very full and frank report, department by department and those reports be placed before Parliament. It should also have the power of contempt, if it is disobeyed. It should also have, of course, the power of right to impose penalties.

Then, the other thing that we would like to point out is this. There is some sort of dichotomy in the powers of the Information Commissioner and the Deputy Commissioners. As per clause 12(8), the Deputy Commissioner is subject to the direction of the Government. We think that the Deputy Commissioner should have exactly the same powers, delegated or even his own, as the Information Commissioner. He should be directed only by the Commissioner, and he should not be directed by the Central Government because, then, even if you have extremely independent commissioner, you may have a Deputy Commissioner who is subjected to another set of governors who would break the chain command, which would create a weaker link over there.

Again, as far as setting it up in different places is concerned, previous permission of the Central Government is needed. Once you set up an autonomous and independent Commission, then, it should not go back to the Central Government within the next ten months to bargain or parley as to where it should be set up. By law, it should already have the roaming jurisdiction as to where it is going to go, how it is going to set up, subject to budgetary constraints. Then, we will be able to judge their performance as to how they are going to use the allocated budget. Very often, we see that the Commissions that we have in the States do not use the budgetary allocations fully, it remain under-utilised and sent back.

Then, the other power which the Commissioner has been given is in clause 15(2). It says, "Where the Commission is satisfied that there are reasonable grounds to inquire into the matter, it may initiate an inquiry in respect thereof". This should really read like this. "Where the Commission is satisfied that there are reasonable grounds to inquire into not 'the matter', but 'any matter'. This gives it a power to act on its own motion without waiting for a complaint. Should it see, for instance, that a department is not singularly uncooperative, it may be a very powerful department or it may be a very obscure department, which is very necessary for rooting-out corruption, so, it should not have to wait for a complaint or direction from somebody else. On the other hand, it should not be subjected to any obstacle being put in its way. It should be mentioned clearly that the Information Commissioner should be so powerful that as far as giving of information is concerned; he can look into any matter. It may not be a matter of complaint. It may be that systems of records keeping have not been put into place, budget sums allocated for e-governance have not been utilised, in which case he should be in a position to do micro-studies or specific studies and put them before Parliament and also inquire and ask the people appear before him.

MS. CHARMAINE RODRIGUES: I would like to inform the Committee that initially this provision was modelled on the Canadian pattern. This power of the Information Commissioner enables him to start his own motion of investigation. They gave the Ombudsman this power because they found that a lot of departments were very slow in processing applications and they wanted to empower the Ombudsman with that power. With that power, he can adjudicate by a single complaint. Recently, this power was given specifically to him to allow his own investigation and he has recently indicated that he will start investigation into Government delays in processing requests.

SHRI VENKATESH NAYAK: If any organisation has to function in an autonomous manner, then, the rule-making power should be vested in that organisation itself. It should not be vested with the Central Government. At present, that important rule-making power is vested with the Central Government. That should be taken away and given to the independent Information Commission itself.

SHRIMATI MAJA DARUWALA: Now, I would like to come to penalty. I feel that this is one of the weakest parts of the Bill. At the same time, it is like the heart of the Bill. We have seen, there is no need to reiterate it, the levels of corruption; we have seen the levels of lack of transparency as well as culture of secrecy that lies within the Government. The whole idea of the Bill is to break that— we cannot break that. We cannot think incrementally while thousands of rupees of developmental money etc., go down the drain, including people's lives go down the drain. This Bill is essentially for the poor to get them into the power game, to get accountability right at the district level. (Contd. by 2e)

kgg/2e/4.30/PPG/14.2.05

SMT. MAJA DARUWALA (contd.): If there is no penalty against getting a no reply or getting half a reply or a wrong reply, then what? If we stop there, then it is as good as having no right. If there is no remedy, then it is no right at all. I feel very strongly about it. You have seen how successful Karnataka, Maharashtra and Delhi are. The reason why this Act is working like a magic and saving the Government of revenue enormously, gaining goodwill for Government, is because we have been able to point to the punishments that are becoming pointers to set the house in order, to give the right information. The seeker of information has already been harassed, waiting for justice for 15 years, 20 years. If this 'harassment' doesn't demoralise the entire bureaucratic cadre, nobody would instil a feeling of responsibility. It doesn't mean that the cadre has lost its enthusiasm; it is only a punishment for a wrong doing. So, I feel, for philosophical reasons, there should be a penalty clause.

The political will of this Government or any Government to really make this Bill into an Act would transform the Governance in this country. It depends on the ability to impose penalties. So, at the present time, I think, the penalty available are failing to influence people to do the right action. What this persistent refusal means is ambiguous. Is it by one person to give information to another person or to many people?

Or, is it persistent refusal of the department to give information constantly? Supposing there is a persistent refusal by an individual or a department, what will happen? Who will judge where is this persistent refusal? Who will be the judge of that? The information that we are asking is being persistently refused. Then how will the other person know there is persistent refusal and then say "I want to charge you"? Suppose, somebody has got half an information. Who will be the holder of that punishment remedy? I think, this is the problem that we are faced. The officer must be clear about different types of penalties for different types of refusal and bad behaviour.

There are three types of penalties. We can ask for very strong penalties for wilful refusal, for flouting the law, for giving wrong information deliberately; such acts are being considered as criminal acts to obfuscate information.

Then there is unreasonable delay that can be of the kind that can attract punishment. But an officer is doing it deliberately and then there are persistent departmental failures. I think, we need to sanction both, the Head of the Department and the person/officer who is failing to give the information.

Sir, on wilful refusal I just would like to point out one thing. Somebody sought information and went to Information Commissioner after 15 years or 25 years. Then he gets exhausted and angry with the bureaucracy, and he approaches the appropriate authority. Then they had to recommend a criminal sanction. Normally, it would have been a departmental enquiry. The seeker had asked for punishment because of a long wait.

MS. CHARMAINE RODRIGUES: If you look at our recommendation, the specific recommendations and the specific wording, these are largely based on a comparative jurisdiction; the most common type of penalty is a penalty for wilful default. It is largely uncontroversial. You can strike there if one deliberately destroys the information. That is clearly a criminal Act, which should be punished. The second penalty, which is unique to India, is based on the Maharashtra model, wherein the Commissioner would say, "We are fully independent and we impose personal penalties on the bureaucrat." They are serious about implementing this Act, doing it right. Then the third set of provision is based on initial suggestion in this Act, for persistent failure. My Director has said about it all. The problem is, one can't know where the department is failing. But once pointed out, then against the individual(s), there should be sanctions. We recommend that even the Head of the Department should be sent a strong message so that officers are put on notice and they do their jobs properly. The Annual Report of the Information Commissioner should be looked into seriously. The Department or the Ministry should take action on that basis. We thought this would be ideal to include the right type of penalties.

SMT. MAJA DARUWALA: It should also be seen how many departments are complying or compliant. Supposing there is a failure to take an initiative. What is the level of reports and preparedness; and how much information you are giving should be part of the annual appraisal of the Head of the Department. Let that be considered for Budgetary allocation also, when they come before the Parliament. This would really scrutinise the functioning of the officers/department as far as right to information is concerned. The department's performance—-how much information was sought and how much have they given in the last year—should be looked into. If there has been a negative statement given by the Information Commissioner, that should reflect in the Budgetary allocation also, not only in the confidential reports. It should be the measure of performance.

Sir, there is the other thorny question, exemptions. We have given details of it in our document. We would be happy to provide supplementary document if you need one. The first thing I would like to point out is, let it be in the concurrent list. But in any way, it is a fundamental right. There is no doubt about that. It is not making anybody special favours but only enabling the fundamental right. This should be stated in the preamble clearly. Then, the logic would demand that the exemptions can't go beyond exemptions of 92. (Contd. by 2f)

KLS/2F-4.40/PPG/14.2.2005

SHRIMATI MAJA DARUWALA (CONTD): Otherwise, we would not be obeying our own Constitution. I think the problem of Cabinet documents is a problem of definition. The word 'Cabinet papers' is too broad. When it is a memo it will turn into a cabinet paper. When it is actually a memo between two people or two departments and when it has cleared the level of confidentiality, that brings it under this blanket exemption. The other thing that I would like to suggest is that, do not have blanket exemptions because blanket exemptions create all sorts of reasons. You have already looked into that. We have exemptions for national security and we have exemptions for foreign affairs, international relations, and all such sensitive matters. So, if a document falls within that sensitivity, take the higher level of satisfaction and make sure that thing is sensitive before you take refusal of disclosure. When we go to section that provides, 'after the decision is made' and then the wording of the proviso of section 8, 'materials on the basis of which'—I will read out it the whole thing. It says, provided that the decisions of the Council of Ministers, the reasons thereof and the materials on the basis of which the decisions were taken should be made public after decision has been taken and the matter is complete or over. Now, in that I want to point out a couple of things, that 'after' does not mean in any time. There should be a time limit. Under the Swedish practice within half-an-hour, after a cabinet decision has been taken, everything is out in the public. It is there. The second thing is that the material on the basis of which decisions are taken is not the same as saying that Cabinet papers will be provided or will be opened. You can make two pages synopsis. That is very deep and very complex and put it to the public as being the material on the basis of which decisions are taken. That makes nonsense about how much revealing at a later time. The time limit and the kinds of paper to put before public all these things have to be looked at. Suppose, there is nothing sensitive or dreadful about those papers why do not you make them proactive? What is the problem? If it is a matter of development or it is a matter of social justice, then it can be done.

MS. CHARMAINE RODRIGUES: Initially, there may be some controversy on this particular exemption. This exemption should be removed. We will review this exemption. They drafted it to protect India from very genuine harm and while at the same time balancing the public interest. Business of the Cabinet is the most important business of the country. When people elect their representatives, they want to know how decisions were taken. They want to know what advice was given. But the key issue to remember is that we have to see carefully and protect the interests. We recognise that there are many cabinet papers pertaining to national security, international relations, managing economy, law and order enforcement, etc. But the definition of paper is very broad. It includes records and deliberations of the Council of Ministers, Secretaries, and other officers. Even if two officers are sitting and talking, actually, they may cover their deliberations under this clause.

SHRIMATI MAJA DARUWALA: We want that this definition should be tightened. On premature decisions, it can cause harm. There can be information, which may harm India. For example, India's economic policy, it should be protected. But there is a lot of information on decision-making. My last point is about security agencies. Now security agencies are given the blanket category sort of information disclosure. Now what should be protected in security agencies would already come under Article 8(1) (a) and 8(2). It would come under national security. So why are our security agencies getting this blanket when they are already covered under national security? In other countries there is no law that gives blanket protection to security agencies. This is not a common practice. But as you all know, not all information of security agencies is sensitive information. For instance, contracts, purchasing, and all sorts of things. We have long list. Defence forces are spending 14 per cent so they should not be outside the public purview. I do not think by covering by blanket clause, you should permit that. And adding agencies, that is another concern. By adding agencies you are diminishing the ability of this human right to have its effect. You add agencies without any criteria, without any rationale. I think the power to add agencies should be circumscribed. (Contd. by 2G)

NBR/2G/4.50.

SMT. MAJA DARUWALA (CONTD.): There should be some rationale and there should be some kind of teeth— whether it is recommended or by a larger body agreed to it. Otherwise, it would just be used as a cover up for anything and there are a lot of segments connected to Defence procurement, readiness, preparedness that we all know about. In addition, there is the whole issue of severability. When someone asks for information, first they have to go through the sensitivity. It is only after that they can be given the information on payment of a prescribed document cost. You can severe the document or you can severe the national security part from the phrase and make available that. So, I think, this is really very important that it should not just let go off because these security agencies have always a holy cow.

SHRI VENKATESH NAYAK: Sir, it is already an established practice. There is a decision of the court of the European Union. A case has come up before the European Union from Finland. The court said that even with regard to sensitive documents, the secret portions cannot be supplied but the other portion can be severed from the document and may be supplied to the party. So, it is a progressive principle and we have to look at that professionally.

SMT. MAJA DARUWALA: There are other minor points and I do not want to take much time of the august Committee. We will supply a brief submission on this to the Committee.

DR. P.C. ALEXANDER: The point is, in your presentation — we have also seen the Memorandum you have submitted to the Committee in writing—you have raised various fundamental issues and not for formal changes here and there. You have raised various fundamental issues on certain matters like what constitute a Cabinet paper and all that. Some of us have handled such type of papers for long years.. I am giving you a simple example. At least, you have made seven or eight major points which need a little time for us to go through carefully and I was suggesting to the hon. Chairman and if he agrees we would like to have one more session with you.

SMT. MAJA DARUWALA: It is up to the hon. Chairman to decide.

CHAIRMAN: Ms. Daruwala, you just wait for some time. Now, we will hear Dr. Jaiprakash and then we will tell you what is the decision of the Committee. We have to have a careful study of the notes that you have submitted.

DR. JAYAPRAKASH NARAYAN: Sir, I will try to be very brief.

First of all, I thank you very much for giving me an opportunity to tender evidence before this Committee on Right to Information Bill, 2004. I will make one broad general point. Then, I will raise one substantive issue and four or five relatively minor, and then open for questions.

I believe that it is a genuine attempt on the part of the Government of India to empower the people. The intention is positive. It is welcome. All the political parties, the system and the Indian State have to be complimented for giving us a reasonably good legislation by giving genuine effect to the Fundamental Right through this Freedom of Information Bill. There is always different perception. Mr. Chairman, you are an experienced Parliamentarian. You have here a former Civil Servant of enormous experience. You have a former Speaker of Kerala. You also have a former Judge of High Court. All of you have performed various rolls. Since you are playing a different roll here, your perception is slightly different and if you are an ordinary citizen, then your perception will again be different.

Sir, this Bill did make a genuine and serious attempt to bring about a fair reconciliation to the citizens' right to information to give effect to the fundamental right to information and the States' duty to protect the citizens, the security of the State and the exigencies of the governance. Therefore, on the whole—well, there are some things have to be proved— exemptions are reasonably drafted in this law. There are some significant and positive things like creation of independent mechanism. For the first time, there is a provision for the Information Commissioner. The Information Commissioner would be appointed, as you have noticed, by a collegium consisting of the Prime Minister, the Leader of the Opposition, Chief Justice of the Supreme Court at the national level. To my mind, this is the first such law provided for such high-powered committee to appoint an independent authority. Not even the Election Commission of India, not even the CVC has such a provision.

Then, I come to the provision relating to Appeal. It is also fair. The first appeal would be to the departmental authority. The second will go to the independent Commissioner. There are reporting requirements. There are pro-active requirements. And, the most important of all is the overriding provision available or should be available. Parliament or legislature cannot deny to the citizen the right to information. But, at the same time, there are some very serious caveats.

Then, Sir, already the issue of jurisdiction has been discussed. This bill sought to limit the jurisdiction or applicability of the right to information to only the Union Subject and the Union Government's jurisdiction. That is, in my judgment, extremely unconstitutional approach. I have heard the discussion about the Entry 97 of List I and Entry 12 and the Concurrent List. To me the matter is simple and straightforward. Time and again, there have been judicial pronouncements and there has been a settled law that the right to information is an extension of the Freedom of Expression. Therefore, it is a Fundamental Right guaranteed under the Constitution. In a number of judicial pronouncements this has been specifically stated. For example in the case of the State of U.P. Vs. Raj Narain in 1975 and in S.P. Gupta Vs. Union of India in 1981 this has been clearly stated. The latest of which is about the disclosure provision. The Supreme Court judgment in the PUCL Case, on 30th March, 2003, held that the citizens' right to information is a Fundamental right. The court has also, time and again, held that right to know is clearly derived from the freedom of speech which seems to be implicit under the right Free of Speech and Expression guaranteed under Article 19(l)(a).

CHAIRMAN: If you don't mind, Dr. Jayaprakash, are you here for one to two days? Or, are you coming from Hyderabad?

DR. JAYAPRAKASH NARAYAN: Sir, I am coming from Hyderabad.

(Followed by "2H")

PK/2H/5.00

CHAIRMAN: If you don't mind, we would like to accommodate Shri Shanti Bhushan. First, we will hear him, after that we will hear you.

DR. JAYAPRAKASH NARAYAN: Sir, I have great respect for a man who inspired us when we were young.

CHAIRMAN: Mr. Shanti Bhushan, good afternoon. We are very happy that we are hearing an eminent jurist and the former Union Minister of law. Sir, we would like to go straightaway to the point because you have to clarify many questions that have arisen during our discussions with different witnesses. Firstly, whether Parliament has got the right to enact a law with regard to right to information binding the States, local self-governments, the bodies which were created through the State Government and other aided institutions like NGOs, etc. Already, you have given your legal opinion, that is, item 97, Part I, will give force to the Parliament as a residual power. They can enact a law but there are differences of opinion. Just now, we have got different opinion from your friends who are sitting nearby. Smt. Maja has given the opinion that we can apply the provisions in the List-III, Concurrent List. According to them that can also be applied. But when we discussed this matter very deeply with other witnesses, we found that they were having a feeling that when this kind of a law exists in certain States, numbering around nine, it may displace that particular law, even though there is a provision that when there is a Central law, that will prevail upon the State law. As you know, Maharashtra law has more powers than this present Bill. Why should we lose the opportunity of having that law? Why are you interfering in that aspect? Why don't you confine yourself with the Union itself? This is one of the problems which has arisen before us. The general opinion of the Committee is that we can have a law which will enforce or implement the fundamental rights which have been enshrined in the Constitution. That is the preamble of this Bill also. The last line of the Statement of Objects and Reasons state, "The proposed legislation will provide an effective framework for effectuating the right of information recognised under article 19 of the Constitution of India." When such is the case, what prohibits us from enacting a law binding on the State Governments. Out of about 29 States and Union Territories, only nine States have come forward. Only one or two States have implemented it, but others have not. There should be an Act which should say that you have to implement it. This is a fundamental right. Since the Parliament could not do it, the executives could not do it, the judiciary could not do it, we want to create an institution by which we want to enforce this particular fundamental right. As you know very well, the Supreme Court has expanded the interpretation saying that this right to information is a freedom of speech. Therefore, at this juncture, we need your eloquence which should satisfy us, so that we could suggest that Parliament has every right to enact this law which would cover all the States, local bodies, which are now a part of the two-three tier system in the Constitution of India and also the bodies which have been created by funds provided by the State Governments. They all are answerable to the citizens. If you have some additional points to make, you can make them. Due to scarcity of time, we are already holding two other teams up and some Members have got preoccupations also. Keeping this in mind, we hope that you will make your presentation within a short time. Now, I request Mr. Shanti Bhushan to make his submissions.

SHRI SHANTI BHUSHAN: May I preface my submission by mentioning in what context and perception the right to information ought to be examined. I think we should remember that we have established ourselves into a democratic Republic. I would like to emphasise 'Republic' because it is my experience that even though we have established ourselves into a Republic, the full consequences of that Act have not sunk in minds, either in the minds of the citizens or perhaps even in the minds of those who govern us. Republic means that the sovereignty in this country resides in the people collectively. Every other organ is discharging functions on behalf of the people. So, people are the masters and every functionary, howsoever high or low it may be, is acting on their behalf. By the Constitution and, by laws, different functionaries have been established which have been delegated by the people some powers to discharge function on their behalf and for their own benefit. This is a crucial question. Therefore, sometimes, it is said, particularly, by bureaucrats that well, we should not be compelled to disclose this information to the people. But, if what I am submitting is correct, namely, that people are the real masters of the country collectively and every functionary is their agent, immediately, the question arises, can the agent have any power to withhold any information from a person who has been constituted master by constituting this country into a democratic Republic except divulging some information which may be prejudicial to the interest of the people themselves? Then, of course, it will be an implication that it will not be in the interests of the people that some information may be brought into the public domain. So, it is from this context that the question has to be examined, namely, first of all, the people must have the right to receive every information as to how its appointed delegates are functioning. Howsoever high they may be, they are accountable to the people. It is for this reason that Justice Mathew's judgement or Justice Bhagwati put the right to information as part of their fundamental right, namely, freedom to expression. They have put it as a part of it. It is a fundamental right. On every fundamental right, only reasonable restrictions can be put, which reasonable instructions can only be in the public interest. (Contd. by 2J)

2J/5.10/SKC

SHRI SHANTI BHUSHAN (CONTD.): It is from this perspective that I would like the provisions of any Right to Information Bill to be examined.

Then, coming to the important question of Constitutionality, whether the Parliament has the right to enact a comprehensive legislation on the right to information, which will not only apply to the Central Government, but will also apply to all the State Governments, etc., the answer is again an emphatic 'yes'. Because, in our quasi-judicial Constitution, the Parliament has been given the right to legislate on every topic, particularly, on account of the residuary entry, unless the topic clearly falls in any of the items in the State List, because, so far as the Central List is concerned, of course, only Parliament has the power. As for the Concurrent List, Parliament has the overriding power. It is only the subjects that are entirely covered by some entry in the State List that are excluded from the jurisdiction and power of the Parliament.

Now, I don't find any item pertaining to the right to information in any of the entries of the three Lists. And none of the entries comes under the State List. A question may be raised: how is it that the States have enacted their Right to Information Acts? The position would be that when they have the right to legislate on a particular topic contained in the State List, they have all 'incidental' powers relating to that law. So, on all subjects on which they have the power to enact the law, they can also enact a provision that any information contained in any Government record, in fact, those subjects, will be made public and the right to information will be governed by them.

Coming to the next question, namely, if the Parliament enacts a law, would not some of the State Legislatures or State Governments get a feeling that there is some kind of interference in the autonomy of the State and why should their law be interfered with, I think there is a very good answer to it. If a provision is introduced in the Parliamentary enactment relating to the Right to Information that the provisions of this Act will be in addition to, and not in derogation of, any laws enacted on the Right to Information by any State Legislature, then the objection will disappear. Because, it may be that some State Legislature laws may be more liberal than the Parliamentary law. Then, in that case, the citizens will have the discretion either to ask for information under the State law, or to ask for information under the parliamentary law.

Under Article 254, if there is repugnancy between the parliamentary enactment and the State enactment, then, of course, a parliamentary enactment will prevail. But if the parliamentary enactment itself said that the provisions of the Act will be in addition to and not in derogation of any provision contained in any State enactment, then the position would be to the extent that the parliamentary enactment is more liberal in regard to the Right to Information. Of course, they will prevail and they will mind all the States, even those States which might have enacted their own Right to Information Act. But if the provisions of the parliamentary enactment were less liberal than the enactment enacted in a particular State, then it would be open; those provisions would not be repugnant to the parliamentary enactment and, therefore, the rights created by those Acts would prevail. So, it is my strong view that the Parliament should enact the Right to Information because many States, many other bodies of the States, may not be governed by any legislation relating to the Right to Information, particularly when the Supreme Court has declared the Right to Information to be a fundamental right.

Secondly, the very concept of a Republic means that people want the truth. They should know what their agents, the functionaries appointed on their behalf, with their authority, are doing. They are entitled to know, except in that rare case, where bringing some information into the public domain may be harmful to the general public interest or harmful to the interests of the nation itself. So, barring that, it is my submission that the right to information should be as comprehensive as possible. It should be made applicable to States also and to all functionaries which are acting, performing, exercising, any function under the Constitution on behalf of the people. That is my second submission.

I have gone through this Bill which is being considered and I have particularly three submissions to make in regard to that. One is that I have already said that it should be made applicable to the States also, but with the rider that the provisions in this Act will be in addition to—this is a technique which has been adopted many times about the provisions of a particular Act—in addition to and not in abrogation of any provision contained in the State enactment. The effect would be that to the extent that this Act would be more liberal for the citizen, he would be able to take advantage of that. But in a rare case in which a State enactment is more liberal, it will be open to the citizen in those States to take advantage of the State enactment.

One more point which I wish to make is, if I may turn to this provision contained in Section 8(1)(i), that there is an exemption from disclosures as regards Cabinet papers, including records of deliberations of the Council of Ministers, Secretaries and other officers, and the proviso, says, "Provided that the decisions of the Council of Ministers, the reasons thereof, and the material on the basis of which the decisions were taken, shall be made public after the decision has been taken, and the matter is complete, or over."

I can quite appreciate this provision. So long as a matter is under consideration, prematurely, what is under consideration need not be disclosed, because various opinions are being expressed. People might like to misuse the information at that stage. So, that information must be made available after a final decision has been taken. But the proviso does not cover everything which is contained in the proposal. My fear is that the notings of the various Secretaries, Joint Secretaries and Deputy Secretaries on the file may not be made public. What I am trying to submit is that once a final decision has been taken on a matter, there is no reason as to why the notings made on the file by the various members of the bureaucracy, namely, the Deputy Secretary, the Joint Secretary and Secretary, should remain confidential. Because, one of the reasons which the Supreme Court gave was that many a time, because things are done in secrecy, the advice will be shared by the Joint Secretary and Secretary in secrecy which will never see the light of the day. Corruption only prospers on this account. A person, an officer, who deliberately gives a wrong advice would not have the courage to give wrong advice if he knows that at some stage later on, what advice he gave is also going to come in the public domain. Sometimes it is said that the bureaucrats will not be able to make notings with honesty. I cannot imagine the ridiculousness of this kind of an argument. If a bureaucrat is honestly saying what he wants to say on the file, why should he be afraid? if he is dishonest, then, of course, he would like to keep his advice secret. Because, if he knows that the advice that he gave has come out in the open, he would be afraid to put his signatures on that. But, many a time, on certain issues, there are two or three possible ways of looking at them; different conclusions may be arrived at. The decision of one person may be agreed to because that would have been the proper thing to do in the circumstances. Another time, he may take a different view.

(Contd. by 2K)

GSP/2K/5.20

SHRI SHANTI BHUSHAN (CONTD.): Another person may take a different view. But neither of them will be afraid because both would be of honest view. Honest difference of opinion is always possible. But even if the honest difference of opinion comes in the public domain, there is no harm so long as they are honest expressions of their opinion. The rationale behind giving the right to information is to prevent any bureaucrat from misusing his powers deliberately. So long as he puts down what he honestly thinks, there would be no risk to him because he would restrict to his views.

But, if he wants to say something wrong, and, then wants to hide it, then the public interest is bound to suffer and corruption can also flourish. Justice Mathew and Justice Bhagwati also held the view that if things are done openly, then there are very little chances of corruption.

If you think over as to who actually has appointed the Secretary of a department, on whose authority the Secretary is functioning; it is the will of the people that elects the Government, that authorises the Government to appoint a Secretary, and, therefore, ultimately, it is the people of India who authorise the Secretary to perform on their behalf. Therefore, if he is acting on their behalf, then they are the principals, and, he is merely a paid agent. This being so, what kind of morality permits him to keep things secret from his own masters except in cases where the interest of the people themselves suffers in disclosing the notings made on the file. Therefore, my submission for the Clause 8(1) is that while the first clause may continue, but the proviso should be expanded to include also the records of deliberations of the Council of Ministers, Secretaries etc. because they would be making the notings on the file, and, ultimately, the Minister would be taking a decision. Therefore, after the decision has been taken, and, not prematurely, what was the advice of the Secretary, what decision the Minister took, all these things must be allowed to come in the public domain, and, people must know those things. They are entitled to know as to why has this decision been taken, what was the recommendation of the Secretary or the Joint Secretary, or, what was the decision taken by the Minister on that matter because all these public functionaries, right from the Minister to the lowest functionary, are actually accounted to the will of the people.

As far as the Section 17 regarding penalty is concerned, I would submit that, of course, the provision is very salutary which creates an offence ultimately punishable by imprisonment of five years, but it is in respect of a matter where the opinion of the Commission is that the public information officer has persistently failed to provide the information. This is a case of persistent default and I appreciate that. But when there is no persistent default—not in the case of criminal case—for every other default, which is justifiable, there should be a minor penalty, and, it can be a fine because it is the only thing that is going to make this Act work. For example, if a person, whose duty is to disclose the information but wrongly fails to disclose the information, then he should be liable to some kind of fine because that acts as a deterrent against withholding of information. Therefore, for every default also, there should be some penalty that should be attached. These are my submissions before this Committee.

CHAIRMAN: Mrs. Daruwala, we have to study the points raised by you. Shri Shanti Bhushanji has also raised the issue of Cabinet papers. We should consider these matters thoroughly before giving any recommendations on this issue.

SHRI SHANTI BHUSHAN: I am not saying that all the Cabinet papers should be disclosed. I am saying that at the time of disclosure, it should be disclosed from the top to the bottom, and, till the time the decision is taken, the Cabinet papers should not be made open. It is my experience that, in many cases, the Ministers only sign the final decision. But they make the Secretary give the particular advice. If you question a Minister as to how did he take that decision, his reply would be that the Secretary of his Ministry advised him to do so. So far as Secretary's advice is concerned, it will not see the light of the day, and, therefore, he is not answerable. That is why it is most essential that after a final decision has been taken, all the notings made by different functionaries must come in the public domain.

SHRI V. RADHAKRISHNAN: As regards the first point, the Freedom of Information Act of 2003 was passed by the 13th Lok Sabha, and, it became an Act. But due to some reasons, it was not notified. In the previous Parliament, this issue was discussed, and, we have taken a decision that the Parliament is supreme as far as enactments relating to the fundamental rights are concerned. Some people raised doubts, and, that is why the matter was referred to you for further clarification.

Secondly, as far as the Official Secrets Act is concerned, any bureaucrat can escape, or, even take shelter as per Section 5 of the Act. My question is: should we abolish that, or, should we make certain amendments for providing some 'exceptions'? That is another point. As far as criminal law is concerned, as you are aware, there are provisions according to which nobody shall be compelled to give evidence. (Contd. by 2)

YSR/5.30/2L/PPG/14.02.2005

There should be no compulsion. If a person is giving information that goes against himself, how can the State function? I want your opinion on this. There is this difficulty because during investigation in criminal offences, it is not good in public interest to use that against oneself. Asking for information about such an item will impede the process of investigation of a case.

SHRI SHANTI BHUSHAN: It is already provided in clause (h).

SHRI V. RADHAKRISHNAN: There is another thing. The rule-making power is exclusively in the domain of the Legislature. The Executive is making the rules and placing them before the Parliament for further ratification. For this purpose, we have a Committee also. Now, there is a suggestion to expand the scope of this rule-making power. The rule-making power should be given to some other body. The Information Commissioner or some other authority, independent of the Government, should make rules. Would it be possible? Why I am saying this is because at present Statute is passed by the Parliament. We are the rule-making body. At present, the rules made by the Executive are to be scrutinised by the Parliament. Now, the point is whether such power should be given to an independent body like the Information Commission or not. These are some of the points, which require further clarification.

Then with regard to the choice, whether the law passed by the Union Parliament will prevail or the law passed by the State Legislature. I am telling you this because some identical provisions are there. The choice is with the applicant. He or she has to choose the law that is favourable to him or her. There is no doubt that he will choose the law that is favourable to him. Sometimes he may refer to the Central Government provisions because it may appear favourable to him and sometimes the State Law. In such a case, is he entitled to change his choice afterwards? Or, there should be some general provision that he can change it at any moment. It should be made clear because the choice is with the applicant either to proceed under the Central law or the State law. This is another aspect on which I want your clarification.

SHRI SHANTI BHUSHAN: With regard to investigation of offence, I think, it is already governed by clause 8, sub-clause (1), sub-clause (h) which says, "Information, the disclosure of which would impede the process of investigation or apprehension or prosecution of offenders." So, it is already protected. There is an exemption. So, while the investigation is going on, such information is not to be divulged, so as not to impede the process of investigation. I think it is a healthy provision. It is already there.

The other point was that nobody could be compelled to be a witness against himself. The Constitution itself gives this protection. But it does not say that any information contained in official records cannot be used against a person even, if he had made that written. In corruption cases, it is common that notings are used against the person but that does not compel him to give evidence against himself. If he is asked to give a statement against himself, he can refuse to be questioned. He can say that he is not going to answer any question. He has the right to remain silent. But if he has written something in some documents, there is no constitutional bar to that document being used against him. That does not amount to an evidence against himself.

SHRI V. RADHAKRISHNAN: Should it not be provided in the Statute?

SHRI SHANTI BHUSHAN: Not necessary. Once every document, unless it is protected by exemptions, is allowed to come in the public domain, then it will be enough; it need not be provided.

Your other point is that if a State law is already there, then what will happen. If one clause is introduced in the enactment that any right to information created by this Act is not in derogation but in addition to the right created under any corresponding State Legislation, nothing further need be said. It will only mean that the State Law will not get repealed or superseded. The State Law will also continue, but the option to proceed under the Central will also be there. He can keep on changing his mind provided he is willing to pay the necessary fee.

The other point was about the rule-making power. The rule-making power has been given to the Central Government. You are saying that there are suggestions that something could be added in the next clause. There may be some details about which the Central Government need not bother itself. Under clause 25, the "competent authority" may make more detailed provisions so long as rules made under clause 25 are not inconsistent with the rules made by the Central Government. So, this could be added in clause 25 to further clarify that the power of making rules of the "competent authority" has to be consistent with the rules made by the Central Government.

SHRI V. RADHAKRISHNAN: Every rule under the Statute will have to be scrutinised by the Legislature. Shouldn't the rules made by the "competent authority" be placed before the Parliament?

SHRI SHANTI BHUSHAN: Clause 26, as it stands today, provides that the rules so made by the Central Government will be laid before each House of Parliament. Normally you delegate the power of making rules. (Followed by 2m)

2M/5.40/KS

SHRI V. RADHAKRISHNAN: After they make the rules, these come before the House. And for that, we have a Committee also, the Committee on Subordinate Legislation. That Committee will have to scrutinise those rules. All these rules are placed before the House.

JUSTICE (RETD.) N. Y. HANUMANTHAPPA: I am talking about the statutory rules.

SHRI SHANTI BHUSHAN: Yes, and which should be consistent with the Act, which cannot detract from anything written in the Act. Rules cannot go beyond that. Rules are only to lay down the procedure.

JUSTICE (RETD.) N. Y. HANUMANTHAPPA: Section 12(5) says, "The Information Commissioner and the Deputy Information Commissioners shall be persons of eminence in public life with wide knowledge and experience of administration and governance". Now, there can be a mischief committed because it is very open-ended. Under all other Acts, where appointments are concerned, you fix the qualification, or, if there is experience, etc., then you say something like he should have been a judge or a senior IAS officer with 30 or 35 years of service and so on. But, here, there is nothing of that sort.

SHRI JAYAPRAKASH: Mr. Chairman, actually, when this Bill was deliberated by the National Advisory Council, there was a lot of discussion on this. Ultimately, if you say that you cannot trust the Government to appoint the right kind of people, no matter what qualifications you prescribe, wrong kind of people will in any case come in. It cannot be our case that just because you put the condition that it should be an IAS officer of such wide experience and so on, people of good record alone will be appointed. In some cases, they may not be.

JUSTICE (RETD.) N. Y. HANUMANTHAPPA: Yes, it may vary from person to person. But you have to define it. Is it not proper to put that a person having so many years of experience and having held such and such position would be eligible to be appointed to the said post and so on?

SHRI JAYAPRAKASH: Yes, Sir. Otherwise, if we keep it so open-ended, there can be people like Mrs. Maja Daruwala who have never worked in Government and so they will never become eligible.

JUSTICE (RETD.) N. Y. HANUMANTHAPPA: Then, even a Tehsildar can claim to be an administrator.

CHAIRMAN: If you read the next Clause, it says, "The Information Commissioner or a Deputy Information Commissioner shall not be a Member of Parliament or Member of the Legislature of any State or Union Territory, as the case may be, or hold any other office of profit or connected with any political party or carrying on any business or pursuing any profession". They are excluding us, Members of Parliament and Members of State Legislatures. Then it says, "...or connected with any political party...".

SHRI JAYAPRAKASH: The last two are unnecessary, I totally agree with that. The last two are not called for.

CHAIRMAN: Then, you read Clause 13(5) which says, "The Information Commissioner or a Deputy Information Commissioner shall, on cessation of his ofice, not be eligible for (a) any diplomatic assignment, assignment as administrator of a Union territory or such other assignment or appointment which is required by law to be made by the President by warrant under his hand and seal; (b) further employment to any office of profit under the Government of India or the Government of a State". They will not be eligible for any further appointment. What does it mean? The poor fellow is being made to lose his career for his entire life if he becomes once an Information Commissioner and he is disqualified from further appointments. He does not have any power at all, even if he wants to prosecute someone. Look at the provisions;

he is being chosen by the highest executive on land, the Leader of the Opposition and so on. If you carefully read the proviso, only retired civil servants can be appointed to these posts.

SHRI SHANTI BHUSHAN: I think, up to the expression 'office of profit' it is all right; the present Members of Parliament have to be excluded. But when it comes to '...or connected with any political party or carrying on any business or pursuing any profession', it means they want to confine these appointments only to the bureaucracy. Therefore, the expressions coming after 'office of profit' should be deleted.

CHAIRMAN: Yes, why should many of those eminent persons who have earlier been MPs be denied? Now, I am an M.P. and I am now getting a lot of motivation to be an Information Commissioner. Why should I be disallowed? They are preventing people from coming forward and serving here.

SHRI SHANTI BHUSHAN: I entirely agree. This last portion must go.

CHAIRMAN: Yes, why should we put this clause at all?

SHRI SHANTI BHUSHAN: Yes. I think it will be all right if sub-clause (5) can be retained.

CHAIRMAN: Can we say that the person should be a dynamic person, somebody as independent as the Chief Election Commissioner or the Chief Justice of India? Because, then only when a petition comes as appeal, he can immediately pass an order and get it executed. Otherwise, he will impose a fine of Rs. 250 and nothing will happen. (Contd. by 2n)

TDB/2N/5.50

CHAIRMAN (CONTD.): My request is, kindly think over it and let us know how best it can be done. Again, I want to stress that except Clauses 12, 13 and 14, nothing can be done to this Bill. The Clauses 12, 13 and 14 give weightage and power to the Commission so that the entire expectation about the right to freedom can be achieved. If you make it very hollow and very meek fellows sit there, occupy the place, retire themselves after five years, nothing will happen. As a result, many petitions will pile up and nothing will be disposed of. On this point, I want to have your suggestion.

Secondly, I want to know whether we can make a provision in this Bill itself for making it compulsory that any activity or any decision made by any department should be made available on the website. If that is made available, then, the rest of the work will be of the straight cases where they may need some information. As soon as the Cabinet takes some decisions, those decisions should be put on the website.

SHRI JAI PRAKASH: It is already covered under Clause 4 of the Bill which provides for notification of the obligations of the public authorities.

CHAIRMAN: You can see sub-clause (d) of Clause 2 which states, "'Information' means any material in any form, including records, documents, memos, e-mails, opinions, advices, press releases, circulars, logbooks, contracts, reports, papers, samples, models, data material; held in any electronic form and information relating to any private body which can be accessed..." What I want to say is, decisions should be made available on the website. If you make it like that, then, there will be no harassment of the lower level bureaucrats; a poor clerk need not be answerable for these types of questions.

SHRI JAI PRAKASH: Sir, under sub-clause (4) of the Clause 4, an explanation has been given, and it states, "For purposes of sub-sections (3) and (4), "disseminated" means making known or communicated the information to the public through notice boards, newspapers, public announcements, media broadcasts, the internet or any other means, including inspection of offices of any public authority."

CHAIRMAN: You look at the website of the CBI. And, then you look at the website of the FBI. You will find all sorts of information on the website of the FBI. On the other hand, if you look at the website of the CBI, you will forget what you want to find there. Why don't you update the website of the CBI and have more and more information about the number of cases pending with it, the number of cases which have been solved by it etc.? All these details should be put on the website of the CBI.

SHRIMATI MAJA DARUWALA: Are you saying that there should be a provision in Clause 4 whereby Cabinet decisions and reasons thereof should be put on the website?

CHAIRMAN: If the decisions of the Cabinet are put on the website, then it would be sufficient for the ordinary people. Only for the purposes of investigative journalism, they would be interested to know how they are working, etc. Even the Members of Parliament are not aware of the decisions taken by the Cabinet.

SHRIMATI MAJA DARUWALA: Clause 4(1)(d), already provides reasons for its administrative or quasi-judicial decisions to affected persons.

CHAIRMAN: That is already available. That has to be communicated to the aggrieved party. If any quasi-judicial decision has been taken, it has to be communicated to the aggrieved party.

SHRIMATI MAJA DARUWALA: You are right, Sir. Perhaps, one or two words need to be put there.

CHAIRMAN: You should give the justification for making it like this. These are the things which are available in the Bill. And some more provisions should be added in the Bill. Why don't you give suggestion for amendment of Clause 2 like this?

I also want to have some clarifications on the qualifications of Commissioners, positions which they are holding, disqualifications and service conditions, etc. Think about modifying all these provisions. Mr. Shanti Bhushan, I would like to know from you one thing. In the Bill, the Commissioner has the power to impose fine. Clause 17 of the Bill talks about right to impose penalty. The Members of the Committee also have some views on it. Their view is that the Commissioner should have the right to imprisonment. The Commissioner should be allowed to pass on the complaint through his officials to prosecute a person who had not furnished the information, who has violated the provisions of the Bill. Can we make such a provision, unless, otherwise, it is made a quasi-judicial commission?

SHRI SHANTI BHUSHAN: I agree with you because if the power is only to file a complaint, like section 340 of the Code of Criminal Procedure, it becomes a useless thing because the trial keeps on going and it does not produce any deterrent. Why can't power be given to him under Clause 17(1) itself to drop proceedings and after hearing him, they will make an inquiry, impose a punishment right there? For instance, the Supreme Court has taken the view in all perjury cases—since section 340 of the Code of Criminal Procedure has failed to do what it was intended to do— if you give a false evidence deliberately or file a perjured affidavit, then, it is also contempt of court and in contempt of court cases, we can straightway take action. Something on those lines be put in Clause 17 so that a person can be punished expeditiously, of course, it should be done after giving him full opportunity of hearing.

CHAIRMAN: The Commissioner will become a quasi-judicial authority. That means, they need certain qualifications for sitting there as arbitrators or as a person who want to pass a judicial order.

SHRI SHANTI BHUSHAN: It is not necessary. He can constitute a tribunal in which some judicial persons can also be included to make that trial. But, that trial should be done under Clause 17 of the Bill by the Commission itself.

CHAIRMAN: When you give him this power, he will enjoy judicial power also. The person is given opportunity of hearing him and then the Commission passes the order. It is done at two levels. One, there is appeal. Second, the Commissioner is coming into the picture. Therefore, we have to think about it.

SHRI SHANTI BHUSHAN: It can be done. It will be open to the Commission to constitute a body to go through the trial itself, and appeal is provided to the Commission.

CHAIRMAN: That means, more or less, as an arbitrator, as an independent body, he is working at two levels. One, at the trial level, and another at appeal level. These two bodies should have judicial or quasi-judicial authority. They should have that power to decide and send the person to prison. That can happen only when the Supreme Court or the High Court accept it, only when a judicial member is there in the Commission.

(Contd. by 20)

kgg/2o/6.00/PPG/14.2.05

CHAIRMAN (contd.): Therefore, we have to look at these matters. If you can help us, it would be very nice. Give us your opinion in a week so that we can consider on that point.

With this, we conclude the meeting today.

(The witnesses then withdrew and the Committee adjourned at 6.02 p.m.)

GSP-SCH/1 A/11.10/16-02-2005

Proceedings of the meeting of the Parliamentary Standing Committee on Personnel, Public Grievances, Law and Justice, which held at 11.00 A.M. on Wednesday, the 16th February, 2005 in Room No. 53, Parliament House, New Delhi.

(SHRI E.M. SUDARSANA NATCHIAPPAN - CHAIRMAN)

Witnesses:

Prof. Bina Agarwal, Institute of Economic Growth, University of Delhi.
Ms. Shruti Pandey, Advocate, Human Rights Law Network
Ms. Poonam Verma, Lawyer, Human Rights Law Network
Mr. Sanjay Dhadwal, Staff, Human Rights Law Network.

Representatives of the Ministry:

Shri N. K. Nampoothiry, Joint Secretary and Legislative Counsel, M/o Law and Justice

Ms. Reeta Vashista, Deputy Legislative Counsil, M/o Law and Justice.

CHAIRMAN: Good morning to everybody, I am very happy that we are starting our discussions on the historical amendment in the Hindu Succession Act, 1956, and, today, Professor Bina Agarwal from Institute of Economic Growth, University of Delhi, who is very vibrant and very much vocal in protecting the interests in the field of human rights, is present here before this Committee. She has taken keen interest in this matter. She has also conducted certain seminars having various representations from various parts of India and also from the women's wing.

The Committee feels that your presentation will be much more helpful for us to know the feelings of the women in different parts of India because in Hindu Law, we have got different systems like Mitakshara etc., and, we are tied up with so many things. We feel that women, the fifty per cent of the population, should get their rights. Rights were not properly given for the past so many years. With a lot of opposition and other things, we could find that during 1956, the Hindu Succession Act has given at least some rights to women. But now it is another step forward for giving more rights to the women. We have gone through your memorandum but even then you can highlight important things through the presentation. (Contd. by 1b)

SK/1B/11.20/PPG/16.02.2005

CHAIRMAN (Contd.): And after making your presentation, our hon. Members will raise certain questions. You can answer such questions immediately, if you can. Otherwise, within a week, you have to send a written reply. And, the usual course is that whatever discussion is taking place here, that has to be kept confidential till we submit a report before the Parliament. I hope you will take 15 minutes for this presentation. If you want to make any other observations, you can make and we will raise the questions thereafter. In the meantime, you can introduce your colleagues who have come along with you.

SHRIMATI BINA AGARWAL: Thank you Mr. Natchiappan and distinguished Members of the Committee. This is indeed a historic occasion for us and we are privileged that you have asked us to depose before you today. It is a wonderful window of opportunity to make an amendment in the Hindu Succession Act after 48 years, when the 1956 Act was passed. I will begin by introducing my colleagues and then present the salient features of the memorandum. Sir, this initiative was taken by myself—I am a professor of Economics at the Institute of Economic Growth at Delhi University—and two organisations, Human Rights Law Network and Housing and Land Rights Network. The Human Rights Law Network is represented here today by Miss Shruti Pandey and Miss Poonam Verma. Both of them are advocates. Mr. Collin Gonzalves, who is the Director of the Network could not come here today. The Housing and Land Rights Network, the Director of which is Mr. Millon Kothari also could not come here today as he is not well. We apologise for them.

The memorandum that we have distributed is a result of extensive consultations across the country with a large number of organisations, women organisations,

organisations working on livelihood and land reforms, organisations working on women rights, organisations working on widows' rights, etc., because we feel that this is an issue which is not concerned just with women, but it is concerned both men and women across the country. It has been endorsed by 50 organisations from Gujarat, Rajasthan, Himachal Pradesh, Haryana, Punjab, Kerala, Maharashtra, Uttar Pradesh and so on. It has also been endorsed by 122 individuals. We are still getting endorsements.

(Then Prof. Bina Agarwal made her presentation with the help of slides)

(followed by 1c)

YSR/11.30/1C/PPG/16.02.2005

CHAIRMAN: After this amendment is carried out, the entire scenario will be changed. Have you thought about it?

PROF. BINA AGARWAL: Well, the Bill is silent on the issue of agricultural land. It does not mention Clause 4(2).

CHAIRMAN: That is true. There is no amendment for this particular section. Now, you see, women are getting equal rights. There is no difference between a male and a female. Earlier women had no right over property, but now they have right over property. The entire scenario will be changed. Agricultural land will also have overriding effect.

PROF. BINA AGARWAL: Thank you, Sir, for this clarification.

JUSTICE (RETD.) N.Y. HANUMANTHAPPA: Property includes agricultural land.

CHAIRMAN: I think this particular section is a barrier. We will consider it at the time of preparation of this Committee's report. We will make necessary recommendations, so that this can also be looked into.

PROF. BINA AGARWAL: Yes, Sir, it is a barrier.

CHAIRMAN: After this amendment is carried out, that barrier should also be removed.

PROF. BINA AGARWAL: Sir, the legal barrier should be removed.

JUSTICE (RETD.) N.Y. HANUMANTHAPPA: Since it is a State subject, States have their own restrictions. Each State Government may have its own thinking over the right to cultivate the land. The law, which prevails in Karnataka, cannot be equally applied to Uttar Pradesh, or Himachal Pradesh, or Haryana, or Delhi. It is left to the discretion of the State Legislature.

(The witness then continued his presentation with the help of slides)

(Followed by id)

VKK/1d/11.40/16.2.20053 PPG

PROF. BINA AGARWAL: Okay, Sir, I will go by the hard copy. Please look at diagram 1a and 1b. You see the situation before amendment and after amendment. If you go in the direction of Andhra Pradesh, Tamil Nadu and Karnataka, in these three States, the wife gets no share on partition. Suppose, you have a situation where a man has coparcenary property of 90 lakhs of rupees. That man has two sons, S1 and S2. Now, each of them will get 30 lakhs as portions. But S1 has a wife, a daughter and a son, So, his share of Rs.30 lakhs will get divided as 15 lakhs to himself and 15 lakhs to his son according to the unamended Act. Suppose, ST dies. Then, his share of 15 lakhs will get divided among his widow, daughter and son. They will get five lakhs each in the notional properties of S1 as class 1 heirs. In this way, the widow gets 5 lakhs, the daughter gets 5 lakhs and the son gets 20 lakhs (5 lakhs + 15 lakhs). So, the son clearly gets much more under the unamended Act.

Now, consider diagram 1b. Sir, if you see, in the case of Andhra Pradesh, Tamil Nadu and Karnataka, where the wife gets no share on partition, after amendment what happens is that if the daughter becomes coparcener, share of S1 which is 30 lakhs....

DR. RADHAKANT NAYAK: It goes to third generation.

CHAIRMAN: This situation will arise only when the first son dies.

PROF. BINA AGARWAL: Yes, Sir. We have given that in the bottom line.

Sir, if you see it after amendment, where the daughter becomes coparcener, the share of S1 goes to daughter, son and himself as 10 lakhs each. And suppose, S1 dies. Then the share of S1, which is 10 lakhs, is divided among the widow, the son and the daughter and each one gets 3.33 lakhs. So, the wife ends up with a smaller share. The daughter and the son get 13.33 lakhs each because of their direct coparcenary. Here, you see that the widow's share after amendment actually falls from 5 lakhs to 3.33 lakhs because the daughter has become coparcener. Sir, this is basically a mathematical calculation.

CHAIRMAN: What you want to say?

PROF. BINA AGARWAL: Sir, by introducing daughters as coparcener, you may increase the share of daughters, but you also have to see that there are other class 1 female heirs, like widow, who lose out by this.

CHAIRMAN: The present law is also not allowing any share for widow.

PROF. BINA AGARWAL: Widows get out of the notional share of man. Sir, the widow gets even under the unamended Act and, therefore, she gets a share equal to that of the son and daughter in the man's notional share. We are saying that if you bring daughters as coparceners, man's notional portion of properties declines and the widow loses as she gets from the notional share only.

CHAIRMAN: What do you want to say?

PROF. BINA AGARWAL: We are pointing out that it is necessary to abolish the Mitakshara system altogether. It privileges the son over other women heirs.

CHAIRMAN: What will happen by that?

PROF. BINA AGARWAL: Equal amounts will go to class 1 heirs of man. We are saying that by this amendment, that is being proposed, the inequality is only partially removed. We request you to go the Kerala way which has abolished the Mitakshara system altogether.

JUSTICE (RETD.) N.Y. HANUMANTHAPPA: There are matriarchal and patriarchal systems prevailing. You cannot ask to scrap it altogether like this. It is there from times immemorial.

PROF. BINA AGARWAL: In Kerala, they have abolished the joint family property system altogether.

JUSTICE (RETD.) N.Y. HANUMANTHAPPA: Now, you have to view all these amendments in the light of Article 14 and other Articles of the Constitution. Since you are bringing an amendment of this nature, you shall have to confine to the Constitution also.

PROF. BINA AGARWAL: Sir, the Constitution says that all men and women and citizens are equal in the eyes of law. I think, by this amendment, inequality still remains. We feel that the widow should have as much claim as the daughter in any legislation. Sir, Article 14 also privileges sons over other categories of heirs.

CHAIRMAN: But here what we could not understand is that there is a widow, a daughter and a son and they are going to get equal shares.

PROF. BINA AGARWAL: Sir, there are two categories of properties. There is the Mitakshara coparcenary property and the notional property in the Mitakshara coparcenary. The daughter, the widow and the son get equal shares in the notional property of the man who dies. But the son, in addition, also gets a direct share by birth, independent of notional property in the first category. So, today, under the unamended Act, the son gets shares both as a direct coparcener and also a part of the notional share. Now, if you also bring the daughter in the direct share, who only has a share in the man's notional shares, she will also get a share just as the son. And the widow will be left with a much less share. That is also very much possible. <u>(Followed le)</u>

RSS/1E/11.50/PPG

JUSTICE (RETD.) N.Y. HANUMANTHAPPA: You see, the point is, once she becomes a daughter-in-law in some other house, what would be the position? Whether she will be in an advantageous position or in a disadvantageous position or she will have double gain. As a daughter, she gets one share, and after becoming a daughter-in-law, she loses. But when the husband dies, again, she will be claiming her husband's rights. In that case, she will be benefited both ways.

PROF. BINA AGARWAL: Sir, the fact is that, law is equal for both man and woman. Woman inherits property as a widow and she inherits property as a daughter. But man also inherits property as a son as well as a widower. The law is equal for both. Both of them inherit property on both counts. If a woman dies, and if she has property, and she has a husband and children, all her property equally passes on to her husband and children on her death. So, there is no inequality. Both of them get their both shares. There is no difference. It is not gender unequal, it is completely gender equal on that account.

DR. RADHAKANT NAYAK: What will happen if your suggestion is accepted?

PROF. BINA AGARWAL: Sir, you do not have the concept of mitakshara coparcenery property in many religions. The Christians do not have a mitakshara coparcenery concept. So, why should we have an ancient archaic system? A lot of people argue that this is for tax purpose.

JUSTICE (RETD.) N.Y. HANUMANTHAPPA: But you must also take into consideration the customs, the traditions and all other things that were existing in the past, and are existing now. After all, the Hindu Succession Law was framed, after taking into consideration all these factors. Straightway, you cannot ask for everything to be abolished and give a new look to the Hindu Succession Act. As a matter of fact, the Indian Succession Act was for a few people. But the Hindu Succession Act covers not less than 80 per cent of the population, and the law is based on, as I said earlier, customs, traditions and all these things. Straightway, you cannot ask to abolish all these things. I am saying this just for the sake of discussion. So, if we do so, it will amount to completely replacing the Act, which will be revolutionary, and there will be a direct conflict between the customs, traditions and the law to be made on the other side. It will lead to disruption of the entire family. The intention of the framers of this law was that the institution of family should remain intact. If we accept your argument, we have to give a go by to the joint family system, and people having the mitakshara concept will not accept this part. They will not agree to give up this concept. All these things will have to be taken into consideration, and not merely the claim of women. You are justified in asking that there should be equal rights for both. But you will have to keep in mind that there are certain pious obligations, which are on sons, not on daughters. Pious obligations are performed by the son only. Are you performing the pious obligations? No. What is your contribution towards discharging the pious obligations?

PROF. BINA AGARWAL: Sir, we had many archaic customs in ancient times. As a modern State, we moved forward very substantially when we drafted India's Constitution. The Hindu Succession Act 1956 itself was a great leap forward in terms of thinking of a modern India where all citizens are equal in the eyes of law. Article 14 was a major leap forward. We had so many customs, which were given a go by with the passage of time. We looked towards modern India. If we go by that, it can be done. Secondly, I have looked at the *Dharamshastras.* I have read their English translation. What I gathered from all the laws that were passed is that the widow claims always came before the daughter. If you look at the ancient mitakshara, that was the case. Now, just making daughters coparceners, and forgetting about widow's share, seems to be overriding the existing tradition. This partial way of making coparceners, has no basis and traditions. Why don't we abolish the joint family system altogether? Then the widow's rights and daughter's rights will be equal to that of a son. We had the practice of child marriage, widow re-marriage. That practice was abolished. A lot of customs, which were not conducive to the society, were abolished. Many things which the women did not have, have been granted to us, and therefore, our plea is that this is a great historic occasion for all of you to play this role and take us forward in that direction.

JUSTICE (RETD.) N.Y. HANUMANTHAPPA: Child marriage is different, widow remarriage is different, but existence and abolition of joint family system is altogether different.

PROF. BINA AGARWAL: Sir, we are not abolishing the joint family system. People can, of course, still live together. What we are saying is that, don't make special privileges for one class.

JUSTICE (RETD.) N.Y. HANUMANTHAPPA: If they live together by way of an agreement or settlement, that will not bind the family. That sanctity will not be there. You did not answer our question about the pious obligations. When a father dies, it is the duty of the son to discharge all the debts incurred by his father. What about discharging the duties taken by the son upon himself by you? Daughters will escape once they go out of the house or are married. It is the son who will discharge all the debts.

PROF. BINA AGARWAL: If the joint family system is abolished altogether, there is nothing which prevents the man from leaving more property to his son, which indeed, is happening. In any case, a lot of property is going to the sons in the form of

'Will' these days. Apart from pious obligations, a lot of parents are depending on daughter's support. Although we have a sociological understanding that sons take care of parents in old days, we find through studies and other sources that sons are not willing to take care of their parents.

SHRI HARIN PATHAK: The scenario has changed. Daughters are taking care of their parents these days.

JUSTICE (RETD.) N.Y. HANUMANTHAPPA: A daughter and a mother is kind to all. But the son has to discharge the debts incurred by the father to meet the legal obligation.

PROF. BINA AGARWAL: If you give daughters the share of the property, then they will be absolutely willing to discharge that obligation as well, once she has equal claims.

JUSTICE (RETD.) N.Y. HANUMANTHAPPA: So far as you are there as a daughter, it is all right, you live with your parents. Once you become a daugther-in-law, what will happen? (contd. by 1f)

MKS/ASC/12.00/1 F

PROF. BINA AGARWAL: Sir, we feel that the daughter should be given an equal opportunity, legally, to discharge all legal obligations relating to her parents, and sons and daughters should have equal obligations if they get equal shares of property.

JUSTICE (RETD.) N.Y. HANUMANTHAPPA: Loving is different from discharging.

PROF. BINA AGARWAL: Married daughters also take care of elderly parents more and more; we find that.

DR. RADHAKANT NAYAK: We are getting into some kind of macro issues like the concept of nucleus family, the concept of joint family and all that kinds of things. How do you react to the western society? It is not only because of equality of rights; that has, more or less, gone down the ages. In many countries, the concepts of nucleus family and single parent family are emerging, and the family is breaking. The number of divorce cases is very high. In some countries, the number of divorce cases goes up to 50 or 60 per cent because of the so-called independence which is given to the individuals. Still people think that Indian families are in tact, they are much better and they have psychologically more sense of security. You are making a logical suggestion for abolishing some of the customs and traditions. How do you think that they will be building a modern society and a humanistic society?

PROF BINA AGARWAL: Sir, firstly, psychologically, we find that in the Indian society also, people are living, more and more, in nucleus families because housing is less. In urban areas, most people are living in nucleus families, but there is nothing to prevent them, if you have equal division of property, from living in joint families. In the Indian society, the family is bound by social norms and social thinking. I think our family system will not break and people will stay together if there is an equal right. Some people say that it is a sad situation if the woman gets an equal share in property. It is a sad comment that inequality is necessary to keep the family in tact. If the woman has some property today, there is a lot of disruption in the family. At the grass root levels, a man can leave the woman; he can marry again, but the woman can't do anything. She has children and she has no property of her own. If the woman has property, the man will try to stay together. There will be a stable marriage. Our reading is exactly the opposite. If the woman gets equal right, the man will stay in the family and will not go elsewhere.

Secondly, I want to mention that there are some States where the widow takes a share on partition or the wife takes a share. After amendment, if you make daughters coparceners, they will all get equal shares. That is prevalent in Maharashtra. What we are, therefore, saying is that in relation to the Mitakshara joint family system property, there are also various anomalies in the Bill. For instance, it only relates to daughters who are unmarried at the time of the passing of the Act and it leaves out already married daughters. The argument that is made is that gifts are given at the time of marriage; therefore, we should not include married daughters. We want to make the plea that the gifts given in marriage are seldom equivalent in value to inheritance shares and rarely include immovable property. We can say that not all parents give such gifts. If you leave out all married daughters, that would be injustice.

Thirdly, the position of an adopted daughter is not clear. Suppose you make daughters coparceners. Would the adopted daughters be counted in the same way as the daughters by birth are?

Fourthly, in a man's notional share, the heirs of the predeceased son are traced to two generations after him as Class I heirs whereas in the case of woman property, the heirs of the predeceased daughter are traced to only one generation after her. That is, in the Mitakshara coparcenary, the son's rights go down to two generations and the daughter's rights go down to only one generation.

Finally, what I have already mentioned is that the coparceners' rights into joint family property will remain in tact. For all these reasons, we are suggesting you to abolish the Mitakshara joint family property system, and if we bring the agricultural interests under the Act, it will create uniformity in all kinds of property.

CHAIRMAN: What about the new concept? The adopted daughter's position is not clear.

PROF. BINA AGARWAL: Our reading is that the adopted son is treated like the natural son. So, the adopted daughter will take the same right as the natural daughter. That is our reading, but it might be made clear.

CHAIRMAN: Naturally, it will go. There is no natural daughter; the adopted daughter is there. Then, she will fill up the place of natural daughter.

PROF. BINA AGARWAL: If the natural daughter is there after her adoption, then what will happen?

CHAIRMAN: That has to be decided by the court. If you pass on a lineage to that family, automatically, the lineage is cut. This girl will become the natural daughter of that particular family. Afterwards, if there is the birth of a daughter, then, the younger daughter can be a daughter along with them. But you can't eliminate that she is not a natural daughter. The son is also treated like that.

PROF. BINA AGARWAL: Our third recommendation is that if you abolish the joint family system, all the property will be subject to wills, and although this is generally a neutral situation in principle; in practice, because of male bias in our society, a lot of people will write their wills in favour of their sons. We want to suggest that there should be a partial restriction on testamentary rights. Place restrictions on half or one-third of the property while allow full freedom of will in the rest. If you look at the systems prevailing in other countries—there are some precedents in India also—under Islamic law, there is a restriction on two-thirds of the property, but we are recommending it on half or one-third of the property. In the European countries, the system that is followed in Germany, Japan, Italy and Spain, there is a partial restriction on the testamentary rights. I believe that only a part of the property can be willed away, and the rest will go to Class I heirs. We are, therefore, suggesting that we should have some restriction on the right to testation so that at least some part of the property could go to Class I heirs. We also discover that Christians in Goa are governed by the Portuguese Civil Court where there is also a restriction on the right to testation, because it is governed by the Civil Law system.

CHAIRMAN: If you go to any Hindu nation, say, Nepal, what is happening there?

PROF. BINA AGARWAL: May I submit, Sir, that if we look at the colonial history and framing of the Hindu laws, the whole right to will was imposed by our colonial Government. There was no right to will. It was part of the Anglo-Mitakshara system. The British Government introduced what was prevailing in England. You have a notion of nodal property. Hundred per cent of the property could be willed away if we really want to follow the Indian tradition. Under the Indian tradition, there was no such thing. It was a colonial imposition. What I am suggesting is we should go back to our own tradition, at least, partially, rather than adopting the colonial system.

TMV/1G/12.10 (Followed by 1G)

JUSTICE (RETD.) N.Y. HANUMANTHAPPA: Irrespective of the Malaysian law, the Hindu law is a Hindu law. The Malaysian law is a Malaysian law. There is a difference. It applies to the Malaysian Hindus and their brethren. You can't ask us to give up our Hindu laws in the light of the Anglo Saxon laws or some other laws. The law might have been codified and brought into the Statute book subsequently. The system was there since time immemorial. The Hindu law was framed in 1956. It was framed following some traditions, customs, conventions, etc. You can't ask, all of a sudden, to change it. If we suggest such a change, stones will be pelted at all of us.

Just now you are saying about the sons, daughters and the daughters-in-law. Let us take the case of the illotum son-in-law, which is a system prevailing in some parts of the country where the son-in-law goes to the house of the parents-in-law. What would happen to him? This system of illotum son-in-law is prevailing in Andhra Pradesh and some parts of other States also. It is not prevailing in all the States. It is prevailing in some Hindu castes in some areas.

PROF. BINA AGARWAL: We completely agree with you that the Hindu law has been changing over time. It has been evolving over time. So, the discussion that we are having today is clearly a central part of that evolution. My answer to your question is simply that we are not turning to Malaysia.

JUSTICE (RETD.) N.Y. HANUMANTHAPPA: What would be the position of the illotum son-in-law?

CHAIRMAN: In some parts of Andhra Pradesh and Tamil Nadu, there is a convention that after marriage, just like the daughter goes away from her family to live with her in-laws' family, the son will go away from his family leaving all his rights in the natural family and live with his in-laws' family. In such a situation, what will happen to the son?

PROF. BINA AGARWAL: Sir, I want to share with you a family situation which already exists in Sri Lanka. It is our neighbouring country, where, in a majority of the Singhalese community, both the son and the daughter have a right to property. There what happens is the couple decides where they should reside. For instance, in a Jaffna family, who are Hindus, where the woman has got a lot of property, say, 70 per cent of the land is owned by the girl. In such a situation, the couple decides, according to the size of the property, where to live and they live where the bigger portion of the property is situated. If the wife has got more property, the couple lives there. If the husband has got more property, then couple lives there. It becomes a flexible system. If you go by that, our system will become much more flexible. Today what happens in North India, and it is very common, is that when the girls are married, they go to a different village and their properties are in a different village. This is not the case with South India. In South India people get married in the same village. In North India the girls are very vulnerable. If the girl has property, there should be a flexible system. Sometimes she goes to the husband's place; sometimes the husband goes to the girl's place. But in the urban context, the couples are not living either with the parents of the boys or with the parents of the girls. They have their typical way of living. They have their own nuclear families. A lot of professional couples whom we know are not living with either of their parents. In fact, very hardly any couple lives with their parents. Therefore, that argument seems to me a very old argument. It was prevalent a long time ago. But today the reality is that people are setting up their own homes. Therefore, I don't say that if the girl has property, we would move towards greater equality.

Sir, our recommendation and partial restriction to the right of testation is linked to our suggestion of abolishing joint family property altogether. If you abolish one and do not restrict the testation, then all the property would be willed away and the daughter would get nothing.

Then, we have one small final concern. In many cases the social reality is that the women sign away their shares to their brothers and other family members because there is a lot of pressure on them to do that. It is often said that a good sister will not ask for her share from her brother's property. There are a lot of cases where it is done under duress. Therefore, we suggest that there should be some legal provision in the Act to protect women from such pressure so that if they are putting their signatures under duress, those signatures should be deemed null and void. Perhaps, such a thing could be done before a Magistrate. This is a suggestion which should be considered, or, there should be some other proper method for doing this.

JUSTICE (RETD.) N.Y. HANUMANTHAPPA: When both are equal in the eyes of the law, where is the question of duress? When both have not only equal right but also equal strength, where is the question of the brother using duress for getting the signature of the sister and making her to give up completely her right in the property? The social reality today is that, as you yourself have observed, when the daughters are married, they go to another house and live there. Once she is married, she will have double strength, one is her own and the other is her husband's support. Now, she is supported by twice more strength. The question is regarding duress or making her to sign under duress. How does it arise? It is a question of figment, whether the signature is put under duress or obtained by fraud or by some such other things. — It is purely a question of figment. This can't be mentioned in the Act. Then you will be putting her on a different platform altogether. That can't be done. When you say both are equal in the eyes of law, you can't ask to put her on a higher pedestal.

PROF. BINA AGARWAL: We wanted to raise this issue. At grassroots levels this issue was raised. This is a serious problem that they face. Many a time they sign away their shares to their brothers under duress. We want to draw your attention to this and some legal provision should be provided. In some countries, if the woman wants to sign away her share, then it is done before a Magistrate to make it legal. So, we want you to flag this issue because we feel that today we are representing not just one group but we are representing a lot of other groups.

JUSTICE (RETD.) N.Y. HANUMANTHAPPA: It would apply to the sons also.

PROF. BINA AGARWAL: It would apply to the sons also.

JUSTICE (RETD.) N.Y. HANUMANTHAPPA: It will apply to the sons, if they are not worldly wise or blind or mute or dumb or suffering from other disabilities.

PROF. BINA AGARWAL: We know that in certain families the younger sons signed away their share to the elder ones under duress. So, the same problem can arise. This is just a social reality that women are much more under duress than men do. So, our recommendation is in the light of that social reality. (Contd. by 1H)

RG/12.20/ppg/l6.2.2005/1 h

CHAIRMAN: Do you have any data on this aspect?

PROF. BINA AGARWAL: I made a study when I was writing my book to look at what is the gap between the law and practice. There is a survey which was done and I found that only 13 per cent of women inherited any land as daughters, which means that 87 per cent of women did not inherit their claims. I also did a survey of Rajasthan because I hail from that State. The Patwaris there said that they discourage daughters from claiming their share. And, the evidence that is coming out is that the ladies very seldom claim their share. If you talk to women, they say, "If we do not sign away our shares, then, our brothers and brothers' wives will not allow us to go to our house if there is a problem in our married life." So, there is a lot of pressure for her to give up her claim. That is the social reality of the situation.

SHRI RADHAKANT NAYAK: Have you made any study whether at the block level, village level or at the district level to see to what is the total land under the occupation of women, even in terms of physical possession?

PROF. BINA AGARWAL: It is a very good question that you have asked because one of the things that we are talking in various fora is this. We have no comprehensive data on land beyond household property. So, whether it is the Agricultural Census or the National Sample Survey or the Cost of Cultivation Data of which I have studied, they do not segregate it gender-wise. And, one of our recommendations has been that you have to collect all these data not just at the household level, but also see how much land and property both women and men can have. So, on the basis of a lot of studies that I did at the village level—I looked at every single village in India, and studied the anthropological and other studies—I found that a very, very small proportion of girls inherit land as daughters. There is a much bigger percentage of women who inherit land as widows. So, one study which I was quoting to you that was done by a socialist, showed that 51 per cent widows inherit land from husbands if they have sons. This still leaves out 49 per cent of women who do not inherit even as widows. So, as daughters, they are very seriously disadvantaged. There is a lot more work to be done in terms of statistics. But the existing statistics show that a very small proportion own or control land or any kind of property.

JUSTICE (RETD.) N.Y. HANUMANTHAPPA: Why do you choose agriculture which is an unprofitable part of property. People are in misery there. Agriculture is not at all profitable. If sons want to keep the land, the daughters can claim the value for their share of property. The fact is still there that they are not accustomed to cultivate land.

PROF. BINA AGARWAL: The fact is that if you look at the data that we have for the past three decades, you find that it is mainly men who have moved out of agriculture and gone into non-farming occupation. And, today, 85 per cent—I emphasise this—of all rural women workers are working in agriculture compared to 78 per cent of rural man. There is a substantial gap, and this gap has been growing. I agree with you that our sisters don't have to do back-breaking work in agriculture. But the reality is that—I am an agricultural economist—it is the women who do the arming and men have moved out of it. But they cannot take the credit for it because credit depends on whether you have the title for it or not. Also, you cannot get access to village level works, access to technology, etc. Even our productivity is suffering because the women, who are farmers, are not getting title of their lands...

CHAIRMAN: In Jammu and Kashmir, all the ladies are having the right, not all the males.

PROF. BINA AGARWAL: That is not the case. The interesting thing is that in Jammu and Kashmir, under the Land Reforms Act, Section 4 (2) which deals with tenancy laws, women have unequal rights in agricultural land. So, in all the North-Westem States—of course, the Southern States are doing much better—the laws are not in favour of women's claim in land. Jammu and Kashmir is included in this.

CHAIRMAN: Jammu and Kashmir has made a law that the daughters' rights cannot be taken away even if she is married to a person of some other State.

PROF. BINA AGARWAL: Right. But the actual fact is that the rights themselves are so limited. My colleague also tells me that the law has not been enacted. I want that all the six States which I have mentioned, namely, Haryana, Punjab, Delhi, Rajasthan, Madhya Pradesh and Uttar Pradesh to be included in the law. Even if we look at various religious communities, although under the Muslim Law, that is, under the Shariat Law, women may have certain rights in the property, as far as agricultural land is concerned, women across all religious communities have very unequal claims. Even, the Shariat Act of 1937 exempts agricultural land from its purview. So, irrespective of whether a person is a Hindu, Christian or a Muslim, women are at a disadvantage. And, this is the most important form of property; be it, in the debates in Parliament or Constituent Assemblies, this one factor is constantly brought in.

To sum up, I would say that we have three basic recommendations. One is to delete Section 4 (2) which restricts women's rights in tenancy laws. The second is restrict testation to part of property and the third is to partially restrict the right to will.

Now, we want to make one additional argument that is about the 174th Law Commission Report of 2000. Prior to this Report, a questionnaire was sent out by the Law Commission in 1999 to non-Governmental organisations, civil society groups and individuals, and a large number of responses were received. I was also one of them who sent in my answer to that questionnaire. In that questionnaire, the Law Commission had asked: Should we or should we not bring in agricultural land under the purview of the Hindu Succession Act? Should we abolish the joint property altogether or should the daughters be co-partners on the same basis as male persons? (Continued by 1H)
1J/12.30/KS

The third was: should we partially restrict the testamentary rights? If you see the responses, it is interesting to see that 88 per cent of those who responded said that agricultural land should be brought under the purview of the Act; 73 per cent favoured the abolition of the Mitakshara coparcenary altogether and 63 per cent have favoured some restrictions on the freedom of testation. So, petitions from various places were already supporting these radical recommendations on our part. But on all these counts, the Commission took the conservative route.

So, while summing up, we would like to say that we urge all of you who are Members of this august Committee that this is a wonderful window of opportunity to make history and to go the very comprehensive route of amending the Hindu Succession Act, including bringing all property, including agricultural land, on par, abolishing the *mitakshara* coparcenary property system altogether and by restricting testation rights. We feel that 48 years have gone by and now we are thinking of amending this Act. If we wait for another 50-100 years to make it gender equal, it would be a long time. Sir, it would also be a signal to all the other communities in India. An argument is often advanced as to when the Hindu Succession Act is unequal, why we ask for gender equality. So, if it is made gender equal, then we can strongly ask for gender equality in all other communities. It will be fully in keeping with article 14 of the Constitution, that there should be no discrimination on the basis of sex. Also, all the mandates that we have under various international treaties that we have signed, like the treaty on discrimination against women and so on, and which we have ratified, we have said that we agree that everybody should be equal in the eye of the law and so on. I think we should all stand together. This is our belief.

JUSTICE (RETD.) N. Y. HANUMANTHAPPA: I need one more clarification. Please help us in the case of what is written here about 'son, grandson or great-grandson' in sub-clause (4) of clause 6. How far it is helpful or not helpful to the children, especially the sons? There is also proviso which says, "Provided that in the case of any debt contracted before the commencement of the Hindu Succession (Amendment) Act, 2004, nothing contained in this sub-section shall affect (a) the right of any creditor to proceed against the son, grandson or great-grandson, as the case may be; or (b) any alienation made in respect of or in satisfaction of, any such debt, and any such right or alienation shall be enforceable under the rule of pious obligation in the same manner and to the same extent as it would have been enforceable as if the Hindu Succession (Amendment) Act, 2004 had not been enacted". Now, for example, the daughter takes her share and goes away. The creditor files a suit against the grandson, great-grandson and so on. Who is at a disadvantage here? Is it not the son who is at a disadvantage here?

PROF. BINA AGARWAL: You are quite right, Sir. The way the Act is working at this time, only the unmarried daughter will have the right to property.

JUSTICE (RETD.) N.Y. HANUMANTHAPPA: Even the unmarried daughter's share is not affected.

CHAIRMAN: Well, this pressure comes only if there is a debt which has been caused before this Act came into force. In such a situation, the debt can be recovered from the sons, grandsons and great-grandsons, but not from the daughters. We thought you would oppose it. But you accept it.

PROF. BINA AGARWAL: We have already said that we do not accept it.

CHAIRMAN: You have not made that point in your presentation. I am surprised.

PROF. BINA AGARWAL: Sir, we have said in our presentation that the 2004 Bill limits coparcenary rights to daughters unmarried at the time of the amendment. This discriminates against already-married daughters whose share will fall. Our plea is that married daughters and unmarried daughters should not be treated differently.

CHAIRMAN: But in the case of the right of the creditors and so on, the son is at a disadvantage; it is unequal.

PROF. BINA AGARWAL: If you are talking about equality, then you are saying that both of them should be equally obligated to repay the debt. Well, we bypass that by saying that what we are thinking of is the joint family property, in which case the debts will be taken out from the total property of the man, and whatever property remains will be divided.

CHAIRMAN: We need one clarification. The Hindu way of life or the system of life as it now stands, is the son gives *pinda* for the father, the grand father and the great-grandfather. That is why the right to property is also of the son because the *pinda* is given by him and, then only, it is believed, goes to heaven. Now, we want to take away that property right from the son and give it equally to the daughter. At the same time, they are taking away the pious obligation also. This is more or less the abolition of the Mitakshara system. Once there is the abolition of the pious obligation, naturally there is no joint family at all. (Contd. by 1K)

TDB/1K/12.40

CHAIRMAN (CONTD.): There is no bondage for the son to say that he is doing all these things which are obligatory on his part, and as a son, he is doing all these obligations. He is giving the *pinda* at a particular time; he is also clearing all the debts of the family; he is managing the joint family and seeing to it that all his sisters are married properly and they are happy with their family; he also sees to it that all his younger brothers are settled in life properly. So, the entire joint family is properly looked after by the son. If there is a debt incurred by the family, that debt would be cleared by the joint family. This is the joint family system. Now, you want to break away that family. That means, we have to take certain practices from Europe and America. We know that the Hindu families are breaking as one family is living in America and another family is living in a village in Rajasthan or Punjab. That is a different matter. But, we have to take a holistic view of the matter. You are touching the religious aspects here. If you want the daughter to have certain rights in the property, then she should also have certain liabilities. There are religious obligations; there are pious obligations. Are you in favour of giving both these obligations to daughters? I want to know from you whether you want the daughters to take all pious obligations and also take the role of a son.

PROF. BINA AGARWAL: Sir, we have three arguments here. Firstly, we feel that the religious obligations and economic factors should be separated. The issue of *pinda* should be separated from the issue of clearing of debts. The issue of clearing debt is an economic one, while the issue of *pinda* is a religious one. There is nothing which is preventing the son from giving the *pinda.* There is no reason why he should not perform the last rites, which, I think, is a privilege. Many daughters would like to have that privilege. My first argument is...

JUSTICE (RETD.) N.Y. HANUMANTHAPPA: Why should the son be restricted? You should say that both son and daughter should have equal rights. Why do you want to shift that burden on the son alone? You want to abolish the entire *mitakshara* joint family system.

PROF. BINA AGARWAL: Sir, we see the giving of *pinda* as a privilege for the son and we see the pious obligation as a responsibility. Let us separate these two things. As far as privileges are concerned, there are many daughters who would welcome being equal on that ground because sometimes you have only a daughter. So, it is not a burden; it is a privilege. Now, I want to address the economic part. As far as the economic part is concerned, even today, because a man has the right to will, he can will away his entire separate property to anybody whom he wants, even if his son is there to give him the *pinda.* I have seen many men who have given away their property to old persons' homes because they say that neither their son nor their daughter looks after them, then why should they give their property to their son or daughter? That is happening in many cases. Already the right to will is there. A man can will away his rights in the notional share in the joint family property. So, as the situation exists today, the man can will away his property to anybody. The notion of Hindu family is already being undermined by allowing the concept of will to exist. This is my second argument.

My third argument is, as far as pious obligation is concerned, I think this is something that the Committee could think about. If you want that daughters to be given equal right as co-partners, then, there can be equal sharing of economic burden. As far as pious obligation is concerned, daughters should also have the right to give the *pinda.* They should not be deprived of religious rights. If they are given all obligations, then they must also have the obligation of economic burden. To me, this argument doesn't seem to be a fair argument.

Sir, our fourth and final argument is, none of this will be a problem if you abolish the *mitakshara* joint family system altogether. It could be a nephew; it could be a niece; it may not be a son; it could be a daughter or anybody, whoever the person feels that they are close to him.

DR. RADHAKANT NAYAK: I have just two small questions. The law plays a small part in bringing about social change. Instead of going through the legal machinery—of course, there are provisions in the Constitution which are aimed at bringing about these changes—don't you think that we have to change our mindset and our traditional views. In order to do that, why don't the women, NGOs and others bring about a big social movement? I want to know whether such a thing is happening in the country.

Secondly, why are you emphasising only on agricultural land? With the increasing emphasis on market economy, productivity is increasing and there is very less agricultural land for women to cultivate. Perhaps, it would be a better argument if you say that daughters should have share in market debentures, in pensions and gratuities of their parents who are working. That kind of an argument, perhaps, would be a better argument, if you want a bigger share of property for daughters. It is much more than what is available in the agricultural land *per se.*

PROF. BINA AGARWAL: You have two questions. You are quite right when you say that there is a big gap between the law and practice. I completely agree with you here. Even though we have progressive laws, we have to change people's thinking about it. As far as your question is concerned, I would like to say that these 50 organisations which have endorsed this are not working on law alone. Some of them are working on legal issues and many of them are working on grassroots livelihood issues. I have done workshops in Gujarat and Delhi. I would like to inform the Committee that all these groups are trying to bridge the gap between the law and practice. In that context, some of the anomalies relating to agricultural land have also come up. So, while agreeing with you, we feel that the law itself plays a role in social change. It is not the only thing, but the law has to lead because the law represents the vision of the society. It is like our Constitution. We have to go a long way in achieving the goals which have been embodied in our Constitution. We have to go a long way before these goals become a reality for every human being in India. We stand proudly in the international forums and say, "Look at our Constitution. We adopted it some fifty years ago. Even at that time, it was so progressive." Similarly, we need to be proud of our laws because they show us the way. Then, we move forward to bridge the gap.

Your second question is, as to why we are looking at agricultural land alone. We agree with you that there should be equality of all properties. We have identified two sources of inequality. One is clause 4(2) which is about agricultural land, and the other is the *mitakshara* joint family system. We are completely in agreement with you that there should be full equality. So, these are the two main constraints to achieve that.

JUSTICE (RETD.) N.Y. HANUMANTHAPPA: Are you in favour of agricultural land or land value? Assuming you are getting the land, then, why are you not using the words 'land value'? If there is 100 acres of land and there are two children, then, you should say that the daughter should be entitled for 50 acres of land or its value.

PROF. BINA AGARWAL: That is understood.

JUSTICE (RETD.) N.Y. HANUMANTHAPPA: But the reality is different. Theoretically it is one way and practically it is something else. We have experienced it because we come from the rural areas of the country. What happens there is this. If there are male and female members in a family, the female members will not take on their hands the job of managing agriculture. (Contd. by 1L)

kqg/1 L/12.50/PPG/16.2.05

JUSTICE (RETD.) N.Y. HANUMANTHAPPA (contd.): Invariably, some other person is employed. As far as the poorer sections are concerned, they are still in land cultivation. As far as agricultural labour is concerned, women do most of the work but the land is cultivated by men. After all, we have to produce the product. That is why, what we are suggesting to you is, in addition to land, you should say, "or its value."

PROF. BINA AGARWAL: I would like to correct the perception that men are doing most of the farming. For the agricultural operation, it is true because of social barrier. Women don't do ploughing.

I have travelled to every State in the poorest parts of the country, because I am basically working in the rural areas. If you look at the reality, women are doing sowing, transplantation, weeding, harvesting, etc. Harvesting is done by both, men and women. Irrigation is done by them. But men do the ploughing. A major proportion of total labour is done by women.

Secondly, if a woman inherits, or anybody who inherits in the share of any immovable property, they can't physically take the possession of that. Suppose, the son has a few acres, if the persons who are benefiting are more, then all the rest would get the value of the land.

JUSTICE (RETD.) N.Y. HANUMANTHAPPA: "Women are better positioned. So, land or its value or vice versa." You can use these words. That means, in case a brother doesn't want to take the land, she can take the entire land and start cultivating.

PROF. BINA AGARWAL: That is already implicit in all forms of immovable properties. Sometimes the share, and sometimes the value. I have talked to women in the rural areas and sometimes, women inherit land and...

SHRI RAASHID ALVI: The lady may have a son and he can cultivate and look after the land. The land must be given, of course.

PROF. BINA AGARWAL: Sometimes, women get the share of the harvest. I met a woman and she said, "I own only two coconut trees. Every year, my brother gives me the value of it." So, the lady should be given an option. That is already there. Suppose, you have only 2 acres of land; and five brothers and no sister. Even they have to find some way of sharing that. The daughter may inherit the land, but her brother can cultivate it and give that value. That would be the share of the harvest.

DR. RADHAKANT NAYAK: Even otherwise, land gives a status to the person who owns it in the rural areas. The land is a living organism to the family. It binds the family together. You can argue from any side. But we have to come to a conclusion.

SHRI RAASHID ALVI: The male member always creates problems.

JUSTICE (RETD.) N.Y. HANUMANTHAPPA: Land issue is very sentimental in rural areas. Suppose, there is a hundred acres of land. A daughter gets fifty acres. The daughter wants to alienate it. So, we say, the preference should be given to the brother in case she wants to alienate it. He should be preferred before any other party. In most of the tenurial laws, this is the condition. The first preference is to the family members.

PROF. BINA AGARWAL: Sir, my understanding is that the right of pre-emption is already recognised. Under the laws of tenure, landholdings under the Land Reforms can't be sub-divided below a certain point. If there are more claimants, there is already a clause built in. Even if you don't bring in daughters, the right of pre-emption is already there and we have no problems on this.

CHAIRMAN: I would like to conclude by raising certain points. You mentioned about allowing claim for equal share to married daughters before the commencement of law. If we go by that, and if we remove the entire proviso, what will be the situation?

A daughter married before 20 years, who has already got her श्रीधन and got value of property share in a joint family, you are allowing her again to claim her share. She would say, “I have got a right from 2005 onwards.” Therefore, you have to give a share in the properties presently available.

PROF. BINA AGARWAL: Sir, gifts could be given by parents to both, son and daughter, before marriage.

CHAIRMAN: We are prohibiting dowry under the law. In every marriage, daughters are given, more or less, equal share of the property value. Things would be given in cash or kind. In some villages, there is a custom that they give land itself. In our own village also this practice is there. We give land share in the public marriage function itself. There are some such conventions. If such is the situation, what will happen? You will open a Pandora’s box. The entire family will go to the court. The daughter, who is now a wife of husband, her husband would say, “Go and demand money or property.” If such situations arise, how would we overcome?

PROF. BINA AGARWAL: Sir, our understanding of the social reality is, in some places of Andhra Pradesh, where the laws have been amended and daughters have been brought in as coparceners, there too the dowry practice is still going on, irrespective of laws. Dowry is a social evil, but it has not been affected by laws. It is also a fact that many daughters don’t get even a dowry. Suppose you are to come up with the clause as it is, we are to exclude married daughters. But the same issue can arise in future. Daughters who are unmarried will claim a share and they might get married too. In the social situation today, dowry is demanded. (Followed by 1m)

Kls/lm-1.00/PPG-16.2.2005

CHAIRMAN: This law will give strength to the girl to demand dowry. That is the effect of this law.

PROF. BINA AGARWAL: But social practice, we find..

CHAIRMAN: That may be. The effect is, you have got a right on the immovable property, you have got a right on ancestral property. Then what is the need for dowry? This is a direct move towards prohibition of dowry.

PROF. BINA AGARWAL: You are right. In some cases, the daughters would have been given dowry. But there are many cases where they have not got dowry. There is no easy way to find an answer to this.

CHAIRMAN: In the same way, if there are four daughters and one is already married and three daughters are unmarried, this Act would help the three daughters and not the one daughter who has gone. We have to take a holistic view. This law is being enacted for the whole of India. The law should not create more problems within the families.

PROF. BINA AGARWAL: Your point is very valid that there could be some families where the daughters are already married and a daughter has been given gifts and all such sorts of things. We would like to some kind of a solution to the total blanket exclusion of married daughters. Our plea is that at the moment, there is blanket exclusion. If some clause needs to be put in, we have not thought in detail about it. If that right cannot be given to the already married daughters, then essentially provision should be made for married daughters.

JUSTICE (RETD) N.Y. HANUMANTHAPPA: The intention is to make it prospective. Let there be some sort of understanding between the brothers, sisters, and also parents. You are asking the Parliament for restrictions. That is not the intention. There will not be a limit for litigations and all that. The idea is to see daughters and sons to live happily without litigation. That is why it is from today onwards. That should be the understanding and that is how it is intended. Suppose, there are two daughters; one readily agrees that when I got married, I got something, but another daughter may like to have a little share in the property again.

PROF. BINA AGARWAL: Already in the current Bill, you are giving all daughters share in dwelling house. There you recognise it. There you are not differentiating between a married and unmarried daughter. It is moving in that direction.

CHAIRMAN: Proviso is given, that will come into effect to the subsequent section at the first stage itself. They are taken away from the scene. When the proviso is given in the first operative part, then subsequent section will say it, 'everywhere'. For example, I have got another doubt. You see sub-section 3. It says that the share of the pre-deceased son or a pre-deceased daughter, as they would have got had they been alive at the time of partition, shall be allotted to the surviving child of such pre-deceased son or of such pre-deceased daughter, as the case may be.

Here pre-deceased, whether it is married or not. Here if the daughter is married in between, that is, from the date of this Bill and the date of the proclamation, when it comes into effect, the daughter may be married, whether their children cannot get it or they will get it, according to this clause. I will put it again,. It says, the share of the pre-deceased son or a pre-deceased daughter, as they would have got had they been alive at the time of partition, shall be allotted to the surviving child of such pre-deceased son or of such pre-deceased daughter, as the case may be.

Here the pre-deceased daughter, it is from the date of the Act coming into force. But the law is already before the Parliament. In between if there is a married daughter going to lose, their family is also going to lose that right.

MS. SHRUTI PANDEY: Sir, it is to be from the date of the Act. There are certain principles of law. The right will accrue from the date of the Act.

CHAIRMAN: Then referring to married daughter, do you want to give any exemption if during the marriage some property is given?

MS. SHRUTI PANDEY: In the present system if a *karta* sells property for the wedding of the daughter, in that case, if the family proves, maybe, the married daughter should not get share in the ancestral property. In many cases no dowry is given, there the married daughters should have share. In case only where some ancestral property has been disposed of for the marriage of a daughter, then she should not get her share.

JUSTICE (RETD) N.Y. HANUMANTHAPPA: It obliterates of all the liabilities of the daughter before the commencement of this Act, as far as rights are concerned subsequent to the enactment of this Act. As the hon. Chairman pointed out to you clause 3(b), you are conferring a right on the already married daughter who has left the house.

(Contd. 1N)

SSS/1N/1.10/PPJ/16.2.2005

JUSTICE (RETD.) N.Y. HANUMANTHAPPA (CONTD.): Because at one stage we say it is a prospective. If you want to give effect to 3(b) you must go back to 2004, earlier to this act. How can it be?

CHAIRMAN: We will discuss it. Another thing we would like to clarify. They have given the date of Tamil Nadu Act only like this, "married daughter". That is the word they have used. The cut off date they have mentioned. Here the date is from where the Act is going to be enforced. Now in clause 4, "pious obligation" is the main part. You were very hesitant when you were helped by your friend also. Yes, we can also do the same. We can also clear the debt. Why don't we be bold enough to say that we are equal, we are ready to do the obligation. In my opinion in all the families, when there are no sons, the daughters are doing it. You need not hesitate about it. Will you hesitate to say that we want to see that the 'pious obligation' part should not be taken away? Some of the Members have this feeling. We can discuss afterwards. If you take away the 'pious obligation', it gives a death knell for the Hindu families. Are you ready to take that pious obligation along with you as a daughter?

PROF. BINA AGARWAL: We want to be equal in religious sense and in economic sense.

CHAIRMAN: Why don't you want it?

PROF. BINA AGARWAL: We want to be equal in both cases and if a married daughter or a daughter does not want to take the pious obligation, she can forego her share. There is always a possibility. Also a man can do that. If sons want to take away pious obligation, can we forego?

CHAIRMAN: No. The first charge is that the head of the family, the *Karta* of the family has got the obligations to do it. Widow, mother and everybody have to look after it. He has to borrow money in the name of the property. When the partition is there all the people have to share the liability also.

MS. SHRUTI PANDEY: The pious obligation is, the son to the extent he took is responsible for the obligations of the father because he took from the father.

CHAIRMAN: He created the debt. The son has to inherit the debt. Hindu property rights lives in spirituality. The property is owned by a family for their livelihood. Even the house is made as a worship place. Rooms are made as a worship place. The entire family's heritage is there. This includes the liabilities also. It is only that there will not be any sex determination.

MS. SHRUTI PANDEY: If you are planning to go along *Mitakshara* coparcenars, if you want to make daughters coparcenars, what about the widow?

CHAIRMAN: We will find out a way. In clause 1, it says, "the woman has children, then the husband and the children get equal shares." But if the woman does not have any children then the property devolves differently. Property goes back to the parents. Property goes back to the husband. When the individual property goes back to the husband, we discussed this difference and we felt that it was important to continue with the difference because given the social reality that dowry does exist, it is important that if the parents had given quite a lot at the time of marriage then that property should go back to them after her death, if she has no children. If she has children it devolves equaily to the children and the husband.

CHAIRMAN: If you allow the pious obligation, if you rectify the mistake for the perfect share for the widower and the widow, then *Mitakshara* family can exist. No problem.

PROF. BINA AGARWAL: Then there are other families. Families can will it away. So there are difficulties there.

CHAIRMAN: Any male member can will away his own share, whatever may be the law. You cannot say that a man cannot will any property or cannot part away with the property. He has got the right to limited share which is available from his share, not from the entire family. I feel you should work out on it. We want to create another problem among the Hindu society. We can go in the same way as Pandit Jawaharlal Nehru started the revolution of the Hindu system. We can take advantage of the Bill and we can think about the widow's right and also we can think about equal participation of male and female in the pious obligation part and we can allow the *Mitakshara* family to live as it is. We need not say that we are abolishing *Mitakshara*. I feel if you allow pious obligation to continue and the widow's right is given in full share then, there is no problem.

MS. SHRUTI PANDEY: Sir, I think in sub-section 4 what it does is, it is doing away with pious obligation except for the limited time period.

PROF. BINA AGARWAL: Sir, there are actually lawyers on inequality in *Mitakshara*. There are several other features. It is very male centred. It gives a lot of privileges to male members. We just feel that it is a very archaic system. Nowhere in the world such a system exists. Best option would be to abolish. If there is no consensus on that….

CHAIRMAN: When you say it has to be abolished it has got its own consequences.

PROF. BINA AGARWAL: What we can say is that you already know our first best option but the second best option would be the direction in which you are talking. First best option is abolishing *Mitakshara* altogether. The second best option is to make sure that the widow does not lose out. The issue of pious obligation does not rise for anybody, whether he is male or female.

CHAIRMAN: Thank you, very much for your participation. Your written submissions should reach the Committee within a week or so.

PROF. BINA AGARWAL: Sir, we need two weeks time to submit the written submissions to the Committee. Thank you.

(The witnesses then withdrew)

(Followed by 1O)

NBR/GS/1O/1.20.

Witness:

Shri T.K. Viswanathan, Secretary, Legislative Department.

CHAIRMAN: I welcome you Mr. Viswanathan. The Committee is considering the Andhra Pradesh Legislative Council Bill, 2004. Having the second chamber means having a bicameral system. Many of the States have abolished the bicameral arrangement and only certain States are continuing with that. The main contention is that there will be a lot of cost bearing on the Assembly Budget and other things. Therefore, we would like to know in which way it — having Legislative Council—would help for the progress of the democracy and in Andhra Pradesh. How the Budgetary demands for the new or revival of the existing Legislative Council are going to be met and how another House will not stand in the way of progress of the State.

So, I call Mr. Viswanathan to make his presentation on this Bill.

SHRI T.K. VISWANATHAN: Thank you Mr. Chairman and hon. Members of the Committee. The Bill before the Committee is for creation of Legislative Council in Andhra Pradesh. As you are aware, to begin with, we had Legislative Councils in the States of Bihar, Maharashtra, Karnataka, Uttar Pradesh, West Bengal, Punjab, Andhra Pradesh and Tamil Nadu and one was created for Madhya Pradesh, but it was never brought into force. Later, the Legislative Councils of West Bengal, Andhra Pradesh and Tamil Nadu were abolished. As you are all aware under Article 169 of the Constitution, Parliament may make law on the basis of proposals received from the concerned State Governments for abolition/creation of Legislative Councils in their States on the basis of a resolution passed by a majority of the total membership of the Assembly and by a majority of not less than two-thirds of the members present and voting for creation of the Legislative Council. The Legislative Councils were abolished in West Bengal in 1969, in Punjab in 1970, in Andhra Pradesh in 1985, in Tamil Nadu in 1986. Subsequently, in the year 1990, the A.P. Legislative Assembly passed a Resolution for reviving its Legislative Council. A Bill was brought before Parliament in the 9th Lok Sabha and it was also introduced. The Rajya Sabha also passed the Bill. But, with the dissolution of the 9th Lok Sabha, the Bill also lapsed. In 1996, the then new Government of Andhra Pradesh did not pursue and hence the resolution was not processed further. The present state of affairs is like this. We have received a Resolution from the Government of Andhra Pradesh for the revival of the same proposal for creation of the Legislative Council in Andhra Pradesh. So, we have brought forward this Bill.

With regard to having Legislative Council or not having Legislative Council, we have two views. Even in the Constituent Assembly debate, the opinion was sharply divided. One opinion was that there is a need for having a second chamber in the States. The other opinion was that it is an unnecessary burden on the public exchequer. There are arguments for and against creation of the Legislative Council. First it was felt that the second chamber is necessary for adequate representation of certain sections of the society not sufficiently represented in the Legislative Assembly. This also helps to ventilate the views and interests of the sections which are not represented in the Lower House and enable the people to express their concern in another public forum. The other argument is that the second chamber will work as a revised chamber. This is a kind of safeguard. Thirdly, there is more time for public debate on measures which are brought before the House if there are two Houses instead of one. It is also thought that if we have another House, it can act as check or advisor or give advice. There is also another argument which says that a second chamber would help in easing the pressure of time on the lower House in as much as important but comparatively non-controversial matters could be initiated in the upper House and after full discussion in the upper House, the matters could be taken to the lower House. After full discussion in the upper House, the lower House would not require much time to dispose of the matter. Further, when the lower House is fully preoccupied otherwise, the time of the upper House can be utilised for discussion of urgent matters for which the lower House is not able to find time. The other argument is that they are not directly elected as a Member of the Legislative Assembly. They are elected by various other constituencies like Teachers Constituencies, Graduate Constituencies, MLAs, etc. The other argument is that it is drain on the public exchequer to have another House. If you have another House, you have to spend a lot of money and it is waste. Thirdly, it is widely felt that the second chamber is used to delay Bills. With the net result, it will add no result. There are Graduate Constituencies and Teacher Constituencies which many of them feel is anarchic. Earlier, it was felt that there was a need to have teacher or Graduate Constituencies. Now, in the present scenario, there is no need to have such a mechanism. There is no justification now to continue that. Even in the Constituent Assembly, eminent people like Shri K.K. Shah were against the second chamber. He said that it makes the Lower House less autonomous and Mr. Shah said that it is another institution to waste the public money. Dr. Ambedkar, when he piloted this Article said that it is purely an experimental measure. We have not, by the Draft Constitution, given the second Chamber, a permanent place, we have not made it a permanent place, we have not made it a permanent part of our Constitution and leave it to Parliament to take a decision in the matter. In those days it was felt that it was a drain of the public exchequer. But, in modern times, the common man has to go to court to get his concern heard. So, one needs more and more public fora like the Legislative Council where he can voice and the representatives can take matters of public importance/interest to the notice of the Government. We feel that it justifies the existence of the second chamber. We feel that the second chamber may be necessary as far as unity throughout the country is concerned. Right now, there is no unity. We have the Legislative Councils in five States — Bihar, Maharashtra, Karnataka, Uttar Pradesh — and States depending upon the party position ask for abolition or creation of Legislative Councils. So, there is no consistency in the approach. Now, it is before the Committee. Sir, even the Sarkaria Commission had made some observation on this. It observed that whenever there is a demand for Council, and where the State Legislature passes resolution, it should be placed before Parliament and that should be voted upon and thereafter the Parliament should pursue.

(Contd. by "1P")

USY/1P/01.30

SHRI T.K. VISWANATHAN (CONTD.): So, these are some of the larger issues. We feel the Second Chamber is necessary. So, we forward this Bill. Now, it is before the Committee.

DR. RADHAKANT NAYAK: There is a lot of literature available on this. But my feeling is, why do you want to over-burden this poor country. In any case, the Second Chamber does not have anything to do in the case of Money Bills. In England, they are also going to abolish the House of Lords. Don't you think it is opportune time that we should do away with this institution?

SHRI T.K. VISWANATHAN: Sir, I beg to differ. The common man does not have access to power. He is driven to the courts because his voice is not heard. I don't think it is wastage of money. Debates take place on matters of public importance. So, the Second Chamber will go on addressing that inadequacy of addressing common concern of the common man. Access to courts is very costly. But MPs and MLAs are easily accessible to the common man. As far as the legislative role is concerned, the role of the Second Chamber cannot be minimised. Bills can always be introduced in the Second Chamber. The Private Members Bills always lead to some action on the part of the Government, sooner or later. So, this is one of the pressure points used to elicit public opinion.

JUSTICE (RETD.) N.Y. HANUMANTHAPPA: If you drop the Second Chamber, you may not have eminent personalities, the men of letter, the men of knowledge in legislature because a doctor, a scientist, a judge may not like to face the electorate. That is why the framers of our Constitution had thought of bicameral legislature. So, the bicameral system should be there.

CHAIRMAN: When you debate on different forums, a lot of ideas come out. Okay, thank you very much. You can join for lunch with us.

(The witnesses then withdrew and the Committee adjourned for lunch)

PK/1Q/2.20

(The Committee re-assembled after lunch)

LIST OF WITNESS:

Ms. Charmaine Rodrigues, Commonwealth Human Rights Institute (CHRI)

CHAIRMAN: Good afternoon, Ms. Rodrigues. We are happy to have your presentation. Already you have made your submissions. At that time, we had raised some queries. Are you in a position to reply those queries now?

MS. CHARMAINE RODRIGUES: Yes, Sir. We are ready for that.

(Followed by 1R)

PB/1R/2.30

CHAIRMAN: The main issue that we had raised the other day was that we have to strengthen the Office of the Commissioner who is to be selected by a collegium of the topmost people of Indian Administration, i.e., the Prime Minister of India, the Leader of the Opposition and the Chief Justice of India. If such is the position, we wanted you to have a comparative study of the laws of other countries in this regard where the similar type of post is occupied. The Committee wanted to know what types of powers the Commissioners are having in those countries and what is the qualification of the Commissioner that is stipulated in their enactments, and how much power they are having. In the same way, we wanted to know whether they are having a quasi-judicial power of even convicting the violator and put him in the prison or their power is only confined to the routine function of asking the violator to pay the fine for a particular violation. Because you know that at the second appeal stage, there is already an appeal. That appellate authority should also have some powers so that it can ask the concerned officer to give the information immediately when there is a demand for it, and he should abide by the regulations which are made by this particular Bill. If he delays or destroys or even avoids giving the required information, then the appellate authority should be in a position to tell that there is an office which sees that something is taking place and it is not just giving certain explanation. We even suggested to you that it should be very much like the Supreme Court where the order of the Supreme

Court is abided by the entire country. It is provided in the Indian Constitution. Such should be the position of the Commissioner. However, when we look at the Bill, we find that very big words are used there, but it is not supported by that type of a very strong office. That is why we wanted to collect information by having a comparative study to show that the Commissioners have got the powers to see that the information is provided at an appropriate time and in a proper manner so that he is able to discharge his duties efficiently.

The second thing is regarding penal provision. The Committee wanted to know whether a penal provision of Rs. 250 or so is sufficient, or, we can increase it to some extent. And, if we want to go in for imprisonment or for any such thing, whether the same forum should have the right and powers for it or whether it should be done by regular judiciary by referring the matter to the Magistrate. If you want that the present forum itself should be strengthened with that power, then there should be a judicial member. Only then the courts will accept it. Therefore, it should be a quasi-judicial tribunal. The Committee would like to know whether that can be a possibility at this juncture. Then, as I have already mentioned, the Committee wanted to have your views regarding the qualifications of the Commissioner. In other countries, what types of qualifications are required for the appointment of a Commissioner?

The third point is regarding the Cabinet papers. You want that every information should be revealed. We want to know from you whether it is possible in a democratic country which is only 58 years old to reveal the entire Cabinet note to the public. Can we expect it in our country? These are the few points which we had raised during our last sitting. You can note down these points and reply to them.

DR. P.C. ALEXANDER: I am sorry, I was not here in the morning. At the last session of the Committee which I attended, I heard you raising an objection to 8(i) which is regarding Cabinet papers. Here it is said, "the Cabinet papers, including records of deliberations of the Council of Ministers, Secretaries and other officers." You have an objection to it in spite of the fact that there is a proviso. The proviso says, "Provided that the decisions of the Council of Ministers, the reasons thereof, and the material on the basis of which the decisions were taken, shall be made public after the decision has been taken, and the matter is complete, or over." What exactly is your objection in giving this exemption for Cabinet papers with this proviso? Once a decision is taken, the decision and the reasons will no longer be considered secret, but be made available. But before a decision is taken, the Cabinet papers cannot be taken out of the list of the confidential or secret papers. For your information, all papers which go to the Cabinet are classified as secret. And, secondly, it is not that a decision is made on every Cabinet paper. There are many cases where the papers go to the Cabinet. And, if some points are raised at a time when the Cabinet considers them, the Ministry is asked to come back with an answer to those points, and then the matter is again discussed. Sometimes, there are long delays between the first meeting of the Cabinet when an issue was discussed and the final decision taken. But obviously, public cannot be given copies of papers relating to a number of discussions spread over several sessions of the Cabinet. Public are interested only in the decision of the Council of Ministers and also the reasons why that particular decision has been taken, either accepting it or rejecting it. I really do not understand your problem.

MS. CHARMAINE RODRIGUES: Thank you very much. Sir, we will not take your questions in the orders they were raised. I think, it might be useful to take the Cabinet discussion first and then go back to the general discussion about the strengthening of the Act. In relation to the Cabinet provision, we have done some more research because we know that this was going to be a key issue. The discussion we were having in relation to that clause is in two respects. The first is that if you look at the initial clause in 8(i), it means not only the Cabinet papers, but the Cabinet papers including records of deliberations of the Council of Ministers, Secretaries and other officers. The initial problem is with the birth of that phrase because the first issue is as to what a Cabinet paper means and how much information could be captured by that. There is no definition in the Act, at the moment, as to what will constitute a Cabinet paper, and that means the perpetual information, the background information, if contained in the Cabinet paper, could be exempt even if it is not sensitive and even it was previously included in some other document. In that, as I have said, the second part of that clause which is very, very broad includes the records of deliberations not only of the Council of Ministers, but records of deliberations of Secretaries and other officers. (Contd. by 1s)

1S/2.40/SKC

MS. CHARMAINE RODRIGUES (CONTD.): 'And other officers' is also not a definite term; they can extend it to any level or rank in the public department. This could, therefore, be interpreted in any way, particularly, when no definitions are in place. It includes almost every record of discussion made within a Government department. We would submit that this provision is much too broad for disclosure to public service and to make such exemptions is harmful to India's interests. Well, it would be alright if the exemptions are granted in genuine cases where release of information could actually harm India.

DR. P. C. ALEXANDER: You don't accept that the proviso given here takes care of the concern.

MS. CHARMAINE RODRIGUES: Sir, the proviso does not refer, in definite terms, to the original Cabinet papers. What we would get is the final decision of the Council of Ministers, and the reasons thereof. That is not enough. That does not necessarily mean the original Cabinet papers; it just means the decision of the Cabinet. In the real sense, we may not be assured of getting the original papers. All we may get is a cut-down summary, not what has happened in the Cabinet and the whole background of the decision. Howsoever definite the papers might be, they might be taken to have been exempted because they were at one stage submitted to the Cabinet. If, as the clause says, the 'Cabinet papers' are exempted from disclosure, then that would mean, that under this clause, they would be protected forever unless they would have happened to be released as the material on the basis of which the decision was taken.

SHRI VENKATESH NAYAK: Sir, to illustrate that with an example, I was involved, as a very small member, in an effort to get the Land Acquisition Act of this country amended in order to include the rehabilitation and resettlement provisions of development projects. The National Human Rights Commission put its weight behind it and referred the matter to the Ministry of Rural Development. It is contained in the Report of the National Human Rights Commission that the draft Bill, which was prepared by the Ministry of Water Resources, has not been shared with the National Human Rights Commission. That is the level of secrecy being maintained. This is, in fact, recorded on the Report of the National Human Rights Commission!

If 'records' is taken for exemption along with the Cabinet papers, it may include important documents of laws or proposed legislation; and if the citizen who has a right to know about it is not provided with the information, then definitely, he would be in an adverse situation. So, the term 'Cabinet papers' as it is mentioned here, does not mean just Cabinet papers. It is my humble submission that it includes a whole range of documents starting from the uppermost level of Government official to possibly the Upper Division Clerks or the Lower Division Clerks. And all these are exempted.

Now, as per the clause, all records are being exempted from disclosure, and that is a cause for concern to the civil society organizations. Here I would like to bring to your kind notice one of the provisions in Sweden, where it says that the agenda for meetings, or committees of Ministers have to be made public one day before the meetings. That kind of provision is not made here. Here, it says that Cabinet papers also include the agenda of the Cabinet, and they cannot be made public. So, what the public gets is readymade decisions. Decisions are taken in the name of the people because people have given the mandate to their leaders. The people do not have the right to know what the Cabinet is discussing! Don't you think this condition is quite contrary to the whole principle behind the Indian citizen's right to know and the concept of democracy?

DR. P. C. ALEXANDER: May I explain to you, for your kind information, what is meant by a Cabinet paper? Probably, that would stop further questions. There is no such thing as 'Cabinet papers'. There is only a 'Note' for the Cabinet, and that is a self-contained note. It first presents the proposal. It contains the views of the Ministry that is proposing it. It also contains the views of the other concerned ministries, and a gist of the reasons as to why they have taken a particular view for or against the proposal. Finally, it contains an analysis of how the views of the various ministries have been taken into account in making the final recommendation. The last paragraph consists of points of decision, a, b, c, d... and so on, and they are summed up so that at one glance you know what it contains. That is a Cabinet Note or a Note for Cabinet.

A Cabinet paper may sometimes cover five to six ministries. It consists of the Ministry from where the proposal has originated. Then, since financial implications are an essential feature of any major proposal, the Ministry of Finance is involved. The Home Ministry is involved to look into the security concerns. Thus, so many ministries are involved. Each Ministry prepares its own notes and they will be sending one note explaining why they have supported or opposed the proposal. So, when the final decision is taken, you will be informed about the Cabinet Note and the decision taken by the Cabinet. It will not be a one-line sentence saying that it was approved by the Cabinet or rejected by the Cabinet, or something like that. It will try to satisfy the request that has been made. But if you say that every single note and every Ministry's note, which has gone into the preparation of the Cabinet Note as well as the final Note of the Cabinet, should be made public, then that would create problems.

DR. RADHAKANT NAYAK: There is also a distinction in some cases. Sometimes, it is called a Cabinet Note and sometimes, a Cabinet Memorandum.

MS. CHARMAINE RODRIGUES: In that case, it is interesting to know that while there is a single Cabinet Note, there are many, many papers produced which could be classified as Cabinet papers. And that is our concern, because it has a definition that is, colloquially speaking, so broad. For instance, in Germany many things are classified as Cabinet papers. I actually met a Member of Parliament there who said she was deeply concerned about exemptions being granted to 'Cabinet papers' even at the preliminary stage. She said that every paper that had been taken inside the Cabinet room was called a Cabinet paper and the papers were simply wheeled out on a trolley by people there; nobody was allowed to have a look at any paper as they were said to be covered by the exemption. Since they had been taken inside the Cabinet, they were granted exemption!

Since there is no clear-cut definition at the moment, it could have that breadth of interpretation; everything is covered under the exemption. It doesn't distinguish the Cabinet Note as such from the initial documents submitted along with the Note. If one particular Ministry produces ten documents that support a Cabinet Note, some of them could be background papers, some of them could be factual details, some could be consultative in nature, and they might contain some very genuine information which is sensitive. And that brings us to the question as to why they were being withheld. One key issue, though, which could be considered, is the need to tighten the provision to protect only against harm that could be caused by premature disclosure of Cabinet documents. That would be preferable.

DR. P. C. ALEXANDER: As things stand today, every paper going to the Cabinet has 'Secret' written on it. Nobody would leak out, the documents of say, a land acquisition case. This new proviso will take care of that.

MS. CHARMAINE RODRIGUES: Then, perhaps, the proviso needs to be reworded to reflect the actual things. At the moment, there is no such distinction and 'Cabinet papers' is a very broad term. The exemption includes the decisions and the material on the basis of which the decisions were taken. Now, Cabinet papers could be interpreted differently based on the material on which the decision was made. If I have ten notes from the Ministry and I send only one note to the Cabinet, then that one note could be released under this proviso. But the ten notes still resting back in my ministry, which were prepared as Cabinet papers would still invoke the exemption, on the basis of which the decisions were made.

DR. P. C. ALEXANDER: We have taken note of your concern.

MS. CHARMAINE RODRIGUES: Sir, the clause actually focussed on the Cabinet papers. The remaining parts of that clause are deeply concerning because they allow considerable information at the Secretary and other officers' level also to be withheld. Any other officer, such as the Secretary and other officers, could also avail themselves of this exemption. This is a very broad provision considering how this bureaucracy functions. How many decisions are made at the lower levels, which involve spending of public moneys in particular? (Contd. by 1T)

KSK/2.50/1TPPG 16-2-2005

MS. CHARMAINE RODRIGUES (CONTD.): So, we would strongly urge to narrow that clause which only covers most sensitive information about decisions. In the context of strengthening penalties, before we start our discussion, I would like to draw your attention to a comparative table of such laws in different Commonwealth countries. It shows what Commonwealth countries have done. Out of 53 countries, it is a study of only 10 countries. If look at this document, a number of countries in the Commonwealth have penalty provisions, and except England, they have provisions of imprisonment. If you look at the submission, we have made our submission on the Bill which is a comparative submission. We have picked up a number of clauses from other countries. The clauses, which we are suggesting, are based on these clauses. One provision, which is very clear and that is there in all the countries having penalty provision, is the penalty for willful non-compliance, destroying the document, falsifying the information, etc. These are considered to be very serious crimes, always punishable by fine and imprisonment and only U.K. does not allow imprisonment. So, that is one of the questions that you asked about other countries allowing imprisonment. Most of the countries allow summary conviction if a penalty needs to be imposed. In that context, we must note that the penalty provisions regarding unreasonable delay are based on laws in Maharashtra, Delhi and Karnataka and they only allow for fine and imprisonment sentence for willful non-compliance.

SHRI VENKATESH NAYAK: Sir, I need not remind hon. Members that the Indian Constitution draws inspiration from Irish Constitution in respect of Directive Principles of State Policy. Ireland has a very important Information Act. It also provides for Information Commissioner. Now, provisions of penalty are there in this law. It says, "(7) A person who fails or refuses to comply with a requirement under this section or who hinders or obstructs the Commissioner in the performance of his or her functions under this section shall be guilty of an offence and shall be liable on summary conviction to a fine not exceeding ₹1,500 or to imprisonment for a term not exceeding 6 months or both." Our submission is that in most countries, the concept of heavy fines and prison terms is used as a deterrent against non-compliance. We think that this provision should be seriously looked at to improve penalty provisions.

DR. P.C. ALEXANDER: In Australia, there is no provision for penalty.

MS. CHARMAINE RODRIGUES: Unfortunately, no. It is a major flaw in the Australian Act, but it has been reviewed and found to be wanting in this area. There was a Commission set up in 1995. If you see some of the recent Acts of Commonwealth countries, for example, U.K. Act also includes fines for these kinds of penalties. We have also asked that Information Commissioner should be given additional power. If he instructs to do something and that is not complied with, that should be termed as contempt of court.

SHRI VENKATESH NAYAK: Sir, I would like to give the example of Russia. There, the Manager and other staff of Government organisations, which are responsible for illegal access to records, are liable under the criminal, civil and administrative law. It is not as if somebody can get away by denying someone his right to information. We will talk about the powers of the Information Commissioner at a later stage.

DR. P.C. ALEXANDER: Every witness, who appeared before us, has pleaded for strengthening the penalty tools. We have taken note of this aspect.

MS. CHARMAINE RODRIGUES: Sir, the Canadian law, which was written 20 years ago, does have penalty provisions. According to this law, any person, who obstructs Information Commissioner in performing his/her duties, is guilty of an offence and liable for summary conviction to a fine. Any person liable for destroying, falsifying the records, concealing a record, or directing the other person to do that, is liable to imprisonment up to two years or fine. That is a major penalty provision which is there for 20 years or more. They actually have an Information Commissioner. Australia does not have an Information Commissioner at the Federal level. In that context, I would draw the attention of the Committee to one additional style of penalty which we are proposing. This style, I think, may be controversial in terms of individual bureaucrats. That is the idea of departmental penalty. We have spoken to some people in the bureaucracy, and there, people are concerned that personal penalty might be too harsh. If there are personal penalties, we would urge you to consider departmental penalties. We are asking for additional departmental penalty which can help at implementation stage to really enforce department to take lead on this rather than just waiting for this to happen. In the last, the question was about strengthening the Information Commissioner. If you look at our written submission, we have tried to suggest some ways, because we feel that there are, currently, loopholes in the law, which need to be tightened. Some more provisions should be added. There are some problems, biggest ones being in clauses 12, 7 and 8. What we understand is that Information Commissioner should be strong, be able to do his or her job autonomously and with authority. But, at the moment, clause 12(7) says, "The headquarters of the Commission shall be at Delhi and the Commission may, with the previous approval of the Central Government, establish offices at other places in India." That means, that could turn into a political issue. (continued by 1U)

GSP/3.00/1 U/PPG/16-02-2005

MS. CHARMAINE RODRIGUES (CONTD.): If they say that there is a need, and, so long as the Budget allows them to set up an office, they should be able to do that wherever it is needed most.

The bigger issue is Section 12(8) according to which the Deputy Information Commissioner shall perform their functions within such areas as may be specified by the Central Government. This could cause huge problems as the Information Commissioner is an independent Commissioner and his deputy is actually working under the directions of the Central Government. The Information Commission itself needs to operate as one unit advocating justice and openness across the country. If the Information Commissioner is independent but his deputy is taking directions from the Central Government, you can easily have a clash there. That is the real issue.

Other issue that we wanted to raise is Section 12(5) where perhaps there must have been lot of concerns. The key point as far as Section 12(5) is concerned is that at the time the Information Commissioner takes oath, he should not be associated with any political party, or, he should not be running a business of profit. Whether at the time of selection, all this was there or not, it should not be an issue because otherwise anyone with a job can never be considered. For being eligible, one needs to be sitting and doing nothing. So, I think it needs to be redrafted. At the time when you are Information Commissioner, you must not be an MP, member of the political party, or, have a business of profit, and, that is what should be there in the Act. Even otherwise, for handling this kind of job impartially and giving one's best, one should not be involved in other things requiring one's time and attention. In our submission, we have added some criteria because at the moment, it is not clear as to who the person should be. The ultimate objective should be that the person selected should be pro-transparency, and, pro-accountability. For example, in Canada, the Information Commissioner is an ex-Member of Parliament. He was a Member of Parliament, and, a Minister for twenty years, and, he is an excellent Information Commissioner. In England, the Deputy Information Commissioner is an ex-public servant. In Scotland, the Information Officer is actually ex-Head of an NGO, Friends of the Earth, and, he is also an excellent Commissioner. So, I mean you must allow people from all walks of life but the only thing is that they must have demonstrated commitment to accountability and transparency, and, they themselves must have a clean record, and, with no criminal charges.

SHRI VENKATESH NAYAK: Sir, regarding the requirement that a person chosen to the position of Information Commissioner, or, the Deputy Information Commissioner should not be connected with the political party, I would like to remind the hon. Committee that this is a provision which is part of the Civil Services Conduct Rules, and, no member of the Civil Service is allowed to be a member of any political party during his service. Therefore, this provision for not allowing the Information Commissioner to be a member of the political party should be retained, and, it should not be taken away from this Bill.

CHAIRMAN: I think a person can also act like a member even if he is not a member. You cannot prohibit him. It is the mental attitude that matters.

MS. CHARMAINE RODRIGUES: Today morning we were discussing this issue with somebody, and, I would like to submit that we should use words, 'demonstrated commitment to accountability'. Even if the candidate is a bureaucrat, there must had been number of activities, and, he would had demonstrated serious commitment to accountability and transparency. So, when someone is nominated, it should be a requirement that the details of previous job showing accountability and transparency must be considered. There may be an instance that a person, who has never performed this way, may say when he comes before the Committee, 'yes, yes, I am also pro-transparency and pro-openness'. I mean he should prove that during the previous tenure in his department, so many people were prosecuted for corruption by him, or, so. There should be some criteria regarding this.

SHRI VENKATESH NAYAK: It is not just a badge of the political party but also the thinking, that matters. In order to overcome these difficulties, USA and Canada have the Senate approvals for every appointment. That is not the situation that we follow in this country.

CHAIRMAN: The entire bureaucracy changes there along with the President. They feel that in a democratic country, the President should have the full control over the bureaucracy or the structure to implement whatever law he wants to make. Ultimately, the politics is the commitment for a particular policy or a programme. For proper implementation of any particular policy or programme, commitment is required. Proper implementation is not possible by simply having the membership, or, putting some political name and that is not the case. What is important is whether they have got the element for which the people have elected the concerned leader or not.

SHRI VENKATESH NAYAK: Sir, according to me, we should see that the process of appointment, or, the process of approval actually provides space for discussing everything that the nominated candidate has done in the past. Otherwise, it is just a list of names by some Government agency, which is, ultimately, approved by the highest department. For example, in the case of selection of the latest Secretary of the State in the United States, the whole discussion that happened in the Senate and the kind of questions that were raised by the hon. Members brought to light the kind of activities the candidate was going through. The space was created for assessing the past performance of the candidate who is being nominated. I am not saying that this should be started here in India as it is for the hon. Committee to look into the matter.

MS. CHARMAINE RODRIGUES: As far as list of criteria is concerned, as we have also suggested in our note, in addition to the requirements started at Section 12(5) and (6), the following criteria should be included in the law to ensure that Commissioners are committed to transparency and accountability. It should say that the person appointed as the Information Commissioner or a Deputy Information Commissioner shall be publicly regarded as a person of integrity and good repute who can make impartial judgements and have a demonstrated commitment to good governance, transparency and accountability. There may be someone who is associated with the political party but is also recognised by the public as someone who can make impartial judgements. (Contd. by 1w)

SK/1W/3.10/PPG/16.02.2005

MS. CHARMAINE RODRIGUES (Contd.): And, this means there is some system which operates as an independent body, which can employ their own staff independently and which don't need to specifically rely on the public service. That is also designed to bring in expertise that they need to be able to support from impartiality. We were also waiting for the Canadian Law recently to refresh our memories. There, salary of the Information Commissioner is equivalent to a Judge of the Federal Court, which, I think, is equivalent to a High Court Judge. And, the Information Commissioner has all the powers of Deputy Head of the Department. So, these powers are higher than what are given in the current provision. They told us that the Information Commissioner is not answerable either to a Ministry or a Government. He reports directly to the Parliament, and, interestingly, therefore, is subject to scrutiny by the Constitution Affairs Committee. The Information Commissioners Act also says that the staff of the Information Commissioner is not a servant of the Crown and the Information Commissioner has the power to determine the salary and the conditions of service of the staff.

CHAIRMAN: Do you want to make any other points?

MS. CHARMAINE RODRIGUES: I have got one more point. In Canada and U.K., they can also submit an additional report. If something very important comes to their attention, which they should brought to the notice of the Parliament, then, they can submit an additional report also.

SHRI VENKATESH NAYAK: There is one more power of the Information Commissioner which has left out here. The Irish Freedom of Information Act, 1997 gives power to the Commissioner to enter any premises occupied by a public body. This is an important power which the Commissioner should have. So, I would suggest that this important provision should be included within the powers of the Commissioner. It does not exist in the relevant clause. I have got one more point. This is related to what has been said earlier by my senior colleague. We have submitted before the hon. Committee not to exempt the entire clause of information or entire department from the purview of the Right to Information Act. There was a list of defence affairs which are mentioned in the schedule to the Right to Information Bill. Sir, I would like to put forward for your consideration the provisions in the Irish Act. It says that the records pertaining to the security of the State, the defence of the State are exempt. But they do not exempt the defence affairs in toto. I have brought the Act with me. Here, they say that the tactics, the strategy or the operations of the defence forces, in or outside the State, will be exempt. But, all other information wiil be put on record. I have also got this European Union case with me. I would like to leave that also. Thank you.

CHAIRMAN: Thank you very much. Mr. Arvind Kezriwal, you can just highlight the specific points because we have got only ten minutes. You can highlight whichever points you want to add. You were there yesterday and you are here today also. Therefore, you need not repeat what has already been told. You can highlight anything which you feel is important for us.

SHRI ARVIND KEZRIWAL: Sir, I would like to start with a small case study to highlight the importance of this Act because whenever we talk of right to information, an impression comes that people would talk for some very great information. Shrimati Triveni is a woman in East Delhi. She has got a ration card but she has not got any ration for so many years. Whenever she goes to the shop, either the shop is closed or she was told that ration was not available in stock. She filed an application asking as to how much ration has been issued against her name. The reply came after a month that 25 kg of wheat and 10 kg of rice had been issued every month and the receipt came with a thumb impression. Now, she was in possession of an evidence with which if she made a complaint, she could get that shop closed. But, before she could do that, the shopkeeper said "बहन जी, मेरी सारी गलतियों को माफ कर दीजिए। अब मैं आप को पूरा राशन दूगा।" This is a two-year old instance. Since then, that lady has been getting full quota of ration at low prices and that fellow does not misbehave with her. What I am trying to say is that for a large number of people in this country, an effective right to information act is basically a means of sustenance. It is right to life for them.

I would just highlight three points. The first point, which I just want to emphasise, is that this Act should be made applicable to the entire country; it should not be limited only to the Central Government Departments. I would not like to go into the theory of all this, as I have been listening all the arguments. It should not be limited just to Central Government's Departments. It should be applied to the entire country, including State Governments.

The second point, which I would like to emphasise, is about the penalty provision. Now, Sir, as far as the penalty provision is concerned, Section 17 of this Act talks about imprisonment of the officer. Proceedings against that officer will be taken place when there is a persistent fault on the part of that officer. Sir, there are two crucial elements which are needed to be there. One is that there has to be an independent appellate body, which exists there in this Act. The other is that there has to be an effective penalty clause which does not seem to be there. We need to have provisions for small penalty also which could act as deterrent. For instance, in Maharashtra, we have seen that penalty has been imposed against 38 officers. I am told that it has actually been deducted from the salary of the officers. Even if it is a penalty of Rs. 50 or 100 or 1000, this will actually act as deterrent. (Contd. by 1X)

VKK/1X/3.20/16.2.2005 PPG

SHRI ARVIND KEZRIWAL (CONTD.): If Information Commissioner is given power, he can order and recover from his salary after giving him an opportunity of being heard on the lines of Maharashtra Right to Information Bill. This acts as a detriment. It could be effectively curbed through the ACR. Sir, if a person gets an adverse ACR for four years, his promotion gets blocked. Because, for promotion, ACRs of the last four years are taken into consideration. Nobody will be prepared for it. No officer would like to risk his own career and most of the Public Information Officers in Delhi are Group-A Officers who are very conscious of their ACRs. I request the Committee to seriously consider it. We need to consider penalty which would be immediately imposed and the Information Commissioner should be given the power to do that.

Now, Sir, the third party clause. This is a new clause which has been introduced in this Act. It says that if any information which relates to any third party, before giving that information to the public, a notice will be sent to the third party and they will be given an opportunity of being heard. This is one clause in this Act which will render it ineffective. Suppose, I ask from the Ration Department to provide me a list of all the cardholders. Now, this information relates to the third party because names of so many people are going to be there in the list. Now, if there are 1,000 people in the list, the Public Information Officer has to send notice to all of them, asking whether they have any objection if their names are disclosed to the public. Similarly, if I ask for the distribution register, which may also contain a list of 2,000 people, do you think that the Public Information Officer will send notices to all of them? It will practically render this Act ineffective. I seriously don't understand how this particular clause has crept in it. It does not exist in any other Act. There is a genuine apprehension that if the Government contains any information which is likely to impinge the privacy of an individual, then that information should not be given. For example, income-tax returns of a particular individual. That should not be provided, but that has already been taken care of. These are my three submissions.

Also, there was one clarification that was sought by the Committee on a day before yesterday that what should be the qualification of the Information Commissioner. I personally feel that he should be from judicial background if it has to be a quasi-judicial body. He has to be from the judicial background, if penalty powers are to be given.

CHAIRMAN: Thank you very much. You have given very solid points.

(The witness then withdrew)

CHAIRMAN: Now, Gujarat officials have come. Mr. Shubh Ratan from the Ministry of Personnel and his colleagues are before us with a power point presentation regarding the natural calamities. We would like to take this particular subject because we realise that citizen-related aspects of the disaster management activities should be looked into. It was proposed that the mechanism for involving beneficiaries, citizens' groups as well as non-Governmental organisations for improving the effectiveness of the disaster management programmes may be considered by the Committee. In this connection, different courses of action were suggested when we were having discussion with the Additional Secretary. One of them is that associations of citizens' groups and beneficiaries may be included in the disaster management. In this connection, the experience of Gujarat Earthquake Management Project was mentioned. It was suggested that the Government of Gujarat may be requested to make a presentation before the Committee in this regard. The disaster management programme of the Government of Maharashtra was also cited, an experience which may be worthwhile going into.

I hope this will be very useful for us to consider under the heading of the 'Public Grievances' because we are facing lot of natural calamities in India and huge funds are allotted and how the funds are utilised by the State Government is to be shown to the public. As a Committee on Public Grievances, especially under the heading of the 'Administrative Reforms', we feel that we should know how the system is working, what is the best system that can be followed. At present, we are facing Tsunami disaster. Huge funds have been collected; even the Government of India has given more than Rs.1500 crores to the affected areas. Whether the people who are affected by such calamities are able to get these funds and also how they are participating in the reconstruction and rehabilitation programmes themselves and how they are well-informed to face the situation, if it arises in future. These are the things we would like to know so that we can also give a report to the Parliament about the existing system and on certain aspects of this public grievance. Many issues are raised in media and people are telling that within a particular period, the rehabilitation work is wind up and everything is left out to the people. There is no system to follow up; there is no system to help them. I hope these issues can be addressed. For that purpose only, we requested the Additional Secretary to make arrangement for this presentation and we are happy that the Gujarat Government was kind enough to send the experts for this presentation. I request the Additional Secretary to start the presentation.

SHRI P.I. SHUBH RATAN: Thank you, Sir. I would like to place a context before the Committee. The Department of Disaster Management is under the Ministry of Home Affairs. We are in the Department of Personnel and Administrative Reforms. Management of disaster, as we discussed, is one area where a variety of public grievances arise. Redressal is a very urgent matter. It is a matter of life and death for millions of people. When we did a survey, we found that it was a one-shot affair. When the disaster came, they reacted to the disaster somehow or the other in that situation. Criticism of the civil services and the bureaucracy has been on account of manning it. Apparently, as a whole, the reports have been quite satisfactory. (Contd. by 1y)

RSS/1Y & 1Z/3.30/

SHRI P.I. SHUBH RATAN (CONTD.): But, however, if you look at the system, which was actually initiated or made possible, the reaction to this disaster, what we found was that these are all *ad hoc* affairs. There is no mechanism to react to disaster. Somehow or the other, we took stock of the situation, mobilized the resources and settled the people. No lessons were learnt from it. It is only when another disaster comes, then again, old services are mobilized, without taking into account what are the lessons learnt from the previous disaster. The Gujarat experiment was useful. They made changes in the system and procedure, and established an authority, which will not only increase the capability of the people to react to disaster, but also involve them in the rescue operations. The final responsibility for reacting and addressing the issues is not on the Government, but on the community itself. When in the last year's Commonwealth Association for Public Distribution and Management, we sent our practices to them, they were quite impressed with the Gujarat experiment. They have said that it is the first case when the community is faced with a very adverse disaster, and instead of buckling down, they reacted in a very positive way and left an institution, a system and a capability, which will enable the community to address similar disaster and crisis subsequently. They won the first prize last year. Now, I request Dr. P.K. Mishra, who has been directly involved in the disaster management, to make his presentation.

DR. P.K. MISHRA: Mr. Chairman and distinguished Members, it is my honour and privilege to make this presentation on the Gujarat Earthquake Reconstruction Programme. I am the Member Secretary of the NCR Planning Board under the Ministry of Urban Development. For the last three years, I was the Chief Executive Officer of the Gujarat State Disaster Management Authority, and right from the earthquake, I was associated with it for the last three years. In that capacity, I am asked to make that presentation. Normally, we have 90 to 100 pages of this document. I will make it as short as possible. This Kutch Earthquake of 26th January, 2001 was one of the major disasters that the country has faced in the recent times. At the very outset, there was a lot of problems and confusion. There was a perception of failure also. A few months after, this perception of failure was converted into reality of success. How it has been done, the processes involved, the public participation, participation of NGOs and how the long-term aspects were taken care of, all these things are being shown on the screen. Normally, the focus is on rescue, relief and immediate action. Then we forget it. The distinguishing feature is that the long-term aspect, the immediate aspect, all have been taken care of. With your permission, I will make the presentation from there. In the first half a minute, there is a video to show the magnitude of destruction. The last slides show how there were smiles on the face of the people after the reconstruction efforts. (Thereafter, slides were shown). (contd. by 2a)

MKS/TMV/3.40&3.50/2A&2B

DR. P.K. MISHRA: (He explained the Task Ahead, the Total Estimated Reconstruction Cost, the Gujarat Emergency Earthquake Reconstruction Programme, the Agency appointed to carry out various works, the Task accomplished, Benefit Monitoring, Urban Reconstruction, International Recognition, the Approach and its Salient Features etc. with reference to slides.)

CHAIRMAN: Have you pooled all the money which was contributed, by the international organisations?

DR. P.K. MISHRA: Yes, Sir.

The World Bank - Rs.3,300 crores; the Asian Development Bank - Rs. 1,600 crores; the Prime Minister's Relief Fund; then, from various Ministries of the Government of

India and the State Governments; altogether, it was estimated to be about Rs. 8,000 crores.

CHAIRMAN: What was the name of the Authority?

DR. P.K. MISHRA: The Gujarat State Disaster Management Authority. Its task was to coordinate all the activities. The power system restoration was done by the Power Department of the Gujarat State Electricity Board; roads by the Roads & Building; housing by the Relief Commissioner. But all these amounts are made available as and when required. The World Bank will basically reimburse as and when the expenses are made.

(Then he again explained the Holistic Reconstruction & Rehabilitation Programme, relocation of villagers, Citizens' Participation in Policy Formulation, training of engineers etc. with reference to slides.)

CHAIRMAN: Is the purchase of materials done in common or individually?

DR. P.K. MISHRA: The purchase of materials is done individually. There is no centralised purchasing.

(He then explained Public-Private Partnership Programme, Multi-Disaster approach, Sustainable Community Based Disaster Management, Training & Capacity Building, Innovations for Sustainability etc. with reference to slides.)

RG/4.00/2C (Contd. by 2C)

CHAIRMAN: Would it be in the knowledge of people to know the seismic measurements; warning systems, etc. You began by saying that people are well equipped to face a situation if there is any recurrence of earthquake. For that purpose, they should know about various seismic readings. More than that, will there be a public announcement telling people in case an earthquake occurs come out of their houses, etc. What type of precautionary measures you have taken for this?

DR. P.K. MISHRA: We have done two or three things. We have some Do's and Dont's circulated in all the areas which will have all the instructions to be followed by people. As regards the warning system, of course, at the district level, there are satellite communication systems.

(He then explained the Redressal Mechanisms that they have envisaged with the help of slides.)

CHAIRMAN: As for the Vision programmes that you have envisaged in the last page of your presentation, kindly give us some more explanation. You can, of course, pass on the information to us. Now the Members would like to see certain clarifications from you.

DR. RADHAKANT NAYAK: I have only one small question to put. During the days when the relief and rehabilitation programmes were going on, the media, particularly, came out very heavily against the Gujarat Government reporting that there have been a lot of discrimination amongst socio-cultural groups, minorities, Dalits and tribals, even in the matter of rehabilitation, that assistance was refused in many cases and the kith and kin of the deceased were not properly taken care of. What was exactly the situation?

DR. P.K. MISHRA: There are two stages of it. One is the relief phase that took place in the first 10-15 days where people were given immediate relief by way of shelter and all that. At the relief phase, certainly, there was a lot of criticism. Of course, in most cases, even at the time of cyclones in Orissa, whatever be the preparedness, because of uncertainty, there may be some amount of chaos. So, that was there. So far as discrimination is concerned, I don't think there was any discrimination so far as the Government efforts were concerned. Actually what happened at the rehabilitation stage was that a lot of NGOs came; at least 250 NGOs came and some of them, of course, contacted the district authorities and they went to various villages. But many of the NGOs went on their own. Of course, it is an independent country and one has to allow it. But then some NGOs were also affiliated with a particular caste or religion. So, they went to those villages where they could focus on people of their caste/religious affiliations. But so far as Government efforts are concerned, there was no such single incident. This has even been checked by the World Bank when they also had this suspicion. In fact, I was told recently that they had to make several trips to find out this aspect.

(Continued by 2D)

Coming to the reconstruction phase, for the last three years, there have been many social impact studies conducted independently by various universities also. In fact, some of the studies show that people belonging to backward castes probably got more assistance than people belong to the majority community and higher castes. That is understandable because poor people obviously get more. So far as housing assistance is concerned, a maximum of Rs. 90,000 was given in rural areas and about Rs. 1.25 lakhs in urban areas. Now, for a poor, an amount of Rs. 70,000 or 80,000 is a big amount. But for a rich person, who has lost his big house and costly belongings gets much less. So, there was no discrimination. The NGOs who are catering to particular castes and communities do feel so.

DR. P. C. ALEXANDER: How did you solve the problem of land acquisition? There was this problem about land acquisition during construction of houses. How did you get over this problem then?

DR. P. K. MISHRA: It was raised by the World Bank also. They had taken it very, very seriously. The cost of relocation was very minimal, because no village was relocated. Only some pipelines and such things were relocated. Land acquisition did not stand in the way at all.

DR. P. C. ALEXANDER: That gives the reply to my second question also, in a way. I am speaking from my experience in Maharashtra. When you relocated people at a new place, a question arose as to the valuation of the land that you were leaving and how it will be compensated. You did not have that problem!

DR. P. K. MISHRA: This is not a problem. It has not yet been fully addressed. What has happened in this case is that about 5 per cent relocation was there and those people whose houses were constructed elsewhere, new houses they got, the old houses they are supposed to surrender, which they did not. It was done on paper only, but people were occupying both.

DR. P. C. ALEXANDER: Yes, in Maharashtra we solved the problem of amending the land acquisition by invoking very special powers.

DR. P. K. MISHRA: Sir, the entire Gujarat experience has been documented in a form of a book. This book will be released on 22ndand this is published by the National Institutue of Disaster Management. We will get a few copies and have them circulated to hon. Members.

CHAIRMAN: If possible, you can expand that last slide about community action. You can send some more details about that. Thank you, very much. We have very much benefited from Mr. Gupta's presentation. We appreciate it. We are thankful to you for having come here.

(The witnesses withdrew and the Committee then adjourned at 4.20 p.m.)

GSP-SC/1 A/4. OO/PPG/1-3-05

Verbatim proceedings of the meeting of Parliamentary Committee on Personnel, Public Grievances, Law and Justice held on 1st March, 2005 at 4.00 p.m. in Committee Room No. 63, Parliament House, New Delhi.

CHAIRMAN: SHRI E.M. SUDARSANA NATCHIAPPAN

CHAIRMAN: First of all, I wish a very good evening to everybody. I am happy that we are going to have clause-by-clause consideration of the Right to Information Bill, 2004. Before we call the officials, I would like to highlight certain points. The Right to Information Bill, 2004 is to be considered on two important aspects. First aspect is that already there is an Act passed by the Parliament, namely, the Freedom of Information Act, 2002. The present Bill is now repealing that Act by changing the very name itself to Right to Information Bill, 2004.

The other important aspect is that the National Advisory Committee has also recommended certain clauses to be included in this Bill. When we heard the witnesses and went through their submissions or presentations, we could find that the recommendations of the NAC were not at all taken into consideration. When those recommendations have not been taken into consideration for correcting the faults, which were found in the Freedom of Information Act, then the purpose of this Bill itself is diluted. There is already a feeling that this Act is not having more powers, and, therefore, there is no purpose of repealing that Act. Because when we go for repealing then we have to see that there is a sea of change. Therefore, we have to stress upon the main points. You would have thought about it. But, I would like to suggest certain aspects, which we have to consider when we are getting the clarifications from the officials. You very well know the procedure. If hon. Members want to give any amendment, they have to circulate it before 27th. If there is anything to be amended, they can suggest it. We have to put it to the officials when they are coming here.

My question is whether we have to go in for a comprehensive enactment, which will cover the Union Government, the State Governments and also the Local Governments. The purpose is to widen the scope of the freedom of speech and to have more knowledge about the day-to-day working of the Government. For the purpose of transparency in a democratic process, this particular enactment is being proposed. As you know very well, at the international level, this is a kind of tool through which a democracy is judged as to whether it is having transparency, or, having something hidden. Many of the countries have come forward with this type of enactment. Sweden is having this kind of enactment since a very long time, USA started it in 1966 and UK started it in the 1990s. So, we have come forward with the suggestion that the democratic process, as it is here also, should be transparent to the knowledge of the people. With this aspect in view, we have to consider whether this Act can be useful not only for the Union Government but also for the State Governments and the Local Governments. Let us suppose that six or seven States are already having the enactment for this purpose. Then, as per the legal system, when both the State Law and the Union Law exist, both of them can go parallel, but in case of a difference, then the Union law will be in force., But here, at the drafting state, we can ask if there is a possibility of giving choice in case a particular person wants to go for the State Law, or, the Central Law. We have to find out if they can do it or not. The very purpose of having this particular enactment is given in Clause 5, and, that is to be found out whether that needs to be incorporated.

Second thing is the qualification of the Commissioner. He is the main person on whom the entire enactment is running around. Therefore, whether the Commissioner will have a specific qualification or, certain things of exclusion should be made in certain provisions this Bill. (Followed by 1b)

SK/1 B/4.05/PPG/01.03.2005

SHRI V. RADHAKRISHNAN: I think, for States also, only one law should be there. Why should we not have a uniform law?

CHAIRMAN: There is a uniform law. A particular citizen can use whichever he wants to use. The question is, can we seek the information from the State Government through the Central Law? Have we got the power? This is not the Bill; this is only a suggestion.

SHRI S.K. KHARVENTHAN: Sir, will the Central Act override the State Act?

CHAIRMAN: It cannot be overriding. But, we are allowing them to have a parallel going, that is, if a citizen wants to get information from the State Government, he can choose the State law also. And, if there is no State law, then, he can use the Central law. If both of them are available in a particular State, as it is there in Tamil Nadu, then, the citizen can choose either of them.

SHRI S.K. KHARVENTHAN: So, we are giving option to the citizens.

CHAIRMAN: Yes, we have to make it. That is one thing which we have to clarify. Another important thing is regarding the punishment. The punishment is enhanced from the earlier Act, that is, the 2002 Act, where there was no provision of imprisonment; and only fine was imposed. But, now, the imprisonment is also given. But giving sentence is not with the Commissioner. He can only ask the concerned official to go and lodge a complaint before the magistrate and then only he can start the process. As it is there in the Criminal Procedure Code, they have to convince the court first. Then only, the complaint can be taken up. We have to examine the witnesses and other things. So, these are the things on which we have to concentrate. Then, another thing is this. When a person is asking for certain piece of information, it should be published, as it is, by way of website or by way of publication. (Contd. by 1C)

YSR/4.10/1C/PPG/01.03.2005

CHAIRMAN (CONTD.): Some of the witnesses gave a very simple example of ration card. If a ration card-holder wants to know how much ration has been supplied to him, then he has to seek the information from the concerned official. Suppose there are so many card-holders, the point is whether this type of information should be displayed, or whether it should be put on the website. These things should be clarified, because every person is not asking for this information. There are only a few people who ask for this kind of information. The very complicated matters are asked only by the media people to write stories. Whether our country is developed to that level or not is altogether a different question. We have to consider this question when we will be asking officials. First, we will discuss it among ourselves and then we will call the witnesses.

JUSTICE (RETD.) N.Y. HANUMANTHAPPA: As the learned Member Shri Radhakrishnan has said, when there are two Acts, why should not we prefer the Central Act. Otherwise, confronting views will be there. Citizens will be in dilemma as to which should they use. Why should not the Central Act prevail over the State Act in order to avoid confusion?

SHRI BALWANT *alias* BAL APTE: We have a federation of States. In certain circumstances, Central law will prevail and in certain circumstances State laws will prevail.

JUSTICE (RETD.) N.Y. HANUMANTHAPPA: Then two views will be there.

CHAIRMAN: Earlier the Bill wants to exclude the States and local governments. The previous enactment, which was made by the Parliament in 2002, allowed the State Governments and local government also as part of it. Now, the general thinking of the witnesses, who have appeared before the Committee, and our own feeling is that we have to include the State Governments and local governments also as is given in the 2002 Act which is in existence. Only seven or eight States are having this Act. Rest of the States have not come up with any enactment. Till then, we have to allow the citizens to get the information through some enactment.

JUSTICE (RETD.) N.Y. HANUMANTHAPPA: The hon. Member's idea was to have a Central Act with some State amendments as we have been doing in C.P.C. and Cr. P.C.

SHRI V. RADHAKRISHNAN: My point is this. The central Act must be there.

(Contd. by id)

VKK/1d/4.15/1.3.2005 PPG

SHRI V. RADHAKRISHNAN (CONTD.): But I don't object because let the citizens have either of these two rights, State law or Central law. Some States have gone to the extent of passing their own laws. We are doing it now. So, let the citizens choose either the State law or the Central law, whichever they find suitable.

CHAIRMAN: Justice Hanumanthappaji, the main problem is when we enact a law, as it is available in the Bill, none of the State citizens is going to have the right to ask the questions from the State Government or the local government.

JUSTICE (RETD.) N.Y.HANUMANTHAPPA: You can incorporate the State enactment.

CHAIRMAN: Whenever they need it, they can bring it.

JUSTICE (RETD.) N.Y.HANUMANTHAPPA: For example, Cr.PC and CPC are Central Acts. We are allowing the States to have laws with same kind of provisions. That can be incorporated.

CHAIRMAN: That is normal. For Concurrent List items, we are allowing like that. We can make it.

JUSTICE (RETD.) N.Y.HANUMANTHAPPA: Mr. Chairman, Sir, after all, this law flows from the freedom of speech and all that. If you go through, we will be considering Article 19 also which gives a right to information and all that. That is how we have to think over this subject.

DR. RADHAKANT NAYAK: My point is that in case you give some kind of an obligation to States to enact in pursuance of this Act, depending on the party in power, they may modify it to the extent that the purpose of the Central law could be defeated. Therefore, in my humble view, we should provide for omnibus law which will have an overriding effect over the State law. In some States, they may amend it to their liking because there are so many factors. There are some Central statutes which are not implemented in some of the States because they do not suit the party in power. Therefore, we have to provide a law which will have an overriding effect down to the grass-root level.

DR. P.C. ALEXANDER: I think Mr. Shanti Bhushan covered in his note the points which we are discussing. I think if we look at the last paragraph of his recommendations, that would resolve the difficulties. It says,

> "It would be perfectly legal and justified for the Central law to be applicable to all public authorities in India, whether they are under Central, State or local bodies. It would also be legal and justified for the Central law to provide that the law provided by the Central Government would be in addition and not in derogation of the right provided by the State law."

If we can have a provision like this, we can also obtain Government's views on this, like some of us have expressed.

CHAIRMAN: Then, shall we call the officials? (Followed by 1E)

RSS/1E/4.20/PPG

WITNESSES

1. Shri A.N. Tiwari, Secretary, Personnel.
2. Shri T.K. Vishwanathan, Secretary, Legislative Department.
3. Shri K.D. Singh, Addl. Secretary, Law.

CHAIRMAN: We had requested all the three Secretaries to appear together. The Law Secretary could not appear because his mother expired. Therefore, our heart-felt condolences to him. But the Addl. Secretary, Law has come. We would like to find out one tning. The Right to Information Act, 2002 is already covering the thing for the

Union, States and local administration, and now, the present Bill confines itself only to the Union Government. The Committee has a feeling that we have to give a comprehensive enactment which will be on the basis of the 2002 Act in this particular aspect, that is, covering the Union Government, the State Governments and the Local Self Governments so that a citizen can have the right to information from any governmental departments or local government departments, and if a State Government enactment is there, then they can have the choice of choosing the procedure, either by the State law or by the Central law, and there need not be any contradiction between the laws. But we are allowing the citizens to have the right to information, in any way, from every part of the Government, that is, whether it is the Union Government or the State Government or the local administration or any through the State Law as well as the Central Law. The Central Law has its own hierarchy and the information can be collected, appealed against and the writ of the law enforced, of the Principal Information Commissioner, the Deputy Commissioner and all. The question is, if all State citizens try to access information in the State Government through the Central Law, will then the writ of the Principal Information Commissioner run on the State Government official? Now assuming, according to the Law Secretary, it cannot happen; we cannot pass a Central Law and make it apply to the employees of the State Government. But, administratively, there can be total anarchy; it can be chaotic. A person will apply for a set of information from the State Law. Suppose the State Law prevents him from getting some information. He applies to the Central Government and keeps coming back and forth to get this information, and creates umpteen problems for both the sets of Law and both the sets of hierarchy. Administratively, this kind of arrangement will be quite a difficult arrangement, but not an impossible arrangement. My submission to the Committee is, apart from the legislative aspect of this arrangement, its administrative aspect should also receive your attention.

DR. P.C. ALEXANDER: Are you suggesting that you want to reexamine it further? Are you clear in your mind that the Central Act can coexist with the State, and without having any resort to an addition to the list or a deletion from the list?

SHRI A.N. TIWARI: We are clear on this point. On legal advice, the two cannot coexist in respect of State Laws.

SHRI BALWANT *alias* BAL APTE: There is a State Government. The Central Law, as it proposes, is confined only to the Central Government agencies. The suggestion has come here that it should cover the State Government agencies also. You have told us the practical difficulties in other administration, where the tax payers money is invested. That is the main purpose of this Bill. Therefore, we feel that this is the purpose of the Right to Information Act, 2002, and the recommendation of the NAC in respect of Right to Information Bill also supports this particular aspect. We know that you have already put forth your viewpoint before the Committee, and the Law Secretary has also expressed his view before the Committee regarding the residuary powers. On that basis, we are enacting it, and there need not be any contradiction between the Central law and the State law. The Parliament has already enacted the Right to Information Act, 2002. But only 7-8 States have come forward in this respect. The other States have not come up with any other amendments, and that is a grey area to know the efforts made by the State Government and the Local Governments.

SHRI A.N. TIWARI: Sir, you are very right in presenting the NAC's advice. Yes, in regard to the information held by the State Government, the citizens would have the option to access that information, either through the Central law or the State law. Now, the first part of your statement that the 2002 Act provides that the Central law shall have an all India applicability, is absolutely right. But beyond that, suppose, we make simultaneously the State law only in relation to the State.... (Contd. by 1F)

MKS/AKG/4.25/1F

SHRI A.N. TIWARI (CONTD.): Suppose we make, simultaneously, the State Law applicable only in relation to the State subjects. There shall be a problem about legislative competence, and that is what the Law Secretary has been advising us all through; it shall be legally indispensable. That is one part. But I would urge for your consideration some of the administrative matters. Assuming, for a moment, we make a citizen to access some information held by the State Government that. But are there any Constitutional difficulties?

SHRI A.N. TIWARI: That is what the Law Secretary has been repeatedly pointing out.

SHRI BALWANT *alias* BAL APTE: Because of that, the learned friend has asked whether you are re-examining it. This is the response given in the papers that you are re-examining it to again find out whether it is possible under the Law. That is your response given in the papers which I have got before me.

SHRI A.N. TIWARI: We received a similar type of suggestion in the Ministry. So, we went to the Law Secretary requesting him. Yes, his view is with us: Why not also consult the Attorney General? To that extent, yes, we are examining it. We are exclusively definite about our position. But as it is, the advice is very clear that there is absence of legislative competence.

SHRI V. RADHAKRISHNAN: I would like to put a simple question. Would you like to have a differentiation between the State matters and the Central matters in the context of fundamental rights? Right to Information is a fundamental right. In the discharge of that function, should they have a Central Authority for implementing the decisions? Of course, there is a State Government, and the State Government officials run its administration. They are governed by their own law.

TMV/1G/4.30 (Contd. by 1G)

SHRI V. RADHAKRISHNAN (CONTD.): In some States there is a State law. Our attempt is to have a Central law, a Union law, applicable throughout India, whether a State has implemented a State law or a State has not implemented a State law. We take a view that this is a matter concerning a Constitutional authority. Therefore, the Commissioner or the authority designated in the Right to Information Bill should have jurisdiction over the State also. What is the difficulty?

SHRI A. N. TIWARI: Sir, the hon. Chairman has clarified that point. The Act of 2002 has this provision which you are mentioning. It has all India application also. If it stops at that, there is no problem. The problem of legislative competence comes when a citizen has got the option to access information either through the State Government law or the Central law. Then the problem arises. That is why an independent law is advised.

SHRI V. RADHAKRISHNAN: This is not a matter concerning administration alone. This is a matter concerning transparency in every activity under the sun. Every activity will be included under this. The citizens have a right to get information on every activity either under the State Government or under the Central Government. Suppose the State law is not adequate. What will be the position? Shouldn't he have a right to get the information from the State? There should be transparency in governance. The State law may be lacking in this respect. The State law may not provide an answer. In such a case, the Union law should prevail. It is with that purpose in mind we are making a legislation covering all the States, whether there is a State law or not. The question of administrative difficulty is immaterial. We take a view that it is a fundamental right. So, the person who is authorised to act under this statute will have jurisdiction over the Union administration and the State administration. What is the legal difficulty? I don't understand it.

DR. P.C. ALEXANDER: Do you have with you the advice given by Shri Shanti Bhushan? The issue was referred to him and he has given a categorical statement—

> "Thus, in my view, it would be perfectly legal and justified for the Central law to be applicable to all public authorities in India, whether they are under the Centre, States or local bodies. It would also be legal and justified for the Central law to provide that the right provided by the Central Act would be in addition and not derogation of the rights provided by any State law. In that case both the Central and State Acts could subsist and complement each other."

This is the advice given to us. Are you going to refer this Bill to some other legal authority based on the views expressed by the witnesses before us as also based on the advice of Shri Shanti Bhushan?

SHRI A.N. TIWARI: Sir, this is the position which was exactly taken by certain NGOs who represented to us in this matter. This is already part of the document which we have submitted to the hon. Attorney-General through the Law Secretary. This is already before him. Presumably, he may give advice on this also.

SHRI RAMJETHMALANI: Has your Ministry taken a view on this Bill? What is the pith and substance of this legislation? To which Entry in the Constitutional List does it relate? According to me, it is a legislation which relates to the residual power which is vested in the Central Government. In that event, an all-India legislation binding on the State is perfectly possible. In fact, it is highly desirable because you are not really conferring any new right on anybody. This legislation, I think, evolves mechanisms for the enforcement of that right which has already been recognised by the Supreme Court in various judgements arising out of the "right to know" under article 19 of the Constitution. Therefore, there is no reason why this should be confined merely to the Centre. "Right to know" exists against everybody. You will create wrong impression on the people that "right to know" is not enforceable in the States. (Contd. by 1H)

VK/1 H/4.35/PPG/1.3.2005

SHRI RAMJETHMALANI (CONTD): Those States which do not have any legislation today will think that they are now immune from making the information public to anybody. If you agree with me that this relates to residuary powers of the Centre, then there will be an all-India legislation. The greatest criticism is that some States have a law which is an advance on this statute. Probably the Maharashtra statute is definitely an improvement on this. Why do we lag behind? We do not have to learn lessons from other State Governments. We should be able to give some lessons to others. Please make changes in this law to make it comparable to the most benevolence legislation that exists in any part of the country; otherwise, you will be sending wrong signals.

The third criticism is this. What is the penalty for non-compliance? If no penalty is provided for, you will ultimately drive people to litigation. They will go to courts again to get their rights enforced. People will interpret the provisions in any manner they like. Even if that turn out to be wrong, there is no penalty. The Maharashtra Act has provisions for penalties. The law must have some teeth; otherwise, it is of no use.

SHRI A.N. TIWARI: Sir, you very rightly said that since it is part of residuary powers of the Centre, there is no legal bar on its application all-over the country provided there is no such law simultaneously coexisting.

SHRI RAMJETHMALANI: If the residuary power vests in the Centre!.

SHRI A.N. TIWARI: I am saying that for getting an information which is held by the State Government, the citizen is supposed to be having the right to access that information either through the State law or the Central law, whichever he finds more convenient. That is not perhaps within the legislative competence of the Centre. What we were asked to do was to provide in the present Act a provision that wherever the State Act exists, then both the Central Act and the State Act will apply, when it comes to the information that is held by the State Government.

SHRI RAMJETHMALANI: So it will apply to the whole of India except where such a law is in existence!

SHRI A.N. TIWARI: We can make a provision like this.

SHRI RAMJETHMALANI: The Bill does no make that provision.

SHRI A.N. TIWARI: It is not there.

SHRI T.K. VISHWANATHAN: Probably, the earlier law was enacted in 1997. But that did not contain any penalty provisions. The present law contains the penalty provisions. Now the problem is in the State List we have various Entries, like public money, police, etc. (Contd. By 1J)

RG/4.40/1J

SHRI T.K. VISWANATHAN (Contd.): Information is related to subject-matter; you cannot detach information and say that we would treat information as a separate entity and then legislate it. In that, we had some difficulty. The State Governments might feel that we are encroaching upon their terrain. That is what they would feel. On the pretext of a legislation, we cannot ask the Government to part with this information which is within their domain. The State Legislatures are equally sovereign. They have to provide transparency in their functioning. They may not like the Parliament telling them. We thought that a situation may arise when the State officials may be punished under the Central law; different political regimes may be there and it may cause Centre-

State friction. That is why we want to avoid this situation, as the Residuary Entry 97 clearly says: "Any other matter enumerated in List II and List III including any taxes in either of those lists, information is tagged on along with the subject-matter." You cannot detach information about Police and say that this is under 97. This is our difficulty. That is the reason why we were hesitant to extend it to the States. I stand corrected if I am wrong.

SHRI RAMJETHMALANI: We have all taken an oath to uphold the Constitution, and the Constitutional right is available against everybody including the State Government. But if we actually say that we want to endorse it, that creates a very wrong atmosphere.

DR. P.C. ALEXANDER: May I add something for the information of the hon. Members? We have examined over 30-40 witnesses on this point also, and the consensus that emerged — I am not saying amongst us as we are yet to make up our mind — from the witnesses is that the Centre is perfectly justified in assuming that Entry 97 provides right to the Centre to bring out such a legislation. Whether such a legislation is to be brought out, which would cover not only the Centre but also the various Authorities of the States, that is the point.

SHRI T.K. VISWANATHAN: We re-endorse our view. It gives us added strength to proceed on those lines.

SHRI A.N. TIWARI: That was the view of the Attorney-General when this Act of 2002 was really passed by Parliament. These points were raised at that time. It was asked whether the Residuary Entry provision made under that would be applicable under the State subject as well. The answer was 'Yes'. So, that point stands fortified by legal opinion as Mr. Jethmalani just now said. But the other point is also important. The point is, when both the State laws and the Central law co-exist for the same set of information. That is the only point about which we need some sort of clarification. On that there is no definitive legal opinion as such.

SHRI S.K. KHARVENTHAN: With regard to penalty, I want to know some thing. Clause 17 (1) of the Bill deals with penalties. It says: "The Commission shall authorise any officer of the Central Government to file a complaint against such Public Information Officer before a Judicial Magistrate of First Class." So, the complainant has to go to the Magistrate Court to file a complaint against a Public Information Officer. As per Section 200 of the Criminal Procedure Code, any person filing a complaint is a private person, and both the complainant as well as the respondent has to go to the Court for the same. Is this penal provision sufficient enough to attract complainant as well as respondent to attend the Court proceedings?

CHAIRMAN: We will go to that clause later.

Now shall we take a consensus on this recommendation that in the clause which deals with the Right to Information, a person will have the right to seek information under the State law as well as under this Act, if the information pertains to a subject under Schedule 7 of the Constitution?

We will take that stand because we are given to understand that you are seeking legal opinion on the question of extending the applicability of the Act to the public authorities under the State Governments as also ensuring co-existence of the Central Act and State Acts where the State enactment is already in existence. In the meantime, the Committee feels that we have to cover both the States and the local administration.

(Continued by 1K)

1K/4.45/KS

DR. RADHAKANT NAYAK: If the present law, which exists in a particular State, is not commensurate with, or, is repugnant to the proposed law, do you think that will not be...

CHAIRMAN: No, no. We have taken a stand that the Union law and the State law can be considered, wherever it is necessary.

DR. RADHAKANT NAYAK: The Union law will not override the State law.

CHAIRMAN: It is not the question of overriding. Actually, as the Secretary has submitted, they have a feeling that there is no administrative set up at the State level. Then, the question arises whether the administrative set up at the Central level can have the power to enforce it. Can that be the remedy? They are raising that sort of question. Let us go into that aspect later. We will not make that recommendation.

Now, we go to Clause 2 (a) pertaining to the definition of "Commission". I think, we should adopt it as it is. Then "competent authority" under Clause 2 (b) is also all right. We adopt it. Then, coming to sub-clause (iii), it says, "the Chief Justice of the High Court of Delhi in the case of the High Court of Delhi". I think we have to amend it to the effect that all the States are included. Then, in sub-clause (iv), we should add the Governor also; and so also the Lt. Governor.

JUSTICE (RETD.) N. Y. HANUMANTHAPPA: Just a minute. Clause 2 (b) (i) says, "the Speaker in the case of the House of the People or the Legislative Assembly of a Union Territory and the Chairman in the case of the Council of States;".

CHAIRMAN: Yes, here we have to cover all the States. (Followed by 1l)

TDB/1L/4.50

SHRI BALWANT *alias* BAL APTE: We are proposing—that is how the amendments are sought to be made—that this legislation should govern the State authorities also. So, the entire enactment requires recasting on that basis. So, from that point of view, do it. You can say it generally, then, you will have to recast it. If you say 'State authorities' everywhere, then, it will have both the Legislative Assembly and the Legislative Council, where there is a Legislative Council.

SHRI T.K. VISHWANATHAN: Sir, you leave it to me. I will recast it and give you a revised Bill.

DR. P.C. ALEXANDER: The Freedom of Information Act of 2002 refers it. It says that in the case of the Supreme Court, the Chief Justice of India; in the case of the High Courts, the Chief Justice of the High Court and the President or the Governor, as the case may be, in the case of other authorities created under the Constitution, like that. It is already there. You will have to bring it over to the Right to Information Bill of 2004. It is a question of drafting only.

CHAIRMAN: Everything is mentioned here. You can simply follow the 2002 Act. We are adopting this by saying that it should cover the Union Government, State Governments and also the local governments. On that basis, you can suggest the appropriate amendments then and there. Here, we can very easily say that the Freedom of Information Act of 2002 has given the definition, and it should be kept as it is here. You can look into this. On that basis, you can make the necessary amendments. In clause 2(c), you have to make the consequential amendments by stating, 'local government or a union territory administration means the Central, State and local administration. As far as 2(d) is concerned, we adopt it as it is. In regard to 2(e), you can make the consequential amendments by creating such posts when the matter goes at the level of the State Government. We can adopt 2(f), as it is. As far as 2(g) is concerned, we have to include the words, 'by any other law made by the State Assembly'. We have to follow the Freedom of information Act of 2002, here. As far as 2(h) is concerned, here also, you have to make the consequential amendments for enabling the State Governments and local administration. (Contd. by 1m)

KLS/1M-4.55/PPG/1.3.2005

CHAIRMAN (CONTD): (iii) any reproduction of image or images embodied in such microfilm (whether enlarged or not); and (iv) any other material produced by a computer or any other device; (j) 'right to information' means the right to information accessible under this Act which is held by or under the control of any public authority and includes the right to — inspection of work, document, records; (ii) taking notes, extracts, or certified copies of documents or records (iii) taking certified samples of material.

DR. RADHAKANT NAYAK: Sir, see the definition of records. I just want to find out if there is any discrepancy. Records include any microfilm, microfiche and facsimile copy of a document or any other material produced by computer or any other business. I think the word records limits the definition of information if we read it very closely.

DR. P.C. ALEXANDER: Information includes records. It is not record limiting the information.

DR. RADHAKANT NAYAK: The definition of information as such is a little broader than the records.

SHRI S.K. KARAVENTHAN: We have to include Indian Institute of Management, Indian Institute of Technology, etc.

CHAIRMAN: It includes any other body aided by the Government.

SHRI S.K. KARAVENTHAN: They are receiving aid. These are the institutions which are receiving funds. They are getting some grants.

SHRI BALWANT *Alias* BAL APTE: We can say, 'substantially funded by the Government.'

SHRI T.K. VISHWANATHAN: It will be quite apt to include those bodies, which receive funding from the Consolidated Fund of India.

CHAIRMAN: We can include the institutions which are aided or getting grants from the Government.

SHRI T.K. VISHWANATHAN: Then NGOs will also be included.

CHAIRMAN: We will specifically say NGOs. They are also getting a lot of money from the Government.

JUSTICE (RETD) N.Y. HANUMANTHAPPA: That is very wider.

SHRI S.K. KHARAVENTHAN: There will not be any scope for mischief.

CHAIRMAN: This is adopted. (Contd. by 1N)

SSS/1 N/5.00/PPG/1.3.2005

CHAIRMAN: In chapter 1, (j), Sub-clause (ii) to (iv), do you want to add anything in this?

SHRI RAM JETHMALANI: In sub-clause (ii) you may add "certified copies of material" instead of "certified copies of documents...".

CHAIRMAN: In (k), "third party", addresses a lot of objection from certain witnesses. What is your opinion regarding this? This allows the dilution of the entire Act.

SHRI T. K. VISWANATHAN: We are talking about the data protection act. We cannot part without the consent of "Third party". That is why it is creating other problems. "Third party" information has to be cautiously handled. Supposing your medical records are there, it cannot be made public. "Third party" occurs in a different context.

CHAIRMAN: We will keep this without adopting till we discuss clause 11. Let it be kept as pending, without adoption. We are keeping it. We are not talking about it. Now we come to Chapter II. Clause 3 says, "Subject to the provisions of this Act, all citizens shall have the right to information". It can be adopted as it is. It is adopted. Therefore, we are adopting clause 3. Now we come to clause 4 (1), "every public authority shall—"...

DR. RADHAKANT NAYAK: What about duty of disclosure for giving information?

CHAIRMAN: It comes in the next clause. (CONTD. BY 1O)

NBR/5.05/1O.

CHAIRMAN: Now, let us take up Clause 4 of the Bill. It is pertaining to Obligations of public authorities. The Clause 4(1) says, "Every public authority shall — (a) maintain all its records duly catalogued and indexed in a manner and form which facilitates the right to information under this Act and ensure that all records that are appropriate to be computerized are, within a reasonable time and subject to availability of resources, computerised and connected through a network all-over the country on different systems so that access to such records is facilitated."

SHRI S.K. KHARVENTHAN: Sir, when we say, 'subject to availability of resources...' the authorities will simply say that records are not available. So, the words 'subject to availability' should be removed.

SHRI T.K. VISHWANATHAN: Sir, it is for computerisation.

SHRI DR. RADHAKANT NAYAK: Then, why should you limit it to only for computerisation? There are some records which need not be computerised.

CHAIRMAN: Mr. Secretary, the words, 'subject to availability of resources' can be omitted.

SHRI T.K. VISHWANATHAN: According to this Clause, we have to computerise records and connect through network for supplying the same to citizens. What you are saying is to be read along with what it says next. It gives a correct meaning.

SHRI RAM JETHMALANI: What constitute 'reasonable time?'

CHAIRMAN: Mr. Secretary, will it have a catalytic effect if we remove that? We are giving a lot of funds for each and every department for computerisation.

SHRI A.N. TIWARI: Sir, the level of computerisation in various States is absolutely different.

CHAIRMAN: I am happy that you are thinking about the States. You think about the Union Government.

SHRI A.N. TIWARI: Sir, this is a very futuristic type of provision. There should be an incentive to do it more and more. I don't think that it is very harmful.

(Followed by "1P")

USY/1P/5.10

DR. RADHAKANT NAYAK: You should not simply limit to computerisation. Even handwritten information is enough. You can include it for future purposes, but what about the present scenario?

SHRI T.K. VISHWANATHAN: Sir, 'computerisation' is not a problem. But the main problem is that of 'network'.

JUSTICE (RETIRED) N.Y. HANUMANTHAPPA: You have used the words, "Within a reasonable time". It should be defined properly, otherwise there may lead to undue delay.

CHAIRMAN: Let us give them some time to develop the system.

JUSTICE (RETIRED) N.Y. HANUMANTHAPPA: We should solve this problem immediately, otherwise it will lead to further delay.

SHRI A.N. TIWARI: Sir, I would like to draw your kind attention to clause 4(i)(a). It says that the computerisation is just for facilitating the maintenance of records. Manual action cannot be replaced by computerisation.

CHAIRMAN: Okay, you try to make it within possible reasonable time. So, hon. Members, should we adopt this?

JUSTICE (RETIRED) N.Y. HANUMANTHAPPA: No, Sir, the words "Within reasonable time" should be defined.

CHAIRMAN: Okay, let us go to the next clause. (Followed by 1q)

VP/5.15/1Q/PPLG/01.02.2005

CHAIRMAN: Now I come to Clause 4(b). It says, 'publish before the commencement of this Act'. This is a controversial clause. No time frame has been given. The NAC has recommended that it should be published within six months of this Act coming into force and, thereafter, update, at least, every 12 months. We can adopt it as it is.

SHRI BALWANT *alias* BAL APTE: That makes it one year. If the Act is passed today, it will come into effect after four months, and, thereafter, you are giving additional six months.

CHAIRMAN: Then the sub-clauses (i) to (vii) are given. Are there any suggestions regarding these aspects?

DR. RADHAKANT NAYAK: As far as sub-clause (vii) is concerned, we can mention 'consultation or concurrence', or, 'consultation and concurrence'. Consultation takes a long time, so, they say that we need concurrence. So, we can say 'consultation and concurrence'.

CHAIRMAN: Mr. Tiwari, here also we would like to draw your attention to sub-clauses (v) and (vi), and we feel that you can consider NAC's recommendations on these.

SHRI A.N. TIWARI: Sir, you just now read out rule (b). You said that after it comes into force, six months time may be given to the officers to publish all these things. This may be slightly contradictory because this rule provides that all these must be in place when the Act comes into force. It would be better that you give six months time for the Act to come into force.

DR. P.C. ALEXANDER: In Britain, an Act was passed and five years time was given to get prepared for it. Actually, it came into force only two weeks ago.

SHRI T. K. VISHWANATHAN: The Act has to come into force in two months. You are saying that six months time should be given.

CHAIRMAN: We have adopted that it should be updated, at least, every 12 months. But you can work it out and tell us. (Followed by 1R)

PK/1R/5.20 PPGLJ 1.3.2005

DR. RADHAKANT NAYAK: Therefore, we can keep it as six months. Four plus six months' time is reasonable.

CHAIRMAN: We will make it like this, "Publish within six months of this Act coming into force and thereafter update atleast every twelve months."

CHAIRMAN: Now, we come to sub-clause (vii). It reads, "particulars of any arrangement that exists for consultation with, or representation by, the members of the public in relation to the formulation of policy or in the administration of the public authority." This is what the NAC has recommended. I hope we can adopt what NAC has recommended. They have expanded some particular aspects. The additional thing here is, "or in the administration of the public authority." The last two words in the Bill are "or implementation thereof". In that place, they have put, "or in the administration of the public authority." So, we can adopt it as it is.

Then, let us go to sub-clause (viii), "a statement listing..". According to the Advisory Committee, this also needs to be expanded. "Statement listing of all Boards, Councils, Committees and other bodies constituted by two or more persons, that are part of, or that have been established for the purpose of advising the public authority, and whose meetings are open to the public, or the minutes of whose meetings are available for public inspection."

I hope, we can adopt it as I have read it.

Then, we come to the next clause, that is, sub clause (ix). It reads "a directory of their public servants from the level of the Head of the Department or his or her equivalent and below." Here we have to give the expanded version. We will adopt it as it is.

Then, we take up next clause, that is, sub-clause (x). It reads, "monthly remuneration received for each position including the system of compensation as established in the regulations."

We can adopt it as it is.

DR. RADHAKANT NAYAK: Sir, with regard to sub-clause (ix), "directory of its officers and employees.." What about the employers?

DR. P.C. ALEXANDER: It is the Government.

DR. RADHAKANT NAYAK: Does it include employers also?

DR. P.C. ALEXANDER: How can you list an employer? It is the Government, public authority, corporation or panchayat..

DR. RADHAKANT NAYAK: Their names should also be included.

CHAIRMAN: Now we come to sub-clause (xi). It reads, "information concerning the object assigned to each agency, including all plans, proposed expenditures and reports on disbursement.

DR. P.C. ALEXANDER: It is already there in the Act.

CHAIRMAN: We can adopt it as it is. (Followed by 1S)

PB/1S/5.25

SHRI A.N. TIWARI: Sir, much of the reading from the NAC's draft is already captured in the Bill itself.

CHAIRMAN: I am just reading it. If it is already there, leave it as it is.

SHRI A.N. TIWARI: Sir, what the NAC has suggested is the language of the common man.

CHAIRMAN: Then, at that juncture, you can tell us. We will rectify it. Then, in clause 4 (1) (b) (xii), it is said, "the manner of execution of subsidy programmes, including the amounts allocated and the details of beneficiaries of such programmes." We can adopt it as is proposed in the Bill.

Then in clause 4 (1) (b) (xiii), the Bill proposes "particulars of concessions, permits or authorisations granted by it." However, in the NAC, it is said, "All concessions, permits or authorisations granted, with their recipients specified." They want to have this inclusion. They are saying, "with their recipients specified." I hope we can adopt it as it is given in the suggestions made by the NAC.

Then we come to clause 4 (1) (b) (xiv). In this connection, I want to read the suggestion given by the NAC. They have given some explanation. They have said, "All information available to the public authority in electronic form or capable of being reduced to electronic form which is not exempt under this Act, subject to availability of resources." However, in the Bill it is said, "details in respect of the information, available to or held by it, reduced in an electronic form." I think, what is said in the Bill is sufficient. So, we can adopt this clause as it is proposed in the Bill.

Then, we take clause 4 (1) (b) (xv). Here also, the NAC has given some explanation. They have said, "the details of facilities available to citizens for obtaining information, including if the public authority maintains a library or reading room that is available for public use, a statement of that fact including details of the address and hours of opening of the library or reading room." But, I find that all this information has more or less been covered in the Bill. In the Bill, it is said, "the particulars of facilities available to citizens for obtaining information, including the working hours of a library or reading room, if maintained for public use." Therefore, I think, we will adopt this clause as it is proposed in the Bill.

Then, we come to 4(1) (b) (xvi). In the Bill, it is said, "the names, designations and other particulars of the Public Information Officers." The NAC has also said the same thing. So, we can adopt it as it is proposed in the Bill.

Then, we come to clause 4(1) (b) (xvii). The Bill proposes, "such other information as may be prescribed." In this respect, the NAC has given some explanation. They have said, "such other information as prescribed by the appropriate government or Information Commissioner from time to time which would promote transparency across public authorities or in specific public authorities, as appropriate." I think, what is said in the Bill that 'such other information as may be prescribed' is widened by the explanation given by the NAC. So, we can adopt this clause as has been suggested by the NAC. We will adopt as per the NAC's recommendations. They have also provided some explanation for that part also. They have said, "On the basis that it shall be a constant endeavour of public authorities to take steps to provide as much information to the public *suo motu* at regular intervals through various means of communication so that the public have minimum resort to the use of this Act to obtain information." I feel it is very important."

(Contd. by 1t)

1T/5.30/SKC PPG - 63 01-03-2005

CHAIRMAN (CONTD.): We could also include 'website' in the provision given in the NAC so that it reads as '...on the basis that it shall be a constant endeavour of the public authorities to take steps to provide as much information to the public *suo motu* at regular intervals through various means of communication **including the website** so that the public have minimum resort to the use of this Act to obtain information.' We can adopt it as in the Advisory Committee's recommendations and include the word 'website'. We can have the provision of website included.

But we have to go to other things. I shall quote the relevant portion. In (xvii) of the Bill it is given that "such other information, as may be prescribed; and thereafter update these publications within such intervals in each year as may be prescribed". We have already adopted that from the NAC. Clause (c) says, "publish all relevant facts while formulating important policies or announcing the decisions which affect public". It is already given in the earlier provisions. It is a repetition. Even then we can adopt it.

JUSTICE (RETD.) N. Y. HANUMANTHAPPA: Sir, we could delete that. Let us not have a repetition.

CHAIRMAN: That may not be needed. It is said in (d) 'provide reasons for its administrative or quasi-judicial decisions to affected persons.'

JUSTICE (RETD.) N. Y. HANUMANTHAPPA: But that is not necessary. When there is the provision of obtaining certified copies, why should they give reasons in the administrative offices?

CHAIRMAN: Is it not necessary for a person to know it? it is very important.

DR. P. C. ALEXANDER: The clause to provide reasons is there in the Act of 2002.

CHAIRMAN: It is a very important clause. We will adopt it as it is in the Bill. According to (e), "before initiating any project, or formulating any policy, scheme, programme or law, publish or communicate to the public in general or to the persons likely to be affected thereby in particular, the facts available to it or to which it has reasonable access which in its opinion should be known to them in the best interest of natural justice and promotion of democratic principles."

We shall keep this provision as it is.

Clause (2) reads as, "It shall be a constant endeavour of every public authority to take steps in accordance with the requirements of clause (b) of sub-section (1) to provide as much information *suo motu* to the public at regular intervals through various means of communications so that the public have minimum resort to the use of this Act to obtain information."

This clause is adopted.

Clause (3) reads, "For the purpose of sub-section (1), every information shall be disseminated widely and in such form and manner which is easily accessible and comprehensible to the public."

This clause is adopted.

Clause (4) reads, "All materials shall be disseminated taking into consideration the cost effectiveness, local language and the most effective method of communication in that local area and the information should be easily accessible, to the extent possible in electronic format with the Public Information Officer, available free or at such cost of the medium or in print cost price as may be prescribed." (Contd. by 1U)

HK/1U/5.35/PPG

SHRI RAKESH MALHOTRA: Sir, it is given that "for the purpose of sub-section (1), every information shall be disseminated widely and in such form and manner as well as language which is easily accessible and comprehensible to the public." In some States where there are certain minority languages or tribal languages, it is mandatory under the Linguistic Survey and other recommendations that any notification or any public information will have to be informed through that particular language that is provided in the Minority Languages Law. Therefore, in any form or manner or language, we have to provide that.

CHAIRMAN: For the purpose of this Section, information should be disseminated widely and in such form and manner which is easily accessible and comprehensible to the public. Here, 'disseminated' means making known or communicated the information to the public through notice boards, newspapers, public announcements, media broadcasts, the internet or any other means, including inspection of offices of any public authority. All materials shall be disseminated keeping in mind the cost effectiveness, local language and the most effective method of communication in that local area and the information should be easily accessible with the Public Information Officer, where possible, in electronic format, free of cost or at such cost of the medium or the print cost price.

SHRI A.N. TIWARI: This has been split into two sub-sections.

CHAIRMAN: The Explanation you have given in the Bill, I hope, will look after this need of the NAC's recommendations. Therefore, we will adopt clause (4) as in the Bill and the Explanation in the Bill.

Now, I come to clause (5). Every public authority shall, within one hundred days of the enactment of this Act, designate as many officers as Public Information Officers in all administrative units or offices under it as may be necessary to provide information to persons requesting for the information under this Act. We can adopt it.

SHRI RAM JETHMALANI: Clause 8 is most important.

JUSTICE (RETD.) N.Y. HANUMANTHAPPA: We can discuss it tomorrow.

CHAIRMAN: We can finish up to clause (7) today. We can sit tomorrow also.

(Followed by 1W)

KSK/5.40/1W PPG 01/03/205

CHAIRMAN: Regarding clause 5(1), I will read the portion of NAC's Bill. I quote,

> "Every public authority shall, for the purposes of this Act, designate as many officers as Public Information Officers, in all administrative units and offices under such authority, as are necessary to render the public body as accessible

as reasonably possible for requesters of information, within one month of this Act coming into force.

An officer at each sub-divisional level or other appropriate sub-district level, shall be designated a Public Information Officer, within three months of this Act coming into force, for the purposes of this Act. He/she shall receive all requests for information, and appeals, both under the State and the Central Acts, and pass them on to a designated authority for onward transmission to the relevant department/agency.

Where applications/appeals are handed over at the sub-divisional or sub-district level, an additional period of five days would be added to the time of response specified under this Act, in order to enable the request/appeal to be communicated to the relevant authority."

They feel that the State and the local administration will also be included. Therefore, when we are expanding the purview of the Act to the State and local administration, we will need officers being appointed in the States and work should be assigned to them.

SHRI A.N. TIWARI: There is a difference between NAC formulation and the formulation in the Bill. I think, the formulation in the Bill is better because it talks about these officers being appointed within one hundred days of enactment of this Act, whereas NAC says, "within one month of this Act coming into force." So, the idea behind 'one hundred days' was that since the Act comes into force within 120 days, these officers should be placed within 100 days. So, the infrastructure will be ready by the time Act comes into force. Now, if we say 'after the Act comes into force', I do not think, that it would help the citizens.

CHAIRMAN: But, how can we take one hundred days after enactment of this Act?

SHRI A.N. TIWARI: In anticipation of this Act being passed, I have written to everybody. Once the Act is passed, we can appoint the officer and within hundred days, officers would be in place.

CHAIRMAN: But, will it not be useful that you make it 'within one month of this Act coming into force'?

(followed by 1x)

GSP/5.45/1X/PPG/01-03-2005

SHRI A.N. TIWARI: Sir, we thought that other infrastructure should be in place before the Act comes into force. If you are giving more time, that is fine. The administration is quite pleased.

SHRI RAMJETHMALANI: Sir, why should we give scope for lethargy if they are trying to be quicker?

CHAIRMAN: Okay, we adopt this as it is in the Bill.

Now, we come to Clause 5(1) which says, "Every public authority shall, within one hundred days of the enactment of this Act, designate as many officers as Public Information Officers in all administrative units or offices under it as may be necessary to provide information to persons requesting for the information under this Act."

Further Clause 5(2) says, "Without prejudice to the provisions of sub-section (1), every public authority shall designate an officer, within one hundred days of the enactment of this Act, at each sub-divisional level or other sub-district level as an Assistant Public Information Officer to receive the applications for information or appeals under this Act for forwarding the same forthwith to it or to the Government:

Provided that where an application for information or appeal is given to an Assistant Public Information Officer, a period of five days shall be added in computing the period for response specified under sub-section (1) of section 7."

DR. P.C. ALEXANDER: I think it would be better to add that it should be passed on to the designating authority for onward transmission to the relevant departments/ agencies.

CHAIRMAN: I think this is a good suggestion. Now, before the proviso, and, after 5(2), we should mention, "He or she shall receive all requests for information and appeals both under the State and the Central Acts and pass them on to the designating authority for onward transmission to the relevant departments/agencies". This can be added there. As far as proviso is concerned, we can adopt it as it is. (Cont. by 1Y)

SK/1 Y/5.50/PPG/01.03.2005

CHAIRMAN (Contd.): "Every Public Information Officer shall deal with requests from persons seeking information and render reasonable assistance to the persons seeking such information". We will adopt it as it is.

Now, we come to sub-clause (4). "The Public Information Officer may seek the assistance of any other officer as he or she considers it necessary for the proper discharge of his or her duties." That can be adopted as it is.

SHRI RAMJETHMALANI: I think that is a very dangerous provision. He can ask any superior officer and then the superior officer is open to assist him.

DR. RADHAKANT NAYAK: My feeling is that it sounds like executive instructions.

SHRI A.N. TIWARI: Sir, I think, the point made by the hon. member, was not taken into account by us.

CHAIRMAN: Then, we have to drop this provision.

SHRI A.N. TIWARI: We will work out on it suitably, Sir.

CHAIRMAN: I think, we can omit the provision 5 (4), that is, "The Public Information Officer may seek the assistance of any other officer as he or she considers it necessary for the proper discharge of his duties".

Now, we take sub-clause (5), "Any officer whose assistance has been sought under sub-section (4), shall render all assistance to the Public Information Officer seeking his or her assistance and for the purposes of any contravention of the provisions of this Act, such other officer shall be treated as a Public Information Officer". This also has to be omitted. So, we can drop clauses 5(4) and 5(5).

Now, we come to clause 6 (1), "A person desires to obtain any information under this Act shall make a request in writing or through electronic means in English or in the official language of the area in which the application is being made, accompanying such fee as may be prescribed to:

the Public Information Officer of the concerned public authority; the Assistance Public Information Officers specifying the particulars of the information sought by him or her..

DR. P.C. ALEXANDER: There is no difference between what is there in the Bill and the NCA advice.

CHAIRMAN: I am reading only the Bill. It says, "Provided that where such request cannot be made in writing, the Public Information Officer shall render all reasonable assistance to the person making the request orally to reduce the same in writing".

DR. RADHAKANT NAYAK: Sir, here you are leaving the discretion to the Public Information Officer. He will give you assistance and then only you can make an oral representation. My point here is this. Suppose he is not able to reduce the request in writing, or, he refuses to give a reasonable assistance, then, what are you going to do? (Followed by 1Z)

YSR/5.55/1Z/PPG/01.03.2005

SHRI RAM JETHMALANI: Then prescribe penalty somewhere.

CHAIRMAN: If you don't mind, please, note it down.

DR. RADHAKANT NAYAK: It is a very tricky provision. What I am trying to say is that oral representation is enough.

CHAIRMAN: They are doing this only for illiterate people. That we will discuss. Kindly note it down.

"(2) An applicant making request for information shall not be required to give any reason for requesting the information or any other personal details except those that may be necessary for contacting him."

We are adopting it as it is.

"(3) Where an application is made to a public authority requesting for an information,—

which is held by another public authority; or

the subject matter of which is more closely connected with the functions of another public authority,

the public authority, to which such application is made, shall transfer the application or such part of it as may be appropriate to that other public authority and inform the applicant immediately about such transfer:

Provided that the transfer of an application pursuant to this sub-section shall be made as soon as practicable but in no case later than five days from the date of receipt of the application."

We are adopting it as it is.

Now, we will meet tomorrow.

(The witnesses withdrew and the Committee then adjourned at 5.58 p.m.)

PK/1A/4.30 PPGLJ 2.3.2005

THE DEPARTMENT-RELATED PARLIAMENTARY STANDING COMMITTEE ON PERSONNEL, PUBLIC GRIEVANCES, LAW AND

JUSTICE MET ON 2ND MARCH, 2005, AT 4.30 P.M. IN ROOM NO. 63, PARLIAMENT HOUSE, NEW DELHI.

(CHAIRMAN: SHRI E.M. SUDARSANA NATCHIAPPAN)

REPRESENTATIVES OF THE MINISTRY:

Shri A.N. Tiwari, Secretary (Personnel),
Shri T.K. Vishwanathan, Secretary, Legislative Department
Shri K.D. Singh, Additional Secretary, Department of Legal Affairs.

CHAIRMAN: Good afternoon everybody. We will start with certain suggestions that have already been made by witnesses. I will just rush through them, and wherever possible, you can make comments on that, thereafter, Committee will take the decision. You can go through the comments and suggestions made on the Bill. You can take that paper. The hon. Members can also have that paper. One Shri Shailesh Gandhi has referred to suggestions on the public authority. (Contd. by 1B)

PB/1B/4.35

CHAIRMAN (CONTD.): It has been said here that Shri Shanti Bhushan, Sr. Advocate and former Union Law Minister, has opined that it would be perfectly legal and justified for the Central law to be applicable to all public authorities whether they are under the Centre, States or local bodies; and, there would be no legal objection if the Central and the State laws co-exist together. Having regard to this opinion, the Bill should be amended so as to cover the Central and State Governments and also the local bodies. This suggestion has already been covered. We have already suggested it.

Then, in clause 3, it has been said by some organisations that the word 'citizens' be substituted by the word 'persons'. That issue has also been decided. We will only have 'citizens'.

In clause 4, it has been suggested that an additional provision should be made for *suo motu* publication of all contracts entered into by public authorities. Now, the response from the Government is that clause 4(2) already contains a general provision for *suo motu* disclosures by public authorities. It would not be desirable on grounds of national security, etc. to put all contracts entered into by public authorities in the public domain. The *suo motu* provision is already there. The provision is there and also the contracts include the documents which are available with the Government.

I am just reading your replies and certain suggestions made by the individual organisations on Right to Information Bill, 2004, a summary of which is with us. We are referring to some of those suggestions which are sent by persons who had appeared before the Committee. We have already covered the first and second page. Now, we are coming to the third page. These suggestions are from Shri Prashant Bhushan, Shri Prakash Kardaley, Ms. Angela Rangad and from institutions like the National Campaign for People's Right to Information and from the Commonwealth Human Rights Initiative. We will go to the rest of the things when we take up the different clauses.

Now, we will take clause 7 which is regarding disposal of request. If any hon. Member wants to make any suggestion in this regard, he can do so. It seems that there are no further suggestions. So, we can adopt it, as it is proposed.

Now, with regard to clause 8, I would like to inform the hon. Members that this is one of the things which we have to discuss. Shri Ram Jethmalani has also suggested some amendments in that regard. Have you received a copy of the amendments suggested by him?

SHRI T.K. VISHWANATHAN: Yes; Sir.

CHAIRMAN: For the ready reference of the hon. Members, I would like to read the amendment given by Shri Ram Jethmalani. It is said, "Nothing foregoing sections will compel any public authority to disclose the following, (a) Information which has been classified as prejudicially affecting, if disclosed, the sovereignty and integrity of India or the defence and security of India or relations with the foreign states in pursuance of an expressed rule or order made by Central Government." The second thing is this.

SHRI RAMJETHMALANI: If you permit, I would like to explain as to why I am suggesting these amendments. (Contd. by 1c)

1C/4.40/SKC PPG - 63 02.03.2005

SHRI RAMJETHMALANI (CONTD.): The idea is that issues affecting sovereignty and integrity, defence or security of India, or relations with foreign States, should not be left to the officers who are going to decide the issue of application of this Act. These are very high-sounding matters, very serious matters, in which the final authority should really be the Central Government. In the American statute, they found after great experience that the best method is, what I have mentioned here, that the Central Government itself must take the responsibility of showing that this particular information must be classified as the one falling under this clause, which affects the integrity or sovereignty or whatever. That decision must come from the Government. The Government must ask for classification and the document must be classified so that it does not leave much room for discussion for the officers concerned The final decision should be that of the Central Government. If somebody wants to challenge the reasonableness of the Central Government, you will have to undertake proper proceedings. But the officer would morally have to see whether it is classified in accordance with the Government's orders. Then, rest of the changes are really verbal and linguistic changes, as the language does not seem to ebb.

Clause 8 (1) reads, "Notwithstanding anything contained, in this Act, except as otherwise provided herein, the following information shall be exempted from disclosure..." This makes no sense. There is nothing in the foregoing sections that will compel any public authority to disclose information. That is as simple as anything can be. Clause 8(a)(i) talks about exemption from disclosure of information which could 'prejudicially affect the sovereignty and integrity of India, security, strategic, scientific or economic interest of the State, relation with foreign State...' Where does one get this from? Obviously, you have tried to copy Article 19 (2) here. But in Article 19(2), these considerations, such as scientific or economic interest and so on, don't exist. These are totally unnecessary and unnecessarily make the exemption too wide. Those words have to be dropped. Keep it strictly within the confines of Article 19(2), which is an exception to the right to freedom of speech.

Then, 8(a)(ii) says, 'lead to an incitement to commit an offence'. Again, this has been taken from Article 19(2). But please, give me one illustration of information, which if supplied to the person, will become incitement to commit an offence. It is true that the freedom of speech under the Constitution is reflected here that you cannot incite commission of an offence. But please, give me some illustration of information that, if supplied to people, will lead to the incitement of an offence. I don't think it is warranted.

CHAIRMAN: Suppose there are some communal happenings.

SHRI RAMJETHMALANI: Communal happenings take place outside.

CHAIRMAN: Mr. Secretary, you could tell us if you have some information.

SHRI RAMJETHMALANI: If there is any such expression which is borrowed from Article 19(2), kindly think about it. I am thinking hard to find that out.

CHAIRMAN: So, you feel that since under Article 19(1) prohibition is already accepted, that will take care of all the three concerns, that is, strategic, scientific and economic interests.

SHRI RAMJETHMALANI: Other clauses take care of it anyway.

CHAIRMAN: I feel that it could hold for simply keeping some trade secrets.

SHRI RAMJETHMALANI: That is already covered under Clause 8(1)(c). 8(1)(b) talks about 'information, which has been expressly forbidden to be disclosed by any court of law or tribunal or the disclosure of which may constitute contempt of court'. The term 'expressly' forbidden can be changed to 'lawfully' forbidden.

(Contd. by 1D)

HK/1d/4.45/PPG

SHRI RAMJETHMALANI (CONTD.): So, anything which has been 'lawfully forbidden', for that you did not make a disclosure. Instead of 'expressly forbidden', we said, 'lawfully forbidden'. The next is the information, the disclosure of which may result in a breach of privileges of Parliament. Then, 'the information, including commercial confidence, trade secrets'. The proposal is that legitimate trade secrets and commercial or financial information obtained from or furnished by a third party on condition of strict confidentiality that alone is entitled to protection and it must be legitimate. Any person who has given you information on condition of confidentiality, you are bound to respect it. That is all. Otherwise, 'information, including commercial confidence', that English is bad. 'Information, including commercial confidence', how does it make good English? Then, 'information available in a fiduciary relationship'. What is this again? Where has it come from? Give me one illustration. So, I would request you to kindly think about it again whether anything serious is sought to be achieved by this. Then, 'information available to a person in his fiduciary relationship', again is the same thing. Then, 'information received in confidence from a foreign Government', that is totally useless. Then, 'information given by anybody on condition of confidentiality', we are deleting it because it is unnecessary. Then, (g) and (h) have to be combined together and made simpler. Now see how they have been combined. 'The information, the disclosure of which will lead to identification of an informer or his source of information or which would endanger the life or safety of any person for having furnished material information useful to the Indian nation or would materially hamper investigation into crimes or other lawful enforcement activities'. This is a simple English. It is understandable, and it avoids all complications. 'Cabinet papers' must remain. That follows from the Article of the Constitution. You cannot avoid it. Then, 'information not related to the operations of the Government or their instrumentalities and disclosure of which would constitute clear and unwarranted invasion of the privacy of an individual'. This is a verbatim copy from the American Statute. I have borrowed strictly from there and it is a much better English and it is much more intelligent.

(Contd. by 1e)

KSK/4.50/1E PPG 02-03-2005

CHAIRMAN: There is one representation given by a witness regarding Cabinet papers. They have suggested that we should either delete it or substitute it by saying that only those Cabinet papers, premature disclosure of which would harm public authority, should be kept secret. And, then, one witness claimed that Cabinet papers should be made public after the decision has been taken, or, the matter is complete or over. But, should we prescribe some time limit? It has been stated that in Sweden, certain time is stipulated.

SHRI RAMJETHMALANI: If an order of the Government is challenged in the Court, the Government is bound to state the reasons. Nobody is interested in knowing what one Minister said or other Minister said. That is a useless enquiry. That will lead to mischief.

CHAIRMAN: They want to know the timing. When it will be made public. Some time limit should be stipulated, or, shall we leave it as it is?

SHRI RAMJETHMALANI: We should leave it as it is.

CHAIRMAN: That will be right.

DR. RADHAKANT NAYAK: We should give a reasonable period of time in proviso (i).

SHRI RAMJETHMALANI: This provision which says, "shall be made public after the decision is taken", is good enough. That depends, when the demand comes. The demand will come after the matter is over.

DR. RADHAKANT NAYAK: Even if there is no demand, it should be mandatory on the part of the Government to disclose the reasons.

SHRI RAMJETHMALANI: There are hundreds of decisions and the Government has no need to disclose reasons for all the decisions.

DR. RADHAKANT NAYAK: Sometimes, if it is a sensitive matter, they may take long time. We should mention something like 'within a reasonable period of time'.

CHAIRMAN: Mr. Tiwari, regarding this amendment, which was given by Shri Jethmalani, what is your opinion?

SHRI A.N. TIWARI: We did not have the time to see the context.

CHAIRMAN: He has made it very concise, deleting only certain things which are being repeated.

SHRI T.K. VISHWANATHAN: I will give presentation on the lines as suggested by Shri Jethmalani. As you said that clause 8 is not happily worded, we will reconstitute it.

(contd. by 1f)

VP/4.55/1F/PPLG/2.03.2005

SHRI T.K. VISHWANATHAN (CONTD.): Certain repetitions, are there. Most of the ideas have been covered. But we would like to add two or three more points. We will discuss the points with them.

CHAIRMAN: Regarding the time limit, a proviso has been given. "Provided that where any question arises to the date from which the said period of ten years has to be computed, the decision of the Central Government shall be final." Shall we accept it as suggested by the Advisory Council?

We will adopt Clause 8 by making an amendment suggested by the hon. Members.

SHRI A.N. TIWARI: There is one factor in this proviso to 8(i) which says: "the material on the basis of which the decisions were taken". This may imply that even the Cabinet papers, on the basis of which the Cabinet takes a decision, shall be disclosed. That possibility exists. The Cabinet papers have all the inter-Ministerial discussions on it. Their objections over-ruling everything are there, and they are all secret. So, that factor you may kindly keep in mind.

SHRI RAMJETHMALANI: After every Cabinet meeting, somebody advises the Press as to what decision has been taken on a particular day.

SHRI A.N. TIWARI: This proviso says that the material on the basis of which the decision was taken will also be disclosed.

CHAIRMAN: Do you want the words, "the material on the basis of which" to remain? What is your suggestion, Mr. Ram Jethmalani?

SHRI RAMJETHMALANI: If there is any serious objection to this, you read Bhagwati's Judgement, and, then, give us your suggestion in that regard. We have considered this article and, then, come to the conclusion. There was some objection that it could not be disclosed in a court. Ultimately, the Supreme Court said, 'No, it has to be disclosed.' So, just read it again. I will also look into it.

DR. RADHAKANT NAYAK: Even if you remove that clause, sub-clause (i) itself says: "the Cabinet papers, including records of deliberations of the Council of Ministers, Secretaries and other officers:" So, these absolutely include the basis on which the decisions were taken.

SHRI A.N. TIWARI: The provision contains an exception to the rule. The proviso says, "being what it is, the material on which the decision is arrived at should be made public."

DR. RADHAKANT NAYAK: But, don't you think this proviso, the material on the basis of which the decisions were taken", is included in sub-clause (i) itself, that is, "Cabinet papers, including records of deliberations of the Council of Ministers, Secretaries and other officers."? (Continued by 1G)

GSP/1 G/5.00/PPG/2-3-05

SHRI A.N. TIWARI: There is some tension between these two, between the proviso and the main clause. Sometimes, the cabinet papers are itself the material on the basis of which the decision is taken. There could be some problem.

DR. RADHAKANT NAYAK: Do you think that this proviso should be removed?

CHAIRMAN: Why do you feel that the proviso will not protect your interest? For example, any decision based on certain material collected on a subject like rural development can be brought to the public knowledge. On the other hand, information relating to defence and external affairs cannot be leaked, and, the proviso will look after the exemptions. So, as far as other things are concerned, the amendment, as suggested by the hon. Member, will look after the interest.

SHRI A.N. TIWARI: Sir, I have seen the Cabinet papers. They are all marked 'secret'. Every department or the ministry gives the opinion for and against a particular proposal that is recorded in the papers, and, the decision is taken on the basis of all these comments.

DR. P.C. ALEXANDER: I think the next sentence "provided further that those matters which come under the exemptions listed in this section shall not be disclosed" clarifies the position.

SHRI A.N. TIWARI: Sir, a room for litigation is there.

CHAIRMAN: As I said earlier also, when you are taking a decision on a subject like rural development then certainly people would like to know about that and that information should be available to the public. Most of the times, it is the media that requires the information. So, I think that the proviso as well as the amendment, as proposed by the hon. Member, will take care of that situation.

Kindly don't make it that the entire material on the basis of which the decision is taken, is taken away. That will lead to taking away some more teeth out of this Bill. Try to keep it as it is. That proviso will surely give protection. The first clause will also give protection. We can exclude those materials from the purview of bringing that to the public knowledge. Once again, I would say that, it is a well-protected proviso. So, we adopt it subject to the amendment proposed by the hon. Members and accepted by the Committee.

As far as Clauses 9, 10 and 11 are concerned, I hope there is no amendment proposed, and, these can be adopted as they stand in the Bill. Now we come to Clause 12 that needs some more discussion. (Contd. by 1h)

SK/1H/5.05/PPG/02.03.05

CHAIRMAN (Contd.): Here, we have to make, as we have seen in the Advisory Committee's recommendations:

(i) (b) The Governor shall appoint or designate, a State Information Commissioner for all matters pertaining to the State. Such appointment shall be made on the basis of recommendation made by an Appointing Committee presided by the Chief Minister, with the Leader of Opposition in the Legislative Assembly and the Chief Justice of the High Court as Members.

(ii) Information Commissioners may be appointed by the President, or the Governor, as the case may be, in consultation with the appropriate Appointing Committee and the Chief Information Commissioner or State Information Commissioners, as the case may be.

(iii) Every Chief Information Commissioner, State Information Commissioner and Information Commissioner shall be a person with wide knowledge and experience of administration and governance, and/or a person with high public stature.

We want to have some discussion over this one. The Advisory Committee also suggests this qualification and that can be considered by the hon. Members. I will just propose certain things. Hon. Members and the Secretary can look into it. Here, the qualification for a Member is given as "shall be a person with wide knowledge and experience of administration and governance and/or a person with high public stature". The special knowledge or practice in respect of such matters, namely—law is not there but I am including it — law, literature, science, art, social science, journalism, management, administration and governance can be included after the words 'experience of administration and governance'.

SHRI RAMJETHMALANI: I think the word 'literature' looks a little odd.

CHAIRMAN: Yes, you are correct. The word 'art' also looks a little odd. But, my feeling is the word 'science' should remain there.

SHRI A.N. TIWARI: Sir, I think, these are really administrative type of posts. This is not necessary that such broad knowledge is germane to the functions. This is a function that you acquire through experience and your work. So, in the process of working, a lot of experience is involved in it. (Contd. by 1J)

YSR/5.10/1J/PPG/02.03.05

SHRI A.N. TIWARI (CONTD.): Sir, I would urge one point here. As we go by, perhaps later on when we consider this too restrictive, we could think of explaining it.

CHAIRMAN: The point is that we are providing here a very high collegium for selecting the people.

SHRI A.N. TIWARI: Sir, even for the Director (CBI), we have that kind of system.

SHRI RAMJETHMALANI: You have not only put 'knowledge' but also 'experience' here. It offers this to ex-bureaucrats. If you say knowledge alone, then it is all right. When you say 'governance', Members of Parliament also have knowledge of it. But when you say 'knowledge' and 'experience', then it means the person must have earlier employed.

CHAIRMAN: I would like to draw your attention towards the point of exclusion.

JUSTICE (RETD.) N.Y. HANUMANTHAPPA: Suppose the duties are quasi-judicial in nature, then what will the scientists do?

CHAIRMAN: This is because these people have gained some knowledge as Director of a particular research institute. We are focussing upon certain categories that can be filled up. Therefore, the area of people to be considered should also be focused.

JUSTICE (RETD.) N.Y. HANUMANTHAPPA: Here, you can also elaborate that ex-IAS Officer, or ex-IPS Officer, or ex-Judge of the High Courts in addition to scientists.

CHAIRMAN: That is why I just borrowed the words from the Constitution (Article 83) and said that these were the areas which would look after the persons who were the High Court Judges or Supreme Court Judges or Chief Secretaries or Cabinet Secretaries. Anybody can be like that.

SHRI RAMJETHMALANI: Cut out the word 'experience' and say who have wide knowledge of administration, governance, law enforcement and science and technology.

DR. P.C. ALEXANDER: When you say law enforcement, then it will limit it to a very narrow area. Only Police people or Judges will be there. Why don't you say persons of eminence in public life?

CHAIRMAN: Do you think sub-clause 6 of clause 12 should be there?

"(6) The Information Commissioner or a Deputy Information Commissioner shall not be a Member of Parliament or Member of the Legislature of any State or Union territory, as the case may be, or hold any other office of profit or connected with any political party or carrying on any business or pursuing any profession."

It means the person should be a useless fellow.

SHRI RAMJETHMALANI: All professionals are excluded.

(Followed by 1k)

VKK/lk/5.15/2.3.2005 PPG

DR. P.C. ALEXANDER: Is it qualifying the selection or just duties after selection?

CHAIRMAN: Yes, Sir, if you see, if a Member of Parliament is elected, then he should resign from the post. That we can accept.

SHRI RAMJETHMALANI: Suppose, you are a scientist belonging to the Indian Institute of Science. He shall not be carrying on any business.

SHRI A.N. TIWARI: Sir, that is a commercial activity. That is what it means that it does not mean a head of a scientific institute. He will be covered by a general condition.

SHRI RAMJETHMALANI: He shall not pursue any profession.

SHRI A.N. TIWARI: Sir, each one of us is pursuing some profession.

CHAIRMAN: That is why we are worried. You can exclude the entire gamut of the people who are working very brilliantly. Why we have to include this? As Dr. Alexanderji told, if it is after appointment, it is correct; but if it is the qualification, I feel it has to be deleted.

SHRI A.N. TIWARI: We can think in terms of deletion.

CHAIRMAN: This clause can be deleted. There is no need of it.

JUSTICE (RETD.) N.Y.HANUMANTHAPPA: A lawyer, a doctor or an engineer, everybody is connected with political party. Only because he belongs to a political party, he is not competent to discharge the duty.

DR. P.C. ALEXANDER: I still feel that once people are selected, they must not pursue any other profession.

SHRI RAMJETHMALANI: Do you follow that he must not pursue any profession?

DR. P.C. ALEXANDER: He will not.

CHAIRMAN: He follows sub-section (5), that is, the qualifications.

DR. P.C. ALEXANDER: When he is in office, he should not be allowed to pursue any profession.

CHAIRMAN: If we delete sub-section (6), nothing will happen. There will not be any disturbance of choosing a person from any field, if he comes, he has to resign from his post.

SHRI A.N. TIWARI: This is a full-time job.

SHRI T.K. VISHWANATHAN: We can delete it.

CHAIRMAN: Naturally, therefore, we can delete sub-section (6). We can take rest of the things as they are.

DR. P.C. ALEXANDER: What about the autonomy of the functioning? Then, there will be problem. Therefore, the suggestion that he should function in an autonomous capacity. Some degree of autonomy has to be given to this officer. Should we not have a particular language as suggested by the NAC? The Chief Information Commissioner and other Information Commissioners shall function autonomously without being subjected to directions by any other authority and would be under the administrative control of this Ministry.

CHAIRMAN: We have to include that also. The Chief Information Commissioner and other Information Commissioners shall function autonomously without being subjected to directions by any other authority. (Followed by 1L)

RSS/1L/5.20/PPG

DR. P.C. ALEXANDER: That is why, the administrative control will be with the Department of Personnel. But otherwise, they should be functioning autonomously.

CHAIRMAN: It further says that it would be under the administrative control of the Government of India, Ministry of Personnel, Administrative Reforms and Public Grievances.

DR. P.C. ALEXANDER: I think, that can be added. Is there any objection?

SHRI T.K. VISHWANATHAN: Sir, we have no objection. We can add that. Our intention is to give him an autonomous status.

SHRI A.N. TIWARI: In the same way, I would refer to sub-clause 4. It says, the general superintendence, direction and management of the affairs of the Commission shall vest in the Information Commissioner who shall be assisted by the Deputy Information Commissioners and may exercise all such powers and do all such acts and things which may be exercised or done by the Commission autonomously without being subjected to directions by any other authority under this Act. Even this sub-clause excludes the Department of Personnel. The DOPT has got CBI and CAT. But they are autonomous. Administrative control, of course, will remain with the Ministry. That is an acceptable part. But that should not be injurious to the fact that this organization must function autonomously. We are not contradicting it. The fact that there is a controlling Ministry does not mean that the Ministry affects the autonomy.

DR. RADHAKANT NAYAK: Take the case of Central Administrative Tribunal. Who will be the controlling Ministry in regard to him?

SHRI A.N. TIWARI: Sir, I provide their staff.

DR. RADHAKANT NAYAK: But the administrative control will be with the particular Ministry for the purpose of posting and transfer.

DR. RADHAKANT NAYAK: Is it a *quasi judicial* body?

SHRI A.N. TIWARI: Yes.

DR. RADHAKANT NAYAK: In that case, you cannot compare CAT with the Director CBI.

SHRI A.N. TIWARI: But, in the case of Director, CBI, postings and transfers are done by him.

DR. RADHAKANT NAYAK: But, the nature of work of the Director, CBI is different from CAT. CAT is a *quasi judicial* body. It is an appellate body. It performs all the *quasi judicial* functions. Is there any full autonomy anywhere now?

MKS/MCM/5.251M (contd. by 1m)

DR. RADHAKANT NAYAK (CONTD.): There is an administrative Ministry where postings are being done.

SHRI A.N. TIWARI: We are challenging the decisions of CAT.

CHAIRMAN: Clause 12 (8). We can delete it. Sub-clause (8) will be deleted. We can adopt rest of the things.

Clause 13 - Term of Office. Any comments or amendments on Clause 13?

SHRI A.N. TIWARI: Our own proposal was that this Commission could be modelled on the Election Commission and the Terms of Office could be on those lines because the Commissioner will have an all-India jurisdiction; he will be dealing with very senior Government offices and he will be extremely intrusive. His nature has to be appropriately high.

CHAIRMAN: Why do we have to select a person, who comes to that office, not useful for other purposes? Clause (5) itself can be deleted.

SHRI A.N. TIWARI: It is also in the Election Commission things.

CHAIRMAN: The Chief Election Commissioner has become a Member of Rajya Sabha. Tomorrow, he will become a Minister.

SHRI A.N. TIWARI: He will not be forbidden.

CHAIRMAN: Why to restrict a person who has got good prospects. He may be a good diplomat.

SHRI T.K. VISHWANATHAN: He should not use this diplomatic status.

CHAIRMAN: I refer to page 2, sub-clause (5). The Committee will also accept sub-clause (5). Even the Supreme Court judges are now being appointed as Governors.

JUSTICE (RETD.) N.Y. HANUMANTHAPPA: Second proviso to clause 13.

SHRI A.N. TIWARI: This is to reinforce his autonomy. To make him autonomous, it is done.

CHAIRMAN: He is not going to be an American judge. The words "up to 65 years" can be deleted.

JUSTICE (RETD.) N.Y. HANUMANTHAPPA: Page 8, clause 13, second proviso, the last line: "Provided further that no Information Commissioner shall hold office after he attains the age of 65 years."

CHAIRMAN: That is okay. There is already a restriction that he cannot have reappointment. Sixty-five years, I feel that restriction of age is to be eliminated.

TMV/1 N/5.30 (Contd. by 1N)

CHAIRMAN (CONTD.): Now, we will go to clause 13. Some suggestions have received from the National Campaign for People's Right to Information. They suggested, "In order to effectively perform the role of the appellate authority for the executive, judiciary and the legislature and the responsibility to oversee the implementation of the law, the Information Commissioner and the Deputy Information Commissioner should be equated to the Chief Election Commissioner and the Election Commissioners". The response of the Government was that the suggestion had been noted for examination and decision at an appropriate level. They want it to be equated with the Election Commission so that its autonomous status can be equated to a status which is apparently known to you.

SHRI A.N. TIWARI: We have no fundamental objection to it, if it is equated with the Election Commission. Then the term of office of the Information Commissioner and the Deputy Information Commissioner should be identical to the term of office of the Chief Election Commissioner and the Election Commissioners.

DR. P.C. ALEXANDER: The Deputy Information Commissioner can be equated with the Joint Secretary and the Information Commissioner can be equated with the Secretary.

SHRI A.N. TIWARI: The term of office of the Information Commissioner and the Deputy Information Commissioner should be identical to the term of office of the Chief Election Commissioner and the Election Commissioners. In the Election Commission they have a term of five years.

CHAIRMAN: Instead of calling Joint Secretary, why can't we give the name which is already in existence in autonomous bodies?

SHRI A.N. TIWARI: The Election Commission is one of the models that can be adopted. We have no fundamental objection to this.

DR. P.C. ALEXANDER: It will enhance their status.

SHRI A.N. TIWARI: Then the Deputy Information Commissioner should also have a term of five years as the Information Commissioner. Otherwise, we can redesignate them as Deputy Commissioner and Commissioner and each will have a term of five years.

CHAIRMAN: I remember that there is some clause which says that though an Election Commissioner becomes the Chief Election Commissioner, he has to retire within the period of five years. You have to look into that. It should be 5 + 5.

DR. P.C. ALEXANDER: In some cases the Deputy Commissioner will be appointed as Commissioner. Then his service as Commissioner will be within that five years.

SHRI A.N. TIWARI: He gets an aggregate term of five years. Each one, regardless of whether he is Chief Commissioner or Commissioner or Deputy Commissioner, should get a term of five years. I think that is the intention of the Committee.

CHAIRMAN: I think this can be added.

DR. P.C. ALEXANDER: What about re-employment?

CHAIRMAN: That will also be removed. So, we will adopt clause 13 with certain amendments and deletions that have been suggested.

I think there is nothing in clause 14 regarding removal of Information Commissioner or Deputy Information Commissioner. We will adopt it as it is.

Now, let us go to clauses 15, 16 and 17. Clause 15 relates to the powers and the functions of the Commission. Clause 15 (1) of the Bill says, "Subject to the provisions of this Act, it shall be the duty of the Commission to receive and inquire into a complaint from any person". Here the complaint can be received by the Commissioner. Then under clause 16 the appeal can be received by the Commissioner. If you go to clause 17, which is the penalty clause, the penalty is only in respect of appeal, not in respect of the complaint. If at the stage of complaint itself there is any violation, then the penalty clause should be operative for that also.

I will explain again. Here the Commissioner is having the authority to receive a complaint. Certain specifications were given regarding the complaint. Then clause 16 says, if there is a Deputy Commissioner, that is, a Public Information Officer, and if he gives an order, there will be an appeal within the Department itself. That can be taken to the Commissioner and that appeal alone will be punishable under clause 17.

(Contd. by 1O)

VK/1O/5.35/PPG/2.3.2005

CHAIRMAN (CONTD): Here the word used is 'appeal'. You see clause 17, line 2.

If there is a complaint before the Commissioner, this clause cannot be used. I suggest that here the words 'complaint and appeal' should be there. If a complaint is lodged under clause 15, there is no punishment. Only when there is an appeal under clause 17, at that time the Commissioner can give punishment. Clause 17 gives right to the Commissioner to give punishment.

SHRI A.N. TIWARI: Sir, your point is quite valid. We can remove the confusion. Here the words should be 'appeal/complaint'. You can use them alternatively, 'complaint/appeal'. We can use it like this.

CHAIRMAN: The punishment provision is silent in clause 15 where complaint is made to the Commissioner.

SHRI A.N. TIWARI: We have been using the word 'appeal' loosely. It covers complaint also. As you are saying, we can make it 'complaint/appeal'.

RG/5.40/1P (Followed by 1P)

CHAIRMAN (CONTD.): There was also a suggestion that a separate heading should be there. But since it is already mentioned in the side as a sub-heading, I think, there is no need for a separate heading.

SHRI RAM JETHMALANI: Regarding clause 17, there are three changes which are required. One is, the word 'persistently' should be dropped. Secondly, the word 'may' shall become 'shall'. And, thirdly, we have to add the words 'without any reasonable cause, the burden of proving which shall be upon him'.

DR. P.C ALEXANDER: What is the idea behind it?

SHRI RAMJETHMALANI: Otherwise, the prosecution has to prove negatively in a criminal trial. These words are there in every law.

CHAIRMAN: That is to be noted.

SHRI RAM JETHMALANI: Normally in other criminal laws, punishment would read as 'imprisonment or fine or both'. Why have these words been reversed here? Fine has been brought first.

CHAIRMAN: Before going to clause 17, there are some specific things regarding clause 16. The Advisory Committee has given certain specific recommendations to cover human rights' violations. You may go through the text mentioned in Page 31 of the Comparative Statement between the Act of 2002 and the Advisory Committee's recommendation.

1Q/5.45/KS (Continued by 1Q)

CHAIRMAN (CONTD.): What I am saying is that the suggestion is that this should be included in Clause 16.

SHRI T. K. VISHWANATHAN: Sir, that would be extremely dangerous.

CHAIRMAN: I feel this recommendation protects the interests of the security forces and the Intelligence.

SHRI T. K. VISHWANATHAN: Sir, almost every single information could be brought within the ambit of some human right violation or the other.

CHAIRMAN: But if you read this, that is also protected. Just like corruption is allowed to be exposed, human rights violations should also be exposed. That is the main contention of the NGOs who have appeared before the Committee, as also of the National Advisory Committee. This is part of this Clause, because they have mentioned it in their own serial numbers.

SHRI T. K. VISHWANATHAN: Sir, this matter was very extensively discussed with the NAC officials by us. I do not believe that this can be the position of the NAC.

CHAIRMAN: But this is their position.

SHRI T. K. VISHWANATHAN: I do not know who has stated this position.

CHAIRMAN: About four representatives had appeared before us. They had produced a letter of the Advisory Committee to the Prime Minister to the effect that like corruption, human rights violation should also be included. (Contd. by 1R)

TDB/1R/5.50

CHAIRMAN (CONTD.): But, no provision has been made here in regard to human rights violation.

SHRI A.N. TIWARI: If this is the NAC's recommendation, then, it is a new thing to me. We are based only on that recommendation. If you take away human rights...

CHAIRMAN: The main thrust is on the human rights' violation which are done by the security forces in certain areas. We have to control it. We are in a democratic country.

SHRI A.N. TIWARI: The point which has been made is this. Secrecy is essential and critical element in the functioning of security forces, including the armed forces. Now, if there is ingress in that information on the ground of human rights' violation, virtually, every single information shall be exposed for that reason alone. I am submitting before the Committee that it could be a very big risk to take. I am just saying that in the name of human rights, let us not compromise their functioning.

SHRI RAMJETHMALANI: You are hearing what has happened in England. These are the people who are now convicted in the civil courts for committing breach of human rights against their detenus.

SHRI A.N. TIWARI: There are certain cases in the Indian Army itself where the Army punished their personnel for human rights' violation. In some cases, the erring personnel were cashiered; in some cases, the personnel were terminated. All these things have been happening here also. As a matter of right, if anybody, who has a right through this Act, wants to get some information, then, it would be like giving some sort of a sweeping fishing rod to him.

SHRI RAMJETHMALANI: In a democratic society, where the Army and the Armed Forces are under the civil society, why should not the people know what is happening there? You cannot do it, unless you offer security interests. That provision you have got there. But, if these are out of the sphere of security; then, why should not that information be given?

SHRI A.N. TIWARI: If it is made like this, then, the security agencies would be answering to the courts thousand times in a year.

SHRI RAM JETHMALANI: On the other hand, today, we are condemning the Americans for what is happening in that Island where they have kept those detenus.

SHRI A.N. TIWARI: Theoretically, what you are saying is all right. As a citizen, I am supporting it. But, if you look at the expediency and practical aspect of it, it is not practical. Sometimes, they have to work on some...

CHAIRMAN: I feel you have to consider it. We want to protect the interest of the country; we also want to protect the interest of the Army, Navy and other security forces. When they are in the battlefield, they have to do something. As the hon. Member said, when they are under the civil authorities' control, they should conduct themselves within certain limitations. You know very well that when emotions play in certain areas, many things happen. If such things are allowed to happen in a democratic country, then, people would say that the Government is not doing its duty properly. The Government cannot tolerate violation of human rights. Why do not you give such type of powers to them? When necessary, the protective clause will protect you. We will not reveal everything to them. We will reveal which can be revealed. If there is a mass agitation; if there is some *lathi*-charge and shooting and some persons have died, then, that information can easily be given to the people. It is not the battlefield information. Therefore, human rights' violation is one of the things which protects democracy from the hands of the armed forces. We have to see that something should be given by way of human rights' information.

SHRI A.N. TIWARI: Sir, I would like to know whether such kind of a provision is there in the law of any other country in the world.

CHAIRMAN: As told by the hon. Member, such sweeping powers are there in America and also in the U.K. (Contd. by 1S)

KLS/1 S-5.55/ppg/2.3.2005

CHAIRMAN (CONTD): That is how they are charged. You have seen in the newspapers that so many people have been tied together and then pulled.

SHRI A.N. TIWARI: There are laws under which they can still be charged. But to add all this in this Bill, will create problem.

CHAIRMAN: We want to protect our armed forces. But they should also not violate human rights. When they are going to protect our country naturally they have to violate human rights. We cannot do it without the violation of the human rights.

SHRI A.N. TIWARI: Sir, my point is that we should not put it in under the Information Act. Army intelligence can take a position that the information which has been sought it is human rights violation. Then it goes to the Commissioner and the Commissioner may take a position that it is human rights matter. Everything starts tumbling out. There can be no end to it.

DR. RADHAKANT NAYAK: We can specify what is the nature of violation. We can spell it out. It need not go into nitty-gritty. Apprehension of the Secretary is very genuine.

CHAIRMAN: I feel that you can protect certain information. But you cannot put it a blanket ban. Somewhere you have to say 'human rights violation'. There can be some provision.

SHRI RAMJETHMALANI: We will consider your point of view.

CHAIRMAN: Just consider that some protection is given against human rights violation. Take into consideration the security and other aspects also. I am not talking about battlefield. We feel that human rights violation is a part of information.

(Contd. by 1T)

USY/1T/6.00

JUSTICE (RETIRED) N.Y. HANUMANTHAPPA: You are making it very wide. Why do you want the third parties to make appeal?

CHAIRMAN: A separate clause — clause 11(1) — is given for the protection of third party.

Regarding clause 17, I would like to say that before making a complaint to the magistrate, there should be a provision of taking some disciplinary action under the service rules or the conduct rules by way of suspension, transfer, termination from the service, etc. We should give some powers to the Commissioner also so that, he is in a position to punish the delinquent officers.

SHRI RAMJETHMALANI: Compulsory prosecution before a court comes in those situations where there is appeal. But supposing there is no appeal, in those cases the departmental action is permissible. That can always exist under the normal rules. But it has not been mentioned here. So, here, we can add 'without prejudice disciplinary action may be taken against the delinquent officers'.

SHRI T.K. VISHWANATHAN: That we can provide. But he himself cannot impose penalty.

(Contd. by 1U)

VP/6.05/1U/PPg/2.3.05

DR. P.C. ALEXANDER: He has the inherent powers of the superior or the Head of the Department to impose penalties.

SHRI A.N. TIWARI: We have got an amending provision in this Bill which says that the Conduct Rules should be amended to bring them in line with the Information Act. So, the Conduct Rules of the various Services will be automatically amended and wherever there is violation, there shall, automatically, be disciplinary proceedings.

CHAIRMAN: Who will do it?

SHRI A.N. TIWARI: Nobody can trigger it. What Shri Ram Jethmalani has suggested is correct. He has suggested that the Principal Information Commissioner or the Information Officer can inform the Head of the Department that there is a violation of the Act. Then, disciplinary proceedings follow.

Suppose, there is a violation within the Department, then, what is the punishment? If the Information Officer himself is denying the passage of information to the hands of the HOD, then, an order will follow and he will have to carry out that order. If he does not carry the order, then, there is a punishment. But in case the Information Commissioner thinks that his act is not of such magnitude as to warrant a draconian punishment, then, there is a provision for this.

CHAIRMAN: Where is the power for that?

SHRI A.N. TIWARI: We can make a provision here that he can recommend appropriate disciplinary proceedings also without prejudice to the other provisions.

DR. P. C. ALEXANDER: There are two aspects of it. One is that if the Information Officer himself is to be found guilty of an offence, punishment has to be given. Secondly, the Information Officer may find some officer in the Department not supplying him information and then, he can recommend punishment for him. So, we can have a general statement in addition to some disciplinary action provided in the appropriate rules. This can also be done. That will take care of it.

CHAIRMAN: The imposition of fine and other things as recommended by the Advisory Council should also be considered, and it is to be included. Clause 17 will be adopted subject to certain modifications, which are to be done. Clauses 18-28 are adopted.

Now we come to the Preamble. There is a suggestion by the Advisory Council that "the Bill to operationalise the Right to Information by setting out the practical regime for people to secure access to information under the control of public authorities, consistent with public interest, in order to promote openness, transparency and accountability, and in relation to matters connected therewith or incidental thereto."

SHRI RAMJETHMALANI: The description of the Act does give some idea of this. But, unfortunately, that is not very adequate. What you have to explain is the essence of the democratic ideal which this Bill seeks to enforce. (Continued by 1W)

PK/1W/6.10 PPGLJ 2.3.2005

SHRI RAMJETHMALANI (CONTD.): I mean, the people who are enforcing this Act must know what kind of paramount duty they are performing. And, then, you have introduced exceptions to right to information. The people should also know that even those are based upon the interests of the people; they are not intended to protect the officers, bureaucrats or some delinquents. People have an interest in an efficient government, people have an interest in maintaining confidentiality of sensitive information. There is a conflict between the interests of democracy on the one hand and smaller interests on the other. The Bill seeks to harmonise them. According to me, the Preamble should explain the grandeur of this legislation. After all, in 1976 when Americans introduced it for the first time, the President Johnson had to call a press conference to explain this is one of the brightest days in the evolution of American democracy and hereafter people will know how they are being governed. It is an important measure which we are adopting. I don't think there can be any objection to the contents. I will read it out "Whereas the Constitution of India has established a democratic polity at the Centre and in the States; and whereas democracy requires an informed citizenry, vital to its functioning needed to check corruption and to hold governments and their instrumentalities accountable to the governed; and whereas this vital public interest is in actual practice likely to be in conflict with other public interests such as effective and efficient operations of all governments, responsible use of limited fiscal resources and the preservation of confidentiality of sensitive information; and whereas it is necessary to harmonize these conflicting interests while preserving the paramountcy of the democratic ideal." I think, at least it is something higher sounding, which brings to the officers the importance of what they are doing.

CHAIRMAN: I would like to draw the attention of the Secretary to the Maharashtra Act. It says, "whereas the right to information has been recognised by the Supreme Court as a part of the fundamental right guaranteed to the citizens under article 19(1) of the Constitution of India; whereas the right to information is the bed-rock of democracy and can pave the way for transparency, openness and accountability in governance of the affairs of the State and ensure effective participation of the people in a democratic society; and whereas it is expedient to make provision for effectively securing and enforcing the right to information in the State of Maharashtra and for matters connected therewith or incidental thereto. Now, I would like to draw the attention of the Secretary to the objectives of the Act, which have been recommended by the National Advisory Committee. This Act has three objectives. One is, to give effect to the fundamental right to information which will contribute to strengthening democracy, improving governance, increasing public participation, promoting transparency and accountability in Union, State and Local Self-Government institutions. Number two is, establish voluntary and mandatory mechanisms or procedures to give effect to right to information in a manner which enables persons to obtain access to records of public authority in a swift, effective, inexpensive and reasonable manner. Thirdly, promote transparency, accountability and effective governance of all public authorities by including but not limited to empowering and educating all persons to: understand their rights in terms of this Act in order to exercise their rights in relation to public authorities; understand the functions and operation of public authorities; and effectively participating in decision making by public authorities that affects their rights."

I think, this can be made as a Preamble.

SHRI RAMJETHMALANI: It is a little longer than it should be.

CHAIRMAN: But it gives a much more comprehensive idea.

DR. P.C. ALEXANDER: Mr. Secretary, you can have a look at it.

SHRI T.K. VISWANATHAN: Sir, we will have a look at it, but what Mr. Ram Jethmalani has proposed looks better because it is concise and brings out the conflict which is lacking in the Maharashtra Act.

Sir, another area that we are, presumably, legislating on is Entry 97.

(Contd. by 1X)

PB/1X/6.15

SHRI T.K. VISHWANATHAN (CONTD.): We have to be consistent. So, we shall not say anything about it. Let the court decide. So, we will remain clear of the State List Acts. We will not go into the merits of the State Acts.

SHRI RAMJETHMALANI: There is a general provision of right to information under the residuary powers. But implicit in every Entry in the State List and in the Concurrent List is also the power to disclose information about how the executive power is being exercised in relation to that particular Entry. So, it is not that the States do not have powers. It has implied powers under each Entry in the State List. The Centre has overriding powers for the entire country under its residuary powers.

SHRI T.K. VISHWANATHAN: Sir, I do not want to say anything about the States. Somewhere they have said, if the citizens have an opportunity to go to the State law, they can go there. I do not provide that in the draft law. This law shall not affect the validity of any law which is in force in the States. So, why should we address this question? We will make the law and keep quiet. That law will prevail and this law will also prevail. Why should we trigger that thing?

SHRI S.K. KHARVENTHAN: I think the suggestion made by the Secretary is correct. It will create further problem.

CHAIRMAN: So, it is sufficient here to mention the local administration, State Governments, etc.

SHRI T.K. VISHWANATHAN: We say nothing about the State legislation. The Preamble looks good, and I will reframe it.

CHAIRMAN: We can adopt the First Schedule and the Second Schedule as it has been proposed here. Clause I, the Enacting Formula and the Title are also adopted, as it is. The only correction which needs to be carried out here is in the year of the Bill. The Title would be 'The Right to Information Bill, 2005'. That correction will be carried out and the rest of the things could be put as they are proposed here in the Bill.

Thank you very much.

SHRI T.K. VISHWANATHAN: Sir, I will show the revised Bill to you after carrying out all these corrections.

CHAIRMAN: Okay.

(The Witnesses then withdrew and the Committee adjourned at 6.18 p.m.)

As per the minutes of 27th Meeting held on 16th March 2005 at 4.00 p.m. in C. Room 63 PH., the Committee did take up the consideration of he draft Report on RTI Bill 2004. But the verbatim record of that day does not show/mention the RTI Bill. Just show SC, ST and OBC (Recreation in Posts and Servics) Bill, 2004.

The Report on RTI Bill, 2004 was adopted on March 16, 2005.

The Report was presented to the Parliament on March 21, 2005.

XXVII
TWENTY-SEVENTH MEETING

The Department-related Parliamentary Standing Committee on Personnel, Public Grievances, Law and Justice met at 4.00 P.M. on Wednesday, the 16th March, 2005, in Room No. 63, First Floor, Parliament House, New Delhi.

PRESENT

1. Shri E.M. Sudarsana Natchiappan — *Chairman*

RAJYA SABHA

2. Dr. Radhakant Nayak
3. Shri Balavant *alias* Bal Apte
4. Shri Ram Nath Kovind
5. Shri Ram Jethmalani
6. Dr. P.C. Alexander

LOK SABHA

7. Dr. Shafiqurrahman Barq
8. Shri Chhatar Singh Darbar
9. Justice (Retd.) N.Y. Hanumanthappa
10. Shri Shailendra Kumar
11. Shri Bhupendrasinh Solanki
12. Shri S.K. Kharventhan
13. Shri Shriniwas D. Patil
14. Shri A.K. Moorthy

WITNESSES

I. Representatives of the Legislative Department, Ministry of Law and Justice

1. Shri T.K. Viswanathan, Secretary
2. Shri Z.S. Negi, Additional Secretary
3. Shri N.L. Meena, Joint Secretary
4. Shri N.K. Nampoothry, Joint Secretary

II. Representatives of the Department of Legal Affairs, Ministry of Law and Justice

1. Shri R.L. Meena, Secretary
2. Shri R.L. Koli, Joint Secretary

III. Representative of Ministry of Personnel, Public Grievances and Pensions

Shri R. Ramanujam, Joint Secretary

SECRETARIAT

Shri Tapan Chatterjee, Joint Secretary
Shri Surinder Kumar Watts, Deputy Secretary
Shri H.C. Sethi, Under Secretary
Shri Vinoy Kumar Pathak, Committee Officer

2. The Committee first took up the consideration of the draft Report on the Right to Information Bill, 2004 and after some discussions adopted the Report.
3. * * *
4. A verbatim record of the proceedings of the meeting was kept.
5. The Committee adjourned at 5.00 P.M.

1a-1b-1c/4:30-4:35-4:40/ysr-vkk/ks

The Department-Related Parliamentary Standing Committee on Personnel, Public Grievances, Law and Justice met at 4.30 p.m. on 16th March, 2005 in Committee Room 63, Parliament House

(CHAIRMAN : SHRI E.M. SUDARSANA NATCHIAPPAN)

Witnesses:

Ministry of Law and Justice (Legislative Deptt.)
Shri T. K. Viswanathan, Secretary
Z.S. Negi, Addl. Secretary
N. L. Meena, J.S. & L.C.
S.R. Dhaleta, Addl. L.C.
KV. Kumar, ALC
Ministry of Law and Justice (Legal Affairs Deptt.)
Shri R. L. Meena, Secretary
Ministry of Personnel and Public Grievances
Shri A. N. Tiwari, Secretary
Shri R. Ramanujam, J.S.
Shri K. G. Verma, D.S.

CHAIRMAN: Friends, we take up the Scheduled Castes, Scheduled Tribes and Other Backward Classes (Reservation in Posts and Services) Bill, 2004. There were more than 112 representations. We have already sent 154. We thought that the Government should reply to these. But I learn, Mr. Secretary, that you are still processing them. Many of the things will require constitutional amendments. Of course, we can definitely recommend certain things. But, at the moment, if you find anything which is relevant to the Clause-by-Clause consideration, then you can make that point.

SHRI T. K. VISWANATHAN: There is nothing substantial in that respect.

CHAIRMAN: All right. We thought that we should move forward so that we can present the report to the Parliament as early as possible. We should not delay it any further. You should send your replies by the 19th so that we can consider them on the 21st and finalise our report. Now, here, I would like to make certain points that we have to prepare ourselves for. Therefore, you try to give us a way out to satisfy the aspirations of the SCs/STs and OBCs. Now, we feel there are some provisions amounting to 'exclusion' in the Bill; you are denying certain people. On those things, you have to tell us what the way out is. When we reserve certain posts for the people and also certain percentage for them, it should be fully without any condition, without any fear that that post may not be occupied by us even though we are qualified for it. That type of fear is there when we see those provisions. (Contd. by 1D)

TDB/1D/4.45

CHAIRMAN (Contd.): Those provisions should also be considered. Hon. Members of the Committee feel that we have to satisfy both the sides. We have to see to it that the people who are going to have reservation are satisfied and the people who are not having reservation should also feel that they are safe in certain areas. That should be the purpose of our legislation.

DR. P.C. ALEXANDER: I have been present at these meetings when the witnesses appeared. Their grievances may be legitimate. But, if I can speak in a general way, I would say that out of 150 memoranda received by the Committee, quite a large number of them pertain to either looking into that 50 per cent limit for reservation or for providing promotion prospects not only for the SCs, STs but also for the OBCs. So, these are the basic issues on which the Committee has to take a view and decide. Though the Committee is not a legislative body, the Parliament has sent this Bill to this Committee for examination. If there are strong views expressed in the memoranda, then, we can refer it to the Government, make a recommendation that these may be considered. But, the Government will have to make its own legislation, in some cases, the Constitution itself will have to be amended because reservation has gone into Constitution. We were discussing this issue last time. Therefore, my suggestion to you would be this. In the next three-four days, you may not be able to deal with each one of these items at length, as you would like it to do. But, that will not help our work. So, my suggestion is, in the next three-four days, you pick up some general principles, examine them and then come back to us. If you could do it, it is fine; otherwise, it will take you quite a long time in examining each and every issue.

SHRI A.N. TIWARI: Sir, generally, what happens is this. When a large number of representations are received, the Committee Secretariat sifts them and categorise them into identifiable areas, where reactions of the Ministry are required. If that initial work is done here, and, then, it is passed on to us, it becomes easy for us to examine those points. As you have rightly said, we cannot give our recommendations on each and every item in the next three-four days. Sifting this number of recommendations itself is quite a laborious process. As you have rightly said, we can definitely give our reactions on the main points.

SHRI BALWANT *alias* BAL APTE: I suggest that we need not hurry through this legislation. If the representatives of the Ministry want time, then, time should be given to them.

CHAIRMAN: We are just postponing today's work in order to give them sufficient time to examine the memoranda. They have got ail the manpower to do it. We have gone through it. What type of problem you are facing here?

श्री शैलेन्द्र कुमार: हमारे माननीय सदस्यों ने SC, ST और OBC का प्रतिशत बढ़ाने की बात कही है, उससे मैं भी सहमत हूं और उसे बढ़ाना चाहिए क्योंकि इस देश में SC, ST और OBC का बहुत बड़ा वर्ग है। अभी जो वर्तमान प्रतिशत है, इसमें बढ़ोत्तरी होनी चाहिए। मेरा दूसरा सुझाव

यह है कि SC, ST और OBC के आरक्षण के पदों की पूर्ति उन्हीं में से होनी चाहिए, अन्य वर्गों से नहीं होनी चाहिए। (1 ई से आगे)

kgg-gs/ppg/4.50/1e/16.3.05

डा. शफीकुर्रहमान बर्क: जहां तक माइनॉरिटीज़ का ताल्लुक है, मुस्लिम माइनॉरिटीज़ का ताल्लुक है, मैने राष्ट्रपति जी के अभिभाषण के समय यह बात उठाई थी कि Muslims of the country are very poor and backward. I demand to provide reservation for educationally backward and economically backward Muslims. इस देश की तरक्की के लिए, मुसलमान भी बहुत बड़ा हिस्सा हैं। इस देश की मुस्लिम माइनॉरिटी बहुत पिछड़ी हुई है और गरीब है। इसलिए उनके लिए रिज़र्वेशन की जरूरत है। जब तक उनको रिज़र्वेशन नहीं दिया जाएगा, उस वक्त तक इस देश की तरक्की रुकी रहेगी। हमारे मुल्क की सोसायटी में अगर कोई भी कम्युनिटी पिछड़ी हुई रह जाती है तो वह कभी हैल्दी सोसायटी नहीं कही जा सकती । इसलिए मुसलमानों की संख्या के हिसाब से उनको भी रिज़र्वेशन की जरूरत है, तभी उनको तालीम मिल सकेगी, सर्विसेज़ में उनको जगह मिल सकेगी और उनकी तरक्की हो सकेगी। अगर मुसलमान पिछड़ गए तो मुल्क पिछड़ा रह जाएगा। मेरी गुज़ारिश है कि मुसलमानों को भी रिज़र्वेशन दिया जाए।

श्री शैलेन्द्र कुमार: SC, ST और OBC के लिए छोटे उद्योगों और व्यवसायों में भी आरक्षण की व्यवस्था होनी चाहिए।

SHRI BALWANT *alias* BAL APTE: Sir, we need not pursue with the discussion the Mandal Commission has recommended, as a consequence of which Muslims are given reservation. Those who are backward are given reservation under the Mandal Commission report and I think, more than 27 Muslim castes come under reservation.

SHRI RAM JETHMALANI: I believe, the Supreme Court has also said that reservations can only be done for those who have been historically, for centuries, victims of oppression and persecution by the higher castes; I don't think reservations for Muslim minorities is permissible. Providing reservation on the basis of religious minorities will require amendment of the Constitution. Kindly check and see whether it is permissible. (Followed by 1f)

KLS/PSV/1 F-4.55/ppG/16.3.2005

श्री छत्तर सिंह दरबार: चेयरमैन सर, माइनॉरिटी के आरक्षण की बात पर चर्चा आई है। अभी माननीय सदस्य महोदय ने सुप्रीम कोर्ट के फैसले की व्याख्या की है। उसके तहत माइनॉरिटी या मुस्लिम वर्ग कोई पीड़ित वर्ग या किसी का सताया हुआ वर्ग नहीं था, इसलिए मैं भी उन्हे आरक्षण देने पर सहमत नहीं हूँ। एस.सी., एस.टी. हैं। वनवासी हैं, जो जंगलों में रहते थे। ये लोग वास्तव में उच्च जाति से या सवर्ण जाति से पीड़ित थे। इनका आरक्षण बरकरार रखा जाए, बढ़ाया जाए।

CHAIRMAN: Thank you very much. We will meet again on 21st. Kindly do not postpone it further because we have to finish certain obligations. Then we have to take up Demand for Grants also. Mr. Vishwanathan and Mr. Meena are also requested to be present in that meeting because we are going to discuss an important subject.

(The Witnesses then withdrew and the Committee adjourned at 5.00 p.m.)

Index